D0482230

THE ISLAMIC BOMB

THE
ISLAMIC
BOMB

The Nuclear Threat
to Israel and
the Middle East

STEVE WEISSMAN
HERBERT KROSNEY

NYT
Times
BOOKS

Published by TIMES BOOKS, a division of
Quadrangle/The New York Times Book Co., Inc.
Three Park Avenue, New York, N.Y. 10016

Published simultaneously in Canada by
Fitzhenry & Whiteside, Ltd., Toronto

Library of Congress Cataloging in Publication Data
Weissman, Steve.
  The Islamic bomb.
  Includes index.
  1. Near East—Military policy. 2. Atomic
weapons. I. Krosney, Herbert. II. Title.
UA830.W46   1981   355'.0217'0956   81-18261
ISBN 0-8129-0978-X   AACR2

Manufactured in the United States of America

10 9 8 7 6 5 4 3 2 1

Contents

FOUR

PAKISTAN

FIVE

IRAQ

SIX

AFTER BABYLON

Foreword

The investigation for this book took eighteen months and spanned four continents. We have been in thirteen countries and an endless string of cities from Washington and New York to London, Paris, Cairo, Jerusalem, Islamabad, and New Delhi.

We have named names wherever we could, but that has not been possible in all cases. All of the countries involved, both the buyers and the sellers, have tough nuclear secrecy laws. Most of the needed documents were highly classified. Some of our best sources from inside the various nuclear programs literally feared for their lives. One of them is now under threat of a treason charge, while another has been fired from his job because of pressure from one of the governments. A relative of one of our sources has also been savagely beaten.

The Middle East, nuclear weapons, and the threat of nuclear war all excite strong passions. No matter how hard-boiled, professional, or objective we have tried to be, we found this was not just another good story, a macho exercise in "investigative reporting." What happens in the newly begun nuclear arms race in the Middle East and South Asia actually matters—to us, to the millions who live there, to the hope that the region and the world can somehow avert the coming of a nuclear holocaust.

The Israeli bombing of the Iraqi Osirak nuclear reactor took place as the final manuscript was nearing completion. Our rather exotic topic—as some thought it—had suddenly exploded into the front pages and was now "timely." This necessitated additional research and writing. As it happens, we had seen the tensions building on the nuclear issue throughout the region and had predicted that such an attack was likely. The Israeli raid put a spotlight on an issue that will determine the fate of the world in the coming years.

We would especially like to thank our editor at Times Books, Ned Chase, whose efforts contributed enormously to the final manuscript, and to those people in The New York Times Company—Jesse Levine, Paul Gendelman, and Sam Summerlin—who handled the project from its inception.

The idea for the book stems partly from the role of one of us— Weissman—on the British Broadcasting Corporation's weekly public affairs program, *Panorama*, and its television film, "Project 706—The Islamic Bomb." This documentary won the British Royal Television Society's award as the Best Investigative Documentary in the year 1980. Later, the two of us worked as consultants to the American Broadcasting Company's *Closeup* series film, "Near Armageddon: The Spread of Nuclear Weapons in the Middle East."

We have enjoyed the continuing cooperation of those colleagues with whom we worked on the television documentaries. This includes in particular: Chris Olgiati, BBC producer of the *Panorama* film and one of the best film documentary makers in Europe; Phil Tibenham, the highly professional BBC on-air reporter; Chris Isham, the able producer for ABC; and Robert Ross, the multilingual ABC researcher whose zest for the pursuit was matched by his skill in getting the facts.

We also owe thanks to the personnel of five other television networks who covered aspects of the story and who more than once pointed us in the right direction: ZDF in Germany, especially Gerhard Lowenthal; NHK Television in Japan (in a report on which we worked), especially producer Sosuke Yasume and reporter Ryojo Katsube; the Canadian Broadcasting Corporation's *Fifth Estate* unit, including Eric Malling, Brian McKenna, Ron Haggart, and Glenn Sarty; Swedish Television's Rome correspondent, Kore Nyblom; and personnel of VARA Television in Holland.

On the print side, we worked closely with an outstanding young French journalist, Fabrizio Calvi of the daily *Libération*; Jose Lenzini of *Le Var Matin République*; Franco Levi of the Italian news agency ANSA; and Karl Van Meter. Several other print journalists have provided leads and contributed to the story, and we have tried to give their names in the course of the book.

We also want to express our gratitude to our three hard-working researchers, Susan Taylor in Britain, Cecilia Todeschini in Italy, and Ada Tsoref in Israel, and to our typist Lisa Guthridge. We appreciate the use of the New York Times Syndication office in Paris, which was a base for pursuing much of this story, and owe the office's two mainstays, Sigrid Russ and Zena O'Shea, a special word for their patience and helpfulness.

To avoid having to write in the third person, and to repeat our names over and over, we have used the editorial "we" throughout the course of the book. In a few cases "we" actually did the interviewing together. In most, only one of us was present. With the permission of Chris Olgiati and Phil Tibenham of BBC we have also employed the "we" in a few cases where they conducted the interviews; and we have done the same where two of our researchers—Cecilia Todeschini and Susan Taylor—led the attack.

Finally, we thank our wives—Anna Weissman and Mary Stewart Krosney—who were always there, even when we were not, and we dedicate the book to them.

ONE

FIRST STRIKE

The Bombing of the Osirak Reactor

I add my voice—and it is not mine alone—to the voices of those who tell you not to do it, and certainly not at the present time, and in the present circumstances.

—Shimon Peres,
Israeli opposition leader (Labor),
May 1981

The reactor was destroyed. All our aircraft returned safely to base.

—Israel Government statement
(from the Prime Minister's Office),
June 8, 1981

It was September 30, 1980, the ninth day of the Gulf War between Iran and Iraq. Iranian Phantom jets had just bombed a power plant on the outskirts of Baghdad, when low on the horizon, two Phantoms came streaking in over the desert sands, rushing headlong at a new target.

The same day, in executive offices in London, Paris, and New York, hapless-looking men in well-cut suits were anxiously adding up the dollars-and-cents damage that the Iranian Phantoms and Iraqi MIG's had done to the refineries and pumping stations at Basra and Abadan. Oil makes the world go round, and the fortunes of the Western world rested on the twists and turns of a far-off war. Only a few of us—a handful of journalists, scientists, and quiet little men in funny government offices—had doggedly kept our eyes and ears on the fate of a very different kind of target, the one that the low-flying Phantoms were now racing to destroy.

From the air, the entire place could not have looked like much—just a few low-slung buildings clustered in a patch of irrigated green some twelve miles east of Baghdad. But to the careful eye, there was one structure that set the site apart—a large, dusty, brown concrete dome, the kind used to cover and contain a nuclear reactor. The Iraqis call the spot Tuwaitah. It is the site of their Nuclear Research Center, and the place where Iraqi scientists were preparing to build the Arab world's first atomic bomb.

The Iraqi leaders had expected an attack, or so they had announced. But they had never set up a proper missile defense, and the small battery of antiaircraft guns provided little protection against the onrushing jets.

As the Phantoms zeroed in, rockets flashed toward the building below. In the noise and confusion, no one seemed to know how much damage had been done. Early announcements said that the rockets had missed the big new Tammuz I reactor and had scored only "minor damage" to some buildings nearby. A later report in the French magazine *l'Express* claimed that the rockets had hit the base of the reactor dome, badly damaging the entire structure. It would set the Iraqi nuclear program back at least a year, *l'Express* suggested.

At the time of the attack, French technicians were still completing construction of Tammuz I, which was not scheduled to go "critical" for at least three months. But a smaller research reactor from France and possibly an older one from the Soviet Union were very much in operation when the rockets struck.

Never before had a nuclear reactor site become a military target in time of war, and perhaps it was the novelty of it all, or the apparent brilliance of the attack, that led *l'Express* to drop a bombshell of its own. The Phantoms hadn't come from Iran at all, the magazine insisted. They were Israeli, and they had taken advantage of the war with Iran to knock out the Iraqi nuclear complex.

The story, as it emerged in *l'Express* and its imitators, had all the spice of a paperback thriller. The Israelis had taken two of their own Phantom F-4-E's, stripped off the Israeli markings, and then sent them streaking due east across Jordan and Syria into Iraq, all at an altitude of under 250 feet to escape detection by enemy radar. Once at Tuwaitah, the pilots brilliantly aimed their rockets at the base of the reactor dome, the least protected and most vulnerable part of the structure, and then flew back to Israel undetected.

The story was "confirmed" by Iraq's Minister of Defense, General Adnan Kherallah, when he announced that he was "fully convinced" that the "Zionist entity," or Israel, had done it. Two months before, in July, the Iraqis had condemned "provocative" Israeli statements about the Iraqi nuclear program as "a threat to launch a military aggression against Iraq, particularly since the enemy possessed U.S.-made aircraft capable of striking at the Iraqi land."

"The Zionist entity . . . was perhaps preparing to launch an air attack on the Iraqi nuclear reactor in an attempt to obstruct scientific and technological development in Iraq, and also to prevent the Arab nation from forging ahead in this field," the official dispatch declared. But there was more.

From London, the well-established *Sunday Times* reminded readers that the Israelis had helped train the Iranian Air Force in the time of Riza Shah Pahlevi, and would naturally have shared the Shah's targeting information on his Iraqi foes, including "a comprehensive survey of Baghdad's air defenses, terrain, and principal targets."

From Paris, the independent leftist daily *Libération* revealed that American military officials at the Pentagon had been expecting "pirate" bombing attacks in the war.

From Tel Aviv, the Israeli radio reported that Radio Tehran had denied the attack.

And from all sides, it was noted that Israel's Chief of Army Intelligence, General Yehoshua Saguy, had set the scene for the attack by publicly urging Iran to bomb the Iraqi reactor. "If I were an Iranian, I too would be worried, knowing that Iraq will unquestionably be a nuclear power at the end of the 1980s," he added. After the attack, the chatty General Saguy was even quicker off the mark, issuing an instant assessment of the damage. "The bombing will put Iraq's atomic option back two or three years," he declared.

A very convincing case had been made that the Israelis had done it. Only it was all argument and innuendo, much of it from French Intelligence, who had their own anti-Israeli axe to grind. No one offered even a shred of proof, as if the very lack of evidence proved just how clever the Israelis had been. And so the story died in a matter of days.

The truth, it seems, was more prosaic. The later-to-be-deposed Iranian President Abolhassan Bani-Sadr, who was also the military commander-in-chief, admitted the Phantoms were his. And according to eyewitnesses, it is likely that the place called Tuwaitah was not even a primary objective, but simply a target of opportunity for those two Phantoms on the way home after the bombing of the power plant on the outskirts of Baghdad.

The Phantoms fired only two rockets, according to these eyewitnesses. One failed to explode. A second hit the reactor housing, damaging the dome and sensitive cooling systems, but little else. The rocket also managed to kill two Iraqi workers who were on their way to a lunch break in the nuclear compound. A third was gravely wounded. It was hardly the kind of expertise for which the Israelis are famous, especially if they had decided to go all out to destroy Iraqi nuclear capability through a lightning attack on Tammuz I.

The September bombing of Tuwaitah was not the first of the violence in the trouble-plagued history of the Iraqi nuclear program, and it would not be the last. Back in April 1979, unidentified saboteurs broke into a storage hangar at a small engineering firm near Toulon on the French Riviera and dynamited the Osirak, or Tammuz, core only hours before it was due to be shipped to Iraq. In June 1980, in a hotel room in Paris, an unknown intruder bludgeoned to death an Egyptian nuclear engineer who was playing a leading role on the Osirak project. In August, a series of bombings and letter and telephone threats against French and Italian engineering firms sparked a continuing campaign of terror.

But the big attack came on Sunday, June 7, 1981, the eve of the Jewish religious holiday of Shavuot, the celebration of the giving of the Ten Commandments to Moses in Sinai. The thoughts of most Israelis were far from the battlefield. Thousands had taken advantage of the long holiday weekend to simply rest at home, visit family in other cities, or head for the packed beaches.

In midafternoon, on the shore of the Israeli resort town of Eilat on the Red

Sea, Bertha Edwards sat with her husband Steve, her friend Sandra, and her two children Guy and Claudia. Suddenly, in the distance, speeding through the sky, she saw a formation of Israeli warplanes crossing the Gulf of Eilat and entering the airspace of Saudi Arabia, somewhere near where the Jordanian and Saudi borders meet about ten kilometers south of the Jordanian city of Aqaba. "It must be some kind of international incident," she joked to her husband. After that, she did not give the planes a second thought. She showered, and began to think about preparing a spaghetti cookout on the Eilat beach.

Earlier that afternoon, Brigadier General Ephraim Poran, military adviser to the Israeli Prime Minister, Menachem Begin, phoned one by one to the cabinet ministers of the Israeli Government. Each minister was told that the Prime Minister wanted to see him personally at 5:30 P.M. Poran caught Aharon Abu Hatzeira, the Religious Affairs Minister, just before he was to leave for his home in the Israeli port city of Ashdod. Abu Hatzeira, who had recently been involved in a corruption scandal and had been declared innocent in a lengthy and controversial trial, was certain that the Prime Minister wanted to demand his resignation from the government. Zevulun Hammer, the Minister of Education, had already reached his residence in the Tel Aviv suburb of Bnei Brak. Informed of the Prime Minister's invitation-by-command, he turned around and drove back to Jerusalem.

As the cars arrived at Begin's tree-lined residence in the Rehavia section of Jerusalem, Israeli secret service agents directed the drivers to park in scattered parts of the city so as not to attract undue attention. When the ministers met in Begin's living room, the atmosphere was much like a surprise party. "What are you doing here?" they asked each other. Each had thought that the Prime Minister wanted to speak to him alone.

Within moments, the Prime Minister himself entered the room. He wasted no time in saying what he had to say, and it was a surprising preholiday message. In a tense voice, he announced, "Our planes are on their way to Baghdad."

One of those present understood him as saying "Damascus." Although the Israelis were in the midst of one of their ongoing crises with the Syrians, this one concerning the placement of missiles in Southern Lebanon, he could not understand why the Prime Minister wanted to bomb the Syrian capital. To remove the missiles was one thing; to hit Damascus straight on, quite another.

The confusion lasted only briefly. The Israeli planes were already en route, and the destination was the Iraqi nuclear complex at Tuwaitah, near Baghdad. It was to be an unprecedented, full-scale, preemptive strike on Iraq's most highly prized foreign purchase, the Tammuz I reactor, which could give the Iraqis the atomic bomb.

The attack climaxed long months of precise military planning. The difficulties were enormous, as the Israeli Air Force knew from experience. During the Six Day War in 1967, they had sent their planes into Iraq to bomb an area known as H-3, near the border with Jordan. The Israelis had succeeded in destroying several Iraqi planes. But they themselves had lost two Vautors and a Mirage in the attack.

Bombing the Tammuz, or Osirak, would be even harder. The Air Force planners had first to pick the best routes for the planes to fly, taking into consideration seven key Arab airfields standing between Israel and the target in Iraq. These presented a very real danger of aerial interception, especially by the Jordanians with their F-5-E's, or by the Iraqis themselves with their Mirage-4000s and MIG-23s and -25s. The Israeli planes would then face added danger at the site itself, as the Iraqis had by now installed French-built Roland and Crotale ground-to-air missiles to add to their stock of Soviet SAM's.

The Israeli Air Force also had to decide which of its own aircraft to use, how many of them, how to provide aerial refueling if needed, and, most important, how to penetrate the strongly built dome to destroy the reactor itself.

All of this took weeks and months to work out, and in the meantime, the Israeli Government was becoming more and more worried about what the French and Iraqis were doing. The reactor was scheduled to go "hot" in the near future—a dispute would later break out about exactly when—and the Israelis had decided they must destroy Osirak before it actually became operational.

The political decision to act had not been easy. A half year before, in December 1980, Prime Minister Begin had discussed the possible bombing of the Iraqi reactor with the leader of the opposition, the Labor Party chief Shimon Peres, the man who looked as if he would win the coming Israeli election. As Begin had expected, Peres opposed the idea. A cautious man and one of the architects of Israel's own "nuclear capability," Peres feared that Jerusalem's increasing diplomatic isolation posed a far greater danger for the moment than any future Iraqi nuclear weapon, and he was worried that a preemptive strike might actually spur the Arab nations to even greater nuclear efforts.

"I speak as a man of experience," Peres had written to Begin in a rather cryptic letter on May 10, the day of the French presidential elections and also the first date set for the bombing raid. "The deadlines reported by us (and I well understand our people's anxiety) are not the realistic deadlines. Material can be changed for (other) material. And what is intended to prevent can become a catalyst."

In his note, Peres begged Begin "to desist from this thing." Otherwise, Israel would be left isolated "like a tree in the desert. . . . I add my voice— and it is not mine alone—to the voices of those who tell you not to do it, and certainly not at the present time, and in the present circumstances."

Yet the final decision on the raid still rested with the government, and particularly with the Ministerial Defense Committee. Begin himself was the chief advocate of action, along with Foreign Minister Yitzhak Shamir, who had led the diplomatic attack against the French, and the Agricultural Minister and former war hero Ariel Sharon. Among their chief opponents were the two representatives of Israel's always influential religious parties, the Education Minister Zevulun Hammer and the inveterate Interior Minister Yosef Burg, who were surprisingly dovish when it came to military action. The Deputy Defense Minister, Mordechai Zipori, while he favored the attack in principle, disputed its timing, arguing that it could complicate Israel's increasingly good relations in the military sphere with the new Reagan Administration in the United States.

In the final vote, Begin won. Israel would go ahead with the plan and bomb the Osirak reactor. As the hawkish Sharon later told the Israeli paper *Maariv*, "This is perhaps the most difficult decision which faced any government during all the years of the State's existence."

All that remained was to set the date, and this was left to three men— Prime Minister Begin, Foreign Minister Shamir, and the military Chief of Staff, General Rafael Eytan. The first date selected was May 10. Since this was also the date of the first round of the French presidential elections, the raid was postponed. There were also one or two other false starts, and finally Begin gave the go-ahead. The attack would come on Sunday, June 7, the eve of the holiday of Shavuot.

The attack itself went strictly according to plan. Late in the afternoon, about four o'clock Israeli time, eight of Israel's new fleet of American-built F-16 jet fighters took off from Etzion air base in the Sinai. Originally designed for high-speed dogfights, the planes had been equipped with extra fuel tanks, to increase their range, and special bomb racks which carried two 2,000-pound MK-84 iron bombs.

Once in the air, the F-16's met up with an escort of six F-15 fighter-interceptors, which were intended to ward off any attacking Arab aircraft should the mission be discovered. The Israelis had also readied an unknown number of other aircraft, including F-15's specially equipped with oversized fuel tanks to provide aerial refueling if it were needed. It was roughly 1,800 kilometers to the target and back, and taking into account the extra fuel needed to make the bombing run, this stretched the range of the F-16's to the very limit. Any deviation from plan, any battle with enemy aircraft, any extra passes over the target, would require additional fuel, and the refueling would have to take place over hostile territory.

The main attack force—the eight F-16's and six F-15's—headed east across the Gulf of Aqaba and along the northern part of Saudi Arabia, near the border with Jordan. By this time, General Saguy's Military Intelligence had discovered the blind spots in the radar systems of the various Arab countries and had determined that the American Advanced Warning and Command (Awac) aircraft stationed in Saudi Arabia would be far enough away, overlooking the Persian Gulf, that they would prove no problem. The intelligence people also provided a comprehensive picture of all commercial aircraft and possible Jordanian and Saudi training flights in the area.

The attack force flew in tightly bunched formations, which would give any Arab radar the impression of a large commercial plane. Crossing over the border into Iraq, the planes sped on past Baghdad to Tuwaitah, approaching low to avoid detection. At least one of the planes, most likely one of the F-15's, initially buzzed the site, probably to draw any antiaircraft fire. In the meantime, the F-16's had swept up into the sky to allow the pilots to take aim, and with the setting sun behind them, they dived over the earthen mounds at their target, sending the bombs hurtling against the side of the dome.

This was the tactic that the Israeli pilots had perfected during months of practice on a mock-up in the Sinai, and it was calculated to take advantage of what the Israelis had learned of the weak points of the dome's construction, and also to prevent the bombs from simply bouncing off the rounded top.

The first bombs to hit the lead and concrete walls had delayed-action fuses. This allowed them to penetrate the dome before exploding, opening gaping holes in the side. The next bombs hit only seconds later, finding the holes with pinpoint accuracy and destroying the reactor inside.

Since the earlier attack in September the Iraqi leaders had taken care to erect massive earthworks around three sides of the reactor dome. But the Iraqi soldiers on the ground failed to fire their Crotale and Roland ground-to-air missiles, and the small battery of antiaircraft guns on the site spattered their ack-ack fire harmlessly into the air as the eight F-16's dived directly out of the sun and came swooping in for the kill.

"I saw the planes hit," recalled Jean-François Masciola, a French electrician who had been working on the Osirak project. "It was very well done," he told us a few days after the attack. "Extremely precise."

Sitting with his wife and baby son in their two-room bungalow in the French compound about half a mile from the reactor itself, the thirty-one-year-old technician had heard the sound of the planes and had rushed out to see what was happening. He saw four of the planes dropping their bombs. The reactor dome seemed to be exploding, he said.

Instinctively, the frightened Masciola rushed back into the house, grabbed up his son, and ran with his wife to a protective wall of sandbags that had been placed near the house for just this sort of emergency. There, behind the sandbags, the three of them huddled, waiting and listening for the bombing to end.

From nearer the site, the Iraqi defenders were spraying the darkening sky with their antiaircraft fire. But in less than a minute or two, the attacking planes had gone. "The Iraqis were shooting at everything," smiled Masciola. "But there was nothing there."

The bombing over, the terrified young family quickly packed their few belongings and headed for Baghdad, where they stayed at the villa of Masciola's boss. The following morning, they took off by car for neighboring Jordan, where they caught the next plane to Paris. "For me, Iraq is finished," Masciola told us a few days later. "I'm not going back. Not until they have some peace there. I'm not a politician. I'm not angry at the Iranians or at the Israelis. I'm just an electrician. I just want to do my job."

Another of the French technicians was just getting into his car about 200 yards from the reactor site when he heard the first explosion. "The very first planes dropped their bombs with great precision," he said, asking that we not reveal his name. As he remembers the scene, great chunks of cement were flying up from the dome, while somewhere above the reactor itself a fire had broken out almost immediately. "The reactor building leaned heavily after the very first bombs," he recalled. "Something like the Tower of Pisa, but even more so."

A third Frenchman got caught in the bombing itself. He was a twenty-five-year-old engineer named Damien Chaussepied, and he had been sent to Iraq to work on the difficult problems of cooling the reactor. After the bombing, Chaussepied's body was found in the wreckage. He had a broken skull, as if his head had knocked into a steel wall, one of his comrades told us. Otherwise his body was unmarked.

Prime Minister Begin had kept in direct touch with Command Headquarters "located somewhere in Israel" throughout the operation. Even though the Air Force had been ordered into action, normal command channels were bypassed in order to limit the number of people who knew about the attack. At one point—no one seems to remember exactly when—someone at Command Headquarters exclaimed to Begin, "It's gone like a Swiss watch. Better than a Swiss watch."

Finally, Commander-in-Chief Rafael Eytan, known as Raful, picked up the telephone and spoke personally to the Prime Minister. He told Begin that the operation was 100 percent successful and the boys were on their way home.

The Prime Minister immediately told his Cabinet, "Our planes are returning in peace." Relief swept the room. But it was not yet time for celebration. Everyone knew that the raid would have serious consequences; as Israelis knew well from their turbulent history, military success did not necessarily mean that political success would follow.

The announcement came the afternoon after the attack, June 8, issued straight from the Prime Minister's Office. "On Sunday, June 7, 1981, the Israel Air Force launched a raid on the atomic reactor Osirak, near Baghdad," read the official communiqué. "Our pilots carried out their mission fully. The reactor was destroyed. All our aircraft returned safely to base."

2

M. Mitterrand's Secret Report

Iraq had no legal obligation not to use the reactor to irradiate uranium. That was a loophole. We wanted to close it.

—French diplomat,
Ministry of External Relations,
June 1981

Why should we put our faith in them [the French] even if they ask us to? Especially after they have been so careless in this entire matter.

—Prof. Yuval Ne'eman,
Israeli scientist and political leader,
June 1981

They're whores. Anything goes in their nuclear industry. Everybody knows it, even the Iraqis. That's why they went to the French to buy in the first place.

—Israeli official,
June 1981

It was only a one-page report, headed with the emblem of the French Foreign Ministry, classified highly secret and for official eyes only. *Had the Israelis known of its existence and believed in the ability of the French to implement it, Prime Minister Menachem Begin might never have sent his F-16 jet fighters into Iraq to bomb the French-built Osirak nuclear reactor on June 7, 1981.*

As one of his first acts, the new French President, François Mitterrand, instructed his Foreign Ministry (officially changed to the Ministry of External Relations on May 10, 1981) to come up with a tough new stance on the Iraqi nuclear buildup. Mitterrand had assumed the powers of office on May 21, eleven days after his election. He named the socialist veteran Claude Cheysson as Foreign Minister on Friday, May 22. By the close of the weekend, Cheysson ordered a full review of the French nuclear contract with Iraq, asking his top diplomats for specific suggestions that would guarantee that the Osirak reactor would be used for peaceful purposes only.

Mitterrand, as the Socialist presidential candidate, had vigorously raised the question of the Osirak in his hard-fought election campaign against the former French President, Valéry Giscard d'Estaing. Long known for his sympathies toward Israel, Mitterrand roundly condemned earlier French plans to supply the reactor with highly enriched uranium fuel, from which the Iraqis could have immediately built atom bombs. His position in writing to official representatives of the French Jewish community on May 8, two days before he swept the final round of the presidential elections, could not have been clearer: "It is obvious, whatever is said, that a country that belongs to the battlefield should not get materials whose military use is evident."

A high-powered task force, headed by the dapper M. François Nicoullaud of the ministry's Subdivision for Atomic Issues, worked feverishly through the next ten days to form a new French position on the Iraq nuclear issue, even as the new government declared to the world that France would honor the terms of all preexisting contracts. For the first time, these diplomats—men like Nicoullaud and his antinuclear-proliferation-minded colleagues in the ministry—had the chance to come out on top in their running battle against the export-minded nuclear merchants within French industry and the French Atomic Energy Commission. The French nuclear salesmen always wanted to sell, and they sold well and vigorously. Their attitude and actions reflected the position "The consequences be damned." The Foreign Office diplomats, highly responsive to pressures from Washington and elsewhere, maintained an opposite posture. They assured the world that their country was not selling the bomb, but only "peaceful nuclear technology" to their wealthy Islamic clients—and France's suppliers of oil.

Far more was at stake than the nuclear contract alone. Twenty percent of French oil came from Iraq, and France's overall imports from Iraq in 1980 had mounted to a stunning 23.5 billion French francs, some $5 billion. The nuclear deal had helped guarantee France a permanent and reliable source of oil supply. In return, the French had become major suppliers of the Iraqi Army, selling everything from tanks and armored personnel carriers to Mirage aircraft and high-powered patrol vessels. French businessmen had made deals in petro-chemical plants, the renovation of Iraqi port and air facilities, highways, and telecommunications. France's exports to Iraq in 1980 amounted to 4.5 billion French francs, about $1 billion, leaving France a yearly deficit of about $4 billion in the two countries' trade balance.

Yet French business in Iraq was growing by a healthy 25 percent yearly, and was a considerable help in correcting the country's chronic balance-of-payments deficit. The key to it all, at least in the eyes of many Frenchmen, was the nuclear contract itself.

In the view of the Foreign Office officials who had to make the decisions, France had to walk a tightrope between two conflicting pressure groups. On the one hand, the wealthy Iraqis wanted nuclear technology, had the money to pay for it, linked the nuclear supply to even more lucrative agreements, and did not like to have their intentions questioned. On the other, the Israelis, and increasingly the Americans, believed that oil-rich Iraq wanted nuclear technology only in order to make the bomb and had no other need for it. The Israelis in particular doubted whether international inspection procedures on the Iraqi facilities could be effective in stopping the Iraqis from getting "the nuclear option."

Mitterrand's election gave the "good French"—those adamantly against giving other countries the wherewithal to make the bomb—a chance to carry the day against the nuclear salesmen. Never published or even discussed in detail, the Mitterrand Government's secret report set out six steps that would have gone a long way to preventing the Iraqis from using their controversial reactor to make the bomb. The diplomatic task force wanted to "close the loopholes" and the mistakes they knew to have been made in the original French contract with the Iraqis.

"The original agreement was made in 1975," one of the diplomats involved told us in an exclusive interview conducted in a stylish fourth-floor office in the Quai d'Orsay, home of the French Foreign Ministry in Paris. He gave us the interview on the basis that his name would not be used. "We looked at nuclear contracts differently then. We looked at the entire system of safeguards and guarantees with different eyes. Since then, people have become more demanding. They've imagined a whole range of what I would call diversion scenarios—how a country might get the bomb. We wanted to close the gaps in the original contract. It was all too open-ended."

What were some of these loopholes that the French diplomats saw and wanted to close? Some of them were shockingly obvious. For one, "Iraq had no legal obligation not to use the reactor to irradiate uranium," the official admitted, almost offhandedly. Sitting in the comfortable French office, far away from the volatile Middle East, we were shaken. The technical meaning was devastating, the political consequences profound. The officer was admitting that nothing in the French contract with Iraq legally prevented Iraq from making the plutonium that would, in turn, make atomic bombs. During eighteen months of research, we had been subjected to constant official French assurances that the Osirak reactor would not, and could not, make the bomb. Now the diplomat was admitting that nothing in the French-Iraqi deal officially prevented the Iraqis from doing just that.

"That was a loophole. We wanted to close it. We wanted a public and contractual commitment that the Iraqis would not use the Osirak to irradiate plutonium, and make plutonium," the official explained.

We could not help but wonder if the French had been uncharacteristically naive in their original dealings with Iraq, or grossly negligent, or conscious accomplices of the Iraqis in their drive for the nuclear bomb option. We asked the official if he felt especially worried by this particular loophole (among others), and he sought to put it into perspective.

"You have to look at the total picture, the whole combination of controls," he told us. "And that total picture was reassuring, at least for the honest observer. The Iraqis could not divert the plutonium for military uses without being seen. Possibly the French could be fooled, for a brief time. The International Atomic Energy Agency, with its inspectors, could be fooled. Iraq could denounce the Nonproliferation Treaty. But Iraq couldn't have diverted for military use without being seen, and there would have been plenty of time for a diplomatic warning."

"How much could they divert?" we asked.

"Stretched to the limit of the imagination, very little. It would be measured in grams, in hundreds of grams, but not in kilos—and the world would have known about it. Really, I don't see how they could divert. Even if they got enough material for one bomb, what could they do with it? That would stop their entire nuclear program. We would have cut off our cooperation. It's just not a realistic possibility."

Then why did the French suddenly want to close the loopholes in the contract that they now admitted existed? "We wanted to do all this to answer the worries of public opinion," the official told us. "We wanted to get assurances that would calm the public, and especially the Israeli public.

"We had no feeling of technical urgency about this new policy," he continued. "We had a political urgency but not, I repeat, urgency on the technical side of things. There were open-ended problems and we wanted to solve them. But there was still time."

The official's answer left open the question of international safeguards on "peaceful" nuclear reactors, and we shall discuss these in detail. What other loopholes did the French see in their nuclear contract with Iraq?

"We also wanted to reinforce the guarantees on the permanent presence of French technicians at the reactor site," the diplomat told us. "There were loopholes in the earlier agreements."

What kinds of loopholes this time? The experience, it turned out, was recent. French authorities in 1979 secretly signed an agreement with the Iraqis specifying that French technicians would be on site at Tuwaitah and available for work and consultation through 1989. That arrangement had been violated within the year. In the fall of 1980, during the first months of the Iranian-Iraqi war—and notwithstanding the 1979 agreement—the Iraqis had restricted and even forbidden French technicians access to the Osirak. "We hadn't gone into all the details on those earlier agreements," the official said. "We would have liked it expressly said that the French are there on a permanent basis. That was another loophole worth closing."

As the diplomat now explained it, the French wanted to guarantee that their technicians would have direct access to the reactor itself on an unrestricted basis, a move that would give the French effective surveillance, if not control, of the reactor's functioning.

The French also wanted to formalize their arrangements on the shipment and delivery of highly enriched uranium, that other substance from which atom bombs are made, and the kind of fuel that powers the Osirak reactor. The French had already decided to limit deliveries, so that each shipment of bomb-grade material would be immediately irradiated (in effect, consumed by the reactor) and extra amounts would never be accumulated and available to the Iraqis to divert to bomb use. That had been a unilateral decision, however, and now the French wanted the Iraqis to sign on the dotted line.

Then, as soon as possible, the French wanted to change the kind of fuel from heavily enriched to a less-enriched uranium called caramel—like the candy—that could power the reactor but could not be used directly for nuclear explosives.

There was also the question of what would happen to the heavily enriched uranium after it had been used as fuel in the reactor. In the original agreement, the status of that heavily enriched uranium was unclear. The Iraqis bought it and owned it. But it could be "reprocessed" from its depleted form of some 60 percent enriched uranium back to bomb-grade 93 percent at the will of the Iraqis, assuming they could find the facilities to do the reprocessing. The French now wanted to guarantee that this fuel would be returned to France, and sent back to Iraq only under the strictest French control. "The original contract was a bit unclear on this point," the French official contended. "It was a gray zone. We wanted to make it specific."

Even with all these weak points in their nuclear contract with Iraq, the French still believed that the Israelis, and their friends, were unduly alarmed about Iraq's real nuclear potential. True, the reactor could produce plutonium, but not in really significant amounts. "There's a battle of the experts on this point," the diplomat pointed out, and he did not want to enter into the fray. His own Atomic Energy Commission claimed only 2.4 kilograms a year. Others said as much as twenty kilograms a year. We ourselves had been given serious, well-worked-out mathematical estimates within this range, which would yield anywhere from one bomb in four years to four bombs in one year.

That was not the case, the Frenchman claimed. The Iraqis could not have done it so soon. They lacked the expertise. And they could not get that expertise without foreign, Western help, and without subjecting the facilities to foreign, international, and especially French control. The idea that the Iraqis could get the bomb in two years was "ridiculous," and revealed a faulty, and "irrational," pro-Israeli bias.

Another French Foreign Office official, Yves Doutriaux, the official spokesman who has spent long hours defending the French-Iraqi nuclear deal to journalists, expressed this viewpoint best when we first telephoned him after the Israeli raid on the Osirak. "If you write that Iraq will have the bomb in two years, it shows a certain pro-Israeli position," he calmly alleged. "Scientists disagree. Some say two years. Others say ten years."

"So," we pressed, "the question of *when* one says Iraq will have the bomb is actually a measure of one's political position."

"Precisely. If you say Iraq can have the bomb in ten years it is one thing," M. Doutriaux answered. "But if you say two years, that is an Israeli position." It was a curious and unsatisfactory exchange, uttered, we should add, with some humor, but suggestive of the emotional investment by each party involved in the issue.

To protect their negotiating position with the Iraqis, the French Government has never revealed the contents or even the existence of their new policy, and the "Nicoullaud Report" is still officially under wraps. That report made it clear to us, though, that the French had finally started to take serious steps to make sure that the Iraqi Government of Saddam Hussein could not use either the reactor or the fuel to produce nuclear weapons.

Still, the new policy was just a position. The French had to put it into practice. They had to convince, and possibly to pressure, the Iraqis to accept the new terms. Nonetheless, we found that Mitterrand and his government were showing an eagerness to work out a stance that would satisfy even the highly nervous and suspicious Israelis.

The Israelis never gave the French a chance. Nicoullaud and his task force completed the report in the week of June 1. The top civil servants at the Quai d'Orsay quickly approved it. It was placed on the desk of the powerful new Foreign Minister, Claude Cheysson, ready for his approval by the morning of Friday, June 5. He lacked the time to discuss the details with the new French leader, François Mitterrand, or even personally to initial it.

Two days later—on Sunday, June 7, 1981—came the attack on the Osirak reactor. "A morally supreme act of national self-defense" declared the Israeli Prime Minister, Menachem Begin. "No fault whatsoever on our side."

The scene was an almost festive press conference in the auditorium of Beit Agron, the government press center in downtown Jerusalem. It was the Tuesday following the raid. The Monday had been the Jewish holiday of Shavuot, the springtime harvest festival. As the star of the show, a supremely confident Prime Minister Begin was at the very top of his form in defending the Israeli "visit" to Baghdad.

"Saddam Hussein, the ruler of Iraq, who with his own hands killed his best friends in order to become the sole ruler of that country, had an ambition," the Israeli leader confided to the world's television and press reporters. "He wanted to develop nuclear weapons, so that he can either try to bring Israel to her knees on behalf of the Arab world, or to destroy her menfolk and infrastructure and the great part of her army, which consists of reservists in the cities. In other words, he wanted to destroy our existence—in fact, our people and our country."

And, said Mr. Begin, the equipment to make those nuclear weapons had come chiefly from two European nations—the French and the Italians. "It is shameful," he declared, "that two European countries, ancient, civilized, but also which saw with their own eyes what happened to the Jewish people . . . should help to develop [for] a bloodthirsty archenemy of the Jewish State weapons of mass destruction."

These harsh words reflected Begin's earlier tirades against the alleged anti-Semitism of the West German Chancellor Helmut Schmidt and the government of former French President Giscard d'Estaing. But Begin's words—like his actions in bombing the reactor—seemed especially brutal to the newly elected Mitterrand Government and to those in the French Foreign Ministry who had tried to create controls to make the Osirak safe.

"The Israelis didn't even approach us after the election of M. Mitterrand," complained the French diplomat during our interview at the Quai d'Orsay. "Possibly they didn't want to take the chance of our telling them that we were engaged in a serious rethinking of our policy. It would have been a risk for them to learn from us that we were doing something about the situation. They didn't want to be caught up in the diplomatic process. They had already decided to act. That is my analysis."

The Israelis were not reluctant to explain their actions. In a number of interviews we conducted with top-level Israeli officials in Jerusalem and Tel Aviv, a single view prevailed: The Israelis were convinced that the Iraqis wanted to make the bomb. These officials with whom we talked were equally convinced that the French—whether from narrow self-interest or pervasive indifference—were helping them to do it.

"When the Iranian-Iraqi war broke out, we could hope that the French would see how mistaken they were giving nuclear bomb-making technology and the bomb to a country like Iraq," said Hanan Bar-on, the Foreign Office Deputy Director General in charge of Israel's diplomatic campaign against the Iraqi-French contract. Sitting in his spare first-story office in one of the low-slung Quonset-type shacks that have become the permanent headquarters of the Israel Foreign Ministry, Bar-on seemed resigned to world condemnation of Israel for the raid, but convinced that his country had no choice. "We hoped against hope that this contract would be cancelled by the French," he told us. "There were pessimists among us, and there were optimists. But when the French technicians (who had been recalled by the French from Iraq in September 1980) began to return to Iraq in February and March, the pessimists were proven right."

What about giving the new French Government a chance to act? Couldn't they have made the reactor safe by demanding the right guarantees?

Bar-on felt not. International controls and inspection procedures were worthless, he contended. The Iraqis would have the nuclear capability, and besides, they could simply leave the Nonproliferation Treaty whenever they so decided. Israel could not trust the international community on a question of national survival.

That was a refrain we would hear time and again. The safeguards were useless. They didn't work. Israel could not trust them. But what about the French? Bar-on, the cagey diplomat, refused to condemn them outright, suggesting that perhaps they had been trapped into a contract that they themselves did not really want to fulfill. Israel had now given France an option, he believed. And with the explosive Osirak issue out of the way and a new administration in France, the thorny relations between the two countries could be improved.

A second Israeli, the soft-spoken but politically militant Professor Yuval Ne'eman, the former scientific head of Israel's own nuclear program and a one-time deputy head of Israeli military intelligence, was more pointed in his criticism. Interviewed in his comfortable home on a tree-lined street in suburban Tel Aviv, Ne'eman did not believe the French were worth trusting. "Why should we put our faith in them, even if they ask us to," he questioned rhetorically, "especially after they have been so careless in this entire matter? From the beginning of this contract, until now, they have done nothing to indicate we could trust them.

"Besides, in matters of our own basic security—and Iraq having an atomic bomb is basic to our security—how can we put our trust in any foreign country, or in any international organization? What would the French do? They would send some pretty blonde to charm the Iraqis, and she would report back and say everything's fine, there's no problem. Are we really supposed to trust that? In some matters, maybe, but not when it comes to an atomic bomb in the hands of a country that has vowed to destroy us."

Professor Ne'eman's criticism brought another question to mind. What about Israel's own nuclear program that had been started with French help and in which Professor Ne'eman had played a decisive role? Perhaps, it occurred to us, the Israelis distrusted the French not only because of their well-publicized political disagreements such as over the Palestinian rights issue, but because the Israelis knew from personal experience just what French nuclear aid could achieve, as we shall see.

A third Israeli official, who refused to be identified by name, was ready to be more specific about the Israeli attitude toward the French, putting it in the phrasing of a deceived lover. "They're whores," he stated with certainty. "Anything goes in their nuclear industry. Everybody knows it, even the Iraqis. That's why they went to the French to buy in the first place."

The French, at least the "good" French in the Quai d'Orsay, bitterly disagreed. They felt that they were now, under François Mitterrand, taking a position that would absolutely guarantee peaceful use only of the Osirak. The Israelis had not given them a chance to take action, and the repercussions from the attack (which had included the death of a young Frenchman) would be serious.

"The bombardment will certainly cast a shadow over our relations," the French nuclear diplomat told us. "It won't be forgotten. Not in a few days, or even in a few months."

President Mitterrand was similarly hurt by Israel's lack of trust in his own good intentions. Even as he condemned the raid—"We condemn the raid, not Israel," he declared—he made sure to announce that France would not sell Iraq a new reactor unless the Iraqis agreed to strict new safeguards.

"For the time being, nuclear cooperation with Iraq has been stopped with a bang," added Foreign Minister Cheysson. "And should there be nuclear cooperation in the future, it will involve, as President Mitterrand has stated, the most stringent controls."

As the French saw it, at the time Prime Minister Begin finally decided to make the raid on Osirak, he was in the midst of a bitter election campaign.

The polls showed that he was still trailing behind the opposition leader Shimon Peres, the candidate of the Israeli Labor Party. And the wily Begin would have been less than human—and less than the consummate political animal that he is—if he had not given at least a fleeting thought to the bombing of Osirak as a way to rally the voters behind his tough-minded and aggressive leadership. As his Labor Party rivals never tired of putting it, the one-time Israeli terrorist was certainly not above trading bombs for ballots.

"They chose this moment for the bombardment purely for electoral reasons," the Quai d'Orsay official told us. "It is not acceptable—not from a serious statesman." We reflected on the irony of French officialdom accusing the Israelis of timing the raid "purely" as an electoral ploy, in view of that same French officialdom's frivolous cooperation in permitting Iraq to attain the means for nuclear weaponry.

In fact, Begin's decision was not just politics. The Israelis decided to act as early as March 1981. Based on a close monitoring of Iraqi nuclear progress, the Israeli decision was founded on analyses and intelligence evaluation strikingly different in key ways from the public stance presented by Begin. Surprisingly, in some aspects of their thinking, the Israeli experts differed not a whit from their French counterparts.

Among the intelligence reports, we discovered, was a highly sober and low-keyed secret paper that reached the Office of the Prime Minister about two months before the Osirak bombing. Completed the last week of March, it was a thirty-three-page personality profile of the Iraqi strong man, Saddam Hussein; it was reminiscent of the famous psychological portrait of Adolf Hitler prepared in 1943 by the noted American psychiatrist Dr. William Langer. This one had been prepared by one of the Israeli intelligence agencies, and it attempted to answer two questions that could become a matter of life and death for the Jewish state: Would Saddam Hussein actually use his atom bomb as a weapon of war against the Israelis? And if he would, under what conditions was he most likely to do it?

The report, and what we have learned of other Israeli secret reports, agreed with the French on one critical question. The Iraqis might be considering a diversion scenario, as the French diplomat called it, but Saddam would seriously embark on it only after the Iraqis had attained "complete nuclear capability" and not before. When Saddam could get along without French or Italian help, he might be tempted to make his move. Before that, he would not. And certainly not while the Iraqis were still dependent on the aid, knowledge, and materials of the Western countries supplying him.

The time span for this "diversion scenario" was not one year, or two years, as Begin claimed in his press conference. At a minimum it would be five years, possibly even seven years, or so the Israeli experts stated, not before.

The report on Saddam Hussein was a strange mishmash of pseudo-Freudian psychology and hard-headed intelligence, with elaborate biographi-cal detail on Saddam's fatherless childhood, his early political experiences as a would-be assassin, his rise to power in the Baath Socialist Party, his power lust and megalomania, his lack of charisma and distaste for ideology, and even his recurring problems with the pains of a "low backache."

Some of the report has since shown up in Begin's public utterances about the Iraqi nuclear threat. Some of it has not. But, as the report proves, the Israeli intelligence analysts do *not* see Hussein as crazy, or "a lunatic," as Mr. Begin called him in his well-publicized letter of explanation to Egypt's former President Anwar el-Sadat. Instead, the secret report portrays Saddam as a hard-headed operator most of the time, an opportunist who tempers his political radicalism with rational calculation, capitalizing on the weaknesses of his enemies and gaining political advantage through the use of strength. The report calls him "cunning, sophisticated, cruel, and brave."

As the Israeli analysts described him, this is Saddam Hussein in his normal political behavior. But, warned the analysts, when Saddam finds himself facing an exceptional situation, he can act very differently indeed. When he sees a chance to fulfill his megalomaniacal ambitions for personal greatness, he is ready "to take risks and drastic action, without weighing all the risks he is actually running in the situation," the report explains.

According to the intelligence analysts, this gulf between Saddam's normal political behavior and what he might do in "exceptional circumstances" would shape his handling of the bomb. "Considerations of conscience and morality would not stop him from using it," the report predicted. "He would not be afraid of creating the image of a cruel and aggressive leader."

In normal circumstances, Saddam would still be influenced "by realistic and strategic considerations of expected losses and gains." But, if he saw the situation as exceptional, rational calculations were out the window. *"If in his estimation the use of atomic weapons would give him the chance to strike Israel, and gain for himself at the same time a leadership position in the Arab world, he would not hesitate to use the bomb,"* the analysis warned. And he would use it *"even if it would cost him similar retaliation from Israel, which would create damage and loss of life in Iraq itself."*

It was a terrifying picture, and it gives an insight into the sense of urgency that Begin and his colleagues felt about the Iraqi nuclear buildup. But, like the Quai d'Orsay's six-point proposal, the still-secret Israeli intelligence report suggests that the Israelis had at least five years before they had to act.

That was how the Israelis saw the nuclear threat from Iran. But even as they defended their bombing raid on Iraq, they took time to warn that Saddam Hussein was not the only one who posed a nuclear threat to Israel's survival, and to threaten that they were prepared to do to other nuclear installations what they had just done to Osirak.

"Does the Israeli raid signal a new Israeli policy that says that Israel will not tolerate for any Arab country, any Arab enemy, to construct nuclear weapons against Israel?" asked one of the reporters at the press conference following the raid.

"I didn't say so," countered the quick-witted Begin. "I said that Israel will not tolerate any *enemy*—not any Arab country, any *enemy*—to develop weapons of mass destruction against the people of Israel."

And if the Iraqis rebuild their reactor? asked another reporter.

"Should the Iraqis try again to build the reactor, through which they can produce atomic weapons, Israel will use the possibilities at its disposal to destroy that reactor," Begin replied.

"And will that apply also to Libya?" a third reporter asked.

"Well, let us deal first with that *meshugennah* [crazy guy] Saddam Hussein," Mr. Begin quipped. "With the other *meshuggenah* [Libyan leader Colonel Muammar el-Qaddafi] we shall deal another time."

Even the far-off Pakistanis, with their steadily advancing nuclear program, were a matter of serious Israeli worry. Begin did not mention them specifically at his press conference, but only two weeks before, on May 27, the Israeli Ambassador to the United Nations, Yehuda Blum, had sent an official note to Secretary General Kurt Waldheim warning that the Pakistanis were on the verge of producing sufficient plutonium to make their first nuclear device. And while there was little the United Nations could do about the warning, the Israelis had shown their concern.

"We will know what to do next time as well," added Israeli Chief of Staff Rafael Eytan, in a talk to a group of schoolchildren in the development town of Kiryat Ono. "And it is not definite that it will be Iraq in particular. It may be somewhere else."

As Begin exited from the press conference at Beit Agron, it was clear to everyone that the problem of nuclear bombs in the Middle East had not ended with the Israeli raid on Osirak. It was also clear that the Israelis had a resoundingly direct approach to its solution.

What was resoundingly unclear was whether the raid had not weakened rather than strengthened Israel's national security by threatening the Egyptian-Israeli peace process and isolating Israel in the community of nations, so many of which had condemned the raid. Within Israel itself, the opposition leader, Shimon Peres, expressed these very fears.

For all the fact that the raid elevated the world's fear of nuclear conflict, paradoxically it had salutary consequences. It dramatized the lack of concern—and therefore the flagrant irresponsibility—of the Western supplier nations, whose help is essential for any Third World country to make the bomb. It challenged the international community and, more specifically, the International Atomic Energy Agency and its system of "safeguarding" the spread of nuclear technology to ensure its peaceful uses. * Furthermore, it bought a few precious years to find an answer to the most important question facing mankind in the latter part of the twentieth century: how the spread of nuclear bomb-making technology to a whole new group of nations, especially in the explosive Middle East, could be stopped or controlled.

---

* On September 25, 1981, the IAEA condemned the raid, cutting off aid to Israel amounting to $100,000 yearly. An Israeli spokesman called the action "arbitrary" and "immoral."

The Bomb: Who Wants It?
How to Make It.
How Not to Stop It From
Spreading.

You have no authority to look for undeclared nuclear materials.
Your job is to verify that the declared material accountancy
balance is correct.

—Roger Richter,
IAEA inspector (resigned),
June 1981

Russia and America are one kettle of fish. But in the Middle East
it's totally different. There the rules of the game are just being
invented.

—Dr. Abraham Friedman,
U.S. diplomat (Paris Embassy),
June 1981

From the sparse hills of beautiful Marrakesh in Morocco to the noisy traffic jams of Cairo, from the oil-soaked deserts of Arabia to the bustling markets of Karachi in Pakistan, the vast area that pundits call the Middle East is perhaps the world's most complex and most bitterly divided region. It is unmatched in its diversity, unrivaled in the richness of its history, and sadly unique in its potential for violent and often irrational conflict.

Even without the threat of nuclear weapons, the danger of political violence and open warfare is always at hand. Whether in Lebanon or in Syria or on the West Bank, the bloody fighting between Israelis and Arabs never seems to end. The hostility between the Arabs of Iraq and the Persians of Iran has lasted for more than thirteen centuries: Perhaps the war between them should not have come as such a surprise to the unsuspecting West. The Pakistanis could as easily square off against their Indian rivals to the south, as they did in 1965 and again in 1971, in the war that broke Pakistan in half and created the independent state of Bangladesh. And any of a dozen other potential wars simmers below the region's surface, from Libya's conflict with Sudan to Syria's ongoing rivalry with Iraq.

Within each state as well, the area is racked with instability. Some states—like Pakistan and even Israel—are the results of a partition that left no one satisfied. Others—like Iraq—were formed by the whim of imperial powers, with little regard for the varied peoples who live there. Often, many different nations, faiths, and sects, each with its own beliefs and its own intricate history, share a single set of borders, fighting and killing to stay on top, or to stay separate, or simply to stay alive. Kurd against Arab, Sunni Muslim against Shiite, Lebanese Christian against Lebanese Muslim—the rivalries fester, the violence flares, the wars wear on.

Throughout the region, the dominant faith is Islam. More than any other single force, it is Islam that makes the region one, from the north of Africa to Islamic Pakistan and even parts of India. Of course, the world of Islam stretches far beyond, as far as Indonesia and the southern islands of the Philippines to the east, and deep into black Africa to the south. But in a way that one can almost touch and feel, it is Islam—and the continuing influence of the Islamic Arabs—that gives life to that otherwise meaningless geographic abstraction that is the Middle East.

Islam as religion. Islam as culture. Islam as civilization. By Western standards, with our generally secular values and our relative separation of church and state, Islam has always been hard to fit into any of our standard categories. More than just a religious faith or set of beliefs, it is an all-encompassing code of conduct, which attempts to regulate every aspect of life, from the role of women to the proper punishment of criminal offenders. Unlike the pluralism that we claim to favor, Islam is holistic, a way of life in which prayer and politics are often disturbingly intertwined, whether in the Iran of the Ayatollah Khomeini, the Libya of Colonel Muammar el-Qaddafi, or the Arabia of the Saudi royal house.

Elegant in thought, rich in tradition, great in accomplishment, Islam was and is one of the truly powerful forces in shaping the history of the world as we know it. Yet for more than half a millennium, since the sack of Baghdad by the Mongol hordes in 1258 and the disintegration of the then dominant Arab civilization in the face of the Ottoman Turks, the entire Islamic world has felt itself in decline, growing ever weaker within and suffering a growing impotence against the incursions of an outside world that despised, exploited, and corrupted the Faithful.

Now all that is changing. Islamic civilization has once again come to life, and not least because of a treasure formed long before the followers of the Prophet burst forth from the Arab heartland. That treasure is oil—a mighty sea of oil, lying beneath those shifting desert sands. Western analysts state that Saudi Arabia alone has potential oil reserves of 300 billion barrels, and proven oil reserves now of 180 billion barrels, a quarter of the world's proven supply. Oil has brought fabulous riches. It has changed the lives and fortunes of those who have it. It has altered the balance of world power.

In a sense, this is the other face of the "oil crisis," and there is no shortage of books and articles that purport to tell us all about it. But one side of the story has been sadly neglected, and that is the nuclear side. For as the Arab and Islamic countries of the Middle East suddenly found themselves with all their present wealth and power, they could buy whatever it was that they wanted. And what some of them—chiefly the Libyans, the Pakistanis, and the Iraqis—wanted most was the bomb. Nuclear weapons would let them "walk tall," as a former Pakistani official told us. Nuclear weapons would put them on a level with the Great Powers. Nuclear weapons would make them equal to the two peoples in the region who were neither Arab nor Islamic, but who already had nuclear weapons or the ability to make them—the Indians and the Israelis.

That was the intent, and it should have been obvious to anyone who listened closely to what the Islamic and Arab leaders were saying. But to get what they wanted, the Islamic countries needed the nuclear technology, and that only the industrialized countries of the West could provide.

From the beginnings of the Manhattan Project during World War II, when the United States built the world's first atomic weapons, would-be bomb makers have used two different nuclear explosive materials. One is enriched uranium; the other is plutonium. Both ways to the bomb start with natural uranium, which can be mined in several different parts of the world. In making the two different kinds of bombs, the bomb makers have to put the uranium through one of two completely different—and extremely complex—nuclear technologies. This was true for the Americans in their war with Japan. It was true for the Soviet Union and the more recent members of the nuclear club. And it remains true for any other nation now trying to join their ranks, whether Iraq or Pakistan, India or Israel.

In the first way, the bomb makers have to take account of two different forms of the uranium, or as scientists call them, isotopes. The first of these is called uranium 238, which makes up some 99.3 percent of the uranium as it is mined and is on its own fairly benign. The other is uranium 235, which makes up the remaining 0.7 percent. The relatively lighter uranium 235 atoms are the ones that most readily split, or "fission," which is what triggers the nuclear chain reaction that creates the big bang.

The trick—and it is one of the most difficult in the entire field of nuclear technology—is to find a process to separate the two different isotopes physically and then to build up the proportion of the rare and highly explosive uranium 235, often to as much as 93 percent. This is called enriching the uranium, and as we shall see, only a handful of the world's most industrially advanced nations have managed to master the complicated technologies involved. Or at least that was the case until now.

For the would-be bomb maker, the major difficulty is to get enough of this highly enriched uranium together at one time to create a "critical mass." In the case of the bomb that the Americans dropped on the Japanese city of Hiroshima in August 1945, the highly enriched uranium came to about twenty kilograms, or forty-four pounds. In later, far more sophisticated designs, American bomb makers have made do with as little as seven or eight kilograms of highly enriched uranium.

The second way to the bomb starts with the same natural uranium. But instead of enriching it, the bomb makers put the garden-variety uranium into a nuclear reactor, either as fuel rods in any standard power reactor or as a "blanket" around the reactor core in a relatively powerful nuclear reactor. The nuclear chain reaction in the core frees millions of rapidly escaping neutrons, which bombard the generally benign atoms of uranium 238 and turn some of them into a new, man-made element. This is plutonium, which can be used either to produce new nuclear fuel or to provide the explosive material for nuclear weapons.

But in this way to the bomb, making the plutonium is only half the battle. The other half is extracting it from the spent fuel burned by the reactor. The plutonium itself can be extremely poisonous. And along with the uranium and the so-called fission products produced in the nuclear reaction, it emerges from the reactor in a highly radioactive state. How, then, to extract it?

Scientists call the process reprocessing, and they undertake it only in the most carefully shielded "hot cells," or specially protected plutonium reprocessing plants. In simplest terms, the process entails taking the irradiated material, which is usually in the form of fuel rods, letting them cool, chopping them up and dissolving them in acid, and then using some basic chemistry to separate the remaining uranium and fission products from the plutonium.

Depending on the sophistication of the weapons design, a bomb maker would need somewhere between five and eight kilograms of the plutonium to make an atomic bomb such as the one the United States used to devastate its second 1945 atomic target, the city of Nagasaki.

Of course, the bomb-making novice would still have to discover how to design and build his bomb, or in other words, how to turn the highly enriched uranium or plutonium into actual nuclear devices. And that is not child's play. In spite of many of the reports that have appeared over the past few years in the press and on television, designing and building an atom bomb is not something that can be done by any bright young graduate student in physics or any ragtag band of terrorists. Yet any nation with the scientific talent to run a sophisticated nuclear reactor could be expected to have or to be able to get the needed skills, and they will find most of the necessary calculations in the open scientific literature.

Enriched uranium, reprocessed plutonium—both are part of normal civilian nuclear programs. Any nation with the money can buy the technology to produce them, and they can often do it openly and with the blessings of the world's number-one nuclear watchdog and regulatory body, the International Atomic Energy Agency in Vienna. Yet that very same plutonium or highly enriched uranium can be used to build nuclear weapons, and that is exactly what a handful of nations in the Middle East are trying to do. As we will show, India, Israel, Pakistan, and Iraq—four nations in the region or on its fringes—now pose a potential nuclear threat. A possible fifth, the Libya of Colonel Qaddafi, is still trying to buy, borrow, or steal its own nuclear weapon.

The Indians were the first, at least publicly, using the plutonium from a Canadian-supplied research reactor to explode a "peaceful nuclear device" in May 1974. This led the way, showing that even a poor and hard-pressed country, given the political will, could make an atom bomb.

In fact, according to what we have learned from Western intelligence sources, the Indians stopped short of making actual weapons, content for the time to let the world know that they could do so whenever they wanted. But now, in the face of the Pakistanis and their nuclear ambitions, the Indians have announced the start-up of their new reprocessing plant at Tarapur, near Bombay. This reprocessing plant is a key facility, as it will enable the Indians to take their enormous backlog of used reactor fuel rods and turn them into a large arsenal of nuclear weapons.

At the same time, leading Indian strategists—such as K. K. Subrahmanyam, the head of the influential Institute for Defense Studies and Analyses in New Delhi—are calling for India to cross the line and openly develop nuclear weapons.

The Israelis also have "nuclear capability," though Israeli spokesmen insist in an almost ritual way that they have held back from actually producing nuclear weapons.

"We are not going to be the first ones to introduce nuclear weapons into the Middle East," declared the former Defense and Foreign Minister Moshe Dayan, in a statement on Italian television following the Israeli bombing of the Osirak reactor. "But we do have the capacity to produce nuclear weapons," he added. "And if the Arabs are willing to introduce nuclear weapons into the Middle East, then Israel should not be too late in having nuclear weapons, too."

In practice, this distinction between "nuclear capability" and actual atomic weapons is largely Talmudic, a question of when a bomb becomes a bomb, of how long it takes to put together the final elements, and of whether or not the final screw has been turned. In any case, such nuances are lost on both the American Central Intelligence Agency and French nuclear authorities, who have long since concluded that the Israelis do, in fact, have the bomb.

Like the Indians, the Israelis have managed to produce plutonium, using a research reactor supplied by the French at Dimona, in the Negev desert. And according to a September 1974 CIA report, which was mistakenly released in 1978, Israel has also made weapons with highly enriched uranium, most likely diverted from a small nuclear installation in Pennsylvania.

The Israelis have done all this without any announced nuclear tests, and their present atomic arsenal—or "capability"—is almost certainly larger than the twelve to twenty weapons that are generally mentioned in press reports. For a time still, the Israelis are the only real nuclear power in the Middle East.

The Iraqis are the latest entrant in the nuclear stakes. As early as September 1975, Iraqi president Saddam Hussein let the cat out of the bag, describing his efforts in France to buy a supposedly peaceful nuclear reactor as part of "the first Arab attempt at nuclear arming." Saddam said this in an exclusive interview in the Beirut magazine *al-Usbua al-Arabi*, and according to the journal, the Iraqi leader never attempted to retract what he had said.

Following the Israeli raid on the Osirak reactor, Saddam Hussein openly called for nuclear weapons. "Peace-loving nations should now help the Arabs to acquire atomic bombs as a counterbalance to those already possessed by Israel," he proclaimed.

In what appears to be one of his periodic fits of caution, the Iraqi leader has since publicly denied that his statement meant that Iraq was actually seeking the production of nuclear weapons. But it was hardly the statement of someone who has turned his back on the bomb, and it does show his thinking. As he explained, the Iraqis want the bomb because Israel has it, and also because they want a stake in a world dominated by nuclear powers. If the Jews could do it, why should not the Arabs? And if the Great Powers could play the game, why not the newly emerging nations of the so-called Third World?

In their pursuit of this deadly nuclear logic, the Iraqis were on the way to being able to produce nuclear weapons from both plutonium and highly enriched uranium. In both ways to the bomb, they were depending on the seventy-thermal-megawatt Osirak research reactor which they had bought from the French, and which the Israelis destroyed.

The first way was highly enriched uranium, which was coming directly from France in the form of fuel for the Osirak and for a second, sister facility—an 800-kilowatt Isis-type "critical assembly," which the Iraqis call Tammuz II. Each of these reactors would have a fuel load of thirteen kilograms of 93 percent highly enriched uranium, which together would give the Iraqis enough for at least one and maybe two nuclear devices, depending on the skill of their weapons designers.

The second, more likely route was to use the Osirak to produce plutonium. To go the plutonium route, the Iraqis would have to find a way to fabricate natural uranium into fuel rods to blanket the reactor core, and a way to reprocess the irradiated uranium rods to extract the plutonium from them. Saddam Hussein had already acquired the necessary fuel fabrication and "hot cell" reprocessing facilities—not from the French, but from the equally willing Italians.

With the Osirak destroyed, the Iraqis will have to start all over again, which Saddam Hussein has sworn to do, and for which his former rivals in Saudi Arabia, in an unprecedented show of Arab unity, have now promised to foot the bill.

The Pakistanis have the Islamic world's most advanced nuclear program of all. Under the leadership of the late Prime Minister Zulfikar Ali Bhutto, the Pakistanis started out on their nuclear quest in competition with their traditional rivals on the South Asia subcontinent, the Indians. In recent years, the Pakistanis have moved increasingly into the Arab world, providing key military advisers and even troops to Saudi Arabia, the Gulf state of Abu Dhabi, and Jordan, as well as to the Libyans. It is Arab oil money—initially from Libya's Qaddafi—that has paid for Pakistan's "Islamic bomb," chiefly to brandish as a threat against the Israelis.

With these donated and borrowed resources, the Pakistanis set out on a most ambitious course—to produce the needed nuclear explosives through two separate, highly sophisticated industrial processes. In the first instance, they have been trying to produce highly enriched uranium with a cascade of rapidly spinning ultracentrifuges. This is similar to the process used by the British-Dutch-German Urenco consortium at Almelo, in Holland, and is based on plans taken from the Urenco plant by an expatriate Pakistani metallurgist, Dr. Abdul Qadeer Khan. The second method extracts plutonium from used reactor fuel using chemical reprocessing technology bought principally from France and Belgium. Both of these processes are the cream of Western technology, and the components to build them have been bought on the international market. Either of them alone will give Pakistan—and its Islamic allies—an entire arsenal of atomic weapons. Not one, but two, three, many Islamic bombs.

American intelligence sources tell us that the Pakistanis could have enough of their own plutonium to test a nuclear device by early 1982. Those in the American Government who have followed the Pakistani nuclear program most closely say that they do not necessarily expect the Pakistanis to carry out a nuclear test. Like the Israelis, the Pakistani scientists might have sufficient confidence to build nuclear weapons without feeling any need for a test explosion. And by foregoing a nuclear test, the Pakistanis would avoid creating any undue political problems for the Reagan Administration in Washington, which is committed to giving Islamabad some $3 billion in military and economic support over a five-year period.

India, Israel, Iraq, and Pakistan—a budding nuclear arms race that now poses an unprecedented threat to the peoples of the entire region, and beyond. Within the region itself, both Iraq and Islamic Pakistan are ruled by repressive, unstable regimes. Both are also sworn enemies of Israel, and any weapon in their hands could threaten the very existence of the tiny Jewish state. The Israelis, in turn, already rely on the veiled threat that they could drop atom bombs on Baghdad or Damascus. With the threatened loss of their atomic monopoly, Israeli strategists might well be tempted to press ahead with their policy of preemptive strikes, such as their bombing of the Osirak reactor. If they are faced by a full-scale attack, they would have the option of nuclear retaliation.

The threat, however, goes beyond the Arab-Israeli conflict. The Iraqis see their "nuclear arming" as a political weapon in their drive to become the regional superpower in the world's most strategic zone, the entire "arc of crisis" from the Fertile Crescent through the oil-rich Arabian Gulf and into the Red Sea and the Indian Ocean. This pits them against their traditional foes, the Iranians, and also other Arab regimes, especially Kuwait and until recent months, Saudi Arabia and the other Gulf states, which have been backing the Pakistanis and their Islamic bomb. The Pakistanis, meanwhile, have their own scores to settle with an already nuclear India. And in India, important voices are calling for the development of an arsenal of nuclear bombs to respond to the Pakistani threat.

As the Israeli bombing of Osirak proves, the very prospect of a nuclear arms race has already raised the level of violence. It also raises the level of tension within each country as well as between them. Iraq is presently a powder keg, with a small ruling group using arms and terror to hold down a well-armed Kurdish rebellion and a growing opposition from the majority population of Shiite Muslims, who are closely tied to the followers of Ayatollah Khomeini in Iran. How would the present Iraqi rulers use the bomb, especially if they were losing a war? And what if the weapon fell into the hands of the Shiite opposition—or their Shiite coreligionists across the border in Iran?

Pakistan under General Mohammad Zia-ul-Haq is the very model of an unstable military dictatorship. The nuclear program is a highly emotive symbol within the country, and it is likely that any group trying to topple Zia would also try desperately to get their hands on the Islamic bomb. This is especially true since the chief opposition group is led by the sons, wife, and daughter of the father of that bomb, the late Zulfikar Ali Bhutto the former Pakistani Prime Minister.

Israel, of these three, is the only one with a truly stable and democratic government. But the very existence of the Jewish state surrounded by Arab enemies—many of which are determined to destroy it—creates the most unstable situation of all. It is made even more volatile by Israel's memories of the Holocaust. If the Israelis ever felt their survival at stake, they could well threaten to unleash their ultimate weapon of destruction.

The result is a new nuclear confrontation even more dangerous for world peace than the present nuclear balance of terror between the atomic giants, the United States and the Soviet Union. The ins and outs, the shifting alliances, the religious fervor, and the basic instability in the region all make a cruel joke of any rational calculation, or of the kind of game theory that Western strategists use to analyze the nuclear conflict between the United

States and the Soviet Union. Both superpowers have vital interests and alliances in the region, and any nuclear conflict could involve them as well, raising the deadly vision of a nuclear Sarajevo escalating by mistake and miscalculation into World War III.

"Russia and America are one kettle of fish," explained Dr. Abraham Friedman, the former Director of International Programs for the U.S. Atomic Energy Agency and now Scientific Attaché at the American Embassy in Paris. "But in the Middle East it's totally different. There the rules of the game are just being invented."

Trying to Halt the Spread

What is to stop the worst from happening? The conventional answer of the community of nations is to rely on the Nuclear Nonproliferation Treaty and the "safeguards" of the International Atomic Energy Agency, a United Nations organization based in Vienna.

The Nonproliferation Treaty, or NPT as it is called, was sponsored initially by the United States, the United Kingdom, and the Soviet Union in the mid-1960s. Finally signed in 1968, it was essentially a bargain between those nations that already had nuclear weapons and those that did not. Those with nuclear weapons promised not to transfer them and "not in any way to assist, encourage, or induce any non-nuclear weapon state to manufacture or otherwise acquire nuclear weapons or other nuclear explosive devices."

Those that had no nuclear weapons similarly promised that they would not attempt to get or to make them, and also that they would open all of their nuclear installations to outside inspections and other safeguards by the International Atomic Energy Agency.

Both sides, the haves and the have-nots, also promised that they would pursue negotiations to stop the present strategic nuclear arms race and to move toward universal nuclear disarmament. This was the celebrated promise to stop what has been called vertical proliferation, a vow that the major nuclear weapons states now honor almost entirely in the breach.

But the treaty really rested on a simple trade-off, which has come to plague the entire effort to stop the spread of dangerous nuclear technologies. As payment for their promise to forswear nuclear weapons and to permit the so-called full-scope safeguards, the nations without nuclear weapons were guaranteed that nothing would stand in their way if they wanted to buy any "civilian" nuclear technology.

"Nothing in this Treaty shall be interpreted as affecting the inalienable rights of all the Parties to the Treaty to develop research, production and use of nuclear energy for peaceful purposes without discrimination," the key paragraph declared. "All the Parties to the Treaty undertake to facilitate . . . the fullest possible exchange of equipment, materials and scientific and technological information for the peaceful uses of nuclear energy."

For all the legalistic words, the basic bargain was clear enough, especially for those nations which did not yet have the bomb, but which wanted to get it. If they promised not to get the bomb, and also allowed certain outside controls, they could get all the supposedly civilian nuclear technology they wanted, even if they intended to use that same technology to build the bomb.

The silliness of the situation is hard to believe. As long as the would-be buyers have signed the NPT, they are assumed to have only the most peaceful intentions, often in the face of the most blatant evidence to the contrary. And to add insult to injury, they can and do claim that the treaty itself gives them every right to buy whatever they want.

Inevitably, this provision creates a double bind for those industrialized nations that export nuclear technology. Either they can fulfill their part of the NPT and supply supposedly peaceful nuclear technology, spreading the know-how and the facilities needed to make nuclear weapons. Or they can refuse to supply the more sensitive technologies, primarily uranium enrichment and plutonium reprocessing—a policy of denial that will undermine the very basis of the NPT and similar international undertakings, such as the Treaty of Tlatelolco, a regional treaty against nuclear profileration in Latin America.

"The general problem is that there is no clear difference between what you can use for civilian purposes and what you can use for military," admitted André Jacomet, the distinguished former Secretary of France's official Council on Foreign Nuclear Policy, who was exceptionally candid with us. "That's the big problem. That's why people are skeptical about stopping proliferation. The only true safeguard is to see that these countries do not have access to the technology," he told us during one of several lengthy interviews at his comfortable home in Paris. He added with a regretful shrug of the shoulders, "But there is competition to sell, and so we do it."

So far, some 114 nations have signed and ratified the NPT. One of the very first was Iraq, which completed the formalities in 1972. Another of those which have taken the pledge is Colonel Qaddafi's Libya, while the Israelis, the Indians, and the Pakistanis have all refused.

That is the Nonproliferation Treaty. The International Atomic Energy Agency and the adequacy of its "safeguards" raise a more complicated set of concerns.

Working under the wing of the United Nations, the IAEA has the responsibility to supervise more than 700 nuclear installations in some fifty countries. This includes all openly admitted nuclear installations in those "non-nuclear weapons states" that have signed and ratified the Nonproliferation Treaty, as well as certain specific facilities in other countries, such as a small U.S.-supplied research reactor in Israel and various power reactors and other installations in India and Pakistan.

In itself, this is an unprecedented and unenviable task. Never before has any international body attempted to involve itself so deeply in the most sensitive area of the economic life of so many nations, each jealous of its own national sovereignty. To make the job even harder, the IAEA has been forced to work within a straightjacket of built-in constraints. It is supposedly the world's top nuclear cop. But it has no police powers. It has no intelligence service of its own. It must depend to a frightening degree on the voluntary cooperation of the various nations it is supposed to monitor, and also on the intensely political decisions of the member nations on its Board of Governors.

Perhaps the biggest difficulty, though, is that the IAEA is expected to play two often conflicting roles. It is supposed to promote the worldwide growth of nuclear power and research programs, chiefly by encouraging the spread of "civilian" nuclear technology and providing technical assistance to nations in the Third World. At the same time, it is supposed to prevent the spread of nuclear weapons.

The conflict is obvious. Yet all too often, IAEA officials deny the difficulty, insisting against the evidence that there is no necessary link between the civilian nuclear technologies that they are promoting and the nuclear weapons that they are trying to prevent.

"It is far easier and cheaper to make a bomb than to launch a nuclear power program," argued the Agency's just-retired number-two man, the highly articulate David Fischer, with whom we spoke. "Historically, the half-dozen nations that have nuclear explosive capacity have acquired it by building a series of specialized plants, dedicated to the production of nuclear explosives. In no case has proliferation resulted from, or even been undertaken under the cloak of a civilian nuclear power program."

Fischer is a persuasive man, a tall, distinguished-looking, and very sophisticated South African, and when we interviewed him at the IAEA's new offices at the "modernistic" United Nations complex in Vienna, we found him forthcoming and one of the few top international civil servants willing and able to break free from the mind-numbing bureaucratese that passes for communication in all parts of the U.N.

But as we discovered during our investigation, Fischer's argument that proliferation has never resulted from civilian nuclear power programs is misleading about the past. The Indians, for one, used a supposedly peaceful nuclear research reactor and reprocessing facilities to produce the plutonium for their "peaceful nuclear explosion," and the celebrated French nuclear deterrent, the *force de frappe*, borrowed heavily from France's initially peaceful efforts in nuclear research and development following World War II. Even worse, Fischer's argument completely avoids what is happening now, especially the budding nuclear arms race in the Middle East.

Both the Iraqis and the Pakistanis are purchasing essentially civilian nuclear technologies to produce nuclear explosives. The Indians have declared that their new reprocessing facility at Tarapur is needed for their civilian nuclear power program, even though they will be able to use the reprocessed plutonium to build a large nuclear arsenal. And all three nations are actually pursuing relatively ambitious peaceful nuclear programs at the very same time as they are pursuing nuclear weapons. In other words, they are going both ways at once. In fact, within the Middle East, it is only the Israelis who have gone straight and single-mindedly for nuclear weapons. Like the Indians, they got the basis of their nuclear option back in the early sixties.

But Fischer's argument is typical. As major promoters of nuclear power, IAEA officials do not like to hear about the dangers of civilian nuclear technology. Their job is not to assess the hidden intentions of nations that have signed the Nonproliferation Treaty, such as Iraq, but only to monitor a country's *declared* facilities and to make technical reports on what they have seen of the country's use of nuclear fuels. In their public pronouncements and private statements, IAEA officials often sound as if they are more concerned to make the world *safe for* nuclear power than *safe from* nuclear weapons. As a result, the Agency seems oddly unprepared to meet the present threat of proliferation, and often irrelevant to any possible solution.

This is even the case in the Agency's main line of defense against proliferation, the so-called nuclear safeguards that are employed to do the monitoring. In practice, the safeguards are a series of measures to keep track of "sensitive" nuclear materials, the processes that produce them, the tanks that store them, and the facilities that handle them. Each nuclear installation under safeguards is expected to keep a record of all such materials and to account for any changes that are produced through nuclear reactions or other processes. The IAEA makes periodic inspections, at times to be agreed on by the Agency and the concerned country, to audit these accounts and to make sure that the material balances are what they are supposed to be.

The inspectors also install and monitor a wide range of technical devices to make sure that nuclear materials cannot be moved or altered without detection. These include tamper-proof locks and seals on materials containers and containment areas and even on parts of reactors, and still and motion-picture cameras and video recorders to watch over sensitive areas and operations. The inspectors also make qualitative checks on nuclear materials, using neutron counters and gamma-ray spectrometers.

The goal of all this prying and poking is simple—to provide "timely detection" of any diversion of a "significant quantity" of bomb-prone materials. The Agency claims there has been no such diversion in the 700-odd facilities it monitors in more than fifty countries. "A significant quantity" of bomb-grade fuel for the IAEA would normally be the amount of any material that would be needed to make a single nuclear explosive device. The Agency presently defines this as a minimum of twenty-five kilograms of highly enriched uranium or eight kilograms of plutonium, though sophisticated bomb makers could make do with less of either one. "Timely detection" is similarly figured to equal the amount of time that would be needed to make a nuclear device, which could be as little as a week with plutonium already in its metallic form.

At best, the aim is to detect the diversion, not to prevent it, and to make the detection in enough time to give the diplomatic community a chance to act before the bomb goes off. As David Fischer has described it, this timely warning is supposed to serve as "a burglar alarm which allows the diplomatic police to rush in and apprehend the offender before he blows open the safe." The hope, of course, is that the threat of detection would deter any would-be nuclear nation from diverting any significant quantities of either plutonium or highly enriched uranium.

How safe are the IAEA safeguards? Do they do even this limited job? The answer is more complex than many critics have suggested.

In the past, the system has worked reasonably well to give continuing assurance that a safeguarded country was not diverting nuclear material. This was useful in the highly industrialized countries, which had easy access to large quantities of highly enriched uranium or plutonium from their own or their allies' nuclear research and power programs. Especially in the case of the three major defeated countries of World War II—Germany, Italy, and Japan—the system helped to remove any lingering fears that they might be attempting a nuclear comeback. In these situations, the safeguards built trust and reduced the likelihood that any nasty surprise might disturb the existing strategic nuclear balance.

Even today, the same highly industrialized nations—from Canada and Sweden to Germany and Japan—could still make nuclear weapons if they wanted, and in a very short space of time. They have the skill, and most of them already have enough highly enriched uranium or plutonium close at hand. But they have all made a political decision not to build the bomb, and the IAEA safeguards tell the world that they are keeping their word.

In those situations, where countries are not building the bomb, the system works well enough. But in countries like Iraq and Pakistan, where they are, the safeguards are anything but safe.

"I believe that the Iraqi nuclear program was organized for the purpose of developing a capability to produce nuclear weapons over the next several years," explained former IAEA safeguards inspector Roger Richter in his dramatic testimony before the Foreign Relations Committee of the United States Senate right after the Osirak bombing. A nuclear engineer, Richter had just resigned as the only American inspector in the IAEA section responsible for safeguarding nuclear facilities in Israel, India, Pakistan, and Iraq.

"The role of the inspector is limited to verifying only material declared by Iraq or France," Richter testified. "You have no authority to look for undeclared material. Your job is to verify that the declared material accountancy balance is correct. You are not entitled even to look at the other facilities if Iraq has not adhered to its obligations under NPT to report to the IAEA that material subject to safeguards is located in these facilities," he warned.

As Richter described it, the inspections and accounting procedures would probably be able to detect any diversion of the highly enriched uranium fuel. But they would probably miss any attempt to produce plutonium by blanketing the Osirak reactor core with natural uranium rods, or targets.

"The IAEA does not look for clandestine operations," the former inspector reminded the Senators. "The IAEA, in effect, conducts an accounting operation."

Even in that, the Iraqis had the upper hand. Like every other country subject to safeguards, Iraq could and did veto inspectors from any country it did not like, Richter reported. All but one of the inspectors approved by Iraq came from the Soviet Union or Hungary. The one exception was from France, which was supplying the Osirak reactor. "As an accepted inspector, you must keep in mind that any adverse conclusions you might reach as a result of your inspection would have to take into account your country's sensitivity to how this information might affect relations with Iraq," he explained.

Next, the inspectors were limited to three inspections a year and had to give several weeks' notice that they wanted to visit those installations that were in fact subject to safeguards. The Iraqis could and did suggest alternative dates, which would give them every opportunity to hide any illicit operations. "Since the entire reactor can be emptied of the clandestine uranium target specimens within days, you as an inspector face the fact that by the time you arrive to verify the declared inventory of fuel elements which power the reactor, all evidence of illicit irradiations could be covered up."

Both the IAEA and the American Government have since criticized parts of Richter's testimony, arguing that negotiations with the Iraqis were still going on and that many of the problems that he was raising were in the process of being solved. But in the course of our investigations, we heard many of the same criticisms of the safeguards system, both from former top officials of the IAEA's Safeguards Division and from outside experts. Some of those on the inside were reluctant to speak as frankly as they or we wanted. Warren Donnelly, a research associate at the Library of Congress, told us why: "The inspectors don't like to be too open about their own criticisms. It's like getting a dentist to criticize the work of another dentist, or a doctor telling you that his colleague messed up on a surgical operation. These are the kind of things you don't say openly, only inside the shop." Any time the criticisms have been made publicly, mainly by former inspectors willing to speak out, IAEA officials offered assurances that, even if there had been problems before, everything was now under control. It should be noted that Roger Richter broke the rules of the club, and was ceremoniously fired from his job in IAEA about ten days after he himself had resigned.

Of course, those of us on the outside have little way of knowing just how effective the controls are, as the IAEA is obliged by its regulations and agreements to keep its reports confidential, and they are never published. This does not seem to us the best way to encourage accountability, or to build public confidence in the system.

The most glaring problem, however, and a fatal weakness of the international safeguards system, is that any country can simply opt out of it after it has the nuclear equipment it wants, and that includes countries that have signed the Nonproliferation Treaty.

"Now, safeguards are not foolproof," explained one highly placed American official, in an interview following the Israeli bombing of the Osirak reactor. "But even if they are somewhat effective, what if Iraq drops out of the NPT? What protection is there against that? There was a piece of paper between Iran and Iraq, all signed and sealed, and what happened there? A war."

Dr. Abraham Friedman, once the Director of International Programs for the U.S. Atomic Energy Commission, raised the same concern. "If a country concludes that for national security reasons it does not want to be part of the NPT, it could give three months' notice," he told us. "The safeguard obligation would still hold in principle, but it could simply say to the IAEA that it was not permitting inspections. The assumption is that, if a country felt strongly enough, it would simply ignore the treaty."

This, then, is the answer of the community of nations to the problem of stopping the spread of nuclear weaponry: Under the Nonproliferation Treaty a nation that wants the bomb can buy whatever nuclear technology it wants. Once it has the goods on its soil, it can leave the treaty at its own discretion, giving three months' notice. No penalties are prescribed within the treaty. It's all legal and fully aboveboard.

What, then, is the good of having a treaty? Signing it is an excellent and not even a particularly clever way to be able to buy the technology to make the bomb.

TWO

WALKING TALL

The Day the Bomb Was Born

> We know that Israel and South Africa have full nuclear capability. The Christian, Jewish and Hindu civilizations have this capability. The communist powers also possess it. Only the Islamic civilization was without it, but that position was about to change.
>
> —Zulfikar Ali Bhutto,
> former Prime Minister of Pakistan,
> 1979

Pakistan stood at the breaking point. Only a few months before, as midnight approached on the 25th of March, 1971, the Pakistani armed forces had moved with stunning brutality to crush the separatist-minded Bengalis in what was then East Pakistan. The soldiers, all from the western provinces of the divided country, had run riot over the Bengali countryside in a frenzy of death and destruction. They had burned Bengali villages, raped Bengali women, killed and mutilated unarmed Bengali men. They had also systematically rounded up a long list of Bengali intellectuals, students, and political leaders—a "cleansing process," the Pakistani military leaders had called it. And they had taken prisoner, to await execution, the man who had just won Pakistan's first free election in years, the leader of the Bengali political party, the Awami League, Sheik Mujib-ur-Rahman.

"Sort them out," the West Pakistan generals had ordered, and a young officer explained exactly what that meant to a Pakistani journalist who was there, a very shaken Anthony Mascarenhas. "We are determined to cleanse East Pakistan once and for all of the threat of secession," said the officer. "Even if it means killing off two million people and ruling the province as a colony for thirty years."

The bloodbath had been the Pakistani military junta's answer to Sheik Mujib's victory at the polls, as well as to the "threat" of his widely proclaimed Six Point Program, which would have given the Bengalis and other provincial groups far-reaching autonomy from the Punjabi-dominated central government. As the world looked on in horror, some 8 million panic-stricken Bengali men, women, and children fled across the border into India, many of them into tattered refugee camps in the area around Calcutta.

The East Bengalis, fighting now for their survival, declared their independence from the government based in West Pakistan. They began to fight a vicious guerrilla war, retaliating against their enemies mainly with savage attacks on non-Bengali communities within their own province. Floods and famine added to the misery, and their situation became desperate. They pleaded with the nearby Indians to aid them.

India answered their call.

Hard-pressed by the flood of Bengali refugees, and eager to cripple their longtime Pakistani rivals, against whom they had just fought a war in 1965, the Indian Army staged what one observor termed an Israeli-style strike. They struck directly at the Pakistani forces in both East Bengal and West Pakistan itself, quickly overwhelming them with larger numbers and greater fire power. It was never a contest. Within a month, on December 16, the once swaggering Pakistani Army meekly surrendered to the Indians at the racecourse in the East Bengali capital of Dacca.

For Pakistan, the disaster could hardly have been more complete.

"In December 1971, Pakistan was divided, defeated, demoralized, and in the eyes of the world, disgraced," wrote the distinguished British historian Hugh Trevor-Roper.

"Pakistan is now dead and buried under a mountain of corpses," declared Tajuddin Ahmad, the first Prime Minister of the breakaway Bangladesh.

Pakistan had lost its eastern wing, nearly 60 percent of the country's population. Would the rest of the country now hang together? Or would the other provincial groups—especially the Baluchi and Pathan tribesmen—try to break away and form their own independent nations?

In what had been East Pakistan, there was now the independent Bangladesh, a client state of India, while the Indians themselves were still holding more than 90,000 Pakistani prisoners of war in the east, and some 5,000 square miles of Pakistani territory in the west. Pakistan seemed permanently weakened, and India was now the undisputed master of the South Asian subcontinent.

Humiliated, the Pakistani military rulers could do little but return to their barracks and hand over the reins of power to the one civilian political leader who had any hope of holding together what was left of Pakistan. That man was the leader of the Pakistani People's Party and the country's best-known political campaigner, the charismatic and highly individualistic Zulfikar Ali Bhutto.

Elegant in dress, flamboyant in manner, arrogant, eloquent, and profoundly ambitious, Bhutto cut a spectacular figure—on the world stage as well as in Pakistan itself. Henry Kissinger, the White House National Security Adviser, had worked closely with Bhutto during the Bangladesh crisis and had found him "brilliant, charming, of global stature in his perceptions." Professor Trevor-Roper, who knew Bhutto as a student at Oxford and again as the Pakistani Prime Minister, found him "the ablest statesman in Asia, with the possible exception of Chou En-lai." Others saw him less kindly, as a demagogue, a megalomaniac, a rank opportunist, and a tyrant.

But in his own eyes, Prime Minister Bhutto was a man of destiny, the heir of the Mogul emperors who had ruled India as an Islamic state before the coming of the British. He was the chosen leader of his people, with unbounded ambition to put himself and his wretched and impoverished nation at the top of the entire Third World.

"I was born to make a nation, to serve a people, to overcome an impending doom," he later wrote from prison, after his military chief of staff General Mohammed Zia-ul-Haq led a military coup in 1977 that finally brought Bhutto down. "I was not born to wither away in a death cell and to mount the gallows to fulfill the vindictive lust of an ungrateful and treacherous man. I was not born to be humiliated and insulted by a barbaric and spiteful clique. I was born to bring emancipation to the people and honor them with a self-respecting destiny."

In many ways, Bhutto came naturally to such an exalted view of himself. Very much to the manor born, he was the son of a rich Zamindar family of large landlords from the province of Sind, near Karachi. His father had served the British Raj and had been knighted for his efforts. The younger Bhutto's education was at the best schools in the West—the University of California at Berkeley and Christ Church, Oxford. And his career was meteoric.

In 1958, when he was only thirty, he was named a minister in the military government of Field Marshal Mohammed Ayub Khan. Within five years he was Foreign Minister. And in 1966, following the war with India and the concluding Tashkent Agreement, which he saw as a sellout to the Indians, he left the government to form an avowedly socialist opposition. This became the Pakistan People's Party, the country's first mass political party, and by 1968, Bhutto was in jail for leading the popular agitation against his former benefactor Ayub Khan.

It was a martyrdom that served Bhutto well. Thanks in some measure to his agitation, a new military junta came to power, headed by the hard-driving General Yahya Khan, who threw the country open to elections in December 1970. Bhutto and his People's Party swept the provinces of West Pakistan, coming in second to Sheik Mujib, who had scored a comparable sweep in the more populous east. This left it to Bhutto to work out a compromise with Sheik Mujib, whom he considered "a windbag." And when Bhutto and Mujib failed to find a way to work together, General Yahya called down the reign of terror on the long-suffering Bengalis.

To a less exalted man, or one with more fastidious sensibilities, the horrors of the bloodbath in Bengal might have sidetracked, at least for a time, what seemed a vastly promising political career. But Bhutto stuck by the generals. As a matter of principle, he shared the Army's opposition to Bengali autonomy, which he saw as a threat to the country's unity. And always one with an eye to the main chance, he stayed loyal to General Yahya, proudly proclaiming on the morning after the massacre began, "Pakistan is saved."

Bhutto also used his eloquence to defend the Army's savage action in debates at the United Nations, and then gratefully accepted the post of Deputy Prime Minister in the government that was butchering the Bengalis. When Yahya Khan was finally forced to step down after the humiliating surrender to India in December 1971, Bhutto seemed to be the destined leader. He could claim not only to have won the majority vote in West Pakistan, which was all that was left of the country, but also to have safeguarded the one vote that counted most—that of the military command.

Once in office, Bhutto wasted no time. Never one to suffer fools gladly, and long eager for a chance to show himself as a Third World socialist, he had quietly chafed under what Henry Kissinger called "the plodding pace of Pakistan's military leaders." Now, with their failure and disgrace, he was finally on top, and his was "the power to level mountains, to make deserts bloom and to build a society where people didn't die of hunger and humiliation."

His ambition—for himself and for his battered country—stretched far beyond what most Western observers would have thought possible. "My vision is that of a Pakistan whose social standards are comparable with those in parts of Europe," he told the British journalist George Hutchinson. "This means a war against illiteracy and ignorance. It means fighting prejudice and obscurantism. It involves the equality of men and women. It demands the mobilization of the people's collective energies. . . . It poses a hundred challenges. It is a long haul. We have braced ourselves for it."

His enthusiasm was catching, and somehow his faith in himself and in his half a country caught on. For a magic moment in their collective history, Ali Bhutto held the people and the power in the palm of his hand. Anything seemed possible.

Hugh Trevor-Roper visited Pakistan in early 1972, three months after Bhutto came to power. He could hardly believe what he saw. "I expected to find a people still reeling from defeat, demoralized and dismayed," he wrote. "Instead, I found a new excitement, a new resolution. Bhutto himself was greeted enthusiastically wherever he went. He was the man who had restored dignity and a sense of purpose to a broken and bewildered people."

But Bhutto's most exciting ambition—and the one that Western observers found the most difficult to believe possible—was in the terrifying field of nuclear science. For in his very first days as Pakistan's civilian ruler, Bhutto set out to build the Islamic world's first atomic bomb.

Bhutto began on his nuclear quest with his characteristic sense of urgency. He had taken power in mid-December 1971, and in January he hastily called together some fifty of Pakistan's top scientists and government officials for what was to be a very secret meeting.

At the time, the new government was still in a state of enormous confusion, and Bhutto's aides originally scheduled the meeting for the town of Quetta, the provincial capital of Baluchistan. As we can testify from personal experience, the town is a backwater, best remembered for its morning camel market. It was January, with winter storms blowing down from Afghanistan to the north, and Quetta had no facilities adequately heated for the selected scientists and bureaucrats to meet in. It was hardly the spot to stir men's souls or heat up their blood, which is precisely what the hard-selling Mr. Bhutto had in mind.

No one complained, then, when the government laid on military planes to fly the freezing scientists south and east to the little Punjabi town of Multan, close to the border with India. The day was crisp and sparkling clear, and Bhutto convened the meeting under a brightly colored canvas canopy, or *shamiana*, on the lawn of a stately old Colonial mansion.

The scientists and administrators who were there were far and away the best brains in Pakistan, and some were as good as could be found anywhere in the world. For all of their desperately poor villages and overcrowded slums, the Pakistanis and their Islamic forebears had historically nurtured a rich scientific tradition, and the country, though in many ways backward, could count on a surprisingly strong scientific establishment. Three names are especially worth remembering.

Abdus Salam—"the professor" to his worshipping younger colleagues— had founded the Third World-oriented International Center for Theoretical Physics in Trieste, Italy, and would go on to win the Nobel Prize for Physics in 1979.

Dr. Ishrat Usmani had gained prominence as chairman of the Pakistan Atomic Energy Commission and would go on to build his reputation as an international civil servant specializing in energy questions at the United Nations in New York.

And the man Bhutto would name to replace Usmani as head of the nuclear program, Munir Ahmed Khan, had just come with high marks from the staff of the very organization that is supposed to stop the spread of nuclear weapons, the International Atomic Energy Agency in Vienna.

These were the men to whom Bhutto would turn as he opened this strange and secret meeting under the tent at Multan.

Until we learned about it several months after we had started our investigations, almost nothing had been known of the meeting or of what had been said there, and it was almost by accident that we chanced to ask about it. The opening came at London's posh and pricey Café Royal over drinks with a man called Khalid Hasan.

A well-worn Pakistani journalist and onetime press secretary to Bhutto, Khalid is in his forties, short and dapper, and a natural entertainer with an Eastern twinkle in his eye and an impish grin continually breaking out from beneath his neatly trimmed mustache. At the time, he was living in Britain and working as managing editor of the *Third World Review,* a commercially funded supplement that regularly appeared in the *Guardian* newspaper. We had asked to see him in the hope that he might be able to point us toward some expatriate Pakistanis who had actually worked in their country's nuclear program.

It was a shot in the dark, really. But we needed people who had firsthand knowledge to appear in one of the British Broadcasting Corporation's *Panorama* films, and as none of us knew any Pakistani nuclear scientists, we could only start out by talking to other journalists—and especially Pakistani journalists—who might be able to steer us in the right direction.

Khalid tried to help, dredging through his contacts book for leads and regaling us with wonderful stories about Bhutto, all brilliantly told. But his list of nuclear scientists ran short, and we were beginning to wonder where to turn next when, after a third Scotch and water, Khalid looked at us and asked, almost as an afterthought, "Of course, you know about the meeting at Multan, don't you?"

"The meeting where?" we asked dumbly.

"The meeting at Multan, when Mr. Bhutto first told us that we were going to get the bomb."

We were floored. Here we had been looking for a list of names, and right in front of us was someone who had been there the day the bomb was born. Why not interview Khalid on camera?

Khalid refused. For all his love of an audience, he did not want to be in the BBC film. He was already on the outs with the new Pakistani rulers because of his association with Bhutto, and he was afraid that they would make trouble for him if he appeared on camera and talked openly about the nuclear ambitions that they were trying to keep secret.

But we would not take no for an answer. Excited by what he had told us, enchanted by his skill as a storyteller, and blindly confident that nothing would really happen to him, we pushed, pressured, connived, and cajoled. Finally he gave us an interview on film, a decision that he immediately regretted and that ultimately cost him his job.

The main commercial sponsor of the *Third World Review* and its stable of related publications for which he worked is the highly visible Bank for Credit and Commerce International, which is run by Pakistani financiers with oil money from the Gulf states. When the BBC finally broadcast the film, the Pakistani Government put pressure on the bank, and the bank put pressure on the *Review* to sack Khalid Hasan. It was too late to say we were sorry.

As Khalid described Bhutto's meeting with the scientists he used the most vivid terms, less a reporter than a raconteur. "The meeting was pure showmanship and vintage Bhutto," he recalled. "It was rather like a jamboree, you know. There was a great deal of enthusiasm and joy."

Bhutto started slowly. He spoke of Pakistan's defeat and humiliation in the war with India, and vowed that he would vindicate the country's honor. He said that he had always wanted Pakistan to take the nuclear road, but nobody had listened to him. Now fate had placed him in a position where he could make the decision, he had the people of Pakistan behind him, and he wanted to go ahead. Pakistan was going to have the bomb, and the scientists sitting under the *shamiana* at Multan were going to make it for him.

According to Khalid, and also to three other participants with whom we have since spoken, the scientists were stunned, "absolutely dumbfounded," as one of them put it. There they were, like a circus under a tent, and Bhutto was asking them to make atomic bombs.

Still nostalgic for those early days of Bhutto's rule, Khalid recalled the mounting excitement with a lingering smile. "So he had all these boys together, these scientists, and there were senior people, very senior people, and junior people, and youngsters fresh with their Ph.D.'s in nuclear physics, and he said: "Look, we're going to have a bomb." Like "We're going to have a party." He said, "Can you give it to me?" So you know, they started shouting like schoolchildren. "Oh yes, yes, yes. You can have it. You can have it."

But Bhutto wanted still more. He pushed them. "How long will it take?" he asked.

The scientists could not agree. Khalid remembered the enthusiasm for what the great leader wanted. Other participants gave us a slightly different picture. They emphasized the doubts, especially those expressed at the meeting by some of the more senior men. Some of them had said that it would be difficult, if not impossible, to predict when such a project could be completed. A few even dared to suggest that the task itself might push Pakistan beyond its scientific and technical capabilities.

The debate continued. Finally one scientist—no one seems to remember who—dared to say that maybe it could be done in five years. Bhutto smiled, lifted his hand, and dramatically thrust forward three fingers. "Three years," he said. "I want it in three years."

The atmosphere suddenly became electric. It was like that moment in an old-fashioned American revival meeting just after the preacher asks, "Do you believe?" Most of those gathered wanted to believe very much.

It was then that one of the junior men—S. A. Butt, who would come to play a major role in making the bomb possible—jumped to his feet and clamored for his leader's attention. "It can be done in three years," Butt shouted excitedly.

A second, more experienced scientist jumped in and broke the magic of the moment. "It isn't like making firecrackers, you know. We don't know how long it will take. It's all nonsense. It can't be done that way."

Others joined in, and the enthusiasm slowly built up again, as Khalid Hasan recalled: "So Bhutto was very amused and he said, 'Well, much as I appreciate your enthusiasm, this is a very serious political decision, which Pakistan must make, and perhaps all Third World countries must make one day, because it is coming. So can you do it?'

"And they said, 'Yes, we can do it, given the resources and given the facilities.' Bhutto's answer was simple. 'I shall find you the resources, and I shall find you the facilities.'

"Those were the early days, and he could have gotten away with anything," Khalid explained, bringing himself back to the present. "His authority was unquestioned. Loyalty to him was unquestioned. He was looked upon as the Great Messiah."

This, then, was the day the bomb was born, the meeting at Multan that set the seal on Pakistan's nuclear future. From that moment, Pakistan would begin a national crash program to get the bomb. It was a historic move. It would result in one of the most audacious forays ever into the world of nuclear and industrial espionage. And we had gotten the story at enormous cost to Khalid Hasan.

The meeting set the stage and also helped to select the actors. Most of the scientists came along. A few did not. Even Ali Bhutto, for all his powers of persuasion, could not convince some of the senior men, including his longtime friend and adviser, the future Nobel laureate Abdus Salam.

According to one of the more skeptical participants at the Multan meeting, Bhutto and his top aides greatly feared that any open condemnation of the project from Salam could severely split Pakistan's nuclear scientists, many of whom revered him. His opposition could also trigger alarm bells among scientists and diplomats around the world. So some time after the meeting, a special emissary was sent to Salam, who had returned to his home in Britain, to brief him on the program and to assure him that it was really peaceful in intent.

The emissary was one of Pakistan's most promising younger scientists, a man who had known Salam for years and who was loved and trusted by him. The younger man talked to Salam in great detail, and in the end, managed to convince him that the Multan meeting was only a circus, and the nuclear program purely peaceful and civilian.

It was a brilliant deception and a painful one, like that of a son who has lied to his father.

"Did you feel bad about lying to Salam?" we asked the younger man.

His answer some eight years after the event was not articulated in words. He simply covered his face with his hands to hide his sudden tears.

A second, lesser obstacle was the longtime head of Pakistan's Atomic Energy Commission, Dr. Ishrat Usmani, who told us his side of the story during a highly revealing session at his United Nations office in New York.

"In fact, Bhutto had asked me to take our nuclear program to its logical conclusion," Usmani confided to us. "But I refused. Pakistan just didn't have the infrastructure for that kind of nuclear program. I'm not talking about the ability to get ten kilograms of plutonium. I'm talking about the real infrastructure.

"Pakistan totally lacked a metallurgical industry," he explained. "There was not a single steel mill in the country. But," he smiled, "if you're playing political poker and have no cards, you have to go on betting."

Given this attitude, Bhutto fired Usmani, kicking him upstairs to the post of Secretary of the newly created Ministry of Science and Technology. He became a figurehead and soon left Pakistan, taking a post at the United Nations. In his place, as the new Chairman of the Pakistan Atomic Energy Commission and the man who would make the nuclear dream come true, Bhutto named one of the enthusiasts, Munir Ahmed Khan.

Trained at the Argonne National Laboratory in the United States and a longtime staff member of the International Atomic Energy Commission, Munir Khan has since outlived his patron Ali Bhutto to become the spirit and the symbol of Third World nuclear ambitions, both on the civilian side and in the proliferation of nuclear weapons. Yet he remains a figure of considerable mystery.

To Usmani, whom he replaced, Munir Khan is a charlatan, a man whose ambitions were purely personal and whose intrigues in the international arena continue to bring dishonor to Pakistan.

To others with whom we've spoken, Munir Khan is a patriot, a man who would do anything and everything to bring atomic power and atomic weapons to his homeland. To those who know him personally and are willing to talk about him, he is a man of charm but lacking in candor, often tricky, and at times ruthless. As a scientist, he is said to be competent, though by no means brilliant.

Our own view is necessarily limited. As a standing rule, Munir Khan refuses to grant interviews on anything to do with nuclear weapons, and he only agreed to see us when we said—with, admittedly, a certain lack of candor—that we might be interested in doing a series for BBC Television on the energy crisis, "as seen through the eyes of Third World decision makers." Even after that got us into his spacious office on the outskirts of Islamabad, he coolly and with great charm refused to let us ask any question that touched on the Pakistani nuclear program.

Still we came away from an otherwise uninformative interview with two overriding impressions. One is that Munir Khan understands the West—and especially the United States, where he worked and studied—and how we think far better than most of us understand the Pakistanis. The second is that, by the standards of either East or West, Munir Khan is a world-class survivor, as he proved by keeping his job even after General Zia overthrew and then executed Mr. Bhutto. Although Munir Khan refused to answer our questions, he made little secret of his disdain for many of his nominal military superiors. Yet he has somehow retained their confidence and is still the man in charge of the bomb project.

Another of the enthusiasts at Multan, S. A. Butt— who predicted, wrongly, that the bomb could be completed in three years—also went on to make a name for himself in the nuclear program. Under Munir Khan's guiding hand, Butt would organize Pakistan's surreptitious purchasing network from a little office on the outskirts of Paris, running the most successful foray into nuclear espionage since the Soviet Union set out to penetrate Anglo-American nuclear efforts during and right after World War II.

Unlike Munir Khan, Mr. Butt never even let us into his office.

Bhutto Tells the World

Zulfikar Ali Bhutto was on his way to the atom bomb. But no one should have been surprised by that, not if they had followed Bhutto's career, heard what he had said, and read what he had written. From the late 1950s, when he was Ayub Khan's Minister for Fuel and Natural Resources, Bhutto had talked openly about the need for Pakistan to have nuclear weapons, and he clearly hardened his position in favor of the bomb by 1964 or 1965.

The timing was significant. In April 1964, the Chinese tested their first nuclear device at Lop Nor, in Sinkiang, and in November the Indian Government took the decision to begin development of their own "peaceful nuclear device," which they would finally test ten years later, in May 1974. The Indians took their decision in the greatest secrecy. But Bhutto appears to have caught wind of what they were doing, and from his position as Foreign Minister and later as opposition leader, he began calling openly for Pakistan to develop its own "nuclear deterrent."

Bhutto's clearest statement of intent can be found in his sometimes brilliant book *The Myth of Independence*. Bhutto finished writing the book in 1967, and it was published in London in 1969. But few in the West ever bothered to read the warning, and no one appears to have taken it seriously.

"All wars of our age have become total wars; all European strategy is based on the concept of total war; and it will have to be assumed that a war waged against Pakistan is capable of becoming a total war," he wrote. "It would be dangerous to plan for less and our plans should, therefore, include the nuclear deterrent."

Bhutto continued his argument at great length, and with obvious disdain for the 1968 Nuclear Nonproliferation Treaty:

"Difficult though this is to employ, it is vital for Pakistan to give the greatest possible attention to nuclear technology, rather than to allow herself to be deceived by an international treaty limiting this deterrent to the present nuclear Powers. India is unlikely to concede nuclear monopoly to others and, judging from her own nuclear programme and her diplomatic activities, especially at Geneva, it appears that she is determined to proceed with her plans to detonate a nuclear bomb. If Pakistan restricts or suspends her nuclear programme, it would not only enable India to blackmail Pakistan with her nuclear technology, but would impose a crippling limitation on the development of Pakistan's science and technology.

"Our problem, in its essence, is how to obtain such a weapon in time before the crisis begins," he insisted.

"India, whose progress in nuclear technology is sufficient to make her a nuclear Power in the near future, can provoke this crisis at a time of her choosing. She has already received foreign assistance for her nuclear programme and will continue to receive it. Pakistan must therefore embark on a similar program."

This was Bhutto writing in 1967, and calling openly and explicitly for nuclear weapons, as a defense against the Indians. Elsewhere, and especially in private conversations with his aides, Bhutto saw the bomb as something much more wide-ranging.

"He wanted the bomb, you know, because he wanted Pakistan to walk tall," his former press secretary Khalid Hasan told us during one of our long series of interviews with him in London. "He knew that proliferation will come, and that more countries will become nuclear, and that there's nothing that can stop it. So, if everybody's going to have a bomb in the basement, he said, 'Okay, if we have the capability, let's do it.'"

This was just the kind of thing that some other Third World leaders would later come to think, if not to say openly, and not so very different from the thinking of French and British governmental leaders who conceived their own "independent nuclear deterrents." Only this was Pakistan, and Bhutto was thinking this back in the 1960s, a full decade ahead of the new nuclear nationalism that we are now seeing in countries such as Iraq.

"I think Bhutto had always been a believer in Third World countries having the nuclear option," Khalid told us. "As a Third World leader, and an intellectual, someone who knew the West well because he had been trained in the West, he questioned the basic assumption that only the Western powers and the Soviet Union were capable of having nuclear weapons and handling them with responsibility.

"I mean, why is it that only the Western countries and the Soviet Union can have nuclear weapons and not be questioned? And why is it that everybody takes it for granted as part of the world as it is?"

Bhutto argued his case forcefully, especially after he became Foreign Minister in 1963. But Field Marshal Ayub Khan, the country's military ruler, turned him down. A soldier of the old school, and generally considered a fair and decent man, he just could not understand why a country like Pakistan needed an atomic bomb.

"What do we need a bomb for?" he would ask, as Khalid Hasan recalled. "You chaps read too many books."

"Pakistan is a poor country. We can't afford it," he would tell Bhutto. "We should put our money into schools, maybe hospitals, and industry."

Just like a general, not to understand progress.

But the final word was Bhutto's, not Ayub Khan's. When Bhutto, the fiery socialist and nationalist, came to power in the wake of the Bangladesh War, it should have come as no surprise that he made the bomb one of his country's first items of business.

The Americans and the Arabs

From the creation of Pakistan in 1947, the country's leaders, military and civilian, had clung firmly to the West. Pakistan proudly called itself the "most allied ally" of the United States. It signed a Mutual Defense Pact with the United States in 1954 and a Mutual Security Pact in 1959. It played a leading role in both of Washington's regional anti-Communist alliances in Asia—SEATO, the South East Asia Treaty Organization, and the Baghdad Pact, or CENTO, Central Treaty Organization.

Less publicly, the Pakistanis also provided the Americans with the Bada Ber air base at Peshawar, near the border with Afghanistan. It was from this base that U-2 spy planes regularly flew over the Soviet Union, and it was from here that the ill-fated Francis Gary Powers began the flight that the Soviets shot down in May 1960.

This particular incident brought the Pakistanis their first real lesson in the meaning of nuclear confrontation, with a pointed warning from the Soviet Premier Nikita Khrushchev: "If you continue to let the Americans fly from your air bases into Russia, then we will not only shoot down the U.S. planes, but we will have to aim our rockets at your bases as well."

At the time the Pakistanis were undeterred, as the doughty Ayub Khan declared a few months later in a celebrated speech before the United States Congress. "If there is real trouble," the Pakistani Field Marshal told the American lawmakers, "there is no other country in Asia on whom you will be able to count. The only people who will stand by you are the people of Pakistan."

In return for all of this loyalty, the Pakistanis got what they most wanted. This was a series of secret pledges, from both the Kennedy and the Johnson Administrations, that the Americans would help and protect Pakistan, and that they would do so not only against "Communist aggression," but also, and far more important to the Pakistanis, against any attack from India.

This was the Pakistan that Washington knew and loved, and that the present Administration is trying to resurrect with its massive offer of "security guarantees" and military and economic aid. This was not the Pakistan of Mr. Bhutto.

From the very beginning of his public life, Bhutto saw things from a very different perspective, and one that shaped his commitment to nuclear weapons. A Third World nationalist, he could never really accept such "toadying" to the West. And far more important, he never believed that the Americans would come through with the protection that they had promised.

"We should not unnecessarily extend the principle of attachment to the United States," he warned his cabinet colleagues in the late 1950s, soon after joining the government of Ayub Khan. "In case of war with India, the U.S.A. is not going to help us."

As Foreign Minister during the 1965 war with India, he had seen the Americans embargo arms to both sides, which he felt had worked "exclusively to Pakistan's disadvantage." As a central figure in the Bangladesh crisis, he had seen firsthand the limits of American power and commitment.

He had himself worked closely with Kissinger at the height of the war. He knew that the Nixon Administration had "tilted" toward Pakistan, even to the extent of sending warships steaming into the Bay of Bengal as a threat against the Indians and their Soviet allies. And he had heard from no less than the Chinese Premier Chou En-lai that it was this American show of force that had stopped the Indian forces from taking even more West Pakistani territory.

Bhutto knew all of this better than most. Yet for all of the goodwill of the Nixon Administration, the Americans had proved themselves unable or unwilling to stop India from tearing Pakistan in half. The Americans had promised to protect Pakistan against India and they had failed. To a realist like Bhutto, that was what counted in the end.

Bhutto applied the same skepticism to other possible allies as well, including the Chinese. He had been the chief architect of Pakistan's alignment with Peking in the 1960s, and had helped in bringing Peking and Washington together. He knew better than anyone how the Chinese had done their best to help Pakistan in the 1971 war with India over Bangladesh. The Chinese had supplied the Pakistanis with arms, and they had even put their armed forces onto a war footing near the Indian border to bring pressure to bear on New Delhi.

But as Bhutto discovered firsthand, there were real limits to Chinese power, especially when nuclear weapons were involved. At the height of the war, when the Chinese help was most needed, India's allies in the Soviet Union threatened to send their missiles to destroy the Chinese rocket and nuclear weapons facility at Lop Nor. The Chinese backed down. Pakistan was not worth a nuclear confrontation with the Soviet Union. For Bhutto, this was another lesson in nuclear deterrence, and in its limitations when the nuclear weapons belonged to someone else. At a time when the very existence of Pakistan was threatened and the country was being ripped apart, the Chinese had failed to protect them and so had the United States. As a result, the Indians were riding high and the Pakistanis were badly in need of a new strategy and a new set of allies. Bhutto's genius was that he saw a solution before most observers saw the problem. The solution was close at hand, and directly involved Bhutto's own nuclear ambitions.

As a country, Pakistan had been purposely created as a homeland for the Muslims of the old British Raj. It was from birth an Islamic state, which separated the Pakistanis from the hated Hindus of India and gave them a shared commitment with most of their Middle Eastern neighbors—with the Turks, with the Iranians, and above all with the Arabs, their brothers in

Islam, whose oil riches were only beginning to shake the world at its roots.

Several of the Arab states had come to Pakistan's aid during the Bangladesh War. The Saudis had loaned them seventy-five fighter planes. The Libyans had loaned them several more. And tiny Jordan, with the approval of the White House, had helped Pakistan get around the official American arms embargo by transferring ten American F-104's.

This aid was all largely symbolic, and had only partially offset India's overwhelming superiority in the air. But to Bhutto, the brotherly support suggested the possibility of far greater cooperation in the future.

The logic was persuasive. Even before the Bangladesh War broke the country apart, West Pakistan had always considered itself part of the Middle East, and foreign policy and defense specialists in London and Washington had always seen it as the protective flank of Western interests in the Middle East.

In addition, the Pakistanis were already part and parcel of the Middle Eastern world. Pakistani traders ran the commerce of the Persian Gulf. Pakistani pilgrims made the haj to Mecca, and also worshipped at religious shrines in Iran and Iraq. Pakistan officers and conscripts manned the armies of the new Gulf states, and would soon run training missions throughout the Arab world. And literally tens of thousands of Pakistani professionals—doctors, teachers, and engineers—held key posts as far afield as Libya.

Bhutto would build on that base. In a history that all of Islam celebrated, the Mogul Empire of South Asia had been a high point, from its brute military power to its building of the Taj Mahal. And now, under his leadership, the descendants of the Moguls would use their undoubted scientific and technical superiority to cement an Islamic alliance with the newly rich and rejuvenated Middle East.

"Pakistan did not have oil, you know," explained Khalid Hasan. "It did not have any of the riches which fell to a number of Middle Eastern countries in the middle 1970s.

"But Bhutto wanted to capitalize on what Pakistan did have—a lot of skills, a very large core of professional people, scientists, technicians."

Exactly the people Bhutto had brought together at Multan. For what better way to whet the appetite and encourage the generosity of all those half-sophisticated sheiks and shahs and soldier-kings than to offer them the one thing that their billions could never buy on their own—the promise of an Islamic bomb.

Colonel Qaddafi's Bomb

A few years ago, we could hardly manage to procure a squadron
of fighter planes. Tomorrow, we shall be able to buy an atom
bomb and all its component parts. The monopoly of the atom will
be broken any day now.

—Colonel Muammar el-Qaddafi,
Le Point,
January 20, 1975

Where would an impoverished country like Pakistan ever find the money to
build nuclear weapons? For Ali Bhutto, the answer was obvious. Only hours
after he had finished meeting with his top scientists under the tent in
Multan, the Pakistani leader set off on a whirlwind tour of the major Islamic
capitals of the Middle East.

"After Bangladesh, Pakistan's name was mud," recalled Khalid Hasan,
Mr. Bhutto's press secretary at the time. "People thought of us as killers,
rapists, genociders, bastards," he told us. "What Bhutto was trying to do was
to say, 'Look, friends, the old order is finished. There's a new Pakistan. So,
really, give us a break.'"

Much was written at that time about Bhutto's grand tour, about his flying
diplomacy, his airport encounters, and his stunning success in "rehabilitat-
ing" Pakistan wherever he went—in Islamic capitals, in other Third World
stops, and finally in the People's Republic of China, where he crowned his
trip by meeting with Chairman Mao Tse-tung.

The schedule was hectic. The stops included Iran, Saudi Arabia, the
United Arab Emirates, as well as Turkey, Syria, Morocco, Egypt, Algeria,
Tunisia, and Libya.

In his speeches on the trip, Bhutto bitterly criticized his country's Western
allies, especially the United States and Great Britain, the two countries that
had previously been Pakistan's closest diplomatic and political partners and
best military suppliers. They had "betrayed" Pakistan, he charged. So had all
the countries in the two Western-backed regional alliances to which Pakistan
belonged, the South East Asia Treaty Organization and the Central Treaty
Organization. "The member countries of CENTO and SEATO slept while
our country was dismembered by violence," he declared.

Bhutto also predicted that Pakistan would leave the British Common-wealth, a threat that he would later carry out. Like so many leaders of former Western colonies, the Oxford-educated Bhutto seemed especially angry at his former "mother country." His passion was that of a son betrayed—disappointed, disillusioned, and looking for an alternative, one that he increasingly came to see in the Islamic world.

This was the public face of the whirlwind tour, the dramatic turnabout in the orientation of a country that had once been the West's most allied ally. But in all that has been written about Ali Bhutto's trip, no one has mentioned the obvious. In making the trip, and opening his Islamic offensive, Bhutto was also taking the first steps toward finding the financing he had promised his scientists at Multan, the monetary support for the world's first Islamic bomb.

In hindsight, this was nowhere more dramatic than in Bhutto's stopover in Libya, where he was warmly embraced by the country's new revolutionary leader, Colonel Qaddafi.

"Oh, the atmosphere was beautiful," remembered Khalid Hasan. "It was evening when we landed in Tripoli and we could see nothing but people. There was a large number of Pakistanis in the country and, of course, they'd all come. And lots of Libyans. People were cheering and singing. Qaddafi was there, and he came onto the tarmac and embraced Bhutto, and I think kissed him on both cheeks."

The visit lasted only a night and a day. But it was the beginning of a close personal friendship between the two men, a friendship that would have the most profound consequences for the entire Islamic world.

It started with a small gesture. Qaddafi had invited Bhutto to stay at his home, where Qaddafi's wife had gone to the trouble to dress in the traditional Pakistani blouse and baggy trousers, the *shalwar kameez*. Bhutto was delighted, and let Qaddafi know it. The visit—and the friendship—were off to a brilliant start.

Outwardly, the two men—Bhutto and Qaddafi—could not have seemed more different. One was a sophisticated, cynical, deeply subtle man of the world, a feudal aristocrat educated in the West and widely admired for the breadth of his world view; the other, a man of the desert, a bedouin and soldier, straightforward and hard-eyed in his distrust of Western ways, and undeterred by his growing image as fool, fanatic, and uncontrollably wild leader of international terrorism.

That, at least, was how we saw the two men at the start, and some of the people who had known one or the other of them went even further. They found it incredible that we could even ask about the two of them in the same breath.

"Comparing Bhutto and Qaddafi is like comparing two men from different planets," we were told by one of Qaddafi's former comrades, now one of the leaders of the Libyan opposition in Cairo and anxious that we not use his name. "It's like comparing the former French President Giscard d'Estaing, with all of his sophistication, to Sheik Seyd of the Sudan. Bhutto's interest in Qaddafi was for one reason only—money. In 1972, and later, Bhutto came to Qaddafi only to get money."

Dr. Ishrat Usmani, the man Bhutto removed as chairman of the Pakistan Atomic Energy Commission, told us much the same when we interviewed him at his United Nations office. "Bhutto was a megalomaniac, and I distrust everything he did in Pakistan," Usmani confided, not without a taste of sour grapes. "But Bhutto had limits to his megalomania, unlike Qaddafi."

Yet somewhere in all these obvious differences, Bhutto and Qaddafi unmistakably struck a common chord, and one that would come to play a major role in the making of the Islamic bomb.

"They really got along very well," recalled Khalid Hasan. "Bhutto had a wild, romantic side, and he could communicate with Qaddafi."

In their own, very different ways, both were strong, charismatic leaders of new Islamic nations, and both saw themselves—and each other—as socialists, nationalists, and revolutionaries. Bhutto had just taken power from a discredited military dictatorship, and was breaking Pakistan free of its historic alliance with the West. Qaddafi had just booted the British and American military out of their Libyan bases, and was spearheading the fight of the OPEC oil producers to break the hold of the Western oil companies— possibly the most historic and revolutionary shift in wealth and power in our time.

Above all, the two men had a vision of personal and national destiny. And for both—for the naive Qaddafi every bit as much as the worldly Bhutto— that destiny included the bomb.

As Qaddafi himself told the Lebanese newspaper *An Nahar* in 1975: "People now say that this country has fifty planes and that country has five hundred. The day will come when they will say that this country has three nuclear bombs and that country has ten. When that day comes, Libya will not be absent."

Colonel Qaddafi's worldwide hunt for nuclear weapons is by now one of the most hackneyed stories in the world press, especially in Western Europe and the United States. Newspapers and magazines regularly report the latest twist in the long-running tale, and there is even a best-selling novel, *The Fifth Horseman*, that tells of the threat by a determined Qaddafi to obliterate Manhattan, not with your average atomic device, but with an even deadlier hydrogen bomb.

Of all that has been written, the most credible account so far comes from a man who knew Qaddafi and liked him, the former editor of the semi-official Egyptian newspaper *Al Ahram*, Mr. Mohamed Heikal. He tells the story at length in his book *The Road to Ramadan*, published in 1976.

Heikal first met Qaddafi in September 1969, only hours after the then unknown Libyan and his youthful band of Free Officers overthrew the faltering regime of King Idris. The officers had contacted their longtime hero, the Egyptian President Gamal Abdel Nasser, and Nasser had sent

Heikal as his personal envoy to meet them. He returned sympathetic but horrified. The young Libyans were "shockingly innocent, scandalously pure."

Some weeks later, Qaddafi returned the visit and, according to Heikal, one of the first questions he raised with Nasser was about nuclear weapons. Still wide-eyed at meeting with his boyhood idol, Qaddafi had urged Nasser to join with him in an all-out war to liquidate Israel. According to Heikal, a close friend and confidant of the Egyptian leader, Nasser replied that the international situation would not allow them to do it. Neither the Soviet Union nor the United States would permit a situation that might lead to nuclear war.

"Do the Israelis have nuclear bombs?" asked Qaddafi, according to Heikal's account.

This was only 1968, but Nasser thought that the Israelis probably did. In response, Qaddafi asked, "Have we got nuclear bombs?"

Nasser's answer was, of course, no, the Arabs did not, and he apparently thought that this was the end of it. But two or three months later, in early 1970, Qaddafi sent his close friend and deputy, Major Abdul Salam Jalloud, on a surprise visit to Egypt. Jalloud asked that the trip be kept secret and explained that his only purpose was once again to consult President Nasser.

What about? Nasser asked.

Jalloud's answer was simple: "We are going to buy an atomic bomb."

As Heikal tells it, Jalloud understood well enough that the Russians and the Americans would be unwilling to sell them the bomb. But what about the Chinese? Maybe they would sell Libya a nuclear weapon. Nasser remained skeptical. As far as he knew, atom bombs were never for sale.

"Oh," said Jalloud, as Heikal reports it, "we don't want a big atomic bomb, just a tactical one. We contacted the Chinese and said we wanted someone to go there and pay them a visit, and they said they would welcome us. So I am going."

According to Heikal, the trip to China remained completely secret. Jalloud traveled incognito on an Egyptian passport, and went by way of Pakistan and India. The Chinese still did not know why he had come, but Jalloud told them soon enough.

"China," he said, "is the pride of all Asian countries. You have done a great deal to help the backward countries, and have proved to the world that you are as strong as the West. So we from Libya have come to you for help. We have no wish to be a burden to you, and we know these things cost a lot of money—we want to buy an atomic bomb."

Heikal was not present in Peking, and probably got the story from Jalloud or secondhand from Nasser. So he can only report that the Chinese Prime Minister Chou En-lai responded "with perfect Chinese courtesy." Chou explained, as had Nasser, that atomic bombs were not generally for sale. The best that China could do was to help the Libyans with their own nuclear research. But any development of nuclear weapons the Libyans would have to do themselves.

Undaunted, Major Jalloud left empty-handed. He returned only months later, in August 1970, when the Chinese turned down a second request, this one for more general nuclear and missile technology.

Mohamed Heikal's personal account revealed Qaddafi's very first efforts to get nuclear weapons, almost from his first day in power. For the sophisticated and cosmopolitan Heikal, this was proof of Qaddafi's "terrifying innocence of how things work in the modern world." But, as time would prove, the "innocent" Qaddafi was simply showing the way to those in the Arab world who lacked his innocence. This became clear following the Arab-Israeli war of 1973, when Heikal himself wrote in *Al Ahram* that the Arab world needed "to build, buy or borrow" nuclear weapons as a deterrent to the Israeli nuclear arsenal.

The Libyans continued their search for nuclear weapons, turning next to France and to the weapons and electronics manufacturers Thompson-C.S.F. On the Libyan side, the negotiations were handled by the then head of their Atomic Energy Commission, a man of Tunisian origin named Turki, and this time they were looking for nuclear technology rather than the weapons themselves.

What the Libyans wanted were some twenty electromagnetic units for the production of enriched uranium. Thompson officials asked for governmental approval from the French Atomic Energy Commission, the CEA. But, in contrast to their later openhandedness toward Mr. Bhutto's Pakistan, the CEA turned the Libyans down cold. The CEA's official spokesman, Alain Varneau, told us that the French rejected the Qaddafi request because it represented a "danger of nuclear proliferation." The sophisticated Bhutto and his able corps of Pakistani scientists were one matter; the boy from the desert, with his obvious desire to have a bomb, quite another.

The Libyan request was particularly interesting because the technology they wanted—electromagnetic enrichment—is rather primitive. The Americans first used it in the Manhattan Project during World War II, and quickly discarded it. So even if the French had approved the sale, the Libyans would still have had a long and difficult time before they actually had any bomb-grade uranium in hand. Why the Libyans wanted to go this route is unclear. But it does suggest that they were still very innocent, not only about how to buy nuclear technology from the French, but also about what to buy.

The Libyans kept trying to buy various kinds of nuclear technology and expertise, and were similarly rebuffed by a long string of suppliers—Canada, West Germany, Italy, the United States, and once again France. By 1978, the globe-trotting Major Jalloud even approached the Indians in New Delhi, offering cash and low-priced oil for access to their nuclear technology. India also refused, and the Libyans retaliated by cutting off shipments of crude oil.

The stories keep coming. Yet in all the fact and fiction, the Libyans themselves have so far scored only a small and relatively harmless research reactor and accompanying laboratories, which they got from the Soviet Union. As is their general policy, the Russians insisted that any used fuels be returned to the Soviet Union, and that the Libyans sign the Nuclear Nonproliferation Treaty, in which they would pledge not to seek nuclear weapons. Libya signed the treaty in 1975, but only ratified it in 1981. The signing was indicative of Qaddafi's lack of success in buying nuclear technology in the open, or even on the black market.

From Mohamed Heikal and others, however, it was clear enough that although Qaddafi wanted the bomb, he never came anywhere near getting one, except in one case. That came out of his friendship, begun in early 1972, with the Prime Minister of Pakistan, Zulfikar Ali Bhutto. In the months following Bhutto's visit to Tripoli, Colonel Qaddafi began to work out an agreement with the Pakistani nuclear program that would make the Libyans, at least for a time, one of its biggest single financial backers.

From the start of our investigation, this Libyan connection was always one of the major challenges facing us. Rumors of it had long troubled Western intelligence agencies. Occasional references to it had appeared in newspapers and magazines, often as the result of officially inspired propaganda from one or another of Libya's many enemies. But into the beginning of 1980, no one had found any hard evidence to back up the claims of Libyan involvement with the Pakistani nuclear program, and some of the more responsible people—including President Jimmy Carter's former antiproliferation chief Dr. Joseph S. Nye Jr.—told us that they tended to doubt that Qaddafi had any hand in what was then already becoming known as the Islamic bomb.

For months we looked, following the same old, tired trails through a maze of rumors, innuendos, and propaganda droppings, talking to dozens of well-informed Pakistanis, several of whom told us that of course the Libyans were paying. Yet they never managed to substantiate their claims. It all seemed to be gossip, and no one knew anything firsthand. We were fast giving up hope, when out of the blue one of our Pakistani sources suggested that we speak to a former colleague who, he said, might know a thing or two. The man lived in a distant part of the world, and after checking flight schedules, and our own finances, we decided to make the investment in a plane ticket and contact him. We found him, and arranged to meet at the local replica of the "Hotel Interplastic," the kind of hotel that could be in Washington, Paris, or Karachi. We cannot give details where for reasons that will become obvious.

Rarely have we seen a man quite so scared.

"Should we sit in the bar?" we asked, thinking that he would prefer to talk in a public place.

"No," he said. "Let's go somewhere private. Perhaps your room."

He was meeting us only because of his faith in our mutual friend, he told us. But the friend knew only a small part of the story. He told us that there was no way we could use his name or even hint at who he was.

"The leaders of my country can be like animals," he said. "They have ways to find you and to punish you, if they want." He was obviously nervous, and yet he had a need to talk—a need to unburden what he had kept pent up inside himself for many years. He had never told anyone the story before, he said. Not even our mutual friend. He had been living his nightmare alone, silently torn by his own sense of guilt for having been involved in what he now saw as the core of evil itself.

As we began to ask him about the Pakistani nuclear program, and the possible Libyan connection, he answered at first vaguely and with reluctance, trying to avoid too many incriminating specifics, yet anxious to get the story out. Finally, after about an hour of cat and mouse, he turned and looked us straight in the eye.

"It's amazing how little you know," he said. "All you journalists. You know nothing."

We pressed him to be specific. What exactly should we know? we asked.

"You mean to say that all these intelligence services, all these journalists, have been following our program for years, and you know so little, just the barest outlines?" he asked, not without a touch of arrogance.

"So why haven't you spoken with any of the Western intelligence services?" we countered. "You have something to tell them. They'd welcome you with open arms."

"I just want to pursue my own life now," he said. "I'm not interested in intelligence agencies."

The interview continued another two hours, with more questions left hanging than answers hammered down. For us, the high point came when we pushed him to tell us about the Libyan connection.

"Yes, of course, the Libyans were involved," he said, moisture now dampening his forehead.

"How do you know?" we asked.

"I know," he said. And he told us.

The Pakistani—we shall call him Mr. K.—told us a rather simple story, one that came from his own direct knowledge. We have since verified his personal credentials and credibility, and have confirmed key parts of what he told us from other sources. We have purposely held back parts of the story that might reveal his identity.

As Mr. K. revealed, the Libyans and the Pakistanis held a formal series of meetings following Mr. Bhutto's trip to Libya. Most of the meetings took place in 1973. They were in Paris. Official representatives of the two governments took part, along with people from Saudi Arabia and the Gulf states, and possibly Iran as well. The purpose of the meetings was to work out the details—technical and financial—of ongoing nuclear cooperation.

The choice of Paris as a meeting place was not by chance, but a matter of convenience. The French were busily engaged in attempting to sell billions of francs worth of warplanes, tanks, helicopters, and whatever else glittered in the eyes of Islamic and other Third World leaders. The reputation of the Mirage fighter jets—spread, ironically, by Israel's dazzling use of the plane against the Arabs in the Six Day War of 1967—had made the French competitive with the Americans. The French were eagerly capitalizing on every Russian-supplied MIG that the Israeli Mirages had shot down.

As a result, military delegations from both Libya and Pakistan were already making France a regular milk stop. Libya's globetrotting Major Jalloud, promoted to Prime Minister in July 1972, was making a dizzying series of trips from Tripoli to Paris in a continuing effort to secure French military equipment. The Libyan Air Force was contracting to buy dozens of Mirage fighters, and preparations were under way for a state visit by Qaddafi himself in early 1974.

Pakistan's Bhutto was similarly busy buying French. He wanted to rid Pakistan of any remaining dependence on the British, and he was determined not to become overly reliant on the Americans as a source of military hardware. He made one trip to Paris on July 25, 1973, when President Georges Pompidou received him at the Élysée Palace. By that time the Pakistani military already had their "Blue Flash" purchasing mission in Paris and were already integrating Mirages into their highly skilled Air Force.

All of this coming and going made Paris the obvious place to meet, and under the very noses of France's supposedly first-rate secret service, the Direction de la Surveillance du Territoire, or DST, the crisscrossing Libyans and Pakistanis held their first nuclear meetings.

The meetings were top secret. Most of the diplomats at the Pakistani and Libyan embassies were purposely kept in the dark, as were most of the military officers on the purchasing missions. In all, fewer than ten Pakistanis even knew that the meetings were taking place.

The Pakistani representatives operated under direct orders from Bhutto and from Munir Ahmed Khan, who had replaced Dr. Usmani as head of the Pakistan Atomic Energy Commission. The Ambassador to France, Yakub Ali Khan, one of Pakistan's leading diplomats and later Ambassador in Moscow, played a leading role in the meetings, as did his successor in Paris, Mahmoud Shiqfat.

The meetings were primarily to set the terms for Libyan financial aid, Mr. K. explained. But they also spelled out what the Libyans would get in return. According to Mr. K., Qaddafi wanted and expected "full access" to the nuclear technology that Libya would be helping Pakistan to buy.

Mr. K. recalled specific requests for the Pakistanis to train Libyan scientists in the operation of "hot cells," which would allow them to reprocess used reactor fuel to extract plutonium for nuclear weapons of their own. Qaddafi also wanted Pakistani help in neutronics and the handling of nuclear waste.

Beyond these specifics, the Libyans were expecting "full access," and "the entire capability." According to K., this would become a source of continuing friction, as Qaddafi came to believe—correctly, as it turned out—that the Pakistanis were shortchanging him and not delivering what he thought they had promised.

The other nations in the meetings—particularly Saudi Arabia and the

Gulf states—also offered money, K. recalled. But they seemed content to let the Pakistanis keep the expertise.

So how much money was offered? we asked K.

"The sums were staggering," he told us. "Well over $500 million." Pakistani expectations mounted. In fact, the normally ragamuffin Pakistanis—the poor relations of their Arab cousins—came to believe that they could eventually raise the figure to several billion dollars if they wanted. But, K. quickly added, "nothing like that amount was actually needed or delivered."

That was the Libyan connection, or more accurately the Arab connection, as seen from the Pakistani side. Could we find confirmation from the Libyan side?

Our best hope was in the growing number of Qaddafi's early revolutionary comrades who have now gone into opposition to him, especially two of them who seemed likely to have played some role with the Pakistanis, or at least known about what was happening.

One was Omar el-Meheishi, a former member of Qaddafi's Revolutionary Command Council, who became Minister of Science and Technology in November 1974. Meheishi handled much of the nuclear negotiations with the Soviet Union and should have been involved with the Pakistanis as well. Meheishi broke with Qaddafi in late 1975, and has since been trying to win support for his opposition movement in Egypt and Tunisia.

The second was Abdul Monham el-Huni, a former intelligence chief, Minister of Interior, and Foreign Minister. We discovered that people close to him, and possibly he himself, were now in Egypt.

Our difficulty here was obvious. Colonel Qaddafi was sending out hit teams to assassinate his political opponents, and there had just been a rather botched-up attempt against one of the men with whom we wanted to talk, Omar Meheishi. As a result, the entire opposition movement was keeping its head down, and certainly none of the leaders wanted to openly talk about Arab or Islamic bombs.

Still, we did manage to make contact with el-Huni's camp in Cairo and to speak off the record with one of the most senior people in the Libyan opposition. He confirmed what we had learned from Mr. K.—that the Libyans met with the Pakistanis and agreed to provide financing for the Pakistani nuclear program. But he denied that either of the present opposition leaders—Meheishi or el-Huni—played any role.

"Qaddafi threw away a lot of money by helping Pakistan," he told us. "But the Libyan people never knew of this financing. Not even Qaddafi's cabinet, his government ministers, knew of it. I assure you, it did not go through his cabinet."

He was also absolutely scathing about Major Jalloud, who has remained close to Qaddafi and continues to play a role in most, if not all, of his major decisions. "Jalloud is Qaddafi's towel," the man said, referring to the Arab custom of keeping a towel by the toilet to clean one's hands.

"A toilet can never be without the towel. If Qaddafi is the toilet, Jalloud is the dirty towel. He carries out whatever Qaddafi asks him to do."

And that, he assured us, included Qaddafi's quest for nuclear weapons.

The Paris meetings laid the groundwork for what would become one of the most important nuclear exchanges of the 1970s—Libyan and other Arab money for Pakistani expertise. But it was not until the following year, in February 1974, that the two leaders—Qaddafi and Bhutto—shook hands on the final agreement.

The timing tells a great deal. Only a few months before, Arab armies had shown new strength in the October War with Israel. Arab oil producers had followed suit with an oil boycott of Western nations, the first real use of the so-called oil weapon. OPEC oil revenues, following Qaddafi's lead, were soaring beyond any earlier expectations. And in this euphoric atmosphere, the leaders of thirty-seven Islamic nations gathered together for a Summit Meeting in Pakistan, in the old Mogul capital of Lahore. Their announced purpose—to find new ways to fight what they saw as Israel's continued occupation of the West Bank, the Gaza Strip, and the Holy City of Jerusalem.

Bhutto, as chairman of the conference, and host, set the tone in a powerful keynote address.* Seen by his peers as the most brilliant of the Islamic rulers, he was staking his claim to lead what he saw as a powerful new alliance of oil-rich Arabs and their less fortunate Islamic and Third World brothers. His starting point was therefore the Palestinian cause and the continued fight against the Zionists, "intoxicated with their militarism and reeking with technological arrogance."

"Israel has gorged and fattened on the West's sympathies, nurtured itself on violence and expanded through aggression," the Pakistani leader told his fellow potentates. But now—with the oil weapon and a new military strength—the balance was shifting. "This may well be a watershed in history," he proclaimed. The Arab world, the Islamic world, the Third World, were for the first time in a position to finance their own economic development. All that was required was a banding together of those who enjoyed the new riches of oil with those who did not.

"We are emerging today out of nearly a half millennium of decline," he announced. "It is time that we translate the sentiments of Islamic unity into concrete measures of cooperation and mutual benefit."

Looked at cynically, Bhutto might have been accused of simply passing the begging bowl, using the flowery words of Islamic unity to cajole his oil-rich Arab neighbors to pay the way for debt-ridden Pakistan. This applied especially to his new friend and fellow revolutionary, Colonel Qaddafi.

In the course of the Islamic Summit, Bhutto named a brand-new football

*The speech is quoted in full in Zulfikar Ali Bhutto, *New Directions* (London: Namara Publications, 1980), pp. 74–92.

stadium after the Libyan leader. He took Qaddafi on a tour of the high spots
of Pakistani development, including the armaments industry at Wah and the
aerospace base at Somniani. And he showed the Colonel overflights of the
best the Pakistani Air Force had to offer—French Mirages, Chinese MIG's,
and even the old American F-86s. Everywhere Qaddafi went he was the hero
of the hour.

A former Pakistani military man now living in the United States, General
A.D. Djalani, told us of the expectations at the time, and from a particular
vantage point. Djalani was under administrative detention at the time,
placed there by Bhutto. The Pakistani Prime Minister was worried about the
possibilities of dissent and rebellion in his armed forces, especially from
Baluchis like General Djalani whose ethnic colleagues were protesting
against their lack of power within the Pakistani regime.

Djalani found that his guards did not share his personal opposition to
Bhutto. Not only that, they were downright ecstatic about Bhutto's new
Islamic friends, people like Qaddafi, who they believed would come to the
aid of their impoverished and beleaguered country.

"The fellows who were guarding me, they said the Messiah had come.
Qaddafi was the Messiah. He would save Pakistan," General Djalani told us.

The country had just been hit by an earthquake, and was in dire straits.
Qaddafi's visit brought renewed hope. As described by Djalani, there was a
belief among millions of poor and simple Pakistanis that the oil gushing from
the Libyan wells would soon be at the service of Pakistan. Libya would give
unstintingly to help its Islamic sister country. Libyan money would pour into
Pakistan. For every Pakistani, there would soon be, if not a chicken in every
pot, at least some rice in every bowl.

Qaddafi did contribute some funds to Pakistan's poor. But Bhutto wanted a
lot more than chicken and rice. His ambitions were nuclear, and for him, as
for Qaddafi, the high point of their public engagements was a personally
conducted tour of Karachi's new Canadian-built nuclear reactor. Their guide
for the tour was none other than Munir Khan, the new head of the Pakistan
Atomic Energy Commission and the man in charge of the Islamic bomb.

The tour of the Karachi reactor was the public face of the shared interest in
nuclear development. But there was also a secret side. For it was during the
week of the Islamic Summit in Lahore that Qaddafi finally pledged himself
to financing the making of the bomb.

One source for this fact is a former Bhutto appointee, who appeared in the
BBC *Panorama* film with his back to the camera and his voice electronically
altered. The man has since died after a lingering illness, and it is now
possible to reveal his true identity—the Pakistani journalist, one-time
diplomat, and former European Director of Pakistan International Airlines,
Mr. Mohammed Beg.

"Mr. Bhutto told me that during the Islamic Summit in Lahore he had
several discussions with Colonel Qaddafi about the manufacture of an
atomic bomb by Pakistan," Beg told us. "He promised Mr. Bhutto that he

would provide however much money was needed. And, in return, he asked Mr. Bhutto if Libya could have the first bomb."

Bhutto told Beg of this request sometime in 1975, when he asked the journalist to take the airline post in Europe. In this position, Beg served as a wide-ranging expediter for the unorthodox Bhutto, and was in a unique position to learn what had come of Qaddafi's financial offer.

According to Beg, Pakistan International Airlines was called upon to make special security precautions for at least two flights from Tripoli to Karachi. One flight lifted off from Tripoli in December 1975; the other in the summer of 1976. Beg knew of the flights because the airline had to make special arrangements with officials in Italy to protect the planes during refueling stops in Rome. The airplane crews were told that they would carry a VIP, possibly Colonel Qaddafi himself.

In fact, the VIP was a special courier from Colonel Qaddafi, and according to Mr. Beg, he was carrying a most unusual gift to Bhutto. "The courier was carrying suitcases full of American dollars," Beg told us in a series of interviews shortly before he died. "He was carrying as much as $100 million on each flight, and I was told that the money was for the nuclear program."

Why did Qaddafi bother to send money this way? One answer seems obvious. By handing over cold cash, the sums would never show up in Pakistan's official accounts, which are closely scrutinized by all of the many Western countries who loan money to the debt-ridden country, and can be perused by eager journalists such as ourselves. No official statistics, no embarrassing questions. And Bhutto could use the money as he liked.

Qaddafi, for all his enthusiasm, was not the only Islamic leader to offer money to the Pakistani nuclear program. According to Mr. Beg, Bhutto had told him of at least one other—King Faisal of Saudi Arabia. It was Faisal's backing of Bhutto—moral, political, and financial—that made it possible for Pakistan to host the Islamic Summit in Lahore in 1974. And Faisal's backing extended to the nuclear program as well.

"Well, according to Mr. Bhutto, the first country that was interested in this was Saudi Arabia," Beg told us. "I'm not sure if King Faisal really wanted Pakistan to have the bomb. But he was very keen that, as the most advanced and progressive Muslim state, Pakistan should have the know-how and the technology to develop one."

Whether for the nuclear program or for more general support, most of the Saudi money appears to have come through ordinary banking channels, as part of a staggering influx of Islamic money into Pakistan in the year beginning July 1973. According to official figures, as published in the government's *Pakistan Economic Survey*, the Shah of Iran gave as much as $500 million in that single year, with lesser sums coming from Saudi Arabia and the Gulf states, and some officially counted money from the Libyans.

The Shah also gave similar amounts in the following year, and was probably the largest single Islamic contributor to Mr. Bhutto's Pakistan. The

Shah was extremely worried that the insurgency among the Baluchi tribesmen in Pakistan might spill over the border into Iranian Baluchistan, and much of the money he gave to Pakistan was earmarked to help Bhutto put down the Baluchi rebellion.

Adding together all of the Islamic contributions, the figures come to several billion dollars, and there is no way that the nuclear program could have spent anywhere near that amount. Even so, the figures demonstrate Bhutto's incredible skill in raising Islamic money, at least in part by holding forth the promise of an Islamic bomb.

Would Bhutto have repaid this money by actually giving Qaddafi or the other Islamic states the bomb? The answer can only be speculation. Bhutto was overthrown and hanged before his bomb was completed, saving him from ever having to make the decision. But as we learned from Mr. K.'s account of the original negotiations in Paris, the Libyans had their worries from the start. It is also safe to assume that anyone as shrewd as Bhutto would have held on to his nuclear trump as long as he possibly could, even with Qaddafi asking for the first bomb.

"Mr. Bhutto was too shrewd a politician ever to commit himself on that," Beg assured us. "But I was quite certain that the first bomb would always remain with Pakistan."

Khalid Hasan, the former press secretary to Bhutto, told us the same. "I do not believe for a moment that Bhutto would have said: 'Okay, send a notice around to all the Arab and Muslim capitals. Tell them we have the bomb and it's up for auction. Ask them how much they are going to pay for it.'

"He would never have done that," Khalid insisted. "He would have used it for diplomatic and political advantage with the Arabs, and even with the Western countries. But he would never have put it on auction. I mean, that wouldn't be Mr. Bhutto. He wasn't a man like that."

Just as President Nasser had told the fast-traveling Major Jalloud before the Libyan's trip to China, nations do not generally sell atomic bombs. At least not if they can help it.

But for Bhutto—and now for his successors—the problem is that a wretchedly impoverished country like Pakistan might not be able to help it. As in the time of Bhutto, the country is still completely dependent on handouts from its Islamic neighbors, as well as on the repatriated earnings of Pakistanis working in those countries. Were even a handful of these Islamic beneficiaries to gang up and demand "the entire capability," what could poor Pakistan do? In the East, as in the West, he who pays the piper calls the tune.

6

The French Connection

If you wanted to be somebody in this world, you had to have a bomb.

—Bertrand Goldschmidt,
French Atomic Energy Commission,
January 1981

Suppose you make a steel plant. Could you ever be certain that none of the steel would ever be used to make a gun? This plant was intended to reprocess irradiated fuel. . . . Then you come and say, "Ah, maybe they will make an atomic bomb."

—F. X. Poincet,
Honorary President, SGN (France),
May 1980

Careless or marginal errors committed on purpose would make possible the concealment of appreciable quantities of plutonium. . . . The efficiency of controls is very debatable.

—André Giraud,
Director, French Atomic Energy Commission,
secret French Government document,
January 1973

Ali Bhutto had found his financial backers in the Arab world, and ever since the "jamboree" in the canvas tent at Multan, he had the commitment of Pakistan's traditionally strong cadre of highly skilled scientists and engineers. But those were the easy bits. To build the Islamic bomb, Bhutto still needed the major components of nuclear technology and the materials. And that could come only from the West.

The Canadians had already sold Pakistan a Candu natural uranium reactor, the one at the Karachi Nuclear Power Plant that Bhutto had shown Qaddafi during the week of the Islamic Summit in Lahore in February 1974. The reactor produced electricity, some 137 million watts for the local power grid, and had been ordered back in the mid-1960s, when Bhutto was still a minister in the cabinet of Field Marshal Ayub Khan. This was at a time when the Canadians were fighting hard to win nuclear export orders, and Canadian General Electric had supplied a ready-to-run, turnkey power plant, with generous financing from the Canadian Government.

The reactor itself, the Candu, is by all the accepted definitions a standard civilian nuclear reactor.* It is generally considered safer than the American light-water reactors, and is in many ways easier to operate. It also has three added attractions, which make it especially enticing to any nation trying to build nuclear weapons on the sly. It uses fuel made from easily obtained natural uranium, without the need for costly enrichment facilities, or any dependence on the handful of outside and potentially antiproliferation-minded suppliers of enriched uranium fuel. It can be refueled continuously, without any need to shut down the reactor, which makes it more difficult for outside observers to know how much fuel has been burned or for how long. And it produces in the used, or irradiated fuel, large quantities of the new man-made element plutonium, which is the most frequently used nuclear explosive and the most likely way for any new nation to build the bomb.

Bhutto's plan, as we were told by the former Pakistani official Mr. K., was to use the plutonium from the Candu reactor to make his first atom bombs. This is the technique the Pakistanis had discussed with the Libyans—as well as with the Saudis and the Gulf states—during the meetings in Paris in 1973. And this is what the Libyan and other Arab financial aid was initially intended to support.

What was needed, then, was a way to get the plutonium out of the used reactor fuel—a *reprocessing plant*. And to get it, Bhutto wisely turned to the one nuclear supplying country most likely to say yes—the export-hungry French.

In matters nuclear, the French have always pursued an elegantly independent course. It is an astonishing and highly innovative tradition when one thinks about it.

From the discovery of radium by Mme. Marie Curie in 1898, and the discovery of artificial radioactivity by her daughter and son-in-law Irène and Frédéric Joliot-Curie in 1934, French scientists have played pioneering roles in nuclear research. First at the Collège de France in Paris, then as wartime refugees at Cambridge University in Great Britain, and finally as part of an Anglo-Canadian team in Montreal, French scientists such as Bertrand Goldschmidt contributed both to basic nuclear physics and also to the work of the wartime Manhattan Project, which developed the first atom bombs.

Even in the early days of discovery, the French found themselves systematically excluded from full partnership in the Anglo-American nuclear effort. The security-conscious Americans feared that the Free French scientists, who were following the leadership of General Charles de Gaulle, might betray nuclear secrets to their French Communist colleagues, such as the Nobel laureate Frédéric Joliot-Curie himself, or directly to the other wartime ally, the Soviet Union. In a more mercenary vein, the British feared that the French might gain the knowledge and experience to become

---

*Candu stands for Canadian deuterium uranium reactor. It uses deuterium oxide, D_2O or heavy water, to cool the reactor and moderate the chain reaction.

stronger competitors in the commercial and industrial development of nuclear energy once the war was over.

In retrospect, this ganging-up against the French was perhaps the first attempt to stop the proliferation of nuclear knowledge and technology, and the effort continued after the war in tightfisted and extremely nationalistic atomic secrecy laws, such as the McMahon Act in the United States and similar measures in Britain. Then as now, the antiproliferation effort failed. The French, proud as ever, came away feeling that they had been wronged, and saw little choice but to strike off on their own, and in the most ambitious way.

This independence and self-reliance have marked the French nuclear program ever since. The French were the first nation to set up a civilian nuclear authority—the Commissariat à l'Énergie Atomique, or CEA, which they established in October 1945. They found their own source of uranium ore in the province of Limousin, and later developed huge uranium mines in their former West African colonies, Gabon and Niger. They built their own atomic pile or reactor, the Zoe, at Fontenay-aux-Roses, which was based on their earlier research with natural uranium. And, of special interest for the future, they used the methods they had developed while working as part of the Anglo-Canadian team in Montreal to begin extracting plutonium from their irradiated natural uranium fuel.

The French are still enormously proud of this pioneering role in reprocessing and the extraction of plutonium, as we discovered when we talked to the leader of the team that made the original breakthrough, Dr. Bertrand Goldschmidt.

A distinguished, pleasant-looking man now in his late sixties, Goldschmidt has just gone into semiretirement, writing and working as a part-time consultant and unofficial historian for the CEA. A Jew and a wartime refugee from the Nazis, Goldschmidt had in his later years been at the center of Islamic and Arab attempts to get the bomb, first as the CEA's Director of International Relations and then as Chairman of the Board of Governors of the International Atomic Energy Agency in Vienna.

We met Dr. Goldschmidt at the CEA's modern, rather sterile headquarters on the Rue de la Fédération in Paris, near the Eiffel Tower. From the window of the office where we talked, we could see the roofs of the city's finely structured older buildings, the new Paris of the high-rises, and the timeless River Seine with its glass-enclosed tourist boats—in all, a nicely mixed message of then and now. We spoke with Dr. Goldschmidt in English. He has a perfect command of the language and speaks with little accent, a reflection of his wartime years in the United States and Canada.

As Goldschmidt explained it, the difficulty in reprocessing irradiated fuel had been to find the best solvent to separate the newly created plutonium away from the fission products and uranium. This was something he had worked on as part of the wartime Anglo-Canadian team in Montreal, where he had helped to perfect what became known as the solvent-extraction method. Back in Paris following the war, he had continued with the same approach.

"I ordered a lot of solvents—and not just the best ones, through the Carbon and Carbide representative in Paris, and we isolated the first milligram of plutonium in 1949," he recalled fondly. "We published a paper on the reprocessing process in 1955. Everyone was furious when we published. But I had no scruples about it because I felt that we had pioneered this extraction work. From then on, the cat was completely out of the bag."

Dr. Goldschmidt's work gave the French an early lead over Great Britain and the United States in plutonium reprocessing, a lead they have maintained and extended to the present day. In reprocessing, France was and is number one.

Another of the early pioneers was Dr. Francis Perrin, for many years the head of the French Atomic Energy Commission. A small, bearded, and extremely lively man for all of his eighty years, Perrin received us at his book-lined Paris office, where he tried to give us a feel for the early days of the French nuclear program.

As Perrin explained it, the goal from the beginning was to develop independence, especially from the Anglo-American Allies. And to that end, he and his scientists were given "complete freedom of action." The government provided plenty of money, and exercised "no a priori financial control." The new CEA had no cumbersome bureaucracy to block quick decision making. Perrin insisted on basic as well as applied research. And the scientists felt that they had carte blanche. "The idea was to prepare France for all applications of nuclear energy," Perrin told us.

At the start, the French nuclear program was also primarily civilian, without any explicit military intention. But to use a phrase that has become something of a nuclear cliché, the program always had a "weapons option" because of the reprocessing know-how and the growing stocks of plutonium waiting to be tapped. Then as now, it was a short step from the option to the weapon, and the decision could be made at the discretion of the political leaders.

That decision came in November 1956 as the result of a national trauma. The French had joined forces with the British and Israelis to take over the Suez Canal in an attempt to wrest control from the increasingly nationalistic Egyptians under Gamal Abdel Nasser. But just as the invasion forces seemed certain of military success, the two nuclear superpowers—the United States and the Soviet Union—ganged up to force France and its allies to withdraw. The shock to French pride was immeasurable, and in response, the Socialist government of Guy Mollet secretly gave the nuclear go-ahead. France would have the bomb. Three years and three months later, on the thirteenth of February 1960, in the depths of the Sahara desert at Reggan in what was still French Algeria, the French staged their first atomic test.

This was the beginning of France's independent nuclear strike force, the celebrated *force de frappe*, as shaped and popularized by the newly resurrected General Charles de Gaulle. "It is indispensable that it is our own, that France defends herself by herself, for herself, and in her own way," Le Grand Charles declared soon after returning to power in 1958. "The base of this force will be an atomic arsenal—that we buy or that we build—but that must belong to us."

One of the key advisers to de Gaulle in the critical years of French nuclear development, Dr. Perrin told us how the General viewed the political importance of having the military weapon. "It is remarkable to think that the only countries to make the financial, military, and industrial effort in the nuclear field, and the ones that now have nuclear arsenals, are precisely the five countries on the United Nations Security Council," he said at one point during our lengthy interview. "First the United States, then the Soviet Union, then Great Britain and China, and then France, because de Gaulle demanded it."

"From France's point of view, it is a little like a meeting of gangsters, where the first thing you do is to put your knife on the table," he smiled. "The meetings were taking place, but until de Gaulle, France was entering them without a knife."

President de Gaulle's knife on the table, and his declaration of nuclear independence, shook NATO and the Atlantic Alliance. It also disrupted the nuclear status quo, the strategic balance in which the Soviet Union squared off against the United States and its willing junior partner-in-arms, the United Kingdom.

Over the years, de Gaulle's view of the *force de frappe*—a bomb that belongs to us—has continued to ring true for other would-be nuclear nations, as France became the model and the provider for those who wanted to follow in its footsteps.

Or, as Dr. Goldschmidt put it to us, "If you wanted to be somebody in this world, you had to have a bomb."

Exports and the Bomb: the Real French View

President de Gaulle had thought in terms of grand strategy. His successors in the 1970s spoke in the less exalted language of economics. But both strategy and economics have forced the French into an all-out effort to find friends and clients in the Islamic Middle East.

The reason is obvious. It can be summed up in a single word: oil. The French need it. The Arabs have it. And the only way for France to pay for it is to sell the Arabs and their Islamic allies what they want to buy.

Not that the French have wanted to kowtow to the sheiks. Far from it. No country in the world has tried harder to reduce its dependence on the import of oil, and in the absence of any significant coal deposits or domestic gas and oil reserves, the key to that effort has been a massive commitment to nuclear power. Under President Valéry Giscard d'Estaing, the French nuclear goal was unmatched anywhere—to generate as much as 60 percent of their electricity with atomic power plants by 1985.

The logic was elementary, as we heard from the chief of the French Atomic Energy Commission, Michel Pecqueur, when he was interviewed for the BBC *Panorama* film in the spring of 1980. A tall, powerful-looking man, Pecqueur was less than happy speaking English to a television camera, and he tended to sound as if he were answering the questions by rote or reciting the received French doctrine, which he was.

"The main target of our nuclear program in France is to fulfill our own energy needs," he told us. "We are a country with very small resources in energy, and it is necessary for us to develop our nuclear program very rapidly to reduce our dependence on oil."

Dr. Goldschmidt told us much the same, and in a far more dramatic way. "Nuclear energy is the only solution against the strangling of the Western world by the Arab countries," he argued. And possibly against an all-out energy war as well. "If there were no nuclear energy, you'd soon have a world-wide fight for energy resources, and possibly a nuclear war," he told us. "No energy is more dangerous than nuclear energy. But not having it is even more dangerous."

It was an argument that we would come to hear over and over within the French nuclear community. Yet in a way that no one seemed willing to admit, the very commitment to nuclear power was, at least for a time, actually increasing France's dependence on the potential Arab "stranglers" who were producing the oil.

Nuclear power plants take time to build. They cost enormous sums of money. To pay for them, the French found themselves looking to sell their own products to the newly rich oil producers. In the meantime, of course, the oil imports were continuing, and the French had to sell even more to earn the foreign exchange to pay for them.

In both cases—to pay for the nuclear power plants and to pay for the oil—the emphasis was on exports, and especially on exports to the Arabs of French high technology, from Mirage fighter jets to nuclear reactors and reprocessing plants.

"We cannot rely on the export of raw materials," M. Pecqueur told us. "We are poor in raw materials. We cannot try to export the usual goods, because wages are high in France compared to the developing countries. So what we can do to pay the oil bill is to develop our nuclear technology and our nuclear industry."

And what about the dangers of nuclear proliferation?

In public, the French have taken a careful attitude. Like many of their friends and potential customers in the Third World, they have refused to sign the Nuclear Nonproliferation Treaty, arguing that it discriminated unfairly between countries that already had nuclear weapons and those who, under the treaty, would not be allowed to reach that lofty status. But, in a clever diplomatic twist, they pledged in 1968 that they would follow the provisions of the treaty, which called for international safeguards on all sensitive nuclear material.

In private, the French attitude was somewhat more cavalier, as we learned in a rather unorthodox way.

During our initial investigations in France, one of our contacts invited us to supper with a man whom he described as at the center of some of the overseas nuclear projects that we had been asking about. We met the man in the parking lot of a café outside of Paris, drove in separate cars to a superb little provincial restaurant that he and our contact just happened to know, and proceeded to stuff ourselves on one of the tastiest meals we ever had, talking all the while of the dangers of nuclear proliferation and the threat of all-out war. We finished with a large cognac each, and as we started to leave, the man—casually dressed and exceptionally well informed—asked if we would excuse him for a moment. He had something in his car that he wanted to give us. A minute or so later, he returned with a neatly photocopied set of documents, and in the light from the rear of our Renault 5, he began to run through one highly classified document after another, all from various parts of the normally leakproof French Government.

We were stunned. What we thought had been a pleasant meal, and little more, had unexpectedly turned into a meeting with our own "Deep Throat." Only this *la gorge profonde* was not just pointing us in the right direction. He was giving us the documents to prove what we had only suspected.

Suddenly, as we stood there on the lonely country road, a large black sedan came slowly up behind us. We froze. It was the police, we were certain. And they had caught us red-handed. But even as we tried to figure how we would explain what we were doing in our rather halting French, the black sedan drove on, obviously lost or looking for a certain house along the road.

Later, after our man had gone and we had driven back to Paris, we laughed at ourselves and our sudden paranoia.

"By the way," one of us asked. "What was his name? I don't think I got it down."

"Neither did I," said the other. "He never gave it."

It seems that we were not the only ones with a bit of professional paranoia. And after we had a chance to study the documents he gave us, we came to understand why.

One of the "leaked" documents—some would say stolen—was the minutes of a meeting on January 4, 1973, of the interministerial Atomic Energy Committee. The meeting included representatives of the Atomic Energy Commission, the Foreign Office, and Électricité de France, and the minutes paraphrased a lengthy discussion on the problems of proliferation. They are marked "Défense Confidentiel," which we learned is the second highest secrecy classification in France; handing them over was in direct violation of France's atomic secrecy laws and could subject the leaker to a lengthy prison term.

Dr. Goldschmidt, the father of French plutonium, led the discussion. As recorded in black and white, he gave the inside view of the French nuclear establishment that proliferation could not be stopped.

As he saw it, no nation could build a real nuclear arsenal in secret. But almost any nation could build a few bombs without anyone knowing. That, he insisted, "was practically unstoppable." So it did not make sense to become too obsessed, as the Americans were, with the clandestine building of a single bomb, since there was really no way to halt it.

The minutes reveal little disagreement with Goldschmidt's basic pessimism on proliferation. In fact, the same view was seconded by the then head of the Atomic Energy Commission, M. André Giraud.

Generally considered the architect of the French nuclear program in the 1970s, Giraud told the others "that the development of nuclear energy is going to increase considerably the quantities of plutonium handled around the world." As a result, "carelessness or marginal errors committed on purpose would make possible the concealment of appreciable quantities of plutonium. In this sense," he insisted, "the efficiency of controls is very debatable."

Is it that easy to make a bomb? asked one of the other participants.

"A primitive device could not be excluded," replied Giraud. "Even if put together from various parts, at the cost of a weak yield or a bizarre explosion."

This, then, was what the French nuclear mandarins really thought. More nuclear power would bring more plutonium. More plutonium would bring more bombs. A few bombs could not be detected. Controls or safeguards did not really work very well. And it did not make sense to try to stop what could not be stopped.

From there, it was only a short step to what became the real French approach on nuclear proliferation. If it could not be stopped, why be the ones to stand in the way? New nations wanted to buy plutonium-reprocessing plants and other nuclear technology. France needed to export to meet the energy crisis. Was it not better, smarter, more realistic, more French, to help French firms make the sales?

The only possible objection that the minutes show to this line of reasoning came from a man from the Foreign Office—a M. Courcel—who insisted on a bit of caution. "We do not want to put ourselves in the position of being accused of helping other countries to make atomic weapons," he warned.

The Foreign Office naturally worried about what other nations would think of France, especially on such an emotive question as proliferation, and the diplomats feared—correctly—that the often careless export of nuclear technology would be seen as leading to the spread of nuclear weapons. As a result, there was a recurring split over nuclear export policy, with the Quai d'Orsay consistently at odds with the exaggerated push for nuclear exports led by Giraud and the Atomic Energy Commission.

In 1973 and for several years afterward, Giraud and his priorities—exports first, antiproliferation last—were winning the fight and effectively shaping French policy, first from his post as head of the Atomic Energy Commission, then as the powerful Minister of Industry under Giscard d'Estaing.

M. Giraud, we might add, was recently honored by the American Nuclear Society and the Atomic Industrial Forum as the Nuclear Statesman of 1980, for reasons that the award's presenter expressed in this prose: "Even today, as Minister of Industry in France, he continues to offer guidance and inspiration to this nuclear program, which in terms of vision, vigor, and ongoing activity is unequaled in any other part of the world."

Established in 1972, the award is intended "to recognize outstanding service in developing and guiding the use of atomic energy in constructive channels."

The Pakistanis Come to Paris

The Pakistanis knew their French, and in seeking a reprocessing plant, they found them especially *sympathique*. Ali Bhutto, the Pakistani leader, was personally a great admirer of France. His library was renowned for its collection of French texts, and he considered himself a student of Napoleon. More broadly, he saw France as offering a happy alternative to Pakistan's former reliance on Britain and the United States. Though still in NATO, and unmistakably "Western," France was increasingly presenting itself as a "Third Force," independent of its allies and unashamedly pro-Arab. And when it came to nuclear cooperation, Bhutto and his advisers wanted expressly "to disentangle themselves from their excessive reliance on Great Britain," and saw the French as their best bet.

Plutonium extraction, or reprocessing, was the French specialty, and the job fell primarily to a highly specialized engineering firm called Saint-Gobain Techniques Nouvelles, or simply SGN. *

Though privately owned until the late 1970s, SGN had been closely tied to the official French Atomic Energy Commission ever since 1952, when Dr. Goldschmidt selected it to build the first French reprocessing plant at Cap de la Hague, near Cherbourg, and also to play the chief role in the thirteen-nation Eurochemic plant at Mol, in Belgium. The Eurochemic plant was really the first attempt to move from the laboratory extraction methods that Goldschmidt had pioneered to an industrial scale. The hope was to make eventual commercial use of the extracted plutonium as part of a new mixed-oxide fuel for nuclear power reactors, especially the so-called

---

* SGN started as a division of one of France's larger private business groups, Saint-Gobain Pont-à-Moussan. It was later incorporated separately as Saint-Gobain Nucléaire (1960); then as Saint-Gobain Techniques Nouvelles (1965); and finally as Société Générale pour le Technique Nouvelle (1977), with the French Atomic Energy Commission taking a 66 percent controlling interest. Throughout all the changes, the firm kept the same initials, SGN.

breeder reactors, which would reproduce more plutonium than it would consume.

Later, SGN would beat stiff British and American competition to build the Japanese reprocessing plant at Tokai-Mura, and would negotiate to build smaller facilities in Taiwan and South Korea, as well as in Pakistan. In all these negotiations and contracts, SGN continued to work closely with CEA scientists, and to share with the CEA the financial rights to the technology they had developed together. SGN was, in sum, the French Government's chosen instrument in the highly sensitive field of plutonium reprocessing.

According to one of the documents that our unknown friend in France had given us on that lonely country road—a "Note" prepared by the Scientific Affairs section of the Quai d'Orsay and dated October 23, 1974—the Pakistanis had actually made their first approaches to SGN in the late 1960s, and the French Government had raised no objections at the time to helping them in the building of a reprocessing plant. But this was before Mr. Bhutto came to power, and the Pakistanis lacked the financing to go ahead.

This time, however, the money was in hand, and SGN undertook a series of contracts to design and help build not one, but two different reprocessing facilities. The better known of these plants—and the one that later stirred most of the controversy—was an industrial reprocessing plant to be located on a desert site near the upper reaches of the Indus River, at a place called Chashma. The plant was to have the capacity to reprocess 100 tons a year of used reactor fuel. At a rough estimate, this would yield some 800 kilograms a year of plutonium, or enough for an entire arsenal of nuclear weapons.

According to another of the French documents—an aide-mémoire to the French Ambassador in Islamabad dated January 24, 1975—SGN signed at least two separate contracts for the Chashma plant. They signed the first—for "basic design"—in March 1973, about the time the Pakistanis and the Libyans were holding their secret nuclear talks in Paris. The second—for "detailed design" and help in the actual construction—was signed in October 1974. In the second, SGN agreed to serve as the principal engineers on the project, providing blueprints and specifications, furnishing some of the equipment, helping in purchasing and procurement from subcontractors, and putting the plant into operation, the all-important "start-up."

This was precisely the kind of high-technology export encourged by André Giraud. According to the aide-mémoire, SGN itself stood to make an estimated 40 to 50 million francs, or about $8 to $10 million given the exchange rate prevailing at the time. French subcontractors expected another 120 million frances, or $45 million, aided by official French export credits. And the Pakistanis as much as promised that SGN's help on Chashma would lead France to the big prize—the multibillion-franc sale of three to four 600-megawatt power reactors, Mirage aircraft, and other costly goodies, not just to Pakistan but to its oil-rich Islamic supporters as well.

Business is business, and that kind of business few nations knowingly turn down. To get a better sense of this particular business from the inside, we went directly to the man who had sold the Pakistanis the reprocessing plant, the former head of SGN, M. François-Xavier Poincet. A big, rounded, jolly, and wonderfully outgoing engineer-turned-executive, and a man who cannot seem to resist the temptation to say what he thinks, M. Poincet invited us to spend an afternoon at his lovely country estate in a wooded village about an hour's drive from Paris.

Surrounded by a long stone wall and an electronically controlled gate that swings open majestically at the push of a button in M. Poincet's Citroën, the beautifully kept grounds stretch out past a small lake and a fine old stable to a two-story, vine-covered house of rough-cut stone. Inside, we found a surprisingly modern open-plan living and dining area, full of stone and polished wood and prized old antiques. Through the window, the little lake glistened. It was the spring of 1980.

We had told M. Poincet as little as we could in advance, which was that we were doing a television program on French nuclear exports. Our goal at that point, especially after seeing his estate, was to get him (and it) to appear in the film and to agree to let us return with our crew and on-camera reporter Philip Tibenham to do a formal interview. But as Poincet pointed out with some suspicion (and rightly so), we had rather quickly steered the preliminary and supposedly general conversation around to the question of SGN's role in Pakistan.

From the classified documents that we had in our possession, which we did not show Poincet, the first big question was about the plant's capacity. When finished, Chashma would reprocess one hundred tons a year of used nuclear fuel, which would produce enough plutonium for dozens of atom bombs. Wasn't that a bit excessive? we asked. Especially when Pakistan's one and only reactor, the Candu in Karachi, turned out only eighteen to twenty tons of used fuel a year? And when the Pakistanis themselves had no reactors that could burn the new plutonium mixed oxide fuel?

Not at all, Poincet replied. The Pakistanis wanted "energy independence." They were talking about buying more reactors. They were also talking about using the excess capacity to sell reprocessing services to other nations, along with a service that no one else was offering—the burial of the remaining nuclear wastes after the reprocessing was finished. According to Poincet, he had heard of these plans directly from the head of the Pakistan Atomic Energy Commission, Munir Ahmed Khan:

"I have something nobody else in the world has—a desert with not a single drop of rain during the entire year," Poincet quoted Munir as telling him. "If I offer reprocessing to other countries, I can also store the wastes in a place where there's no danger of any radiation spreading. It's a good business."

It sounded a bit farfetched, especially as the Pakistanis had no experience in the still difficult art of preparing nuclear wastes for long-term storage. But in any case, didn't M. Poincet know that Mr. Bhutto had set his heart on nuclear weapons? And that he had even announced his intentions to the world before he came to power?

That was clearly a question M. Poincet had answered before. "This is another idea that has spread all over, that Pakistan wanted to make an atom bomb with the help of this plant," he replied briskly. "In my view, it's completely unproved. First of all, if you wanted to make an atomic bomb, you wouldn't need to resort to such an expensive and complicated thing as a reprocessing plant. There are far easier ways to make a bomb, and far cheaper."

In part, Poincet was right. The Pakistanis really did not need the industrial plant at Chashma to build a single bomb. Chashma would allow them to build an entire arsenal. For a clandestine bomb in the basement, there were easier ways, and cheaper, as we will show in the following pages.

But whichever way the Pakistanis got the plutonium, had it never crossed M. Poincet's mind that Pakistan might use it for anything other than purely peaceful purposes?

"Obviously I can't say that," Poincet shot back. "Suppose you make a steel plant. Could you ever be certain that none of the steel would ever be used to make a gun? This plant was intended to reprocess irradiated fuel," he went on, getting more and more animated. "Pakistan has a source of irradiated fuel. They have one reactor, and are planning to have more. So they make a reprocessing plant. It's quite normal. Then you come and say: 'Ah, maybe they will make an atomic bomb.' Well, maybe they will use the steel to make a weapon, a gun, a pistol. Who can say?"

It was an argument that we would hear over and over again. The businessman's stock reply: "Nuts and bolts can make a bomb. So where do you draw the line?" As Poincet saw it, drawing the line was a job for government, not for the individual businessman. And as he stressed, the French Government had been very much involved at every step of the Pakistani reprocessing project.

From the beginning of negotiations, the French Atomic Energy Commission, the CEA, worked closely with SGN engineers and also directly with the Pakistan Atomic Energy Commission. The French and Pakistanis had signed an earlier agreement on nuclear cooperation, which Bhutto revived when he came to power. This covered various scientific exchanges, such as visits by French experts to Pakistani nuclear facilities, and technical assistance in upgrading a small U.S.-supplied research reactor at the Pakistan Institute for Nuclear Science and Technology from the original five to eight or ten thermal megawatts. The French also agreed to train as many as a hundred Pakistani technicians, many of them at the SGN-built reprocessing plant at La Hague.

Did the French know from an early stage that Pakistan wanted to build the bomb? Our conversation with one Pakistani insider—who cannot be named or identified—indicates that at least certain Frenchmen did. This especially well-placed Pakistani contends that the French scientists and technicians at the Atomic Energy Commission were "not naive" and were necessarily aware of Pakistani intentions, because in 1973 and 1974, the Pakistanis asked the French for certain types of "mass" or "criticality" analyses that would be relevant only in the production of a nuclear weapon. The Frenchmen, after checking with their superiors inside CEA, returned to the Pakistanis with a surprising answer. Yes, they said, they could give the data, but only at a fee. The quoted sum, according to the Pakistani, was "ridiculously large," and the Pakistanis, still feeling under a financial constraint, concluded they could develop the analyses themselves, and thus rejected the French offer. "The French knew exactly what we were doing," the Pakistani told us, "and they knew exactly what they were doing too."

Anxious for the sale of the reprocessing facility and eager to insure a good name for French diplomacy, the French government felt that the main task was to negotiate an agreement specifying how the plant would be safeguarded. What kind of international inspection and controls would the Pakistanis accept? This was delicate in the extreme. The Pakistanis did not want their hands tied, while the French had to look over both shoulders. The Quai d'Orsay did not want France to be seen by its allies to be helping the Pakistanis build the bomb. But if that was what Pakistan wanted to do, André Giraud and the export lobby did not want to lose the sale, or the promise of future sales.

The negotiations went on behind closed doors in Paris and Islamabad, and there was little mention of them in public statements or in the press. In our pile of purloined documents, however, we happened to have some of the diplomatic correspondence, which offers an intriguing view of the ins and outs of the newly developed nuclear diplomacy.

As the correspondence shows, the French were trying to toe a terribly slippery line. They knew that Pakistan had refused to sign the Nuclear Nonproliferation Treaty and had no intention of signing in the future. They also admitted, at least in the secrecy of their classified correspondence, what M. Poincet had tried so artfully to deny: that the hundred-ton-a-year plant proposed for Chashma was rather large for a country with only a single small power reactor, whatever the plans on paper for future reactor purchases or reprocessing services to sell.

French officials also realized from the start that the Pakistanis were extremely reluctant to submit the Chashma plant to international controls. This is clearly recorded in the January 24, 1975, aide-mémoire, which notes that the Pakistani nuclear chief Munir Khan had made a show of his "surprise" and "displeasure" at French requests for "multilateral controls" by the International Atomic Energy Agency. Munir Khan's position, backed in part by SGN, was simple: Leave the question of controls "until the plant had gone into operation, or at least until the construction was completed."

As the aide-mémoire showed, the position was transparent, even to the

French. And we heard much the same on a personal level from Dr. Bertrand Goldschmidt, who was at the time of the negotiations the CEA's Director of International Relations.

"I never trusted anything Munir Khan said," Goldschmidt confided to us when we spoke with him at the CEA's headquarters in Paris. "He could lie while being charming. I never believed a word he said."

A second aide-mémoire, dated January 30, 1975, and addressed to Goldschmidt's attention, gave the French assessment of the potential danger in even more dramatic terms: Once the Pakistanis had the detailed design in hand, they would be able to build the Chashma plant without further French help, "either by their own means, or by calling on non-French suppliers for certain equipment."

"*SGN is well and truly involved with the Pakistanis*," the document warned. And worse: "*The Pakistanis have the firm intention to complete the installation, with the help of SGN or without it.*"

The warning—the emphasis was there in the document—would prove prophetic. At the time, however, the French thought that they could hold the Pakistanis in line by insisting on international safeguards, while the Pakistanis continued to drag their feet. The stalemate continued, and finally in the early months of 1975 the French Government forced the issue with a little Gallic guile.

We heard the story from M. Poincet, during our first afternoon at his home. "We got the information from the French Government in March 1975 that we had better slow down, because the Pakistanis had not entered into agreements with the International Atomic Energy Commission," he told us with a wink.

But a simple, unexplained slowdown might have made SGN look bad in the eyes of their Pakistani clients, which was something that the businessman in Poincet wanted to avoid. So to get his company off the hook, he arranged for the Foreign Ministry to write an official letter to the company, formally threatening to cut off the contract if Pakistan did not accept the safeguards. Poincet quietly showed the letter to his Pakistani friends and it had the desired effect.

"It forced the Pakistanis to enter into negotiations with the IAEA," explained Poincet. "The negotiations took a year."

In the meantime, SGN continued to work on the design, and quietly protected itself on the other side by getting guarantees from the Pakistanis that they would still pay even if the negotiations, and the contract, should fall through. According to Poincet, SGN held back on any actual construction until after the negotiations were completed and the IAEA had approved the project. "We continued to make drawings," he told us. "But you must realize, it wasn't a question of pouring concrete the next day."

The negotiations on safeguards finally ended toward the end of 1975, and the International Atomic Energy Agency gave its approval in early 1976, as marked by a formal tripartite agreement signed by the Agency, the French, and the Pakistanis. By IAEA standards, the agreed safeguards seemed rather strict.

Pakistan undertook that none of the reprocessing equipment or the material produced "shall be used for the manufacture of any nuclear weapon or to further any other military purpose or for the manufacture of any other nuclear explosive device." The Pakistanis consented to submit the Chashma plant to international safeguards, including regular visits by IAEA inspectors. They also agreed that the same provisions would apply to any future facility based upon the same type of reprocessing technology, which was defined as any facility using the solvent extraction method. This was a key understanding, and would come back to haunt both Pakistan and the IAEA.

At the time, though, no one knew what the future would hold, and most observers thought that the French and the IAEA had managed to tie Pakistan's hands for at least the next twenty years.

For their part, the Pakistanis were ecstatic. The final approval came in March 1976. Bhutto was in Canada visiting the Parliament when his friend and former press secretary Khalid Hasan gave him the news.

"And you know, his face lit up and he relaxed," Hasan told us during our interviews with him in London in the spring of 1980. "He was very pleased. And later in the afternoon at the press conference, he said: 'Look, why are you asking me so many questions about the reprocessing plant? The IAEA has cleared it. So what are your misgivings?'"

The Pilot Plant

That was the Chashma plant, which would soon become the center of a huge international storm. But even as the Pakistanis were negotiating for Chashma, they were already beginning a second, more secret reprocessing facility—a small pilot plant next door to the Pakistan Institute for Nuclear Science and Technology, or Pinstech.

Little has been written about the pilot plant, and it somehow has managed to escape most controversy. But if American intelligence estimates are right, and the Pakistanis do complete their first nuclear facility by the beginning of 1982, this is where the explosive material, the weapons-usable plutonium, will come from.

As SGN's Poincet had told us when we asked him about Chashma, "If you wanted to make an atomic bomb, you wouldn't need such an expensive and complicated thing as a reprocessing plant. There are far easier ways to make a bomb, and far cheaper." The pilot plant was that easier, cheaper way.

A certain mystery and confusion continue to surround the plant, especially about who helped the Pakistanis to build it. No one seems to want the credit for giving Islam the bomb, not when the explosion could come shortly, at a time to be chosen by the Pakistanis. The French, who would seem to be the most likely suspects, insist on blaming their neighbors in Belgium, while the Belgians go to particularly great lengths to put the blame back on the French.

In fact, they both seem to be right. As we were able to establish during our investigation, the French firm SGN engineered the reprocessing facility itself, while their Belgian counterpart and sometimes competitor Belgonucléaire designed the overall building, which is simply called the New Labs.

The trail that we had to follow went back to the beginnings of the 1970s, when the Pakistanis first started reprocessing with a very small-scale facility, which was designed for them by the British. According to a senior official of the state-owned British Nuclear Fuels Limited, Dr. Donald Avery, the lab would have had a maximum capacity of 360 grams of plutonium a year, and the design was "virtually finished by 1971."

But as Dr. Avery told us, the Pakistanis wanted a far larger pilot plant, and in 1970 they asked the British to help them build a facility that could process as much as thirty tons a year of used reactor fuel, which would have given them 240 or more kilograms a year of plutonium.

The British refused, Dr. Avery recalled. They did not want to go beyond "small-scale operations" with Pakistan.

In the meantime, the Pakistanis were building the facility called for in the original British design. This was in the basement of one of the wings of the Pinstech building. We were told by a European engineer who worked on the construction of the lab that the basement was wholly unsuitable. It was too crowded, and it made the handling of the irradiated fuel extremely difficult. "The British designers gave the impression that they liked it that way," the engineer recalled with a smile.

That was probably true, and as a result, the Pakistanis grew unhappy with the British and started approaching, among others, the Belgian firm. Partly owned by one of the world's most powerful financial groups, the Belgian Société Générale, and part by the Belgian state, Belgonucléaire has its headquarters in Brussels and is run by its hard-driving managing director, Jean van Dievoet.

We telephoned van Dievoet from London in November 1980, hoping to conduct an interview on the phone, and the next thing we knew, he had persuaded us to take the plane to Brussels the following morning to speak with him in person. He wanted to tell us his side of the story.

A tall, trim, good-looking man in his forties, van Dievoet looks like Marcello Mastroianni playing a young and very ambitious corporate executive who still has places to go. He had a deceptively open manner; was quick to laugh, though never too much; and repeatedly made little jokes at his own expense. He told the story without waiting to be asked.

The Pakistanis had first approached Belgonucléaire back in the 1960s, when they were starting out on their nuclear power program, van Dievoet told us. They wanted some basic information, and in response, the company prepared "a ten-page study" on what it could do for the Pakistanis in three areas—reprocessing, the treatment of radioactive wastes, and the turning of reprocessed plutonium into the new mixed oxide reactor fuel, a process called fuel refabrication.

At the time, the Pakistanis lacked the necessary financing, and Belgonucléaire heard nothing more. Then, sometime in the early 1970s, the Pakistanis came back. Would Belgonucléaire be consulting engineer for a new set of labs that would include both reprocessing and fuel refabrication?

Belgonucléaire readily accepted, and the project got under way. As van Dievoet told us, the Pakistanis themselves did the construction. Belgonucléaire's job was to prepare the design and to help the Pakistanis buy the needed equipment. This involved drawing up lists of specifications for various pieces of equipment and advising on the evaluation of offers from would-be suppliers.

The lab's facilities had initially been planned for space inside the Pinstech building, the Belgian told us, which fits with what we had heard of the original British design. But according to van Dievoet, the Pakistanis had moved the facilities to a new building next to Pinstech, and Belgonucléaire was given the added job of designing the basic services for the building, including the ventilation, water, heating, and the like.

As Mr. van Dievoet first told us, the new labs included both a fuel refabrication lab and a pilot reprocessing plant, and a Belgonucléaire publicity handout dated December 1977 appears to take credit for both. But, as he talked to us at greater length, the Belgian executive gave the story a slightly different twist.

Belgonucléaire designed the overall laboratory and the fuel refabrication lab, he admitted. But not the pilot reprocessing plant. "We wanted to do the reprocessing facility as well," he told us, "but we never even got the chance to bid. The Pakistanis gave the job to SGN.

"We had nothing to do with it," he insisted, looking us straight in the eye. "That was all SGN's."

Van Dievoet is a dynamic, persuasive salesman, and for all the obvious self-interest in telling us the story his way, he made a convincing case. After all, the Pakistanis were giving SGN the contract for the industrial reprocessing plant at Chashma. Did it not make sense that they would give the same firm the contract for the pilot plant as well? What is more, van Dievoet's story meshes with a slightly less forthright account that we managed to extract from the former SGN chief, M. Poincet.

"We finished a lab started by a British company," he told us in our first, off-camera interview. "The Pakistanis decided that they didn't want to continue with the British, and asked us to take over. This was a chemical laboratory—for nuclear chemistry—located next to Pinstech. The British had brought it to the drawing stage, and the Pakistanis had already built the walls and the building."

Poincet insisted that the facility was just a simple lab for nuclear chemistry. In our investigations, though, one of our sources gave us the copy of a letter from SGN to the Pakistan Atomic Energy Commission. It was dated July 7, 1973. It was addressed to Mr. M. Afzal, a key deputy to the PAEC chairman Munir Khan, and in it SGN offered the Pakistanis a multipurpose "Universal Machining Unit."

This was a highly sensitive piece of equipment for reprocessing facilities. As the SGN letter explained, it would allow the Pakistanis to cut up and remove the cladding from the irradiated fuel rods taken from the Candu reactor. This is the first step in reprocessing the used fuel to extract the plutonium.

According to the SGN letter, this was explicitly intended for Pakistan's "Reprocessing Pilot Plant." But by whatever name—pilot plant or nuclear chemistry lab—this was the facility that would give the Pakistanis the plutonium for their first bomb, and we now have the evidence that the French authorities had every reason to know that this was exactly how Pakistan intended to use the facility.

The backing for this rather harsh judgment is in one of our French Government documents—a secret telex from the scientific staff of the Foreign Ministry in Paris to the French Embassy in Brussels. It is dated July 28, 1975, and it quotes the Pakistani nuclear chief Munir Khan, who had just been on a visit to the French capital.

According to the telex, Khan had stated that "his country would henceforth be in a position to equip itself with a workshop atelier able to manufacture—using the irradiated natural uranium produced by their Canadian reactor—the few kilograms of plutonium necessary for an explosive device." The telex goes on to say that Munir Khan was referring to "the pilot reprocessing facility being built in Pakistan with the help of Belgonucléaire."

So the French Foreign Office knew of the pilot plant and of Munir Khan's statement that it could be used to give Pakistan the bomb. The only thing the Foreign Office appears not to have known is that the pilot reprocessing plant was being built by both Belgonucléaire and the French firm SGN. In any case, the Quai d'Orsay certainly knew enough of Pakistani capabilities and possible intentions to stop the much larger Chashma facility, and that was something they were not—at the time—willing to do.

In fact, the Foreign Office did just the opposite. The diplomats used the existence of the pilot plant as a rationalization for going ahead with the larger reprocessing plant at Chashma. After all, just as Poincet had argued, if the Pakistanis already had a pilot plant, they did not really need a big plant such as Chashma just to make a bomb. So why stop them from having it?

For their part, the Belgians appear to have been equally remiss. Belgonucléaire certainly had more than a passing involvement in SGN's pilot plant, and the fuel refabrication lab is itself a terribly sensitive facility. It handles the plutonium from which the atom bombs can be made. But neither Belgonucléaire nor the Belgian Government required safeguards or inspections by the International Atomic Energy Agency. The Belgians were content to give their help with nothing more than a letter from the Pakistani

Ambassador in Brussels, who assured them that "the installation would only be used for strictly peaceful ends."

This, in turn, very much worried the Quai d'Orsay. Not that Pakistan would build a bomb. But that their Belgian competitors had not insisted on even the pretense of international safeguards, which put the French, who were insisting, at a decided disadvantage.

7

The Butcher of Baghdad

The Arabs must get an atomic bomb.
—Naim Haddad,
Iraqi Revolutionary Command Council,
1977

We knew very well that some of the Iraqis were interested in the military aspect, the military potential of the reactor they wanted to get. But those were the Army people. You have to understand that in a country like Iraq, if you have a big budgetary expenditure, the Army has to approve it. That's the way it works.
—Yves Girard,
Vice President, Technicatome,
July 1981

Libya and the other Arabs were paying. France was providing. And Pakistan was on its way to the Islamic world's first nuclear bomb.

"We are emerging today out of nearly half a millennium of decline," Pakistani Prime Minister Ali Bhutto had told the February 1974 Islamic Summit in Lahore.

Almost 500 years of decline, and Islam was destined to come back with a nuclear bang. But of all the countries in the Islamic fold, of all the oil-rich Arab states, there was one that clearly would not let Bhutto take the nuclear lead unchallenged. That was Iraq.

"Baghdad was one of the first stops on Mr. Bhutto's trip in 1972," his former press secretary Khalid Hasan told us during a series of interviews in London. "And you know, we couldn't even agree on a standard joint communiqué. They were fighting over commas. The plane was delayed for hours, and in the end there was only a short statement. But no communiqué."

The incident was trivial, Hasan admitted, and on the surface had nothing to do with the two nations' nuclear programs. Yet it symbolized the deep divide between the direction the Pakistanis were taking and the course the Iraqis were setting themselves.

The Pakistanis, even under the secular leadership of Ali Bhutto, were stressing Islamic solidarity; the Iraqis emphasized the unity of the Arabs and the historic leadership of Baghdad. The Pakistanis were praying—or paying lip service—to Allah; the Iraqis, to the highly secular Arab nationalism of the Baath Socialist Party. The Pakistanis were looking for money; the oil-rich Iraqis had it.

The differences were pointed even in 1972, and the Iraqis did not really consider backing the Pakistani nuclear program. Let Pakistan build its Islamic bomb. The Iraqis would build their own, the first nuclear device in purely Arab hands. Here in the cradle of civilization, the primordial land of the Tigris and Euphrates, the Arabs of Iraq would buy and build the most far-ranging nuclear complex, which in a matter of years would give them their own nuclear weapons.

Saddam Hussein is the strong man of Iraq. He is a plodding, systematic, highly determined forty-three-year-old ruler. He has effectively exercised that rule since shortly after the Baath Revolution of July 1968, first as the man behind the aging President Hasan al-Bakr, and from July 1979 as President of the Iraqi Republic and Chairman of the all-important Revolutionary Command Council.

Saddam is also the father of the Iraqi nuclear program, and, more than anything else, it is his strengths and his weaknesses, his memories and his dreams, his foresight and his blind spots, that have so far shaped the making of the Iraqi bomb.

Like the Pakistani leader Ali Bhutto, Saddam Hussein has been an enormously controversial figure. To his admirers, he is the great leader, the new Nasser, and even "the perfume of Iraq." To his enemies, those who are still alive, he is a thug and killer, a Hitler in the making, and "the butcher of Takrit," after the rather impoverished area in northern Iraq from which he and his political clique emerged. To the outside world, he is the man who in September 1980 gave the orders for Iraqi planes and troops to wage war on the neighboring Iran of the Ayatollah Ruhollah Khomeini.

In whatever way one sees him, Saddam Hussein is a man dedicated, determined, driven to make Iraq a modern industrial state.

In his rapid rise to power, Saddam has shown himself quick and ruthless. Born in 1937 in the area of Takrit, he joined the Baath Socialist Party as a student in 1955. Four years later, in 1959, he made his first mark in Iraqi politics when he and a small group of comrades attempted to kill the country's then chief of state, General Abdul Karim Qasim.

The attack came in broad daylight. General Qasim's heavily armed car was moving through the streets of Baghdad. Saddam and his team of assassins moved in. They fired. Qasim fell wounded, shot in the shoulder bone. One of his guards was killed.

Saddam escaped in a waiting car. But he too had been shot, the bullet lodged in his leg. According to those in the car with him, he took the bullet out with his own knife.

Fleeing back to Takrit, he made his way to Damascus, in neighboring Syria, and then to Cairo, where the Egyptian Government gave him the status of political exile. While in Egypt, he was arrested for allegedly threatening to kill a fellow Iraqi. But he was released by the Egyptian President, Colonel Nasser.

Saddam returned to Iraq in 1963, the year his Baath Socialist comrades finally succeeded in killing Qasim and taking power in their first, bloody, and short-lived period of rule. Saddam worked as a party activist, organizing Baathist cells around the country. This gave him the contacts and political base for his rapid rise to power when the chance came.

It came quickly enough. In July 1968, in a two-stage coup, the Baath returned to power, this time to stay. Two years later, the ex-terrorist took control of Iraq's internal security apparatus, a post where he rapidly gained a reputation for ruthlessly removing anyone who stood in his way. This made Saddam the power behind the throne until mid-1979, when he emerged publicly as Iraq's number-one man.

In his rise to power, Saddam has sounded the extreme Iraqi nationalist. For him, Iraq was "the radiant center" of the entire Arab world. The Iraqis had descended from all the great people who had lived and died in Mesopotamia in the past, even before the dawn of Islam. The Iraqis of today were the inheritors of the Sumerians, the Akkadians, the Assyrians, the Babylonians. And Saddam himself was "the grandson" of Nebuchadnezzar, of Hammurabi the lawgiver, and of Sargon, as well as of the Prophet Muhammad.

"The glory of the Arabs stems from the glory of Iraq," he declared in 1979, shortly after becoming President. "Throughout history, whenever Iraq became strong and flourishing, so did the Arab nation. This is why we are striving to make Iraq formidable, invincible, and highly developed. And when this is achieved," he concluded, "Iraq will turn into the radiant center of the whole Arab nation."

These feelings of passionate Iraqi nationalism have been at the heart of Saddam's long-simmering conflict with the Persians of neighboring Iran, a conflict which Saddam pushed to full-scale war in a drive to reclaim Iraqi rights to the disputed Shatt al Arab waterway, as well as to Iran's chief oil-producing province, Khuzistan, which is populated mainly by people of Arab origin.

The same feelings have fed his ambition to replace the late Shah of Iran as the dominant power, if not the policeman, of the disputed Persian Gulf.

And they have inspired his rivalry with neighboring Syria, his territorial claims on Kuwait and the other Gulf states, and his barely concealed contempt for the Saudis, as well as his militant opposition to "the Zionist entity," Israel.

In theory at least, Saddam combines, or perhaps tempers, this Iraqi nationalism with a commitment to the broader, pan-Arab goals of the Baath Socialist Party. Started in Damascus at the end of French rule in 1946, the Baath, or Arab Resurrection Party, has been the classic expression of pan-Arab nationalism. It has been most active in Syria and Iraq, and has preached the unity of all the Arabs without the present national divisions, their freedom and independence, and a rather middle-class kind of state socialism. In practice, the party has been bitterly divided, especially between the rival Baath regimes in Baghdad and Damascus.

From his student days, Saddam has used the party organization, and has at least paid homage to the wider Arab nationalism of the party line. "Our aim," he proclaims, "is to build a powerful, able, socialist Iraq and turn it into a liberated base that would eventually carry the whole Arab nation to its final goals: Arab unity, liberation (from imperialism and Zionism), and socialism."

More relevant, perhaps, Saddam and the Iraqi Baath also preach a very different kind of line—a secular, almost Western commitment to science and technology, to economic development, and to "modernization." This is in sharp contrast to the religious fundamentalism of so much of the often competing Islamic revival, as seen in various forms in Saudi Arabia, Iran, and Pakistan.

The results are impressive. Under Saddam's leadership, the Iraqis have made huge investments in highways, the railway system, airfields, and ports. They are planning to build new chemical and petrochemical plants, new industries such as textiles and food processing, and large-scale irrigation and flood-control systems, recalling those of the ancient Mesopotamians.

The same push has also inspired the modernization of the military, with large investments in Soviet MIG-23's and MIG-25's, French Mirage F-1's, and an impressive range of helicopters, mainly French-built, including the Alouette III, the Super Frelon and the Gazelle. The Iraqis have also made huge purchases of tanks, tank carriers, artillery, and armored vehicles.

These have made the Iraqis the strongest and most modern military force in the Gulf, and probably in the entire Middle East, with the exception of Israel.

"There is a great, almost violent push for modernization," we were told by a top Western businessman now active in Iraq. "They have the attitude that they are now in a position to acquire technology from the more advanced countries because of the bargaining power their oil gives them. They say: 'If we wish to become a modern country, we have thirty years in which to do it.'"

All this is possible, of course, for only one reason. And that is oil. Iraq is sitting on top of the second-largest oil reserves in the entire Middle East, second only to those of Saudi Arabia. Present estimates speak of reserves of more than 100 billion barrels of oil, and the figure is constantly being pushed higher. This is more than enough to last Iraq well into the twenty-first century. Or, in the words of Saddam Hussein: "One of the last two barrels produced on earth must come from Iraq."

Income from all this oil has soared spectacularly since the Baath came to power. In 1970, oil revenues stood at $500 million. In 1980, when the Iranian-Iraqi war broke out, they were expected to hit $15 billion. Experts predict that the figure could reach $30 billion by the mid-1980's.

In part, these phenomenal increases were simply due to OPEC price hikes. But the Iraqis themselves have played a strong role within the Organization of Petroleum Exporting Countries, and also in the fight to gain greater control of their own oil production through the nationalization of foreign-owned oil companies in Iraq.

Oil and modernization—these are the twin themes of Baath rule, and nowhere more dramatic than in their nuclear program, where they have used their oil power to force nuclear exporters to sell them the technology to develop both civilian nuclear research and the ability to build an Iraqi bomb.

The Iraqis set out on this nuclear road in secret—and in silence.

In sharp contrast to Zulfikar Ali Bhutto in Pakistan, Saddam Hussein had not written or spoken very openly of his nuclear ambitions, at least until his outburst following the Israeli bombing. His aides have similarly held their tongues, and the handful of scientists who might now want to speak out are in absolutely no position to do so.

The only verbal hint of Iraqi intentions, of what they really have in mind, has come in a few chance remarks. The first was in Saddam Hussein's September 1975 interview with the Beirut magazine *al-Usbua al-Arabi*, when he described his search for a supposedly peaceful nuclear reactor as part of "the first Arab attempt at nuclear arming."

A second came from a senior member of Iraq's Revolutionary Command Council, Naim Haddad. "The Arabs must get an atomic bomb," he insisted in a 1977 statement. "The countries of the Arab world should possess whatever is necessary to defend themselves."

For the most part, the Iraqi nuclear buildup seemed entirely innocent, especially at the very start. This was in the mid-1960s, before the Baath Socialists returned to power in their 1968 Revolution. The government at the time prevailed upon the Soviet Union to provide various nuclear research facilities, and this included a small two-megawatt research reactor. The reactor began operating in January 1968 at the newly built Nuclear Research Institute at Tuwaitah. The reactor and accompanying facilities fell far short of giving the Iraqis the ability to get their hands on any significant amount of nuclear explosive material, whether highly enriched uranium fuel or plutonium.

In general, the Soviets were following—and still follow—a very stern policy against proliferation. They do not like to sell large reactors in the Third World. They insist that all fuel remain under the control of Soviet technicians. And they demand that used fuel be sent back to the Soviet Union under Soviet guard.

This stops the spread of nuclear weapons, and also keeps Soviet satellites and other client states from becoming too independent.

In addition, the Soviet Union insists that nuclear clients join in the Nonproliferation Treaty, which the Iraqis signed in 1968 and ratified in 1972, one of the very first nations to do so.

In signing the treaty, and especially in agreeing to Article II, the Iraqis explicitly pledged themselves "not to manufacture or otherwise acquire nuclear weapons or other nuclear explosive devices; and not to seek or receive any assistance in the manufacture of nuclear weapons or other explosive devices." The Iraqis also agreed in the treaty, and in subsequent agreements, to open Tuwaitah to regular inspections and other safeguards by the International Atomic Energy Agency.

The Iraqis said that they would not do what they could not do anyway at the time, and amiably consented to international controls. But in the meantime the Baath had taken power, the new oil revenues were beginning to pour in, and the Iraqis had a change of heart. Like the Pakistanis, they turned to the one country most likely to give them what they wanted.

Choosing a Reactor

In December 1974, Jacques Chirac traveled from Paris to Baghdad.

Newly named Prime Minister of France, M. Chirac was the leading political heir of Charles de Gaulle, and was intent on strengthening French ties to the Arab world. The French were still hurting from the OPEC price hikes and the 1973 Arab oil boycott, and they were madly scrambling to secure oil supplies and search out new markets for French weapons and other high-technology exports.

Chirac's host in Iraq was the Deputy Chairman of the Revolutionary Command Council, Saddam Hussein, and the two men got on exceptionally well. Chirac later spoke of Saddam with considerable affection, and called him "a personal friend." Saddam apparently felt the same, though he was quick to point out that, at least in Iraq, friendship paid off.

"Those who pretend that this trip of M. Chirac to Baghdad did not produce concrete results are ignorant, either of politics or of the relationship between M. Chirac and myself," he explained the following March, during a short stopover in Paris. "If all of his trips produced such results, M. Chirac would spend all of his time in foreign countries."

The "concrete results" were, in part, a string of contracts for French industry worth as much as 15 billion francs, according to M. Chirac. Even more "concrete," as it turned out, were the talks in Baghdad about French nuclear sales to Iraq.

In fact, the Iraqis had already begun shopping around, and had turned first to their friends in the Soviet Union, who had already provided the small research reactor and other facilities at Tuwaitah. The Soviets were also supplying Iraq with MIG's and other military equipment, as well as technical assistance to the nationalized oil industry, and in 1972 the two countries had signed a fifteen-year Treaty of Friendship and Cooperation. As a result, many observers in the West had already written Iraq off as the next worst thing to a Soviet satellite.

But the Soviets—"the number-one friend of Iraq," as Saddam Hussein

once called them—were unwilling to give the Iraqis the new nuclear
equipment that they wanted, consistent with their general antiproliferation
policy. Saddam Hussein then turned to the French, and to his new friend
Jacques Chirac. As the former head of the Council on Foreign Nuclear
Policy, M. André Jacomet, told us, "If Iraq came to France, it means that
they couldn't get what they wanted from the Russians."

But the French were not the only ones trying to sell what the Russians
would not. There was competition among the nuclear salesmen of a number
of different nations for the Iraqi business: among them, Germany, Italy, and
Canada. French nuclear officials knew that they would have to offer the
Iraqis the very best nuclear equipment that France could supply in order to
get the lucrative contracts in the offing.

"It was a time of great confusion," recalled Yves Girard, who accompanied Chirac on his trip to Baghdad. "Everything that there was to be sold
could be sold. And we wanted to do the selling. We were determined to keep
an inside track on the contracts."

Now a vice president at the state-owned Technicatome and at the time an
adviser on nuclear affairs to the French Department of Energy, Girard gave
us an inside view of the negotiations, in which he had played a leading role.
We interviewed him in the lounge of Paris's main Hilton Hotel, just around
the corner from the headquarters of the French Atomic Energy Commission.

"We had plenty of competition," he told us. "And not just in Iraq.
Everyone in that part of the world wanted to buy nuclear—the Iranians, even
the Saudis. And everyone wanted to sell."

As Girard described it, the smell of Iraqi money freshened the Baghdad
air, and the pursuit after it was hot and heavy. The nuclear merchants
wanted to get a piece of the Middle Eastern action, and it did not really
matter what were the ultimate intentions of the customer. That was a
question for the politicians, and the whole structure of international
safeguards and controls, but not for the salesmen. Even so, Girard conceded,
it was within the realm of salesmanship to point out the virtues of the
product under discussion, including its ability to produce plutonium. That
was just a normal part of selling.

He was especially critical, though, of the surprisingly competitive
Canadians for doing so; they made a number of trips to Baghdad, he related,
where they sat around their hotel puffing the virtues of the Candu natural
uranium reactor to their potential clients, hinting broadly at its excellence in
producing the deadly substance, and even more broadly at the possibilities of
keeping safeguards to a minimum. What bothered Girard most about them
was not that they had tried to sell the Candu that way. It was their later
hypocrisy in pointing to the French sale as a danger for nuclear proliferation,
when actually they had desperately wanted the sale for themselves, and had
indicated no concern whatsoever whether Iraq got the bomb or not.

Not to be outdone, the French started out by discussing the possibility of
selling the Iraqis a very distinctive piece of nuclear equipment indeed—a

500-megawatt natural uranium reactor, a gas-cooled, graphite-moderated type like the one the French military had specially developed to produce plutonium for their own independent nuclear arsenal, the *force de frappe*.

This was the reactor the Iraqis wanted, and it would have been ideal for making the bomb. Chirac, the Gaullist, agreed. But some French scientists and a few of the "good French" in the Quai d'Orsay had their qualms about the deal. A natural uranium reactor like the gas-graphite would give the Iraqis plutonium, and one that was 500 megawatts would give them an awful lot of it.

Later, French diplomats and officials would tell us time and again as proof of their concern about nuclear proliferation that the reason the French did not sell the gas-graphite reactor was because they thought it would give the Iraqis the bomb. Several of them, including the official spokesmen of both the Foreign Office and the Atomic Energy Commission, even went so far as to suggest that Chirac had agreed to the sale so readily out of technical ignorance. We discovered, however, during interviews with some of the people who had actually been involved in making the decisions about the sale, that the question of nuclear proliferation really was not that important. The French concerns were far more prosaic, and reflected the kind of practical economic considerations that so often lie behind great political decisions.

The first big problem was the actual difficulty of building the reactor. The special team that had built the gas-graphite reactor for the French military had long since been disbanded, and Framatome, the big reactor company, was now busy constructing pressurized light-water power reactors under license from the American giant, Westinghouse. An Iraqi order for a single gas-graphite reactor would require Framatome to reassemble a new production team, and would disrupt the ongoing work. From Framatome's point of view, it was hardly worth the effort, no matter how high the price tag.

But Framatome was not the only one with its own reason to oppose selling Iraq a gas-graphite reactor. The state-owned Électricité de France also opposed the sale. EDF had just emerged out of a long, drawn-out fight with the Atomic Energy Commission over selecting a single kind of power reactor that could be built both for use at home and for export abroad. In this fight, EDF had opposed the gas-graphite reactor in favor of light-water reactors, and they saw the Atomic Energy Commission's eagerness to build one for Iraq as a way to bring it in through the back door.

"EDF thought that we were opening up the battle again, and they jumped on it," recalled Dr. Bertrand Goldschmidt, the doyen of the Atomic Energy Commission. "They claimed that the gas-graphite reactor was proliferating," he told us, "that it could give Iraq the plutonium for a bomb. But they only used that argument to fight the CEA. They succeeded in convincing the higher authorities to cancel the sale because of proliferation. But, the sale was really cancelled for internal French reasons that had nothing to do with nuclear proliferation."

In the end, the French President Valéry Giscard d'Estaing did intervene, deciding between the two warring factions in favor of EDF. He decided not to sell the Iraqis the reactor they wanted. And the French could claim they had acted out of concern for nuclear nonproliferation.

In truth, it was a difficult decision, and the French were fearful that their backtracking would offend the Iraqis. France depended heavily on Iraq for its oil supplies, and the Iraqis were linking a permanent and reliable source of oil to the nuclear contract. Dr. Francis Perrin has even suggested to us that a main reason that the French-Iraqi nuclear accords were never published was because this linkage was explicitly spelled out in the contract between the two countries.

There were other deals pending, too, in areas ranging from military hardware to petrochemical plants to port development, and the French desperately wanted to keep their commercial and political relations with Iraq intact. As a result, Yves Girard was packed off to Baghdad to tell the Iraqis the gas-graphite deal was off, and to try to convince them that some other French reactor could still serve the purposes they had in mind.

"We knew very well that some of the Iraqis were interested in the military aspect, the military potential of the reactor they wanted to get," Girard told us, in an admission startling for its candor. "But those were the Army people. You have to understand that in a country like Iraq, if you have a big budgetary expenditure, the Army has to approve it. That's the way it works."

The French suggested that the Iraqis consider the purchase of an advanced research reactor. The Iraqi scientists could sell it to their bosses in the government and in the Iraqi military and get budgetary approval for it, since it did have a plutonium-producing capacity, and they could say that it would give Iraq the "nuclear option."

To be fair, Girard also contended that the Iraqi scientists themselves did not state they wanted to make a bomb, at least in the short run and in regard to the specific sale. "They wanted a tool that could provide Iraqi scientists with the training to enter the nuclear world. They knew the stage scientifically and technically that Iraq was in," he claimed, "but the scientists also knew they had to please the military to get the money to buy the reactor."

The French, in spite of Saddam and the Iraqi military's desire for the bomb, remained eager to sell. Negotiations went on until September 1975, when Saddam Hussein made an official visit to Paris. The French received him with the honors generally accorded a chief of state, and entertained him royally. They also took him on a special visit to the nuclear research center at Cadarache, where he showed particular interest in experimental reactors.

Two months later, on November 18, representatives of the two nations met in Baghdad and signed an agreement for nuclear cooperation, and on August 26, 1976, Iraq signed a contract worth more than 1 billion francs with a consortium of French nuclear firms for the construction of two new research reactors. The first and most important of these was a seventy-thermal-megawatt experimental reactor, one that was in most ways similar to the Osiris reactor at the Center for Nuclear Research at Saclay, just outside of Paris. The second was a tiny 800-kilowatt "critical assembly" of the Isis type, which had the same basic core as the larger reactor and could be used in training Iraqi technicians.

The French had named their Osiris reactor after an ancient Egyptian god, the king and judge of the dead, and they initially dubbed the new one Os-Irak, or as some pundits put it, O-Chirac. Saddam Hussein and his comrades gave it the name Tammuz I, after the name of the month in the Arabic calendar in which their regime took power in the Baath Revolution of July 1968.

Isis, the smaller "critical assembly," was also classically named, after the goddess of fertility, who was also the sister and wife of Osiris. But, for the Iraqis, the name seemed to create certain problems. "The Isis could not exactly be called Isak, so we just called it Tammuz II," a French scientist explained wryly.

The Osirak, or Tammuz I, was essentially a large, open swimming pool with the reactor core at the center, and was designed primarily to do experiments and to test specialized metals and other structural materials under conditions of intense radiation. The materials to be tested would be placed in the pool around the reactor core, where they would be subjected to an intense and continuous bombardment of neutrons from the nuclear chain reaction. This kind of testing is generally done in designing and building nuclear power reactors in the more advanced industrial states, and when completed at the Iraqi nuclear center in Tuwaitah, the seventy-megawatt Osirak was to be one of the most powerful and sophisticated materials test reactors anywhere in the world.

"The large advantage of a swimming pool reactor is its flexibility," explained Yves Girard. "It can give a large choice of experimentation. The Iraqis wanted Baghdad to be the nuclear center of the Arab world. And they wanted any scientist from any of the Muslim countries to be happy and ready to come to Baghdad."

Even by nuclear standards, this was a fair-sized project, and the firms in the consortium that would build the two reactors were—and are—the stalwarts of the French nuclear industry.

Technicatome, which would provide the designers and supervising engineers, is state-owned, 90 percent by the Atomic Energy Commission and 10 percent by Électricité de France.

Constructions Navales et Industrielles de la Méditerranée, which would build the reactor cores, is an old firm of shipbuilders and ironworkers and has supplied the core elements for several French reactors, including the Osiris.

Comsip, which would provide the automatic controls, is a big name in electronic information systems.

La Société Bouygues, which would do the civil construction at Tuwaitah, is a specialist in major engineering and construction projects, with a great deal of experience in Iraq and other countries of the Middle East.

Saint-Gobain Techniques Nouvelles, the old standby, would provide waste-handling equipment and a laboratory "hot cell," which could be used for analysis, measurements, and a limited amount of reprocessing of the used fuel.

These were all highly respected, reputable firms. But they were not above a bit of fast dealing, especially on the question that most concerned the Iraqi military. Could the Osirak produce plutonium for nuclear weapons, like the gas-graphite reactor the French had refused to sell?

"Some of the Iraqi scientists misled the military into thinking so in order to get a nice research tool," Technicatome's Yves Girard admitted to us. "But that is the way it works in Iraq," he hastened to add. "The scientists really knew that this reactor was not the best way to make the bomb. But the Iraqis wanted the best, and the Osirak was excellent for their needs."

Did the French have any reservations, we questioned, about the way the Iraqi scientists had sold the reactor to Saddam Hussein and the generals on the basis of its military potential?

Not really, claimed Girard, because even though the Osirak has a plutonium-producing capacity "it doesn't have it in large amounts, not in its present configuration, in the configuration in which it was sold to Iraq."

Girard firmly believed that the Osirak was an excellent research tool and not the way to build a quick and dirty bomb. He also had doubts that the Iraqi scientists could deliver the goods, if they were asked, "not in the present stage of scientific development in Iraq."

But why did you decide to give the Iraqis highly enriched uranium fuel, we pressed, with all the risks that entailed?

"That's very simple," Girard answered. "The Osiris, or Osirak, is a high-powered research reactor. That's the kind of fuel it takes. There was no alternative when we sold it. And even today, that's the fuel that gives the best performance in this reactor."

With hindsight, though, Girard did have some second thoughts about the sale and his role in it: "Of course, we should have resisted. We could have said, 'This tool is too good, look for something more reasonable.' But everyone was ready to sell—the Italians, with their poor reactors, and the Germans, and the Canadians.

"You don't say to a client, 'My computer is too good, don't buy it.' That is not the way it works. It's easy to criticize the deal afterward. But it was not so easy at the time, not to make the deal."

Eager to sell, Girard and his colleagues convinced themselves that the Iraqis would not and did not want to make the bomb. What difference if the Iraqi generals believed that Osirak would give them their nuclear weapon? The Iraqi scientists knew better, or at least they said they did.

Not everyone shared this sanguine view, however, and especially not in Israel.

"The first glimpse of danger was the type of reactor they chose," Professor

Yuval Ne'eman recalled to us. He was the former scientific director of Israel's own nuclear program and also the former Deputy Director of Military Intelligence.

"It's a swimming pool reactor, a very good one for making the bomb," he told us during a lengthy interview at his comfortable one-story home in Tsahala, part of suburban Tel Aviv. It was a few days after the Israeli bombing raid, which the well-placed Ne'eman had been pushing for during the past year and a half.

"Why did the Iraqis need this particular reactor?" the Israeli-born scientist asked us rhetorically. "Why seventy megawatts? What kind of experiments were they going to do? Come on, anyone could see what they were doing. For the kind of experiments that the Iraqis would need to do, they could do with a one-megawatt reactor, and that would be enough for them for twenty years. I know that a lot of countries buy white elephants in nuclear research, and in other areas, just for the prestige," he conceded. "But just look at the pattern of what they were doing. Just look at the pattern."

The French were not overly concerned about the pattern, largely because of their considerable skepticism concerning Iraqi abilities. The most charitable view of Iraqi competence, as expressed by a Frenchman, came from Yves Girard, who told us, "They don't have any Nobel Prize-winners among them. But the top ones are competent; they're good physicists. What they lack is depth—the whole range of technicians that feed a nuclear industry. They needed years of training to attain that."

Other Frenchmen were even more skeptical of Iraqi scientific capability. An Israeli friend of ours working for the United Nations later chanced on one of the top French engineers on the Osirak project in a Cairo hotel, where the Frenchman was pursuing a new French nuclear deal with the Egyptians. It was after the Osirak bombing, and the Frenchman sharply criticized the Israelis both for the bombing and for an inflated view of Iraqi capability. "You Israelis don't know what was really going on out there," the Frenchman told the Israeli. "Building an atomic bomb? Those goddamn Iraqis can't even change a light bulb. That bombing was as needed as knocking off my three-year-old daughter."

The Israelis, at least some of them, differed. One Israeli scientist, who refused to be identified by name, told us that he believed the Iraqis far more able than the Europeans thought, and he offered a singular reason to back up his evaluation. "The Iraqis are good, even very good, as scientists. You can always judge a nation's ability by the Jews who have come from it. The Iraqi Jewish community [now almost entirely in Israel] has some of the best Jewish minds that I know. Their abilities were formed in Iraq, and the level there was high. I believe that the Iraqis are highly able, and we shouldn't take them lightly."

Yet for this scientist, and for Professor Ne'eman and other Israelis, the immediate concern was not the level of Iraqi science, but something far more specific. This was the nuclear fuel that the French had agreed to supply, the 93 percent, highly enriched uranium, perfect for making nuclear weapons.

The Osirak and Isis were both designed to take a fuel load of uranium metal in alloy with aluminum, which would contain about thirteen kilograms of the highly enriched uranium. The Osirak would use about three loads of fuel a year, while the low-powered Isis could keep its load going almost indefinitely. The French had initially agreed to supply Iraq with six loads, or nearly eighty kilograms by the end of 1981, which would have given the Iraqis enough for anywhere from four to nine Hiroshima-type bombs, depending on how the bombs were put together.

True, the Iraqis had signed the Nuclear Nonproliferation Treaty, and at least in theory any diversion of the highly enriched uranium fuel would become obvious to the inspectors from the International Atomic Energy Agency. Yet, the possibility of diversion remained, and as time went on, the highly enriched uranium fuel would become the first focus of concern about the Iraqi nuclear project, and the French contribution to it.

To Italy for Reprocessing

The Iraqis had chosen well. They had gone to France for nuclear reactors, and even if the French had refused to sell the big gas-graphite natural uranium reactor, they had offered Iraq the Osirak and eighty kilograms of highly enriched, bomb-grade uranium fuel. Oil wins friends, and the Iraqis were not above using what they had as a lever to get what they wanted.

Saddam Hussein called this leverage "a strategic price." But Saddam was far too clever to lock himself into depending on a single source of supply, and soon the Iraqis were casting fond eyes on export-hungry Italy, which like France depended on Iraq for about 20 percent of its oil supplies.

At the time, in the mid-1970s, the Italians had a small but growing nuclear program. They had three nuclear power reactors on stream. There was a fourth on the way, and they were starting to experiment with fast breeder reactors and an advanced prototype of the Candu natural uranium reactor. They had also tried a hand with two small pilot reprocessing plants, and there were several Italian engineering firms able to compete for nuclear projects anywhere in the world.

On the economic side, the Italians were also hard hit by "the energy crisis," and were even hungrier than the French to export high technology, especially to the Arab oil producers on whom they depended for a large part of their oil supply. In their economic need, the Italians were in even less of a position than the French to turn down a deal that could possibly lead to a bomb for Iraq.

"We are trying to eliminate the deficit in our balance of payments," said the suave and urbane Umberto Colombo, the current head of the Comitato Nazionale per l'Energia Nucleare, or CNEN, the Italian nuclear agency, during an interview in his comfortable office in CNEN's Rome headquarters. "We are also trying to give our nuclear industry work, and it needs to work if we are to develop it for the future," he told us.

Unlike the French, the Italians had signed the Nuclear Nonproliferation Treaty, and they insisted from the start that their nuclear customers accept international safeguards, which the Iraqis, who had also signed the treaty, were willing to do.

As the Italians saw it, the Iraqis were starting small. They wanted Italy to sell them some basic laboratories and workshops for research and training in what nuclear people like to call the fuel cycle, which is everything from the mining of the uranium to the reprocessing of the irradiated fuel and permanent storage of the radioactive wastes.

The buying and selling began in April 1975 in Baghdad, when the Iraqis made their international nuclear debut by hosting a conference on "Peaceful Uses of Atomic Energy for Scientific and Economic Development." We learned that at the conference, the Iraqis spoke to officials from CNEN. The Iraqis had two rooms available, some 400 to 500 square meters, in a building where they already had various chemical labs, apparently the ones provided by the Soviet Union. They wanted to use the rooms to do research and experiments for training in the chemistry of fission products and in analytical methods with "hot," or radioactive, substances. Could the Italians submit a proposal for equipping the two rooms?

CNEN, the nuclear agency, was willing, and in August 1975 they turned to a well-known Italian engineering firm called SNIA Viscosa. SNIA had worked on the two Italian reprocessing plants, as well as on the Eurochemic reprocessing plant in Belgium. They had also built labs, or "hot cells," for working with radioactive materials, and could easily do the job.

A top SNIA official, who has asked that we not identify him by name, told us that the firm submitted its proposal at the end of 1975, offering to supply and install equipment for "a radiochemistry lab." This would include three small, interconnecting, lead-shielded hot cells ($2 \times 1.5 \times 1.4$ meters each), ten glove-boxes for remote manipulation of radioactive material, and some Pyrex Micromixer-settlers with Tygon or Teflon tubes.

The lab would permit easy and safe handling of highly radioactive substances. It could also be used for dissolving irradiated uranium oxide, such as in spent nuclear fuel, and extracting the plutonium. Or, in other words, reprocessing—one key to a bomb.

SNIA's price for all this was a modest $2,300,000. The Iraqis offered $1,670,000, and SNIA took it. For SNIA, this meant working near cost and just barely breaking even. But Italy's own nuclear program was going through one of its periodic crises, which left SNIA's nuclear personnel without work. So the SNIA management decided to take the Iraqi job "just to keep our people employed."

In the meantime, in January 1976, CNEN had sent one of their top men, Professor Enzio Clementel, to Baghdad for further discussions. This led to a ten-year agreement, in which CNEN promised to help the Iraqi Atomic Energy Commission in the peaceful applications of atomic energy. The agreement covered a wide variety of areas, including reactor physics and the nuclear fuel cycle.

Both the CNEN agreement and the SNIA contract were signed in April 1976, and SNIA completed its work on the radiochemistry lab two years later, though according to officials at CNEN, the hot cells were not fully working.

"The hot-cell lab has actually been there since 1978, and is not yet really operational," Dr. Achille Albonetti, CNEN's skeptical director of foreign relations, told us in September 1980. "Everytime the Iraqis touch something, they break it. We have to do maintenance from two thousand kilometers away. It's the desert, both literally and in terms of standards."

Even so, some time in 1976, when SNIA was just starting on the hot cells, the Iraqis asked them to submit a second proposal. This was to supply four more laboratories for work in other areas of the fuel cycle.

This was a much bigger job, and the negotiations dragged on. SNIA came in with a price just over $67 million. The Iraqis shopped around, and apparently got better prices from Poland and India. SNIA then dropped to $55 million, and finally signed the contract for just over $50 million. That was on February 10, 1978.

According to the SNIA official, the $50 million price tag was extremely low, and very close to the knuckles. But they took it. They still had to keep their people at work. The Iraqis had proved themselves shrewd bargainers.

"As with all Oriental people, they're good negotiators," said Dr. Albonetti, the foreign relations man at CNEN. "They pass from the utmost rigidity to a quick decision. They'll stick to their position, believing you can go farther in meeting their demands. Then you wait a month, two months. . . . And four months later, they'll come back and tell you, 'Yes, we agree.'"

On the Italian side, SNIA was now sharing the contract with one of the nuclear industry's most important firms and biggest exporters, Ansaldo Mecanico Nucleare. Ansaldo would handle the machinery, the circuits, and the materials-testing equipment. Other subcontractors would do much of the actual construction. And SNIA—now SNIA Techint—would act as the main engineer and contractor.

The four new labs were all "cold labs," without the shielding needed to work with irradiated plutonium or other highly radioactive substances. According to officials at SNIA and CNEN, the Iraqis were getting a quite complete set of facilities: a fuel fabrication lab, to fabricate natural or low enriched uranium into uranium oxide fuel pellets; a chemical engineering lab, to try out equipment for the nuclear fuel cycle on an industrial scale; a radioisotope lab, to make radio-isotopes for medical and industrial uses; and a materials-testing lab, to test structural materials for use in power reactors.

The four new labs were scheduled to be completed by the end of 1980 or the beginning of 1981, though this was delayed by the war between Iran and

Iraq. The fifth—the radiochemistry lab, with three hot cells—was also expected to be operational before the end of 1981.

In the meantime, the Italians agreed to train some one hundred Iraqi technicians and scientists, about twenty in each of the five types of laboratories being supplied. The Italians insist that the five labs are all part of a normal nuclear research and power program, and that they are geared to train Iraqi scientists and technicians for the future.

"The Iraqis want mastery of the fuel cycle," we were told by the CNEN chief, Dr. Colombo. "They are now starting to get lab experience in the fuel cycle. Then if they get a full power plant, which would take nine or ten years to function, they can be moving toward independence in the fuel cycle.

"The Iraqis are, in our opinion, looking forward, as they must, to a time when oil will be finished," he added. "They want to develop their independence. They don't want to depend on outside support for their fuel cycle."

Independence in the fuel cycle—a worthy goal, no doubt. But it was a goal that would inevitably bring with it the experience, the expertise, and the equipment to move perilously close to nuclear weapons. And the Italians knew it.

According to the SNIA official, the five labs working together would allow the Iraqis to go from natural uranium to fuel pellets, which the Iraqis could irradiate in a suitable reactor to produce plutonium and then reprocess in their "hot cells."

In this scheme, one of the most sensitive facilities would be the fuel-fabrication lab, which could make up the natural uranium pellets to irradiate in the reactor. The Italians saw this possibility at an early point, and insisted that the Iraqis agree to extra measures of physical protection to secure the lab against theft or the threat of terrorism. And they demanded that the Iraqis promise to keep the lab under continuing safeguards even if Iraq should decide to pull out of the Nuclear Nonproliferation Treaty.

At first, the Iraqis refused the new demands. They had signed the NPT. They had agreed to accept inspectors and safeguards from the International Atomic Energy Agency. And they did not see why they should be asked to do anything more. But the Italians persisted, and finally the Iraqis accepted the additional measures.

That covered the fuel-fabrication lab. But, there was a second, extremely sensitive facility—the original radiochemistry lab, or the "hot cells," where the Iraqis could reprocess the irradiated fuel pellets and extract the weapons-usable plutonium.

This is a subject of considerable controversy, and the people at SNIA and CNEN were suitably sensitive when we asked them about it.

According to an official statement from SNIA, the lab is simply for study and chemical analysis, and is just like those used in various countries at the very beginning of their work in nuclear energy.

CNEN officials similarly insist that the lab is very small, "in *piccolissima scala*," that it is only a university type of lab for the training of Iraqi scientists and technicians, and that it is "completely unsuitable for the production of significant quantities of plutonium."

How much, then, is "significant"? What quantities could the lab, with its three hot cells, actually produce?

To make a Nagasaki type of plutonium bomb, the Iraqis would need anywhere from five to eight kilograms of plutonium metal. That would be "significant quantities."

As for the quantities the three hot cells could produce, the Italians are adamant that the Iraqis could never produce anywhere near the amount needed for a bomb. "With difficulty, 300 to a maximum of 500 grams of plutonium per year," a top SNIA official told us. And that, he said, was based on the best estimates of technicians at the nuclear agency, CNEN.

Anything more would require additional equipment, such as specialized tanks and possibly a small chopping machine, none of which the Italians appeared to be supplying. But as we shall show in the case of Pakistan, the Iraqis would have little trouble buying what they needed, even in Italy itself. Or they could even adapt it from equipment already in use in their relatively advanced petroleum industry.

As the SNIA official told us, the Iraqis might adapt normal oilfield pipe choppers to chop up nuclear fuel, and they could use tanks and vessels from their oil refineries to make a nitric-acid dissolver for reprocessing the chopped-up fuel. The SNIA man admitted that he had seen this kind of equipment and expertise already in Iraq, though he is assured that the Iraqis have "no evil intentions."

Dr. Colombo, at CNEN, shared the same view. He said he had been together at an American university with the current vice chairman of the Iraqi Atomic Energy Commission, Dr. Abdul Rizam el-Hashimi. They were old chums.

"And," said the trusting Dr. Colombo, "there was no doubt the way Dr. Hashimi explained it to me that Iraq wanted peaceful nuclear energy."

Perhaps they do, we conceded. But even if the present labs fall short of producing those significant quantities of plutonium, the Italians admit that the labs will help the Iraqis learn how to do it for the future. Is this what the Italians want to be doing? we asked.

Not really, we were told. But all the facilities are under safeguards and cannot be used to make the bomb. We concluded that oil is persuasive, and the need for it leads to enormous competition, as well as some ready answers.

"Everything is dangerous for proliferation," explained Colombo, "even buying a book, if you have the intention to proliferate. Italy is not giving something that is not available elsewhere. Should we withdraw, a lot of people will take our place. We have stiff competition for this work, especially from France."

An aide to Colombo readily agreed. "The real problem in nuclear sales comes from the French, especially in the sales to Iraq," he told us.

The French firmly disagreed. "Italy is ready to sell anything," countered André Jacomet, the former Secretary of the Council on Foreign Nuclear Policy in France, in our interview with him in Paris. "We expressed our worries to the Italians about what they were selling to the Iraqis. But they are not concerned about nonproliferation. We French are far more concerned."

THREE

THE AGE OF OF PROLIF- ERATION

8

The Making of the Israeli Bomb

It has always been our intention to develop a nuclear potential.
We now have that potential.
—Ephraim Katzir,
President of Israel,
December 1974

We believe that Israel already has produced nuclear weapons.
—United States Central Intelligence Agency,
September 1974

A day may come when the Zionist enemy would even use the
atomic bomb against the Arab world and the Arab Nation.
Saddam Hussein,
President of Iraq,
October 1979

Saddam Hussein does not say much about his Iraqi bomb, at least not in public. But when he does give a hint of what he has in mind, he usually speaks of another bomb not so far away. "Our struggle against the Zionist enemy will be cruel, bitter and prolonged, and a day may come when the Zionist enemy would even use the atomic bomb against the Arab world and the Arab Nation," he warned on October 26, 1979, as quoted in Baghdad's *Al-Thawra* newspaper. "So we as Arabs should be resolute in every way, and . . . insist on the creation of all necessities required for victory over those who took our sacred land in beloved Palestine."

Yet for all Saddam Hussein's obvious enmity toward Israel, and all of Menachem Begin's fears about his making the bomb to obliterate Israel, the Jewish state was only one of the Iraqi's concerns in building nuclear weapons. Like Pakistan's Ali Bhutto, Saddam Hussein saw the spread of nuclear weapons as "inevitable," especially in the Middle East. And the impact of this regional nuclear proliferation—as the Iraqis advised the Arab League in a memo delivered in 1977—would reach beyond the Arab-Israeli conflict to the Persian Gulf, Africa, and the Indian Ocean.

In other words, nuclear weaponry could make Saddam Hussein's Iraq the major political force in the Persian Gulf region and its perimeters, with all its oil wells, shipping lanes, and growing Great Power rivalries. Just as the Saudis feared, Iraq's nuclear ambitions might have less to do with Israel and more to do with Iran and the Arab states themselves, at least in the short run.

Other Arab and Western observers shared this view of Iraqi intentions, as did many knowledgable Israelis. "Their first priority is to build a power base, including the nuclear installations, that will give them political dominance in the Persian Gulf and over Syria," an Israeli official told us several months before the Israeli raid into Iraq. "Once they have that, perhaps a decade from now, they would turn their attention to Israel."

But, whatever the priorities and the timing, the Iraqis have at least one eye on Israel—and on Israel's own rapidly developing nuclear arsenal. A spur to Iraq as well as a constraint, Israel's nuclear arsenal indisputably represents the first nuclear weapon in the Middle East, and will for some time yet be the only one.

The history of the Zionist bomb has never been properly written. There are only hints and leaks, many of them from the American Central Intelligence Agency, as well as from the Israelis themselves. If there is one thing the Israelis have down pat, it is the way they keep everyone guessing, especially the Arabs and the Americans. It is a form of psychological warfare that can be summed up in the phrase: On the one hand, deny; on the other, imply.

To be a bit more formalistic about it, Israeli nuclear policy, or the public-policy aspect of it, is marked by "deliberate ambiguity," as a U.S. State Department official put it to us. "The Israelis want the Arabs to believe they have the bomb, while at the same time they want to assure their friends in the international community that they don't. The perception of their bomb, in their view, keeps the Arabs from attacking full-scale," the State Department official elaborated. "Clearly, the Israelis think the maintenance of ambiguity contributes to the deterrent effect, while it enables them to keep their hands clean internationally, and they can maintain a public stance against nuclear proliferation for anybody."

Officially, the Israelis do not have the bomb per se. In their calculated word play, they have never admitted its existence. They continued to repeat their by-now ritual formula: "Israel will not be the first to introduce nuclear weapons into the Middle East."

But Israeli officials have, on occasion, hinted rather broadly that they do have a bomb in the basement. The first and most telling of these hints came at a reception for visiting science writers in Jerusalem in December 1974. The host—the Israeli President Ephraim Katzir, a noted biophysicist and former chief scientist for the Ministry of Defense.

"It has always been our intention to develop a nuclear potential," admitted Katzir. "We now have that potential."

Katzir made the statement only in response to repeated questions from the science writers. Pushed farther, he added that the capability could be turned into fact "in a short time—even a few days. If we should have need of such arms, we would have them."

The grandfatherly Katzir was sorry the moment he said it. For all the prestige of his position, it was the first and only time he made international headlines during his five years as President.

The Israelis may have had the need—and the arms—only the year before, in the early days of the October War of 1973. According to *Time* magazine (April 12, 1976), Prime Minister Golda Meir had given the order to make the bombs ready in the early hours of October 9.

For the Israelis, the war was going badly. The Egyptian attack had taken the Israelis by surprise. Their own counterattack in Sinai was failing; the Syrian tanks were threatening to pour across the Golan Heights. Over the next seventy-eight hours, says *Time*, the Israelis assembled thirteen 20-kiloton atomic bombs at a secret underground tunnel and rushed them off to specially equipped Phantom and Kfir jets, which were standing ready to use them. But before the Israelis could unleash the weapons, the battle on both fronts turned in their favor. According to *Time*, "The thirteen bombs were sent to desert arsenals, where they remain today, still ready for use." The Israelis officially denied the story and there is no independent evidence the event occurred. Yet the story came from official sources, possibly close to the then Defense Minister Moshe Dayan, and we can state flatly that Israelis purposely leaked the story, true or not, probably as part of their ongoing psychological warfare.

The background facts fit. As early as 1968, the American CIA had drawn up a National Intelligence Estimate reporting that Israel already had atomic weapons.

The CIA report was top secret, and remained under wraps for years. But Carl Duckett, the CIA's Deputy Director for Science and Technology from 1967 to 1977, revealed the information in a secret briefing to the Nuclear Regulatory Commission in February 1976, and the Commission mistakenly included part of Duckett's briefing in an unclassified 550-page report two years later.

Duckett stated in his briefing that the CIA had varied evidence for its 1968 report. In part, Israel's A-4 jets were going through a special type of bombing practice, "which would not have made sense unless it was to deliver a nuclear bomb."

The CIA had also followed up a disturbing rumor. American scientists returning from Israel were worried by signs that the Israelis appeared to be working with bomb-grade highly enriched uranium. The scientists informed the CIA, and the CIA put to work some highly sophisticated equipment to monitor air and soil samples from around Israel's nuclear facility at Dimona. The "sniffers" and other instruments proved what the CIA most feared: Israel had highly enriched uranium, and the CIA concluded that Israel had enough of it to make several bombs.

Duckett told the nuclear regulators that he had taken the report to CIA Director Richard Helms, who took it directly to President Lyndon Johnson. According to Duckett, the President told the CIA chief to sit on it.

"Don't tell anyone else," Duckett quoted Johnson as saying. "Not even Dean Rusk and Robert McNamara." Dean Rusk was Mr. Johnson's Secretary of State, and Robert McNamara his Secretary of Defense.

Mr. Helms, the former CIA chief, would neither confirm nor deny Duckett's account of these events. "I don't say they didn't happen," he told *The New York Times*. "I just have no recollection of them." But in July 1970, Helms also told a closed-door hearing of the Senate Foreign Relations Committee that the CIA believed that Israel already had the capacity to build nuclear weapons.

The CIA continued to monitor Israel's nuclear capability, and in September 1974 they updated their assessment in a second report. This was a wide-ranging study, and the summary was called "Prospects for Further Proliferation of Nuclear Weapons." The summary covered the world, not just Israel, and it set the tone for official American thinking about proliferation for the next several years.

"We believe that Israel already has produced nuclear weapons," said the CIA. "Our judgment is based on Israeli acquisition of uranium, partly by clandestine means; the ambiguous nature of Israeli efforts in the field of uranium enrichment; and Israel's large investment in a costly missile system designed to accommodate nuclear warheads."

The CIA did not expect the Israelis to test their bomb or to threaten to use it "short of a grave threat to the nation's existence." Instead, the Agency expected them to concentrate on improving the design of their weapons, on perfecting weapons for aircraft delivery, and on building missiles of longer range and greater accuracy.

As with the 1968 report, the 1974 study was highly classified. But once again there was a foul-up, this time by the CIA itself, and in 1978, the Agency released the summary under the Freedom of Information Act to an ecology group, the National Resources Defense Council. As one CIA source told colleagues working on an ABC *Closeup* film about the nuclear arms race in the Middle East, the spooks had intended to release only two paragraphs and keep the rest secret. But after the two paragraphs had been marked, a CIA employee released the entire document with only the two safe paragraphs deleted.

In the meantime, the Israelis appear to have shifted tracks, at least according to CIA estimates. Whereas the first Israeli bombs were believed to come from highly enriched uranium, by 1976 the CIA analysts concluded that the Israelis were using plutonium from the research reactor supplied by the French at Dimona.

The source for this is again Carl Duckett's briefing to the Nuclear Regulatory Commission in February 1976. According to Duckett, the CIA was no longer worried about the possible theft of highly enriched uranium because the Israelis were already producing plutonium weapons from their reactor.

One final word from the CIA also came from Duckett, and this time the fault for leaking it was entirely his own. It happened in early 1976, when the CIA held a lavish cocktail party and buffet supper for 150 members of the high-powered American Institute of Aeronautics and Astronautics. This was part of the CIA's new "public relations" campaign, and as part of the entertainment, Deputy Director Duckett ran an "unclassified" state-of-the-world intelligence briefing. In the question-and-answer session that followed, someone asked the obvious: Were the rumors that Israel had the bomb true?

Duckett answered straight out. Israel, he said, "has ten to twenty nuclear weapons ready and available for use."

Duckett said this inside the CIA headquarters, in what he thought was an off-the-record chat. Four days later, the world saw what he had said printed in *The Washington Post*. The reaction was explosive. Senator Frank Church, at the time Chairman of the Select Committee on Intelligence, called it "the biggest goof in the history of leaks." Former CIA chief George Bush, now Vice President, was horrified. Shortly afterward, Duckett retired from the CIA—for reasons of health, he said. But no one in the Agency denied Duckett's numbers.

Several bombs in 1968. Ten to twenty in 1976. That is the story as it came from the CIA. But how good a story is it?

Some observers have their doubts. We were constantly surprised in our own investigation by the lack of specific information that has emerged concerning the Israeli bomb, and by the extent that American authorities seemed to rely on deduction rather than hard facts to make their assessments. The CIA has worked closely with the Israelis (and still does), swapped information with them, and even had a special Israeli Affairs Section under the longtime counterintelligence chief, James Jesus Angleton. But the sharing stopped at the nuclear door. This is where the American spooks had to snoop on their own.

As one highly placed American official told us, "The evidence on Israel comes from a variety of data, and a lot of it is not nuclear at all. You have to look at their scientific level, their motivation, their negotiating pattern, their delivery systems, their reactor, their situation, and then you come up with the conclusions."

Certain influential Americans think the Israelis are bluffing. "There's too much smoke for there to be a real fire," one of the CIA's former Deputy Directors, Dr. Ray Cline, warned in an interview we had with him back in 1979. "I'd believe it more if there weren't so much noise about it, or so many leaks. And none of them with any hard information."

Others think the Israelis are even more advanced than anyone has given them credit for. A former staffer for a congressional subcommittee, who has had access to certain classified files, told us flatly, "Israel is the third most advanced nuclear weapons country in the world, about equal with the French and well behind the United States and the Soviets."

He could not—or would not—back up his belief with specifics. But he did say that his analysis was based not just on American intelligence information (which he did not think comprehensive), but on confidential discussions with French and Israeli officials. It turned out that we had spoken with some of the same people, at least in France.

Most published estimates of Israel's nuclear weaponry are based on Duckett's 1976 statement that Israel has between ten and twenty warheads, a figure that the Israelis point out is based on deduction and not hard proof. An Israeli scientist of impeccable professional credentials whom we interviewed claimed that the estimates published by the CIA are "ridiculous," and not based on actual knowledge of Israel's nuclear program. "Anyone can do the arithmetic," he stated, and proceeded to do it himself on a paper napkin, adding up the optimal running time of the Dimona reactor and how much plutonium can theoretically be produced over the period.

After arriving at the theoretical conclusion that Israel had more than twenty bombs, he tore up the napkin and declared this was "nonsense." Israel had not, he said, made the bomb from "any plutonium that theoretically could be produced. There is no Israeli bomb."

Yet on balance, the CIA leaks are persuasive. And even if some of the specifics turn out to be patchy, it is hard to reject the bottom line, that the Israelis do have at least a small arsenal of nuclear weapons.

The Americans and the CIA may not be the best source, however, on the actual capacity of the Israeli nuclear program. The French, who sold them their nuclear reactor at Dimona and provided nuclear aid, know far more, at least about the early stages of Israel's atomic progress.

"We are sure the Israelis have nuclear weapons," the former chief of the French Atomic Energy Commission, Dr. Francis Perrin, told us in our wide-ranging interview with him at his Paris office in October 1980. "They have sufficient facilities to produce one or two bombs a year."

The French—and not just Dr. Perrin—believe the Israelis have the bomb. The Americans believe it. Most knowledgeable Israelis believe it, even though Israeli officials will not confirm it. Every Arab we spoke with believed it (it was evident that the Israeli "leakers" had done their job well). And for all their denials, the Israelis have moved men and mountains to get the nuclear materials needed for atomic bombs. Moreover, they have done it with a panache and derring-do that stands as a model for their Islamic imitators.

The French Agreement

If ever there were a nation that needed the bomb to ensure its very survival, or could argue that it did, that nation is Israel. Surrounded by Arab countries with vast territories and far larger populations, the Israelis could never hope to continue matching the Arabs man for man, mile for mile, dollar for dollar. Their only hope, as they saw it, was to rely on quality: on their morale, on their highly skilled manpower, and on the most highly advanced weapons. From an early date, that included what the Israelis like to call "the nuclear option."

"Albert Einstein's revolutionary discovery of the identity of matter and energy, and the research that laid bare the complex structure of the atom, have placed untold treasures of energy at the disposal of the human race," wrote the Israeli Prime Minister, David Ben Gurion.

"This wonderful achievement will not remain the heritage of the Great Powers alone, and the increased cooperation between scientists all over the world in atomic research is a good omen for our generation." Significantly, he added, "It is not impossible for scientists in Israel to do for their own people what Einstein, Oppenheimer, and Teller—all three Jews—have done for the United States." *

J. Robert Oppenheimer was, of course, the father of the first atom bombs, while Edward Teller developed the thermonuclear, or hydrogen bomb.

The Israelis had apparently considered the nuclear option from as early as 1952, when they set up their Atomic Energy Commission under the umbrella of the Prime Minister's Office. They also signed an agreement with the United States in 1955, which provided for a five-thermal-megawatt "swimming pool" research reactor to be located south of Tel Aviv, at Nahal Soreq. The Americans agreed to supply the reactor with small quantities of highly enriched uranium fuel, which is weapons grade. In return, the Israelis were forced to accept regular outside inspections, and later IAEA "safe-guards," at the Nahal Soreq facility.

But as with Ali Bhutto and Saddam Hussein in later years, Ben Gurion saw his best chance with France, which was beginning to treat Israel as a friend and ally. At the time, in the mid-fifties, the French still saw Israel as helpful in their war against Algerian independence. French Socialists under Guy Mollet felt a special bond with their comrades in Ben Gurion's Mapai Party. And throughout France at the time, there was a general feeling of sympathy for the Jewish state, which had come into being largely as a result of the Nazi Holocaust in Europe.

The payoff came in 1956, when France provided the Israelis with arms and airplanes as part of the buildup to the invasion of Suez. At the same time, and in secret, the Guy Mollet Government made the decision to sign a nuclear contract and thus help Israel on the road to the bomb. According to Bertrand Goldschmidt, of the French Atomic Energy Commission, the government's decision came in September, which was even before the go-ahead for their own *force de frappe*. The dates are not coincidental, as the Israeli and French nuclear programs were interwoven at the start.

---

* David Ben Gurion, *Israel: Years of Challenge* (New York: Holt, Rinehart & Winston, 1963).

The 1956 French governmental decision gave French industry the green light to build the Israelis a twenty-four-thermal-megawatt natural uranium reactor. Paris and Jerusalem signed the agreement in October 1957. Construction began shortly afterward in the Negev desert, a few kilometers from where the Israelis were building a new town called Dimona, from the Hebrew word for imagination. The town, and the reactor, were products of the imagination of one man, Ben Gurion.

The Israelis and the French kept the agreement and the construction of the reactor at Dimona completely secret. When asked what was being built there, in the heart of his beloved Negev, Ben Gurion replied, "a textile factory."

Only later would his little lie confirm the obvious—that this was to be primarily a military reactor, one dedicated to the production of weapons-grade plutonium. It was to be Israel's ace in the hole—in Ben Gurion's eyes, the guarantee of the Jewish state's survival.

Curiously, neither the French nor the Israelis made even the pretense of agreeing to any outside inspection or control of the Dimona facilities. The Israelis, and possibly the French as well, had something they wanted to hide, but the original agreement also reflected French interests: The French had resisted outside controls in their own drive for nuclear independence, and did not want to be seen imposing on Israel the very "safeguards" that they themselves were resisting under pressure from the United States and Great Britain.

"We were still in the camp of the thieves," smiled Bertrand Goldschmidt during our visit with him at the Paris offices of the French Atomic Energy Commission. "Actually we were rather pleased when the Israelis insisted on secrecy, because the firms participating could have been subject to the Arab blacklist. This enabled our firms to do the work freely."

As a result of Dimona, the Israelis and the French cooperated on a wide range of nuclear activities. Professor Israel Dostrowsky of the prestigious Weizmann Institute had earlier perfected a new way to produce heavy water, so necessary for most natural uranium reactors, and Israel made the process available to France on a commercial basis. Israeli scientists had also found a new way to extract uranium from the phosphate deposits at the Dead Sea, and this, too, the Israelis patented and sold to the French.

The Israeli aid to the French also extended into the military sphere, and *the Israeli involvement in the creation of the French bomb*, details of which are revealed here for the first time, was a decisive one. Sources in France and the United States, all of whom wanted to remain nameless in this book, told us that the French military men had used Israeli help to get their program started. Partly, the agreement with the Israelis helped the French military men to push their own military program within the French political establishment. Partly, it gave the French access to some of the best military and scientific brains available to the Western world.

The key to the aid was this: Israeli scientists were already making startling advances in weaponry, especially in guidance-control mechanisms perfected

in the early sixties in the Israeli-invented Shavit and Jericho missile systems.
Now some Israeli scientists turned their attention to the design of the French
nuclear weapon, and played a leading role in its planning and development.
(This aid, revealed to us by an American source, has been denied, we should
add, both in Jerusalem and Paris. But we believe it to be true.) That would
make the *force de frappe* a very kosher weapon, and the French were
obligated to offer the Israelis a substantial quid pro quo.

What kind of help did the Israelis get in return? In the first place, they
received their prized reactor at Dimona. They were also given access to
much of the French nuclear program, and especially to vital data in the
French military nuclear program that would be indispensable to the Israelis
in creating their own bomb. And they also received some other key
technology that has been largely overlooked, including at least a starting
hand in building a small facility to reprocess plutonium from the spent
reactor fuel.

The French role in the plutonium facility was confirmed to us by Dr.
Francis Perrin, when we interviewed him for the first time in September
1980. "France helped Israel very much," he told us. "The construction of
the reactor and other facilities was done with a large contribution from the
French Government. We also participated in the building of a plutonium
extraction plant."

The French Government did not participate in the agreement to build the
plutonium factory, Perrin emphasized, but it did permit French industry to
help the Israelis in this endeavor. The name of the company so authorized,
according to a source in the International Atomic Energy Agency familiar
with the project, was the French pioneer SGN, our old friend that later
would be so decisive in helping the Pakistanis and others to attain
reprocessing capability.

The cooperation continued into the new government of Charles de
Gaulle, and Ben Gurion was clearly pleased. "My view," he wrote, "was that
this was our first opportunity to find an ally." *

Moshe Dayan saw it a bit differently. "When de Gaulle routinely declared
that Israel was an ally, Ben Gurion clung to these words as if de Gaulle and
he himself had actually signed some sort of an agreement," Dayan wrote.

The crunch came in 1960, just after the first French nuclear test, and that
was not happenstance. By then, France had gotten whatever it wanted from
the Israeli scientists. Or perhaps the French had simply gotten religion now
that they had joined the nuclear congregation.

De Gaulle later described the change in French policy in his memoirs: "I
put an end to the improper military collaboration established between Tel
Aviv and Paris after the Suez Expedition, which permanently placed Israelis
at all levels of the French services." * *

What did de Gaulle mean by "improper military collaboration"? Informa-

---

* Ben Gurion, *op. cit.*
* *Charles de Gaulle, *Memoirs of Hope: Renewal and Endeavor* (New York: Simon &
Schuster, 1971).

tion sharing on an intelligence level? Arms deliveries? Joint training? We believe differently. France's nuclear test in 1960 established two countries, not one, as nuclear powers. *Part of that quid pro quo between France and Israel was that in return for their part in designing that French bomb, the Israelis also got unrestricted access to the French nuclear test explosion data.*

This would help explain one of the greater mysteries that has puzzled nuclear investigators for the last two decades—how Israel got the bomb, but decided never to publicly test it. The Israelis did not have to. They had the French test results to work from. As far as basic knowledge goes, they did not really need that much more.

"There were a lot of stories about the Israelis sending observers to the first French nuclear explosion," one source, who must remain nameless, told us. "These stories are irrelevant. The Israelis didn't have to be there, there was no scientific reason for it. The Israelis got the test results data from the French, and that was one basis of the Israeli nuclear program."

But France, or at least *le grand général*, Charles de Gaulle, had second thoughts about this "improper military collaboration" once France had entered the nuclear club. Shortly after the French test explosion in February 1960, Foreign Minister Couve de Murville signaled the change in policy by calling the Israeli Ambassador into his office at the Quai d'Orsay. He informed the Israeli that the French had decided to limit their nuclear cooperation with Israel. They would no longer be willing to supply the natural uranium fuel for the reactor they were helping the Israelis to build at Dimona. They also wanted the Israelis to give up the secrecy and make the construction public. And, most disturbing to the Israelis, they wanted the entire facility opened to foreign—possibly international—inspection. The Israelis may have received the data and the knowledge, but they were not about to get the goods as well.

Ben Gurion was deeply worried. He requested a special meeting with the French President, and on June 14, 1960, the two men met for the first time in the Élysée Palace. The giant de Gaulle towered over the tiny Ben Gurion. But the two men got on famously. *

For the French leader, Ben Gurion was "one of the greatest statesmen of our time," and, with Germany's Konrad Adenauer, one of "the two greatest leaders in the West."

"From the very first moment, I felt sympathetic admiration for this courageous fighter and champion," de Gaulle later wrote. "His personality symbolized Israel, which he has ruled since the day he presided over her creation and struggle."

Ben Gurion was equally *galant*. "I had a strange image of de Gaulle," he later remarked. "I had heard that he is an old, hard, closed man. And I found him a lively, humane man with a sense of humor, very alert, and much kindness."

---

* Michael Bar-Zohar describes the meeting in his *Ben Gurion* (London: Weidenfeld and Nicolson, 1978), pp. 267–270.

In the meeting, the French President grandly, though rather vaguely, promised continuing military aid. But he somewhat baldly dismissed any Arab military threat, much to Ben Gurion's distress.

"Do you really fear that an Arab coalition might endanger you?" he asked. "I do not presume that they can overcome you."

"I think you exaggerate with regard to the danger facing you," he added in a second meeting. "Under no circumstances will we sanction your annihilation."

This kind of vague reassurance from de Gaulle was not especially comforting to the practical Israeli Prime Minister, and on the nuclear side the conflict remained more basic. Ben Gurion wanted the nuclear option; de Gaulle wanted distance. In the end, they found a compromise, which was worked out in the following months by Ben Gurion's protegé and now the leader of the Israeli Labor Party, Shimon Peres.

On the Israeli side, Ben Gurion solemnly assured de Gaulle that the Israelis had no intention of manufacturing nuclear weapons. He also agreed to make a public statement about the construction of the reactor at Dimona, and agreed to official French withdrawal from the plant. In return, the French agreed not to press for international inspections and to permit French firms to continue to supply equipment that had already been ordered.

De Gaulle added this observation about his decision to limit nuclear aid to Israel: "So ended, in particular, the cooperation offered by us for the beginning, near Beersheba, of a plant for the transformation of uranium into plutonium, from which one fine day there could emerge some atomic bombs." *

In fact, the break was not quite so abrupt, nor was the plutonium plant the whole story. According to officials with whom we spoke in both countries, French nuclear engineers were still working in Israel as late as 1966. This certainly helped the Israelis complete the Dimona reactor, which went into operation in December 1963. And it was likely that French blueprints and specifications, if not continuing consultation, helped the Israelis go ahead with their reprocessing plant.

This remains a matter of mystery, as there was no direct evidence of what became of the original plant described by Dr. Perrin. French nuclear officials did not want to talk to us about it, probably for fear of antagonizing their present Islamic clients. The Israelis denied to us that they had a reprocessing plant, French or otherwise. The few official visitors to Dimona came away convinced that the Israelis were not reprocessing their spent reactor fuel at the installation. And in all the CIA material that came out, there was no clear reference to just how or where the Israelis were extracting the plutonium.

The only clear statement came from *Time*, in the magazine's April 1976 article about Israel assembling the thirteen bombs in 1973. And that made no reference at all to the initial French help.

---

* De Gaulle, *op cit.*

The article claimed that in the years before the Six Day War of 1967, the Israeli leadership had split on whether or not to build a reprocessing plant. Ben Gurion and Shimon Peres wanted it. Levi Eshkol and Golda Meir and Yigal Allon did not. But, said *Time*, the actual decision was taken in the wake of the 1967 War by the then defense minister Moshe Dayan, who secretly and on his own ordered construction started.

Dayan's *fait accompli* was supposed to have overridden a formal government veto of the project, and according to *Time*, the plant was completed in 1969.

Time's story would certainly fit with the CIA's estimate that the Israelis had plutonium bombs by 1976, if not sooner. But it seemed strange that Dayan could have, or would have, taken such a strategic decision on his own. And it seemed even stranger that the Israelis would have waited until after the 1967 War when they had given the French plant the go-ahead in 1957, ten years before.

From the start, the main purpose of the French reactor at Dimona was to produce weapons-grade plutonium. That is why the French offered a reprocessing plant to extract the plutonium, and when they withdrew, the most logical thing for the Israelis would have been to complete it on their own. Why, then, a pause until 1967?

Again, this was not a subject on which the Israelis encouraged investigation. But if there was a pause, one possible reason might have been American pressure. In late 1960, in the closing days of the Eisenhower Administration, the CIA had gotten wind of the "textile factory" at Dimona. Aerial photographs from a U-2 spy plane confirmed suspicions that the construction was for a nuclear reactor. And on December 9, the U.S. Secretary of State summoned the Israeli Ambassador in Washington to express America's grave concern.

There was also a calculated string of "leaks" from the American Government, and the world's press headlined the birth of the Israeli bomb— within as little as five years, reported *The Washington Post*.

Ben Gurion had still not made the public statement he had promised the French, and the new uproar forced the Israelis to join with the French in a joint communiqué. Yes, they were building a reactor. No, it was for entirely peaceful purposes. In the meantime, the Egyptian President Colonel Nasser declared that he would mobilize four million soldiers to invade Israel and tear down the nuclear installation. With the crisis growing, Prime Minister Ben Gurion was forced to go before the Israeli Knesset, or Parliament, where he insisted that the reactor would be used entirely for scientific, medical, and industrial purposes, as well as to train Israeli scientists and technicians for the future construction of nuclear power stations.

In retrospect, this was the first official Israeli denial of nuclear weapons, or of any intention to have them. Not surprisingly, neither their friends nor their enemies believed what they said.

The Americans were especially skeptical. The new American President,

John F. Kennedy, pushed particularly hard to force Israel to permit American scientists to visit Dimona to check that there was no weapons research. The scientists found nothing, probably because the reactor did not go into operation until the end of 1963.

President Lyndon Johnson similarly insisted on regular visits to Dimona by American scientists, and also offered to give Israel a nuclear-powered desalinization plant if they would completely dismantle any nuclear weapons program. But he too lacked any hard evidence of what the Israelis were really doing, and the offer came to nothing.

Quite possibly, this pressure strengthened the hands of those in the Israeli Cabinet who did not want to go ahead with the reprocessing plant, at least until after the 1967 War. That is if there was a pause, as *Time* suggested. But it seems more likely that the Israelis simply completed the plant the French had started, and as quickly as they could.

In any case, the Israelis might have gotten their first plutonium not from their own reprocessing plant, but from someone else's. *The shipping of reprocessed plutonium back to Israel was another part of the French quid pro quo for Israeli help in making the French bomb.*

The initial clue came from Ben Gurion himself. Back in January 1961, when the Americans first started to bring pressure, they had demanded answers to five questions. The first, and most important, was the most obvious: What was Israel planning to do with the plutonium generated by the Dimona reactor?

According to his biographer, Michael Bar-Zohar, the Prime Minister's reply was slightly enigmatic. "As far as we know," he said, "those who sell uranium do so on condition that the plutonium reverts to them."

The French had agreed to provide natural uranium fuel for Dimona, true, and Ben Gurion was right in suggesting that the spent fuel, with its plutonium, was to be returned to France. But the wily Ben Gurion failed to mention the key point—that the contract called for France to reprocess the fuel and send the separated plutonium back to Israel, where the only real use would have been to make nuclear weapons.

Two extremely well-placed sources confirmed this to us in exclusive interviews in Paris and Jerusalem. One was a top official in the French nuclear program in the 1950s who dealt directly with the Israelis. The other was a senior Israeli official who had cause to know.

This was a startling admission on the part of both the French and Israeli officials. At the time, however, French officials saw little harm in spreading plutonium, and we learned that such a provision would have been run of the mill for a nuclear contract signed in the 1950s. As far as we know, no other journalists have ever bothered to ask the obvious question of what happened to the spent fuel from Dimona and whether or not it stayed in Israel. It is amazing that this twenty-year-old story has never before seen the light of day.

The answers we got to the question indicate that the actual disposition of the plutonium is a matter of some debate, as our Israeli and French sources agree on the nature of the contract but do not at all agree on what happened in the implementation.

According to the French source, the Israelis sent forty tons of the irradiated fuel back to France. But the French returned only about half of the reprocessed plutonium, or enough for some fifteen to twenty bombs of the size that destroyed Nagasaki.

"We made the shipment on the material coming from the first twenty tons," he told us, drawing on his own firsthand knowledge. "But we decided against sending back the plutonium from the second twenty tons. The Israelis rightly protested," he added. "They said we were breaking a commercial agreement. And we were."

According to the Israeli source, the French never sent back any of the plutonium at all. They were supposed to. But they did not. "On the *Sefer Torah*, the Holy Bible, the French story is bullshit," the Israeli told us emphatically. "What happened was that when the French broke the agreement, we kept the fifteen or so tons of uranium that was still in Israel. By this time it was around the Six Day War, and the French were cutting off everything."

The Israeli also suggested that the Frenchman had planted a half-truth on us, as part of a French counterpropaganda war against the Israeli press and diplomatic campaign on the Iraqi bomb. This, we granted, was not beyond the realm of possibility. Which source, then, should we believe?

The best evidence comes from the *défense confidentiel* minutes of the January 1973 meeting of France's interministerial Atomic Energy Committee, handed over to us by a French scientist who believed that his country was a recurring nuclear proliferator, and that what had been started with Israel was being continued even more dangerously with Iraq and Pakistan. As summarized in the document, André Giraud, then the nuclear chief and later the French Minister of Industry, was talking about proliferation. He noted matter-of-factly that Israel already had "appreciable quantities of plutonium." Dr. Bertrand Goldschmidt, his colleague, added that this would give the Israelis "the means to fabricate several bombs."

How would they know? Either they *believed* that the French-assisted reprocessing plant had been completed in time to do the job. Or they *knew* that France had supplied the plutonium directly.

In either case, the French had given a substantial quo for the Israeli quid, and created a pattern for future Islamic purchases of French nuclear technology. The scientists and military men of many nations began to believe that anything goes in France, so long as you have the money to pay or anything else that is vital to the French, such as oil or knowledge. In return, you can get the atomic bomb.

Or, as summed up by an American source who supplied and confirmed some of the above information, "The French nuclear industry is like a French virgin who's been seduced. She's gone to bed with one and promised her heart to him. But she's found out she likes it and now she'll go to bed with them all."

Whether or not Israel actually assembled the bomb—and the Israelis continue to deny it—they had the major portion of their "nuclear option" by the mid-sixties, even before the Six Day War. They also did not waste time in preparing or buying systems to make the delivery of the bomb possible. Some of them came from abroad and some of them came from the Israeli arms industry, today the seventh largest in the world.

The Jericho and Shavit missile systems with their outstanding guidance-control mechanisms were homegrown Israeli products, first tested in the early sixties and capable of delivering nuclear weapons. Even at that time, the Israelis could use their French-supplied Mirage to deliver the bomb in a pinch, and they later built domestically the Kfir fighter bomber, based on the plans of the advanced Mirage V. The American A-4 Skyhawk fighters could also deliver the bomb, and the CIA had noted the Israelis using them in nuclear-type exercises in their 1968 report.

Later, the Phantom fighters, the F-15's, and the F-16's supplied by the United States also had bomb-delivery capability. In 1980 the Israelis announced the existence of the Lance missile, a system they had actually developed some fifteen years before.

The above potential delivery systems are only part of the story, since they reflect only what is known and published about certain areas of technology—such as missile systems—in which the Israelis are among the world's leaders. The Israelis like to announce "new" weaponry only a decade or more after it has actually been in use, and we can only speculate on what else they might have in their delivery arsenal.

On one point, however, we are certain: The Israelis do not stay content with fifteen-year-old weaponry or materials, either in the nuclear area or outside of it.

The Apollo Affair

When the CIA first reported that Israel had nuclear weapons in 1968, they apparently knew little or nothing of the French plutonium. What they did know was that Israel had the other bomb material, highly enriched uranium. Their "sniffers" and other fancy instruments had found unmistakable traces of it in waste taken from Dimona. The question was, where did the Israelis get it?

The Israelis themselves had already begun their own research in uranium enrichment. But they had no known facilities for enriching uranium to bomb grade. Only five countries in the world had the capacity at the time, the big five nuclear powers, the United States, the Soviet Union, Britain,

France, and China. And of the five, only the United States exported any significant quantities.

The assumption, then, was that Israel had gotten the uranium from the United States, and the CIA had a "strong opinion" of exactly where they had gotten it. This was a small fuel fabrication plant in Apollo, Pennsylvania, called Nuclear Materials and Equipment Corporation, or Numec, run by a nuclear chemist with close ties to Israel, Dr. Zalman Shapiro.

The exact amounts have never been clear, even to the CIA. But Agency officials were convinced that Shapiro and Numec had supplied Israel with more than 200 pounds of highly enriched uranium, or enough for several atomic bombs.

Other American Government agencies were less certain. In all, there were more than ten investigations of Numec, and not one ever led to a criminal prosecution. The possible crime—unlicensed transfer of uranium to a foreign government—carried the threat of a death penalty at the time.

Dr. Shapiro himself completely denied the charges and called them "utterly ridiculous." His lawyer told David Burnham of *The New York Times* that his client's position was "very simple: He never diverted a single microgram of nuclear material to Israel or anyone else, and does not believe that anyone else did at the plant."

But even without a criminal case against Shapiro, the suspicion lingered. And the case of Numec and the Israelis entered the lore as one of the most intriguing cases ever in the history of nuclear espionage.

Much of the story comes from the writing of two American journalists— John Fialka of the *Washington Star* and *New York Times* man David Burnham. Fialka and Burnham have followed the story since the mid-1970s, and they have consistently offered the best coverage and the most extensive culling of official government sources.

The leading man in the drama was Numec's founder and president, a figure well known and widely liked in the American nuclear industry, Dr. Zalman Shapiro.

Born in Canton, Ohio some sixty years ago, Shapiro was the son of an Orthodox Rabbi from Lithuania and had himself been a longtime activist in Zionist organizations. As a scientist, he had helped get money, information, and equipment for scientific work in Israel, and had kept in close touch with Israeli officials in the United States.

A Ph.D. in chemistry from Johns Hopkins University in 1948, Shapiro won his spurs at Westinghouse where he worked on the reactor for Admiral Hyman Rickover's first nuclear-powered submarine, the *Nautilus*. This would later open the door for continuing involvement with the nuclear submarine program.

Numec was Shapiro's bid to start a business of his own with two other veterans of the American nuclear program. They started in 1957, in an old factory in Apollo, a small industrial town located about thirty-five miles east of Pittsburgh. Their idea was to fabricate uranium oxide fuel for commercial atomic power plants, which were expected to spring up everywhere in the euphoric afterglow of President Dwight Eisenhower's Atoms for Peace program.

In its early years, the company appears to have flourished, and Shapiro spoke of becoming "the du Pont of the atomic fuel industry." But much of the actual business came from Washington, D.C., including an ongoing contract to turn government-owned bomb-grade uranium into fuel for Admiral Rickover's nuclear subs and a projected nuclear-powered rocket, the Nerva.

Numec had several foreign clients as well, It shipped highly enriched uranium to France, Germany, the Netherlands, and Japan, all with permission from the American Government. It drew up plans for Japan's first plutonium fuel lab, at Tokai-Mura. And not surprisingly, it worked very closely with Israel.

The firm initially served the Israelis as a technical consultant and a training and procurement agency in the United States. Shapiro then started a subsidiary in Israel, which irradiated strawberries and other fruits and vegetables to prevent spoilage. The subsidiary was called Isorad, Israel Isotopes and Radiation Enterprises Ltd., and Shapiro's partner in it was the Israel Atomic Energy Commission.

Numec itself employed at least one Israeli, a metallurgist, and the Apollo plant received frequent visits from Israeli officials, including the Science Attaché at the Embassy in Washington.

As part of its business, Numec had access to various highly secret processes. It also handled large quantities of weapons-usable plutonium and highly enriched uranium, all under license from the U.S. Atomic Energy Commission. But Numec's security was notoriously lax, and Atomic Energy inspectors expressed concern from the early 1960s. According to an AEC report in 1962, the inspections "have disclosed numerous security discrepancies attributable to lack of effort on the part of Numec management."

The Commission specifically chided Shapiro for mixing government-owned uranium with commercial stocks and for failing to keep proper records. They also expressed concern about the number of foreign and especially Israeli visitors, as well as the employment of the Israeli metallurgist.

By 1964, the CIA became concerned, especially after the Chinese set off their first nuclear device. Until a U-2 spy plane finally discovered that China had its own enrichment plant at Lanchow, some CIA officials feared that the Chinese had somehow gotten their bomb-grade uranium from Dr. Shapiro's Numec plant in Apollo.

But the big scare came in the Atomic Energy Commission inspections of 1964 and 1965. The inspectors had an exact figure of how much bomb-grade uranium the government had shipped to Numec. They also knew exactly how much Numec had shipped back in the form of nuclear fuel, and they could measure how much Numec still had in stock. Just basic accounting, really. But between the amount "in" and the amount "out" or "on hand," there was a gap. In fact, as of October 31, 1965 there was a gap of exactly 361.6 pounds, or enough to make a number of atomic bombs. Where had it gone?

This was the famous "MUF," Materials Unaccounted For, and Dr. Shapiro had a ready answer. It was in the trash. Numec had mistakenly buried it with the radioactive wastes. The Atomic Energy Commission waited while Dr. Shapiro's men dug up the waste and took samples of it. That accounted for about 10 percent of the missing uranium. Where was the rest?

Dr. Shapiro could only guess that it had been lost in the processing, stuck to the pipes, or otherwise melted away. As he later explained, "If you're cooking a small thing in a large pot, then you have material that sticks to the pot."

The Atomic Energy Commission agreed in part, and generously allowed for these losses. But they demanded to know exactly what had happened to something over 200 pounds.

Theft of that amount—or "diversion," as it is politely called—would have been child's play. Highly enriched uranium is only slightly radioactive, and it is incredibly dense. Two hundred pounds could easily be carried away or even mailed in a series of small packages, and then sent out of the country in an embassy's diplomatic pouch.

The matter was literally a question of life and death. If a foreign country had gotten its hands on the uranium, it could easily make several bombs. If Dr. Shapiro (or someone else at Numec) had given it to them, he could face a possible death sentence under the atomic energy laws.

But somehow the investigation of the loss showed less than an all-out determination to find out where the 200 pounds had gone. The Atomic Energy Commision ran two investigations, in 1965 and 1966, and questioned present and former Numec employees, though without insisting on written statements. The Commission's verdict: "No evidence [of] unlawful activity or that special nuclear material had been diverted." The Commission, of course, had itself been responsible for giving Numec its license and allowing it to continue operating in spite of continuing security violations.

Congress staged its own investigation, sending in the General Accounting Office to see what they could find. Their report: "No evidence of diversion," though they added that Numec kept such poor records and had so many records missing that it was impossible to tell when the losses actually happened.

The Federal Bureau of Investigation, which should have handled the case, did not. The Bureau apparently considered the matter for a week and simply decided not to investigate.

Numec was in the clear. The only inconvenience was that Dr. Shapiro was compelled to pay the Atomic Energy Commission for the uranium he had "lost." The bill came to just under a million dollars.

Shortly afterward, in 1967, Dr. Shapiro sold his interest in Numec to Atlantic Richfield, which later sold it to the engineering firm and reactor manufacturers Babcock and Wilcox. The Numec plant has continued its record of laxness in security and record keeping, while Dr. Shapiro returned to a job in Westinghouse, though deprived of his old security clearance.

And so the case was closed, and would have been forgotten if not for the CIA. The turnabout came in 1968, when Carl Duckett and his CIA analysts found that Israel had somehow gotten a certain quantity of bomb-grade uranium. This was just after the 200 or more pounds had gone missing at Numec, and once again the finger pointed at Zalman Shapiro.

The CIA is not supposed to conduct domestic intelligence operations within the United States, and so CIA Director Richard Helms called in the FBI. Ramsey Clark, the Attorney General, authorized electronic surveillance, and soon FBI agents were looking at and listening to the movements of Dr. Shapiro.

What they found appeared persuasive. On one occasion, Dr. Shapiro held a meeting of American Jewish scientists at his home in Pittsburgh, at which a suspected Israeli intelligence officer asked them to get specific information for Israel. Another time he met with the same Israeli at the Pittsburgh airport.

Yet in all the damning circumstantial evidence, the FBI found no proof that Shapiro had diverted the uranium, or done anything else against the law. Again, there was no prosecution. The case lapsed until 1975. That was the year Congress disbanded the old Atomic Energy Commission and divided its functions between the newly created Energy Research and Development Administration and the Nuclear Regulatory Commission. In this new setup, the NRC decided to put together a historical study of the effort to protect nuclear materials since the Atoms for Peace program started in 1954.

The man in charge of the study was a rather tense thirty-year-old nuclear engineer named James Conran, who immediately began plowing through the old AEC files. When he came to the Numec file, he found it was so secret that it was kept somewhere else. And when he asked to see it, he was told he had "no need to know."

Conran continued to push, and after butting his head into any number of bureaucratic brick walls, he finally got the NRC Commissioners to request a special meeting with the CIA, which had most of the Numec files. This was the briefing by the CIA's Deputy Director Carl Duckett, in which he revealed that the CIA had the "strong opinion" that Numec had given Israel the uranium.

Various investigations followed, both by the FBI and by committees of the U.S. Congress. But none of the inquiries proved anything conclusive against either Numec or the smiling Dr. Shapiro. Numec had lost bomb-grade uranium. And no one could ever say for sure that it went from here to there.

Yet the top experts we spoke with in Washington were convinced that

Israel had, in fact, received this enriched uranium. The CIA's former Deputy Director, Carl Duckett, confirmed this publicly in an interview on the ABC News documentary on which we worked, stating that all his "senior analysts who worked on the problem agreed with me fully. . . . I think that the clear consensus in CIA . . . was that indeed, Numec material had been diverted and had been used by the Israelis in fabricating weapons."

By now, of course, the trail is old, and only the suspicions linger. But wherever the Israelis got their highly enriched uranium, the CIA believed they had what they needed to make the bomb as early as 1968.

Operation Plumbat

For the CIA, the question of the highly enriched uranium quickly became passé. By 1976, the Agency was convinced that the Israelis were making bombs of plutonium reprocessed from the Dimona reactor. Yet that still left a question, one of nagging interest to journalists if not to the spooks. If the Israelis were taking plutonium out of Dimona, where did they get the natural uranium to put in as fuel? The French had dramatically cut off their supply at the time of the Six Day War in 1967. The Argentinians and the South Africans had sold the Israelis a bit, and the Israelis themselves produced small, expensive quantities as a by-product of their phosphate industry. But the Israelis needed more, much more. And their sources of foreign supply— not just of uranium, but of military weapons as well—had proven to be unreliable after the Six Day War. As a result, the Israelis badly needed a new supply of uranium, and they got it—200 tons of it—through one of their greatest nuclear coups, Operation Plumbat.

The story of Plumbat is worth telling at length, as it sets a stage for the subsequent exploits and nuclear intrigues of Israel's Arab and Islamic foes. It is also worth telling right, as the tale has been told widely and wrong, in breathless and wholly fictional accounts of how Israeli commandos hijacked a ship at sea and heisted the needed uranium ore.

In fact, the Israelis did not steal the uranium. They had already bought and paid for it, using an intricate and somewhat ironic cover. And they did not hijack the ship, they owned it all along.

The story comes in large part from a well-documented book by the Insight Team of the *Sunday Times* in London. It is called simply *The Plumbat Affair*, and the authors are Elaine Davenport, Paul Eddy, and Peter Gillman. Of all the books that claim to tell the story, theirs is the only one that is not fiction.

The tale begins with a firm that we have already met, the parent company of Belgonucléaire, the Société Générale de Belgique. Long active as the power behind the throne in the old Belgian Congo, Société Générale, through its minerals subsidiary, was sitting on a virtual mountain of uranium oxide, or yellow cake, all safely stashed away in a silo near Antwerp.

This was the uranium the Israelis wanted to buy. But there was no way that they could buy it directly. The Dimona reactor was not open to international inspection. And Euratom, the Common Market nuclear agency, would never have permitted the sale.

So the Israelis were forced to find a "front," and one that no one would suspect. This was a small West German chemical firm called Asmara Chemie, which was run by a World War II Luftwaffe ace named Herbert Schulzen. The authors of *The Plumbat Affair* say Israeli recruiters had first approached Schulzen in 1964, inviting him on an expense-paid holiday in the Holy Land and following up with a few small orders to his firm. But this time the Israelis asked Schulzen to go much farther. Would he approach Société Générale and place an order for 200 tons of uranium oxide?

It should be remembered that Asmara was a small firm, that it normally sold industrial soaps, softeners, and decontaminants, and that it had never before bought uranium. But Société Générale did not seem to care. In fact, the giant firm had only one question: Could Asmara pay? Schulzen replied by giving the name of a small bank in Zurich, into which the Israelis had put the needed 4 million dollars. The bank quickly confirmed that Asmara had the money on account.

Euratom was only slightly more difficult to satisfy. What did a small chemical company want with so much uranium? asked one puzzled Euratom official. Schulzen answered that Asmara Chemie was about to go into mass production of petrochemicals and wanted to use the uranium as a chemical catalyst. The powerful Société Générale backed him up, and Euratom agreed to the sale in October 1968. Euratom also agreed that the uranium could undergo special processing, and gave permission for Asmara to send it by ship to Genoa, and then on to a paint and chemical company called Saica in Milan.

That was the uranium. The ship was even easier, as the Israelis relied on an old friend, a Turkish-born shipowner and sometimes arms dealer named Burham Yarisal.

According to *The Plumbat Affair*, Yarisal had worked with the Israelis as far back as 1947, when he helped run the British blockade with surplus arms and equipment for what would become Israel's Independence War against the Arabs. His new task was similar, to find a small cargo ship capable of carrying 200 tons of uranium from Antwerp into the Mediterranean.

By September 1968, Yarisal had found what he wanted—a ten-year-old 2,600-ton German-built vessel called the *Scheersberg*, which he renamed the *Scheersberg* A. The ship cost just under 160,000 pounds, which was paid through a bank in Hamburg.

Next came the crew. Yarisal hired a ragtag bunch of Spaniards, Portuguese, and Moroccans, and they were soon joined by a young English-speaking captain who called himself Peter Barrow. The new captain put the crew through a shakedown cruise to Naples and back to Rotterdam, where out of the blue he laid them all off. That was on November 11.

What happened next is the key to the Israeli plan. Euratom had cleared the uranium for shipment from Société Générale's storage silos to the port of Antwerp, and from there to Genoa and Milan. So Asmara's Schulzen hired one of Belgium's best-known transport firms to pick up the uranium from Société Générale and carry it by special train to Antwerp, where it was loaded on a waiting ship. This was the *Scheersberg* A, just in from Rotterdam with a brand-new crew and the same young English-speaking captain called Peter Barrow.

The *Scheersberg* A loaded the uranium—560 specially sealed oil drums marked with the mysterious word Plumbat—and just after midnight on November 17, the elusive Captain Barrow set sail for Genoa.

The ship—and the drums of uranium—never arrived. Instead of going to Genoa, Barrow headed straight for the Eastern Mediterranean between Cyprus and Turkey, where, according to *The Plumbat Affair*, an eyewitness saw the *Scheersberg* A transfer the uranium cargo at sea to an Israeli freighter escorted by armed gunboats.

The Israelis had their uranium, and no one was the wiser. A few hours later, on December 2, the *Scheersberg* A steamed into the little Turkish port of Iskenderun, and then to Palermo, where she was met by a new captain and the old crew of Spanish, Portuguese, and Moroccans. The Israelis had pulled off the perfect operation, or so it seemed.

Euratom, which is supposed to keep track of such things, did not even begin to suspect that the uranium might be missing—not until six months later, in April 1969, when Professor Enrico Jacchia of the Safeguards Division picked up the telephone and called Saica, the company in Milan that was supposed to have received the uranium for processing. Why had Saica not submitted the necessary papers on receiving the uranium? the Professor asked. Saica's answer was vague. Then, in June 1969, a letter from Asmara Chemie confirmed what Professor Jacchia was now beginning to suspect. The uranium had never gone to Genoa and Milan.

Where had it gone? Schulzen could not say. Asmara Chemie had purchased the uranium "on instructions of a client," who had first wanted the shipment sent to Saica in Milan and had then "decided differently," he explained.

Who, then, was Asmara's client? Euratom demanded in a terse follow-up letter. The reply came from a big law firm in Bonn. The name of Asmara's client was a "commercial confidence," which Euratom had no right to know.

Time passed, and after a year or so, Euratom finally admitted defeat. They simply did not know what had happened to the missing uranium. The European Commission, the highest authority of the Common Market, followed suit, deciding in a secret session simply to close the files and hush up any mention of the case. As one commission official later admitted, "It would have made our security regulations look a little ridiculous."

And there it was, except for a strange footnote.

In July 1973, in the little Norwegian town of Lillehammer, an Israeli hit team killed a North African Arab called Ahmed Bouchiki. They had mistaken the ill-fated Bouchiki for Ali Hassan Salameh, one of the leaders of the Black September terrorists who had seized and killed eleven Israeli athletes at the 1972 Olympics in Munich. Then, to make the botch-up complete, the Norwegian police captured five of the Israeli agents, including one of the world's least likely hit men, the luckless Dan Aerbel.

Something less than a tight-lipped James Bond, Aerbel had been born in Copenhagen right before the start of World War II, and had been forced to hide from the Nazis cramped up in a dark cellar. This left him with a classic case of claustrophobia, and after a single night in a Norwegian jail cell, the terrified man broke completely and told his Norwegian captors everything he knew about the killing in Lillehammer and the Israeli network in Europe. He also told them about a small cargo ship called the *Scheersberg* A.

"I owned the *Scheersberg* A," he said. "It carried the uranium to Israel."

Aerbel's admission meant little to the Norwegian copper who was questioning him. But the higher-ups in the Norwegian Intelligence Service soon understood all too well. Dan Aerbel, a member of the Israeli hit team in Lillehammer, had also been used to help cover up Israeli ownership of the uranium ship, the *Scheersberg* A.

Using the alias Dan Ert, a shortened form of his original family name Erteschiek, he had taken over ownership of the *Scheersberg* A from the Turk Burham Yarisal. This was in October 1969, according to a document prepared by a notary public in Zurich. Aerbel sold the ship in Bilbao in 1970, carelessly leaving his name on the register of the city's Hotel Carlton.

There it was, just waiting for some serious investigative journalists to find. Aerbel had taken over the ship after it had taken the uranium. But once it was clear that the Israelis had owned the ship—and not hijacked her—it was much easier to go back and unmask the initial purchase of the uranium by Herbert Schulzen and Asmara Chemie. Owning the ship, the Israelis had only to get someone to buy the uranium for them and have it loaded, and as *The Plumbat Affair* now shows, that is exactly what happened.

To add spice to the story, it turned out that Aerbel also confessed that the Israelis had used the *Scheersberg* A in a second operation while he was the owner of record. This was the spiriting away of five embargoed French gunboats, previously purchased and paid for by the Israelis, from the port of Cherbourg on Christmas Day, 1969. According to Aerbel, the Israelis had used the ship to refuel the five gunboats as they passed off the Basque coast of Spain on their long voyage to Haifa.

The Israelis, of course, denied the whole Plumbat affair. "Just stories," an official Israeli source told us, shaking his head from side to side. But Operation Plumbat scored an enormous coup. It got the uranium to fuel the French reactor at Dimona. And this, in turn, could produce the plutonium to make atomic bombs.

Israel was the first to show that an essentially minor power could build a nuclear arsenal. Many people even sympathize with the effort. After all, the Israelis need the bomb, do they not? And they *are* responsible. They would never use it unless they had to.

The Israelis, for their part, continue to deny the bomb. They have not publicly announced or tested it. And when asked, they keep repeating that they will never be the first to introduce nuclear weapons into the Middle East.

They could be right, though only in a Talmudic sense. The British had already stored atom bombs in nearby Cyprus, and ships of America's Sixth Fleet regularly patrol the Eastern Mediterranean fully armed with nuclear weapons. So the Israelis could never be the first, or even the second. But they are the third.

There was also a technical question. When did a bomb become a bomb? In their best-selling novel *The Fifth Horseman*, Larry Collins and Dominique Lapierre suggested the Israeli answer. The scene was dramatic. It was a moment of nuclear crisis, and the Israeli soldiers were putting together the separate segments to make the bombs.

"As one team removed [the plutonium cores] from the container, another was wheeling in the high-explosive cladding, the jacket into which each was designed to fit," the authors wrote. "Their separation was a strategem. Since an atomic bomb only existed when the two halves were assembled, Israel had always been able to maintain publicly that she had not introduced nuclear weapons into the Middle East."

The last screw had not been turned. No screw, no bomb. Small comfort to Israel's Arab and Islamic foes. They saw the Israeli bomb as all too real, pointed at them, and preventing their ever winning an all-out military victory over Israel or ever restoring Arab supremacy in Palestine—not without risking their own nuclear destruction. They could either accept the Israeli bomb, which would mean discarding their military option against Israel or even making peace with the Jewish state as President Sadat of Egypt did. Or they could try to change the balance, and gain new clout in the world pecking order by getting their own nuclear arms, which is what the Iraqis decided to do.

And so the nuclear arms race was on. Yet for all the consequences in the Middle East, the Israeli bomb sent few serious shock waves into the wider world. Perhaps because the Israelis never staged a test explosion, or perhaps because the CIA kept the secret safe so long, Israel's bomb raised no major alarm about the dangerous spread of nuclear weapons. It had small impact on the new thinking about the problem, and less on the new measures to meet it.

That was for another country to do. And for another time. Only this time there would be a nuclear blast.

9

"The Buddha Is Smiling"

> I hope Indian scientists will use the atomic force for constructive purposes. But if India is threatened, she will inevitably try to defend herself by all means at her disposal.
> —Prime Minister Jawaharlal Nehru,
> June 1946

> The Canadians assured me continually that it was all fine in India, that there were no problems, that we had nothing to worry about.
> —Dr. Ishrat Usmani,
> Former Chairman, Pakistan Atomic Energy Commission,
> April 1980

The explosion came from deep inside an L-shaped trench in the vast wastes of India's Rajasthan Desert. As Prime Minister Indira Gandhi looked on in sari and sunglasses, the blast shook the surrounding scrubland, forcing a large hillock to rise eerily from the desert sands. According to Indian scientists, the yield registered fifteen kilotons (close to the size of the Hiroshima explosion), and was produced by a small nuclear device made of plutonium.

Back in the capital city of New Delhi, seismographs recorded the strange quake, while the Foreign Ministry received a prearranged telegraphic signal of success. It read: "The Buddha is smiling."

"A peaceful nuclear explosive," the Indians insisted. "Not a single thing in it was foreign."

The test was on May 18, 1974, at 8:05 in the morning. For India, it was a high point of a long, hard grind, going back nearly thirty years to the closing days of World War II. For the world, it was, in the words of the German writer Robert Jungk, "the beginning of the Second Atomic Age, the Age of Proliferation."

"The short period during which a few atomic powers had held each other in check was over, and an era of world-wide, incalculable competition in nuclear armaments had begun," warned Jungk in his book *The Nuclear State*. "The probability that before the end of the century atomic bombs might be used in regional or local conflicts had drawn closer." *

---

* Robert Jungk, *The Nuclear State* (London: John Calder, 1979).

The shock waves shattered all the standard images. India was the world's largest democracy, the land of Nehru and Mahatma Gandhi, the altar of nonviolence and nonalignment and pious calls for universal nuclear disarmament. It was also the home of the desperately poor and diseased and yet, of all the poor and backward lands, the one that had most pinned its hopes for the future on nuclear power and the promise of the supposedly peaceful atom. And now this same India was also the first of the less-developed countries to test a nuclear device.

The beginning of both the nuclear test and the nuclear power program goes back to the years before Independence, to the creation in 1945 of the private Institute for Fundamental Research. The money for the Institute came from India's leading industrial barons, the Tata family, and the scientific leadership from an outstanding physicist educated at Cambridge, Dr. Homi Bhabha.

A student and colleague of many of the pioneers in nuclear physics in the West, Bhabha made the Institute a center for basic research and a springboard for starting and shaping a comprehensive nuclear program for the newly independent India. Over the years, he headed every major nuclear body in the country, and with the backing of Nehru, set India on a surprisingly ambitious nuclear course.

Under Bhabha's leadership, the Indians looked to their own supplies of uranium, and also to their own much larger reserves of a second mineral suitable for nuclear reactions, thorium. They built an industry to mine and mill the uranium and thorium ores, as well as a fuel-fabrication plant, some small heavy-water plants, and two of their own small research reactors located at Trombay, on the coast about thirty-five miles north of Bombay.

But Bhabha's greatest success was in winning aid and support from three of the world's major nuclear exporters—Canada, the United States, and France. Probably no other country in the world, and certainly no other underdeveloped country, received such wholehearted help in building its civilian nuclear program—or in building its military nuclear potential.

From Canada, Bhabha got a large and sophisticated research reactor—the forty-thermal megawatt Cirus, which went into operation at Trombay in July 1960. Similar to the reactor that France supplied to Israel at Dimona, the Cirus was a heavy-water reactor that burned natural uranium fuel. It also produced plutonium, which the Indians used to build their "peaceful nuclear explosive."

As part of the Colombo Plan to help the economies of the former British colonies in southern Asia, the Canadian Government paid all of the foreign-exchange costs of the Cirus. Ottawa also held back from requiring any international inspections or safeguards. The Indians simply promised that "the reactor and any products resulting from its use will be employed for peaceful purposes only."

The Canadians also helped the Indians with their heavy-water plant and a nuclear fuel complex, and started construction in Rajasthan on two nuclear power plants of the Candu type, which were to serve as the prototypes for two Indian-built power reactors at Narora and Madras.

From the United States, Dr. Bhabha got almost as good, including a key element for the Canadian reactor—some twenty-one tons of heavy water. And still without any international safeguards.

The Americans also provided heavy water for another experimental reactor, and two complete light-water reactors for the Tarapur Atomic Power Station, also near Bombay. These were each rated at 200 megawatts of electricity, and were built by General Electric for a reported $118 million, much of it paid by the U.S. Agency for International Development. The deal included a thirty-year agreement to provide a continuing supply of low-enriched uranium fuel for the Tarapur reactors, a promise that would become a continuing bone of contention.

Washington similarly provided heavily subsidized loans, research grants, and training programs. In all, more than 1,300 Indian scientists and technicians received training at nuclear facilities in the United States.

Above all, the Americans helped to build an essential facility on the way to the bomb—a small reprocessing plant at Trombay, which allowed the Indians to extract the plutonium from the irradiated fuel of the Cirus reactor. The plant was built from declassified blueprints of the Purex solvent extraction process developed by the United States, and the Indians received further help from at least one American corporation in its construction. The Americans also trained at least twenty-four Indians specifically in reprocessing.

The French helped as well. In 1951, they signed an agreement for nuclear cooperation with India, which provided for special training and exchanges of personnel, especially of chemists and metallurgists. Dr. Francis Perrin told us about this often overlooked aspect of the Indian nuclear program when we interviewed him at his Paris office in the Collège de France.

"We were very close to India from the beginning," he confirmed to us. "It wasn't only Canada that helped the Indians. France also had a responsibility in this area." And much of the responsibility, he added, was in "teaching them about the extraction of plutonium from spent nuclear fuel."

With all of this foreign help, Dr. Bhabha built a fully rounded program of civilian nuclear power and research. But he also strongly favored nuclear weapons, and his attitudes were widely known by his foreign benefactors. As early as 1958, he told the British Nobel Prize-winner Lord Blackett that he hoped to develop nuclear weapons, and he frequently told other friends that he wanted to keep the nuclear option open.

Dr. Bertrand Goldschmidt, the former head of international relations for the French Atomic Energy Commission and one of those friends, told us straight out: "Bhabha always wanted the bomb." As Goldschmidt saw it, "The Indians could have made an explosion from about 1968."

Bhabha's enthusiasm was kept in check by Prime Minister Jawaharlal Nehru, who prided himself on his role as a leading voice for nuclear disarmament. But even Nehru, the apostle of nuclear nonviolence, was prepared to keep the weapons option open. As early as June 1946, he explored the military possibility in a public speech in Bombay. "I hope Indian scientists will use the atomic force for constructive purposes," he declared. "But if India is threatened, she will inevitably try to defend herself by all means at her disposal."

Two years later, in April 1948, he went even farther in the parliamentary debate on the Atomic Energy Bill. "Indeed, I think we must develop it for peaceful purposes," he urged. "Of course, if we are compelled as a nation to use it for other purposes, possibly no pious statements of any of us will stop the nation from using it that way."

In later years, Nehru tended to take a more unequivocal public stand against ever using atomic energy "for defense or destructive purposes." But as Prime Minister, he continued to back Bhabha's leadership of the nuclear program, and carefully avoided safeguards on the Cirus reactor and reprocessing plant. He also left an important loophole in all his promises that the Indian nuclear program would pursue only "peaceful purposes."

That loophole was the "peaceful nuclear explosive," or PNE. From the first atom bombs, scientists and engineers had looked forward to using the vast explosive energy of the atom in large-scale earth-moving projects, such as deepening harbors, diverting rivers, and digging reservoirs for dams. The Americans ran a series of nuclear tests in the 1960s specifically to try the idea, and the Soviet Union is reportedly still interested in it. But in their essentials, "peaceful nuclear explosives" are little different from military bombs, and in all of their statements, the Indians were careful to keep open this particular option, which was both "peaceful" and "explosive."

As the Indian journalist Shyam Bhatia has shown in his excellent study of India's nuclear bomb, * the actual decision to press ahead on the weapons side came in late 1964, following China's first nuclear test in October. Nehru had died. The Indians were still feeling humiliated by their defeat in the 1962 border war with China. And many leading politicians, especially within the ruling Congress Party, were actively pushing for an Indian bomb.

This was Dr. Bhabha's big chance. In London when he heard that the Chinese had tested a nuclear device, he hastily called a press conference and announced publicly that Indian scientists could also produce a nuclear bomb, and within eighteen months.

The pressure fell on Nehru's successor as Prime Minister, the mild-mannered Lal Bahadur Shastri, who tried to hold back as long as he could. But the pressure mounted, and in late November, he finally gave Bhabha the green light—not for an all-out commitment to nuclear weapons, but for the development of a "peaceful nuclear explosive."

By this time, the Indians already had the Cirus reactor and the

---

* Shyam Bhatia, *India's Nuclear Bomb* (Bombay: Vikas Publishing House, 1979).

reprocessing plant at Trombay, all developed without safeguards and under the cloak of peaceful nuclear research. But Bhabha's estimate of eighteen months proved wildly optimistic. He and Shastri both died. Nehru's daughter, Indira Gandhi, took power. And technical problems continued to delay the program, right up to the underground test in May 1974.

The Indians pushed ahead with this ten-year buildup in secret. But it was a very open secret indeed, and when the blast finally came, it hardly came as a surprise.

Mr. Bhutto, in Pakistan, got wind of the Indian plan almost as soon as they started, when as the Pakistani Foreign Minister he first publicly began pushing for nuclear weapons to counter the Indian threat. The Pakistanis also spent great effort in trying to convince other countries of the danger.

Dr. Ishrat Usmani, the former head of the Pakistan Atomic Energy Commission, told us that he had expressed his anxiety on several occasions to the Canadians, who had supplied reactors to both Pakistan and India. And at least once, he spoke directly to the Canadian Prime Minister Pierre Trudeau.

"In 1971, Prime Minister Trudeau was on his way to the Commonwealth Conference in Singapore," Usmani explained to us. "He specifically diverted from his trip to see the Karachi nuclear program. It was the ninth or tenth of January 1971."

"I invited him to lunch," Usmani went on. "He said he didn't want to make it an official occasion, and I was delighted and arranged for a family meal at the Intercontinental Hotel.

"I expressed my concern with the Indian program," Usmani told us, "but I failed to persuade him. The Canadians assured me continually that it was all fine in India, that there were no problems, that we had nothing to worry about."

In fact, as the Canadians later admitted, they were plenty worried themselves. Trudeau had asked Mrs. Gandhi for assurances that India was not planning to use the plutonium from the Canadian reactor to make any kind of nuclear explosive, peaceful or otherwise. But the motherly-looking Iron Lady refused point-blank. The original agreement between Canada and India had not prohibited peaceful nuclear explosives, she insisted. And to change the original agreement in any way would be "discriminatory."

The Indians took the same position in the negotiations for the Nuclear Nonproliferation Treaty, which had been taking place in Geneva from 1964. Originally favorable to the idea of such a treaty, they balked at its ban on "peaceful nuclear explosives."

"The Indian delegation does not deny that the technology involved in the production of nuclear weapons is the same as the technology which produced a peaceful nuclear explosive device," the Indian delegate told the negotiating conference. But, he insisted, that was not the issue.

"Dynamite was originally meant for military use," he argued. "That does not mean therefore that only the poor and developing nations should be denied all technology for fear that they might use it for military purposes."

After all these warnings and denials and evasions, the nuclear test itself must have seemed to inside observers something of an anticlimax, and the first official reactions from India's foreign supporters were hardly cries of outrage.

According to a well-placed source in the French Atomic Energy Commission, the French sent a telegram of congratulations, and followed up by suggesting that France might help the Indians build a fast breeder reactor, which would greatly increase India's supply of plutonium.

The Americans officially accepted India's claim that the device was just a "peaceful nuclear explosive." The hope in Washington was that this acceptance might make it easier for the Indians to stop there and not go any farther down the road to actual nuclear weapons. This tended to blur the line that the United States had so carefully drawn against "peaceful nuclear explosives," and it is not clear whether the soft response in any way affected subsequent Indian decision making. In fact, the Indians did hold back from building a nuclear arsenal, at least until the present.

The Americans also tried to hide their own chief contributions to the explosion—the heavy water for the Cirus reactor and the help for the reprocessing plant. Rather than penalize the Indians in any way, Secretary of State Henry Kissinger insisted that the United States continue to ship nuclear fuel for the two General Electric power reactors at Tarapur even without any new assurance from the Indians that they would not use either the reactors or the fuel in producing any further nuclear devices.

Only the Canadians, who had supplied the reactor, seemed at all upset, and they spent several months trying their best to give the Indians a second chance. Would Mrs. Gandhi sign a new agreement promising not to use the plutonium from the Cirus reactor in explosives of any kind? The negotiations dragged on. The Indians continued to refuse. Finally the Canadians took the ultimate step and cut off all further nuclear supplies, which hampered completion of one of the Candu reactors in Rajasthan. But with all the earlier help from the Canadians and other foreign suppliers, the Indians already had a largely self-sufficient nuclear industry, and were even considering going into the nuclear export business themselves.

These were hardly the sweeping sanctions to convince the world that proliferation does not pay. There was never any attempt to link continuing aid to India's general development with the nuclear issue, and the Western industrial nations announced within a month of the nuclear test that they would increase their support of India by some $200 million.

These were just the immediate reactions. In the longer run, the Indian explosion marked a major turning point. This was the Third World's first nuclear device, and its full meaning would not be lost, especially on the

United States. Within weeks, some of America's brightest policy thinkers were taking a fresh look at the entire problem of proliferation, and their answers on how best to stop it, or at least to slow it down, would soon come to haunt other budding nuclear powers, particularly the Pakistanis, and in time the Iraqis as well.

10

America Takes the Lead

It is not enough to take this weapon out of the hands of soldiers. It must be put into the hands of those who will know how to strip its military casing and adapt it to the arts of peace.
—President Dwight D. Eisenhower,
Speech to the United Nations General Assembly,
December 1953

By 1985, according to their 1975 plans, nearly 40 countries will have enough chemically separable plutonium for a few bombs in the spent fuel produced by their electric power reactors.
—From *Moving Toward Life in a Nuclear Armed Crowd?*
(The Wohlstetter Report),
1975

The United States is deeply concerned about the consequences of the uncontrolled spread of this nuclear weapons capability. . . . We believe that these risks would be increased by the further spread of reprocessing capabilities of the spent nuclear fuel from which explosives can be derived.
—President Jimmy Carter,
April 7, 1977

"It's good for us but not for them"—that has been the opening line and the curtain call for the Great Power play to curb the proliferation of nuclear weapons. In the Nuclear Nonproliferation Treaty, the big three—the United States, the Soviet Union, and Great Britain—with a grudging assist from France and more recently from China, banded together to attempt to stop anyone else from joining the nuclear club while gaining implicit official international recognition of their own nuclear weapons monopoly.

For all the Cassandra-like cries that nuclear weapons would spread unstoppably, for all the dire warnings that proliferation would run rampant, the spread has been surprisingly slow. Very few nations have the bomb. And there is a certain logic, a certain limit, to those that do.

As the former French nuclear chief Francis Perrin reminded us when we spoke with him in Paris, the first five nations to get the bomb—the United States in 1945, the U.S.S.R. in 1949, Great Britain in 1952, France in 1960, and China in 1964—were all within the same magic circle. In the world that had emerged from World War II, they were the Great and Middle

Powers. They were—once the problem of admitting Red China was solved—the permanent members of the United Nations Security Council. They were the ones with the veto.

Many more nations had the technology to join the nuclear club, nations such as Canada and Sweden and, of course, those that had lost the last war—Germany, Italy, and Japan. But all of these others decided, or were forced to decide, to leave nuclear weapons alone. And so the limits seemed to be holding, the wall seemed to be standing, at least until the Israelis got their "nuclear capability" by 1968 and the Indians set off their "peaceful nuclear explosive" in May 1974.

The Indian explosion, in particular, changed the entire picture. While pundits could argue over whether the Israelis actually had the bomb, or only the "capability," the Indians demonstrated publicly and with great drama that they had a nuclear device. Where the Israelis were always a special case, located in the Middle East but not really part of Third World politics, the Indians proved that Third World nations, with all their poverty and wretchedness, could still get the bomb. Where the Israelis set out with the primary purpose of developing a military capability, the Indians produced their nuclear device out of a fully rounded civilian nuclear power and research program.

This link between the civilian and the military uses of atomic energy was hardly new. The promise of civilian nuclear power was born in the original sin of Hiroshima and Nagasaki, and almost from the start, American scientists and policy makers understood the unbreakable bond between the peaceful and the warlike.

The American Department of State certainly understood the connection by 1946 at the latest, when they put the link at the very heart of their first postwar effort to stop the spread of nuclear weapons. This was the Baruch Plan, presented to the United Nations by the investment banker and elder statesman Bernard Baruch. Radical even by today's standards, the plan called for international management and control of all potentially dangerous civilian nuclear activities, including the enrichment of uranium and the reprocessing of used reactor fuel.

In retrospect, the plan itself never had a chance. Whatever its good points, it remained a rather obvious attempt to preserve for the foreseeable future the American monopoly in nuclear weapons, while demanding outside inspection of both civilian and military nuclear development in Britain, France, and the Soviet Union. Then as now, nonproliferation had to mean monopoly, like it or not, and at the time the Soviets did not like it at all. For all its faults, however, the Baruch Plan still reflected an acute realization of the miltary dangers of civilian nuclear activities, especially those that could in any way make available plutonium or highly enriched uranium.

The insight would stand the test of time. Yet in the years that followed the formulation of the Baruch Plan, the official American awareness of the link between civilian and military nuclear activities somehow slipped from sight, whether lost, lied about, or covered up. The new thinking, if it could be called that, completely denied the link, and invented a make-believe barrier between "the fearful engines of military might" and the pretty promise of peaceful nuclear power.

"Atoms for Peace" was what the Americans called this new approach, as unveiled by President Dwight D. Eisenhower in a speech to the United Nations General Assembly in December 1953. "The United States would seek more than the mere reduction or elimination of atomic materials for military purposes," declared the ever likable American war hero. "It is not enough to take this weapon out of the hands of soldiers. It must be put into the hands of those who will know how to strip its military casing and adapt it to the arts of peace."

What Ike was offering was nothing less than the transfer from the United States to the rest of the world of the most advanced nuclear technology. The Americans would open the door to their nuclear secrets. They would provide technical assistance, training, subsidized research reactors, and even supplies of highly enriched uranium. And they would take the lead in setting up and paying for an International Atomic Energy Agency, which would act as a nuclear watchdog and also promote the worldwide development of civilian nuclear power.

"The United States knows that peaceful power from atomic energy is no dream of the future, that its capability, already proved, is here, now, today," proclaimed the American President. "Who can doubt, if the entire body of the world's scientists and engineers had adequate amounts of fissionable material with which to test and develop ther ideas, that this capability would rapidly be transformed into universal, efficient, and economic usage?"

In brief, the United States would become the Johnny Appleseed of the Atomic Age, and the Atoms for Peace crusade was launched with considerable imaginativeness and even idealism.

Yet Atoms for Peace and its celebration of the safe, peaceful, nonmilitary atom had less lofty roots as well. The Soviets had just exploded their first thermonuclear (hydrogen) bomb, and the Eisenhower Administration saw Atoms for Peace and its promise of civilian nuclear power as the perfect propaganda to counter them.

Ike's advisers also hoped to soften the negative image of all things nuclear, and to set the tone for opening the government's monopoly ownership of atomic energy to private enterprise, as provided in the Atomic Energy Act of 1954. The Atoms for Peace foreign aid programs moved in a similar direction overseas, paving the way for America's new nuclear industrialists to capture the world market.

Atoms for Peace on one side, the atoms for war on the other: in the logic of the crusade, the two had to be seen as different, distinct, completely separate. The needs of Cold War propaganda and the hopes for a new nuclear industry demanded the separation. Any earlier insight into the dangerous and inseparable link between civilian and military nuclear energy had to be discarded, filed away, forgotten. It simply did not fit in with the needs of the time.

This was a deception, and one especially important aspect of it lingers on. This is the widespread belief that the plutonium produced by the irradiation of uranium fuel in ordinary nuclear power reactors could not be used to make nuclear bombs. The idea actually goes back to the time of the Baruch Plan, but it became the "Apostles' Creed" of Atoms for Peace and of the new nuclear power industry.

The logic was simple. Any nuclear reactor that burns uranium fuel will produce some amount of plutonium, as the isotopes of uranium 238 absorb stray neutrons from the chain reaction and change into plutonium 239. This is the plutonium isotope that is used in nuclear weapons, and it is usually produced in reactors specially dedicated to the purpose. But if the plutonium stays in the reactor over a certain period of time—which it would in the normal operation of a power reactor—it absorbs still more of the stray neutrons, changing into plutonium 240 and other heavier isotopes. These are for the most part highly unstable and produce weak and often premature nuclear explosions.

So the argument seemed ready-made. Power-reactor plutonium could not make a bomb. It had been "denatured" by the presence of the unstable plutonium 240. It was safe, secure, and wholly confined to the peaceful pursuit of civilian nuclear power.

Scientists began to say it. Governments said it. Reactor manufacturers said it. And the Atoms for Peace program acted as if it were true, even to the point of declassifying the secrets of how the United States reprocessed used reactor fuel to extract the plutonium for subsequent experimentation or for the making of the new mixed-oxide fuel.

It was not until 1977 that awareness of the reality finally caught up. This was when Washington officially announced that as far back as 1962 the United States had exploded a successful nuclear device made of low-grade plutonium, exactly like the stuff that comes out of standard civilian light-water nuclear reactors.

And still the myth persists, though in a new and altered form. Perhaps reactor plutonium could be used, the diehards say. But there are so many easier, faster, cheaper ways to make the bomb that no one would go the civilian nuclear reactor route.

"Trying to divert nuclear power plant fuel into weapons production is the most expensive, clumsiest and inefficient way for any nation to make a weapon," declared Representative Mike McCormick, a leading defender of nuclear power in the U.S. Congress, according to the *Los Angeles Times*.

"If a maverick foreign government should decide to establish its own weapons material production capability, the civilian nuclear power route would be among its least attractive choices," proclaimed Mr. Chauncey

Starr, President of the industry-based Electric Power Research Institute. *

"It's not practical to build a major stockpile of nuclear weapons on the basis of a civilian nuclear program," insisted Dr. Carl Walske, President of the Atomic Industrial Forum, in the pages of *International Security*.

Perhaps. But, practical or not, the Indians had drawn on their civilian nuclear program to create their "peaceful nuclear explosive." The Iraqis were looking to their civilian research reactor. And according to the former Pakistani official Mr. K., the Pakistanis were explicitly planning to get their weapons plutonium by reprocessing the used fuel from their nuclear power reactor in Karachi.

Civilian nuclear power facilitates atom bombs—this was the unhappy link that Atoms for Peace had tried to ignore. But the Indian explosion brought it once again to the forefront of American nuclear thinking.

The Wohlstetter Report

Of all the new thinking and torrents of commentary and debate on the spread of nuclear weapons, no single study matched the provocatively titled "Moving Toward Life in a Nuclear Armed Crowd?" The product of a private consulting firm called Pan Heuristics and a widely known political scientist at the University of California, Professor Albert Wohlstetter, this single study radically altered the antiproliferation strategy of both the Ford and Carter Administrations. * *

"Rarely has scholarly research been so immediately influential for changing government policy," wrote Dr. Fred C. Ikle, then Director of the United States Arms Control and Disarmament Agency, which sponsored the study. "This study, far more than any others on the topic, revolutionized the thinking in the United States (and in other countries as well), leading the way to the radical new departure in the U.S. nonproliferation policy that took place during the Ford Administration."

The report itself was a bulky, poorly written hodgepodge of fact and argument, complete with complicated equations, extrapolations, tables, graphs, and flow charts. But its argument was dead simple.

Too many nations were getting the capability to build nuclear weapons whenever they wanted to do it. Their supposedly peaceful civilian nuclear programs already had stocks of the two nuclear explosives, highly enriched uranium and plutonium. Their stocks were growing. So were their facilities—reactors, reprocessing plants, and enrichment plants—to produce still more. And, warned the report, most of this proliferation was taking place

---

* "Nuclear Power and Weapons Proliferation—The Thin Link," speech to the American Power Conference, April 19, 1977. Reprinted by Atomic Industrial Forum.

* * Albert Wohlstetter et al., "Moving Toward Life in a Nuclear Armed Crowd?" Final Report. Prepared for the United States Arms Control and Disarmament Agency by Pan Heuristics, April 1976. Revised Edition.

within safeguards, and by nations that had signed the Nuclear Nonproliferation Treaty or the Treaty of Tlatelolco, which provided for a nuclear-free zone in Latin America.

"The real problem of proliferation today is not that there are numerous countries 'champing at the bit' to get nuclear weapons, but rather that all the non-nuclear nations, without making any conscious decisions to build nuclear weapons, are drifting upwards to higher categories of competence," the report argued.

"That means that any transient incentive in the ebb and flow of world politics which inclines a country to build nuclear weapons at some point in the future will be just that much easier to act upon."

After the blind and profligate optimism of Atoms for Peace, it was back to the reality of original sin. As the Wohlstetter group made clear, there were not two atoms, one peaceful and the other military. There was just one, and peaceful nuclear programs were opening the door to military nuclear weapons, especially in the case of reprocessing plants that could extract the plutonium from irradiated reactor fuel.

"By 1985, according to their 1975 plans, nearly 40 countries will have enough chemically separable plutonium for a few bombs in the spent fuel produced by their electric power reactors," the report explained. "About half of these countries have been planning a capacity by then to separate at least that much plutonium from the spent fuel."

Wohlstetter was offering a different and radically disturbing way to look at proliferation. For him, the problem was no longer just the spread of the weapons themselves. He was warning about the proliferation of the capability to make them. "The direct connection between weapon development and civilian nuclear reactors has been demonstrated by India," he insisted in the report. "If events continue on their present course, this demonstration may well be repeated by numerous other countries in the years ahead."

The Wohlstetter Report named the specific countries that it expected to pose the greatest threat. These were primarily countries of the Third World, and especially "those that feel threatened and fear abandonment. The most likely countries to decide for nuclear weapons appear to be outcasts, dropouts or fading members of alliance systems, especially the U.S. alliance system," the report predicted.

The list of likelies showed few surprises, though the report tended to underestimate nationalism as a motive force and to overemphasize America's post-Vietnam weakness as the prime reason that several new nations might go nuclear.

South Korea had lost confidence in American guarantees after the rout in Vietnam.

Taiwan was also worried by the collapse of U.S. power in Southeast Asia, and by Washington's new friendship with Peking.

Iran under the Shah was edging slowly away from the United States and beginning to pursue a policy of "independent nationalism" in the Gulf.

Pakistan was "feeling unhelped" by the United States and Britain against India, and had dropped out of the South East Asia Treaty Organization.

Argentina and Brazil were showing their independence—and also their traditional rivalry—in a Western Hemisphere no longer held together by Uncle Sam.

The report named two nuclear candidates not in the Third World—Spain, still out of NATO, and South Africa, the white man out in an increasingly Black Africa. It also mentioned Israel, claiming not to know whether or not the Israelis had already gone nuclear, and repeating "rumors" that they were just a "turn of the screwdriver" away.

The only obvious name missing was Iraq, which was just starting down the nuclear path when the report came out.

Wohlstetter and his team claimed to have drawn up their list from information available in public sources. But the countries named are roughly the same as in the CIA's September 1974 memo on "Prospects for Further Proliferation of Nuclear Weapons," which we mentioned earlier in reference to Israel. *

For these nations, Wohlstetter saw little problem in actually fabricating a nuclear weapon. That was the easy part, the report argued. The basic designs were known. Most of the necessary equations could be found in the open scientific literature. Any country that could run a sophisticated nuclear power program would have little trouble learning how to do it. And the actual time the bomb makers would need to put the bomb together would range from a few days to a few weeks.

The hard part was getting enough of the explosive material. That was exactly what Professor Wohlstetter and his group wanted the United States to make more difficult, especially in the case of plutonium.

The logic was clear. Any country with spent reactor fuel and a reprocessing facility could get the plutonium stocks fairly quickly, and "without any necessary violation of the clearly agreed-on rules," the report noted. Any country with plutonium stocks could easily turn them into weapons, and in a very short time. So whatever the country's original intent, it was never more than a few days or weeks away from having the bomb if it wanted.

The rules about nonproliferation could make matters worse. Nothing in any of the IAEA safeguards agreements or the Nonproliferation Treaty outlawed or forbade in any way reprocessing or enrichment plants, plutonium stocks or plutonium fuel rods or stocks of highly enriched uranium. As long as these were under safeguards, the rules of the game permitted—even encouraged—them all. A country could build up its stocks of weapons-usable material within the rules, while the safeguards would

---

* United States Central Intelligence Agency, "Prospects for Further Proliferation of Nuclear Weapons," September 1974. Released 1978.

continue to assure the world that since there had been no obvious diversions
of the materials, everything was quite all right.

"The critical time to make an explosive has been diminishing and will
continue to diminish without any necessary violation of the clearly agreed-on
rules—without any 'diversion,'" the report argued. "The I.A.E.A. safeguards
system, which is designed to detect diversions, may actually muffle signs of
the critical changes taking place without diversion."

It should be noted that the French Government's Nicoullaud Report,
described in Chapter 2, was an acknowledgment that these kinds of faults
existed in the nonproliferation system, as well as an attempt to close them in
the specific case of Iraq.

Wohlstetter's attack on the perils of plutonium was extremely radical,
going against the thinking of the entire nuclear industry. From the
reprocessing of plutonium for the world's very first atom bomb—the Trinity
device that the Americans tested in July 1945 near Alamogordo, New
Mexico—the idea of reprocessing had always been taken for granted. Nuclear
scientists had looked forward to recycling the reprocessed plutonium in a new
mixed-oxide fuel for standard light-water reactors, and the nuclear industry
saw the recycled plutonium as a substitute for the costly and relatively rare
uranium.

This reuse of plutonium had seemed an important saving of money and of
uranium, especially when seen against the industry's double-barreled forecast
that nuclear plants would spread like wildfire, while the world would soon
run out of suitable uranium reserves.

All of this made plutonium seem like terribly valuable stuff, not to be left
wasted in used power-reactor fuel. But by the mid-1970s, a big change in the
nuclear industry was promising to make reprocessing and plutonium far
more important.

The change was the planned introduction of a new generation of fast
breeder power reactors, which would burn a fuel mixture containing
plutonium to produce electricity. But even more important, the breeder
reactors would produce an even larger amount of new plutonium than they
would consume, generally by burning a fuel mixture of plutonium and
uranium oxides within a "blanket" of natural uranium. This natural
uranium blanket, which is 99.3 percent uranium 238, would absorb vastly
greater quantities of stray neutrons, and this would breed the new plutonium. With breeders, reprocessing would be a must, both to produce the
original plutonium for fuel and to extract the new plutonium from the spent
fuel.

In a sense, this almost magical breeding of plutonium would substitute for
the extremely costly mining of uranium ore and and the even more costly
process of enriching it. As a result of the continual recycling of used fuel, it
would also multiply by as much as fifty times the use of the available
uranium, and thus extend the life of present uranium reserves for hundreds
of years.

For the international nuclear industry, this was the wave of the future. Britain and the U.S.S.R. already had experimental fast breeders. Germany and Japan were planning theirs. The United States had experimental fast breeders and was planning to start up a commercial prototype at Clinch River in Tennessee in 1982. The French already had a 250-megawatt prototype supplying electricity, and were building two more: a larger commercial prototype due to go into operation in 1985 and the giant 1,200-megawatt Super-Phenix at Creys Malville, near Lyon. If all went well, the French hoped to be selling commercial fast breeders to public utilities in the 1990s, which would boost their reprocessing sales as well.

For Wohlstetter, this planned shift to breeder reactors presented unprecedented dangers for nuclear proliferation. Plutonium would be everywhere—in fuel rods, in spent fuel, in reprocessed fuel. Any country with breeder reactors would have a good argument for having its own reprocessing plant and its own standing stocks of plutonium, from which it could make nuclear weapons in the shortest possible time. This was the grim prospect of "life in a nuclear armed crowd."

The Wohlstetter Report challenged the whole business. It was against the use of reprocessing and the recycling of plutonium as a fuel in the present generation of power reactors, especially in the Third World. It pleaded for a postponement on the introduction anytime soon of the new generation of fast breeder reactors, with their automatic increase in reprocessing plants and plutonium stocks. The risks of nuclear weapons proliferation were too great, the report argued, and the economic benefits were far smaller than the nuclear industry had led the world to believe.

The economic analysis was a sweeping tour de force. As the report showed, nuclear power was not growing anywhere near as fast as the nuclear optimists at the IAEA and elsewhere were projecting, especially in the Third World, while uranium was proving far more available than the nuclear industry had warned. Therefore reprocessing and the recycling of plutonium made little economic sense with the present generation of power reactors, and even less with the small scale of nuclear facilities in most Third World nations. As for the fast breeders, they would not be competitive for many years. Even if the French were successful in selling them in the 1990s, there would be no need for reprocessing until that time.

The implication was clear. Reprocessing had been oversold. In any case, there was absolutely no need to rush into it. The world could wait, and try to use the time to find a solution to the risks that would come with having so much plutonium available around the world.

Reprocessing, then, was the place to draw the line against creeping proliferation. The United States should delay its own commercial development of reprocessing and the fast breeder, the report recommended. And Washington should throw its weight against reprocessing in other countries, especially in the Third World.

This was the Wohlstetter Report, a brilliant and extremely influential call to nuclear arms control, and one that still rings true today.

America Fights Its Case

Awakened by India's "peaceful nuclear explosion," the United States took the ideas of Professor Wohlstetter and other academics to heart and broke sharply with the blatant nuclear encouragement of Atoms for Peace.

"In the past, the U.S. was the principal sinner," admitted Dr. Fred Ikle, head of the Arms Control and Disarmament Agency under the two Republican Presidents, Richard Nixon and Gerald Ford. "We trained thousands of scientists and engineers and we sent research reactors to many countries—Chile, South Korea, the Congo, Vietnam—and even information kits describing how to make plutonium. In the future, we simply won't be doing a lot of these things."

Secretary of State Henry Kissinger took the lead in the new American approach, telling the opening session of the United Nations General Assembly in September 1974 that nuclear weapons proliferation was one of the most serious threats to world order. He also gave his backing within the government to new restrictions on nuclear exports. Though ad hoc, these measures effectively stopped all exports of enrichment know-how, which had remained highly classified in any case, and also of know-how and hardware in the formerly wide-open area of reprocessing.

Applications for export licenses on any nuclear technologies now had to run the bureaucratic gauntlet of several different government agencies— ACDA, the State and Defense Departments, and the two successors to the old Atomic Energy Commission, the Energy Research and Development Administration and the Nuclear Regulatory Commission. This reached a high point in March 1975, when the Nuclear Regulatory Commission halted all exports of nuclear fuel and reactors pending a case-by-case evaluation of physical security against possible terrorist attacks.

The new tightfisted stance quickly brought howls of outrage from friends of the nuclear industry, especially the last Director of the Atomic Energy Commission, Dixie Lee Ray. Dr. Ray had just resigned as Assistant Secretary of State under Kissinger, largely over her strong disagreement with the restrictions on exports of sensitive nuclear technologies.

"ACDA and State are taking the U.S. out of the world nuclear market," she warned. "The only thing that happens when we hold up a sale is that a foreign country takes the business away from an American company. The only way the U.S. can hope to influence proliferation is to be a factor in the market."

Fortune magazine made the same complaint in a December 1975 article on "Our Costly Losing Battle Against Nuclear Proliferation." "It seems clear that we are sacrificing too much of our foreign policy on the altar of nonproliferation," argued the article's author, Tom Alexander. "Instead we should be trading our superior nuclear technology for other things of value, economic and political."

The attempt to stuff the nuclear genie back in the bottle was doing nothing to stop the spread of nuclear weapons, the critics charged. But it was losing America the biggest reactor orders ever.

"The deals that the government has so far blocked, discouraged, or delayed included some big ones," reported *Fortune*'s Alexander. Among them were a $4 billion-plus reactor sale to Brazil and a $7 billion sale to Iran, as well as other sales to Libya, Taiwan, and South Korea. "Foreign competitors have already snapped up several of the deals. Some foreign consumers don't even shop for bids in the U.S. anymore, while American vendors decline to offer their wares in several parts of the world."

No wonder the business critics were screaming bloody murder. But the loss of reactor sales was not entirely the fault of antiproliferation efforts.

The initial difficulty started when Richard Nixon was still President, and well before any great concern with the problems of proliferation. At the time, the Atomic Energy Commission was enriching almost all of the uranium fuel for public utility power stations throughout the non-Communist world, and Washington used this near-stranglehold to insist on relatively strict safeguards and also to promote the sales of American light-water reactors. It was a sensible system from the point of view of the American nuclear industry, and it had worked well over the years. But in the early 1970s, President Nixon decided to go even farther in a pro-business direction and to open the potentially lucrative government monopoly in enrichment to private interests, which would be allowed to build a new generation of enrichment plants.

The results were disastrous. The Atomic Energy Commission held back on enlarging its own enrichment plants, and at the same time made a sweeping change in its rules for selling enrichment services. Customers would now have to sign long-term contracts eight years in advance and specify exactly how much fuel they would want to enrich and when. This was a complete break with the previous flexible system, and it created a major crisis for utility executives, who were already reeling from the 1973 OPEC oil embargo and fourfold price hike.

Predictably, the utility executives panicked. Just to be on the safe side, they placed orders for far more enriched fuel than they would ever need, and far more than the Atomic Energy Commission and its unenlarged enrichment plants could ever provide.

But that was just the start. In July 1974, Dr. Ray and her Atomic Energy Commission officials compounded what was really only a paper problem. They announced publicly that their order book was closed, and told the world that they could not guarantee delivery of what had been ordered.

The cutoff angered foreign clients, and was widely seen as a ploy in

Nixon's campaign to open enrichment to private enterprise. It also shook any confidence in America's reliability as a nuclear supplier, and the faith was hardly restored when, in July 1974, President Nixon gave his personal guarantee that the United States would in fact fulfill all enrichment orders. As foreign clients no doubt noticed, Mr. Nixon gave this pledge right before he was forced to resign for his less-than-trustworthy handling of the Watergate scandal.

As might be expected, the loss of confidence carried over into the sale of American reactors. Because of their anxiety over fuel supplies, several prospective purchasers began looking to buy their own enrichment and reprocessing plants, and when the United States now refused to sell such sensitive know-how, the would-be purchasers promptly took their business to those who would.

The clearest case—and the one that would set the stage for the subsequent American intervention in the case of Iraq and Pakistan—was Brazil. The Brazilians had been shopping for as many as eight new power reactors in the 1,300-megawatt range, which represented one of the most ambitious programs of nuclear expansion anywhere in the Third World. With the world's tenth largest industrial economy, and a surprisingly long history of nuclear research in both thorium and uranium technologies, Brazil was looking primarily to ensure its future energy requirments.

The deal seemed a natural for the Yankee traders. Westinghouse was already building Brazil's first power reactor, and was widely believed to have the inside track on the new order. But the Westinghouse reactor was supposed to get its fuel enrichment from the U.S. Atomic Energy Commission, which was now refusing to guarantee the fuel supply. Shaken, the Brazilians asked to buy an enrichment plant of their own, and the Americans, as part of their new antiproliferation policy, refused flat out. The Brazilians then took their business to more eager sellers, and in February 1975, they concluded the nuclear "deal of the century"—not with Westinghouse, but with a group of firms in West Germany.

In the biggest single nuclear deal up to the time, the West Germans agreed to sell Brazil both an enrichment plant and a pilot reprocessing plant, a pilot and a commercial fuel-fabrication plant, and up to eight large power reactors—two by 1985, with an option for six more later.

The German firm Kraftwerk Union, a subsidiary of Siemens, would build the reactors, and the enrichment plant would use the new jet-nozzle system perfected by Professor Erwin Willi Becker, a system that the Germans were also supplying to South Africa. The Germans would provide training for Brazilian technicians, and would work with Brazilian firms in constructing the various plants.

The two countries would also form joint companies to prospect for and mine Brazil's uranium riches, largely on the northern fringes of the Amazon River. The Germans would get at least 20 percent of the final uranium production to help offset the enormous cost of the reactors, and also to enable West Germany to build up its own nuclear power-generating capacity.

The price of all this came to a minimum of $4 billion. But if the Brazilians ordered all eight reactors, the final figure could reach more than $14 billion.

European suppliers were also picking up smaller nuclear sales, and the promise of bigger ones to come, and they were doing it by sweetening the deals with the very technology that Washington would not allow American firms to sell. Self-interested or not, the warnings of Dr. Dixie Lee Ray and the American nuclear industry were proving true. In the wake of Nixon's disastrous effort to open enrichment to private enterprise, the Ford Administration's antiproliferation stance was doing nothing to stop the spread of dangerous nuclear know-how. But it was stopping American firms from doing the spreading.

Washington was clearly in a bind, especially as Brazil was one of the countries most likely to want nuclear weapons as a by-product of their civilian nuclear power program. The country's military dictators had refused "as a matter of principle" to sign the Nuclear Nonproliferation Treaty. They had signed, but not ratified, the Treaty of Tlatelolco. They had committed themselves for the last ten years to carrying out a program to develop "peaceful nuclear explosives," like the one set off by India in May 1974.

The country also had a history of interest in the nuclear option. At one point in the 1950s, the Brazilians had flirted with the top brains in Hitler's atomic weapons project, and had offered safe haven to three of them—Otto Hahn, Paul Haartich, and Wilhelm Groth.

Admiral Alvaro Alberto Motta e Silva, the father of the Brazilian nuclear program, had pushed the German connection even farther, going to Occupied Germany in the early 1950s to buy three gas centrifuges, which could be used for enriching uranium. At the last moment, the American Occupation authorities halted the deal and seized the centrifuges as contraband. But the story of Admiral Alvaro Alberto's quest is still celebrated as a key point in the long and detailed history of frustration that has dogged Brazilian nuclear development.

The nuclear deal with West Germany promised to end that frustration, and also to give the Brazilians the capability to produce nuclear weapons. The West Germans themselves were also under suspicion, at least in some quarters, as the deal might allow them to use a willing Brazil as a secret way around their promise never to build nuclear weapons on German soil.

Washington fought against the sale. American officials first tried to persuade their German allies and competitors that the deal was too dangerous to carry through. But the Germans saw the argument as an attempt to cloak America's economic self-interest in the pious language of antiproliferation. The Americans then considered a major confrontation, which would threaten the Western Alliance and probably fail anyway. In the end, they retreated to the high ground of principle, urging the Germans to press Brazil to the strictest safeguards and, if possible, to some form of joint control of the more sensitive fuel-cycle facilities, especially enrichment and reprocessing.

On the question of joint control, the Americans got nowhere at all. The Brazilians were shifting to nuclear power to reduce their dependence on foreign oil producers, and they were adamantly opposed to any idea of putting themselves back into the position of relying on a new foreign master once they had established their own nuclear industry.

On safeguards, the Americans got more of what they wanted. The Brazilians promised to accept the IAEA safeguards on all German-supplied facilities, and also on any new plants they might build with the same technology during the next twenty years. They agreed not to give any of the know-how to any other country without approval from West Germany and the application of new IAEA safeguards, a provision that would become important in Brazil's later dealings with Iraq. And they promised not to use the German-supplied facilities to build any nuclear explosive device, peaceful or otherwise.

This was still short of Brazil's accepting safeguards on all of its nuclear installations, as would have been required by the Nonproliferation Treaty, and it did nothing to allay the fears that Professor Wohlstetter had raised about the steady upward drift in levels of nuclear capability. Whatever Brazil's intentions when they bought the German technology, they would certainly have what they needed to build the bomb whenever they wanted. And there were certainly Brazilians who saw it just that way. As one official spokesman told us with typical eloquence when we asked him about his country's nuclear intentions: "Take a scenario in the year 2000, when Brazil will be the third power in the world after the United States. We'll be ahead of Japan economically, and almost the double of what Russia is today. And so, with the military consequences of being the third power in the world, how can you answer for that?"

But whatever the risks in the future, there was little the Americans could say. Brazil was playing by the rules of the game, and in early 1976, the IAEA gave the "deal of the century" its blessing. This was at the same time it gave a similar go-ahead to the French contract to build the reprocessing plant in Pakistan.

The failure to stop West Germany from selling reprocessing and enrichment technology to Brazil showed the weakest side of Washington's antiproliferation stance. The world had changed since the heyday of Atoms for Peace, and the United States no longer had the power to dictate what would and would not happen in the world's nuclear industry. Competition was now king, and the best shot at stopping nuclear proliferation was to convince the world's major nuclear producers to set some form of limits to the more dangerous forms of competition.

The Ford Administration set out to bring the nuclear competitors together even before the West Germans clinched the deal with Brazil. The initiative originally included France, West Germany, Great Britain, Canada, Japan, and the Soviet Union, and the "secret seven" met together for the first time in London in April 1975. The group later expanded to fifteen nations and continued to meet every few months. The new participants were Belgium, Italy, the Netherlands, Sweden, Czechoslovakia, East Germany, Poland, and Switzerland.

The Americans had two major purposes in calling together this nuclear OPEC, as it was called by the press. They wanted to reach an agreement that none of the nuclear suppliers would cut any corners on safeguards in trying to coax a sale. And they wanted to convince their competitors to join with the United States in limiting, if not entirely banning, the export of enrichment and reprocessing technology.

The agreement not to skimp on safeguards came fairly quickly. Only the year before, the Swiss energy expert Dr. Claude Zangger had headed up an international committee to specify which nuclear exports should automatically trigger safeguards under the Nonproliferation Treaty. The new Nuclear Suppliers Group, or London Club, tightened and extended the Zangger List, and in November 1975, they agreed on a new set of "Guidelines for Nuclear Transfer."

The guidelines were not a treaty, but a "gentleman's agreement" that each of the nuclear exporters would follow the same set of rules in making sales to any country that did not already have nuclear weapons. Initially secret, the guidelines and "trigger list" were expanded and finally published by the IAEA in 1978.

In accepting the guidelines, the exporters pledged to insist on IAEA safeguards and adequate levels of physical protection against terrorist and other threats before they would sell to another nation any of a long list of sensitive technologies. The list emphasized three of the most dangerous— enrichment and reprocessing, and also heavy water, which could be used in an easy-to-make and easy-to-hide "swimming pool" reactor for making secret stocks of plutonium.

The exporters would also insist that their customers give formal assurances that they would not use the exported technology to make any nuclear explosives, even "peaceful" ones, and that they would permit safeguards on any new facilities based on the same technology.

These provisions all found their way into both the West German agreement with Brazil and the French agreement with Pakistan. But the failings of the London Club were equally apparent in both agreements. The nuclear suppliers were unwilling to insist that their customers permit safeguards on all of their nuclear installations, the so-called "full-scope safeguards" required by the Nonproliferation Treaty. Most telling, the Americans failed completely to convince the London Club to place an outright ban on all exports of reprocessing and enrichment technology.

* * *

Once again, the new American campaign against the spread of nuclear weapons appeared to have come too late. The London Club guidelines would help in the future, no doubt. But they would not undo the damage that the European exporters had already done. That would take more than talk, and in at least two countries the Ford Administration attempted with some success to reverse an already existing danger by taking direct and decisive action. One was South Korea, the other Taiwan.

In South Korea, the military dictatorship of General Park Chung Hee had decided in the early 1970s to build its own nuclear bomb. The Park government was losing faith in its American protectors, who had already started their long withdrawal from Vietnam and were also reducing their troop commitments in Korea itself. Fearing that the Americans would pull out altogether, the Koreans set out to buy a reprocessing plant to extract plutonium from their reactor fuel, and like so many others, they turned to France.

Quite by accident, some of the Korean story turned up in the French Government documents that we had been given on that lonely country road, and the broad outline was not that different from the case of Pakistan. As early as mid-1972, the Koreans were discussing with the French the possible purchase of a large reprocessing plant, ostensibly to meet the needs of the Far Eastern market from 1980. The following year, they extended the project to include a fuel-fabrication plant, and in early 1975 they signed contracts for both facilities. The French firm CERCA was to build the fuel plant. The old standby SGN would build the reprocessing plant. And as South Korea had signed the Nuclear Nonproliferation Treaty, both facilities were to be covered by IAEA safeguards.

During all the negotiations, the South Koreans kept their ambition to build the bomb strictly to themselves. Like the Pakistanis, they were simply building up their peaceful nuclear industry and hoping to sell nuclear services to other nations in their area. But the Americans were not so easy to keep in the dark.

As the world later learned during the U.S. Congressional hearings on the activities of the millionaire Korean wheeler-dealer Park Tong Sun, the Central Intelligence Agency and the electronic wizards of the National Security Agency had the South Korean capital in Seoul wired for sound. Much of the evidence against Park and his alleged attempt to bribe American Congressmen had come from tape recordings of incriminating conversations inside the South Korean presidential mansion, the Blue House, and it appeared that the U.S. Embassy in Seoul could listen in on its Korean ally's highest-level discussions almost at will.

This was the situation following India's nuclear explosion in 1974, when Washington sent a team of intelligence and technical experts to various American Embassies around the world to look for any hint of nuclear intentions. In Korea, the experts found plenty, and on March 8, 1975, the American Ambassador, Richard Sneider, passed the word to his French counterpart, Pierre Landy.

As Ambassador Landy telexed his Foreign Ministry the same day, "In effect, M. Sneider specifically told me that the United States has no doubts that the Koreans have in mind putting to ulterior military ends what they can make use of, such as plutonium."

This is from highly secret French diplomatic correspondence now in our possession. But in June 1975, the South Korean President Park Chung Hee came close to admitting his nuclear intentions in an interview with *The Washington Post*. If the Americans were to withdraw their nuclear umbrella, South Korea would develop its own nuclear arms, he warned, adding, "We have the capacity to do it."

In the following months, the Americans began putting on the pressure, warning Seoul that they might cut off all aid if the Koreans did not give up their nuclear plans, and by the end of the year South Korea officially canceled the contract with France for the reprocessing plant. According to one South Korean diplomat, quoted in the French press, the American pressure "bordered on threat."

Later, the French President, Valéry Giscard d'Estaing, put a good face on the whole affair, telling a press conference in the United States that he personally had vetoed the deal. But the lesson was not lost on either Seoul or Paris, as the French journal *Eurasie Exchanges* summed it up: "The cancellation by Seoul of the order from France of a plutonium plant proves that, in spite of efforts to diversify trading partners, South Korea remains America's private hunting ground."

In Taiwan, the danger had gone even farther. As early as 1969, the Nixon Administration had refused to let an American firm sell the Nationalist Chinese Government a reprocessing plant, and in response the Nationalists did what everyone else was doing, which was to turn to France. Most details of these negotiations have so far remained secret, but the French Government documents now in our possession offer a good insight into what happened.

One of the documents, dated February 5, 1973, is from Dr. Bertrand Goldschmidt, the Director of International Relations for the French Atomic Energy Commission, and is addressed to M. Gilles Curien, the Chief of Scientific Affairs at the Quai d'Orsay. In the note, Dr. Goldschmidt writes of a project for Taiwan of a reprocessing plant able to handle one hundred tons a year of used fuel, the same size as the plant the French would help the Pakistanis to build at Chashma. The Taiwan plant was to be built by the same firm—Saint-Gobain Techniques Nouvelles, or SGN—which was facing keen competition from West Germany and possibly elsewhere, and the note suggests that, as in the case of the Pakistani pilot reprocessing plant, SGN had already supplied the Taiwanese with some sort of smaller reprocessing facility.

"We think that it would be a shame for our industry not to receive the fruits of the action already promised at the time of the furnishing of a reprocessing laboratory," wrote Dr. Goldschmidt. "In effect, we have every reason to believe that German industry is taking a very active interest in the plant, and it is desirable economically that Saint-Gobain is able to get it."

In fact, SGN ended up going into the deal with one of its German competitors, a firm called Uhde-Lurgi. But before anything could come of the project, the Americans effectively vetoed it by threatening a cutoff of military and economic aid to the Nationalist Chinese, thus forcing Taiwan to withdraw.

Taiwan continued its interest, however, and the Americans continued to watch with growing suspicion. In September 1974, in its "Prospects for Further Proliferation of Nuclear Weapons," the U.S. Central Intelligence Agency was extremely clear in its assessment. "Taipei conducts its small nuclear program with a weapon option clearly in mind; and it will be in a position to fabricate a nuclear device after five years or so," the Agency warned. "Taipei's present course probably is leading toward development of nuclear weapons."

Some time later, in June 1976, the French newspaper *Le Monde* reported that inspectors of the International Atomic Energy Agency had visited a research reactor in Taiwan and found ten barrels of used fuel containing 500 grams of plutonium were missing. In August, officials of the U.S. Arms Control and Disarmament Agency and the Energy Research and Development Administration told *The Washington Post* that intelligence reports indicated that Taiwan had been secretly engaged in reprocessing for some time and was producing plutonium for a nuclear weapon.

It is still not clear exactly where the Taiwanese were doing the reprocessing, or if they were using the reprocessing laboratory mentioned by Dr. Goldschmidt as coming from SGN. But as in the case of South Korea, the Americans set out to stop Taiwan from continuing, to the point of actually forcing the Taiwanese to dismantle the facility they were using. According to one nuclear engineer who followed the events in an official capacity, the Americans demanded that Taiwan return certain equipment that the United States had previously supplied, and he quoted one Taiwanese scientist as telling him, "After the Americans got through with us, we wouldn't have even been able to teach physics here on Taiwan."

Clearly, as in South Korea, the United States still had the clout to get its way, and officials in Washington told us in 1981 that, at least for the moment, Taiwan is not an immediate proliferation risk.

Carter Pushes the Issue

India's nuclear test in May 1974 marked the turnabout in American policy, the start of a serious effort to stop the spread of nuclear weapons, especially to countries of the Third World. But in the popular mind, the real revolution seemed to come only with the election as President of the peanut farmer from Georgia who had been a nuclear engineer, Mr. Jimmy Carter.

"We have recently seen India evolve an explosive device derived from a peaceful nuclear power plant, and we now feel that several other nations are on the verge of becoming nuclear explosive powers," President Carter warned in his first major nuclear policy statement on April 7, 1977. "The United States is deeply concerned about the consequences of the uncontrolled spread of this nuclear weapons capability. We can't arrest it immediately and unilaterally. We have no authority over other countries. But we believe that these risks would be increased by the further spread of reprocessing capabilities of the spent nuclear fuel from which explosives can be derived."

Carter's efforts to stop reprocessing began on the home front. "We will defer indefinitely the commercial reprocessing and recycling of the plutonium produced in U.S. nuclear power programs," he declared. The President also took steps to curb the plutonium-producing fast breeder reactor, promising to suspend construction of the demonstration prototype at Clinch River in Tennessee and to delay any decision on the commercial development of a new generation of fast breeder reactors.

Mr. Carter had already opposed reprocessing in a campaign speech in September 1976, and had helped push the then President Gerald Ford to postpone commercial reprocessing, at least temporarily. But the new President's even stronger stand confirmed fears abroad that he was going to escalate the war against plutonium technology everywhere, which he was. His first target was Brazil, and then Pakistan.

To be fair, the attack on plutonium was far from the all-out war on nuclear power that many had expected. As a candidate, Mr. Carter had painted himself as mildly antinuclear, and had openly bid for the support of the growing antinuclear movement. Now, as President, he was trimming. The United States would have to use nuclear power to fill the gap left after developing coal and conserving energy, he declared. According to Administration figures, the gap would be enormous, requiring as many as 400 to 550 light-water reactors in the 1,000-megawatt range by the year 2000.

"The President's energy program envisages a substantial increase in our nuclear power generating capacity," explained Dr. Joseph S. Nye Jr., a Harvard professor whom Mr. Carter brought to the State Department to lead the antiproliferation effort. As Dr. Nye saw it, Washington would oppose only "the premature entry into a plutonium economy."

Even on that, however, the President and Dr. Nye showed signs of barking far worse than they were willing to bite. Their difficulty was obvious. They were treading a very fine line.

On one side, Mr. Carter's more antinuclear supporters and advisers were arguing that the only sure way to put an end to nuclear proliferation was to put an end to nuclear power. They wanted the President to go all the way and set an example for the rest of the world by renouncing nuclear power at home and urging its abandonment abroad. In effect, this would have pitted President Carter against the leaders of West Germany, France, Great Britain, and Japan, and put him in the unlikely position of appealing over their heads to antinuclear sentiment in each country to overthrow established nuclear power programs. It was a revolutionary approach, to be sure, and one that might even have worked, given the strength of the international antinuclear movement at the time.

On the other side, the leaders of the Western industrialized nations and the international nuclear industry were rushing headlong toward the most rapid possible development of reprocessing, the fast breeder, and the very plutonium economy that Carter opposed. The Allied leaders had all committed themselves to large nuclear programs in their own countries, and were determined that antiproliferation measures not get in the way of nuclear exports. Whether or not other countries, especially those with huge oil reserves, really needed to buy nuclear know-how to meet their energy needs, the French and West Germans in particular wanted to export it, both to cover the cost of their own nuclear programs and to pay for the ever-rising price of their oil imports.

Trying to bob and weave between these two opposing camps, the Carter Administration ended up losing credibility with both. In retrospect, it is clear that Mr. Carter never seriously considered the revolutionary antinuclear approach, not with the risk of wrecking the Western alliance and relations with Japan. Antiproliferation just was not that important to him. Yet even if Jimmy Carter was something less than the Ayatollah Khomeini of the antinuclear revolution, that is how many on the pronuclear side came to see him.

Carter's way out was to give in before the battle had begun. Even as he was making such a fuss about reprocessing, he quickly accepted the fact that Europe and Japan might have a need to reprocess plutonium and also to develop their fast breeders, which posed far and away the greatest long-term threat of proliferation.

"We are not trying to impose our will on those nations like Japan and France and Britain and Germany which already have reprocessing plants in operation," the American President conceded in his April 7 statement. Carter pointed out that "they have a special need that we don't have" because of their lack of any domestic oil or gas.

Dr. Nye, his antiproliferation man, went out of his way to assure the Allies in the same fashion. "We are not anti-breeder," he told the Germans early in the new Administration. "We believe that a breeder program is an important energy insurance policy. . . . What we oppose is premature movement toward a breeder economy."

The retreat was most obvious in the way Carter pulled back from using his biggest gun, the continuing American control over much of the world's nuclear fuel. On this he started strong—and never finished.

The United States had lost much of its earlier monopoly on enrichment, mostly to the Soviet Union, which was now supplying as much as two-thirds of the fuel enrichment needed by nuclear power plants in Western Europe. But the Americans were still major suppliers, and even more to the point, Washington still had legal control over what would happen to any of the enriched fuel they had supplied in the past. If Washington said no, none of the already used U.S.-enriched fuel could be sent for reprocessing. Since most of the fuel waiting to be reprocessed in Europe and Japan had been originally enriched in the United States, the Americans had a life-and-death hold over the future of most of the world's major reprocessing facilities.

This control of new and old fuel gave the Americans enormous clout, and for a time it looked as if they intended to use it. The Ford Administration had already stopped all further shipments of enriched fuel in July 1976, pending a full-scale review of nuclear export policy. In September, in his campaign for the presidency, Mr. Carter had gone even farther, promising not to sell any more fuel to any country that insisted on going ahead with its own national reprocessing plan.

Once in office, the new Carter Administration followed through, and continued to hold up the fuel shipments. This was not an announced policy, and in February 1977 the State Department denied that there was any official embargo. But the Administration meticulously subjected each shipment to an endless process of approval, and the delays and interruptions slowed the fuel shipments to a trickle.

On reprocessing, the initial line was even tougher. As Dr. Nye announced it, the United States would consider any request for permission to reprocess U.S.-supplied fuel on a case-by-case basis. He added, though, that Washington would give approval only in cases of "clear need." The country making the request would have to show that it had to send the spent fuel for reprocessing in order to keep its reactors running, or to relieve extreme congestion in fuel storage.

The new strong-arm measures upset the normal running of research and power reactors, especially in Western Europe. They also directly threatened the opening of the new Tokai-Mura Reprocessing Plant in Japan and the expansion of the Windscale Reprocessing Plant in Britain and the Cap la Hague facility in France. And they endangered the future of the fast breeder reactor, to which Japan and much of Western Europe were committed. All of this made the Europeans and Japanese extremely angry.

"For twenty years, we have followed U.S. guidelines on nuclear policy," a Japanese diplomat told the Americans, according to one press account. "Now you are saying you made a complete mistake."

"The Americans sit on 30 percent of the world's coal, and say there is no economic necessity for Japan to recycle plutonium, and develop fast breeders," another Japanese authority noted. "We call that hypocrisy."

The Germans and French complained even more bitterly. This was an American *diktat*, an attempt to stop superior European technology, like the denial of landing rights to the Concorde, they charged. As they saw it,

President Carter had given encouragement to the light-water reactor, in which America led the field. But he was coming out against reprocessing and the fast breeder, where European technology was far ahead.

"France is definitely going ahead with advanced nuclear technology, including the construction of fast breeder reactors," one French official explained at the time. "Unlike the United States, we have little coal and no oil resources. We must develop nuclear technology to meet our energy needs."

Even the Eurocrats of the Common Market raised their voice, sending Commissioner Guido Brunner to Washington to protest against the "political embargo" on fuel shipments.

The outcry was far greater than anything the Administration had expected. The Europeans and Japanese were not about to let a peanut farmer from Georgia tell them how to run their nuclear program, and Carter's attempt threatened to become the single most divisive issue among the Western industrial nations.

The European-led protests had an effect. Carter softened his bark, and in May 1977, right before the Allied Summit Meeting in Britain, Washington eased up on the fuel stoppages. Soon after, the Administration also gave up altogether on trying to stop reprocessing in Europe and Japan, and even admitted defeat in its effort to stop the West German sale of enrichment and reprocessing technology to Brazil.

This last was perhaps President Carter's greatest defeat. In his election campaign, he had singled out the Brazilian deal as especially dangerous, and in his very first weeks in office he used the fuel stoppage expressly to put pressure on both West Germany and Brazil. Vice President Walter Mondale made a personal visit to West German Chancellor Helmut Schmidt in January, and Under Secretary of State Warren Christopher visited both Brasilia and Bonn in March in order to limit the deal.

It was all to no avail. The new effort failed, as had those of President Ford, and in April 1977, even before Carter formally announced his new policy on proliferation, the West Germans announced that they had already begun to send to Brazil the blueprints for both the enrichment and reprocessing plants.

The only offsetting gain for Washington came three months later, in June, when Chancellor Schmidt announced that he would join France in stopping any further exports of reprocessing technology, at least temporarily. But Schmidt made clear that the pledge was only "on the assumption that agreements made in the past concerning the delivery of nuclear fuels will be observed." And he excluded any ban on the present contract with Brazil, or a future ban on the export of enrichment technology.

Brazil would have the bomb if they wanted it. But what of Pakistan? The French contract with the Pakistanis was the one major remaining test where American policy had any chance of winning, and the test was to prove the most interesting of all.

FOUR

PAKISTAN

The French Say No!

If India builds the bomb, we will eat grass or leaves, even go
hungry. But we will get one of our own. We have no alternative.
—Zulfikar Ali Bhutto,
1965

China, India, the U.S.S.R., and Israel in the Middle East possess
the atomic arm. No Muslim country has any. If Pakistanis had
such a weapon, it would reinforce the power of the Muslim
World.
—General Mohammed Zia-ul-Haq,
July 1978

You are breaking a contract. I never thought the French would
do this.
—General Mohammed Zia-ul-Haq,
July 1978

Ever since Prime Minister Zulfikar Ali Bhutto asked his scientists to build the Islamic bomb, the Pakistanis had posed a major threat to any hopes of stopping the spread of nuclear weapons. Pakistan had the scientific skill. It had the financing from its Arab allies. And it had the determination—in part to walk tall in a world dominated by the nuclear superpowers, in part to stand strong against its traditional rivals, the Indians.

"If India builds the bomb, we will eat grass or leaves, even go hungry," said Mr. Bhutto as far back as 1965. "But we will get one of our own. We have no alternative."

Once the Indians had staged their nuclear test in May 1974, the die was truly cast. Only a few months later, in September 1974, the CIA's "Prospects for Further Proliferation of Nuclear Weapons" put the Pakistanis on its list of likelies. The report suggested that Pakistan "would need at least a decade to carry out a nuclear weapons development program," which would have put the target date in 1984. But, the CIA warned, they "might detonate a demonstrative device earlier—perhaps considerably earlier by using purchased materials or by obtaining extensive foreign assistance."

The CIA's estimate came a year after the Pakistanis had signed their first contract with SGN for the industrial reprocessing plant at Chashma, and only a month before they would sign the final contract.

The Americans continued to watch the situation closely, and in December the U.S. Embassy in Islamabad brought to Washington's attention two newspaper interviews with Prime Minister Zulfikar Ali Bhutto. In both, Mr. Bhutto appeared to be denying any real desire to go nuclear. He was, it seemed, simply using the threat to get the Americans to lift the arms embargo they had imposed at the time of the Bangladesh War, and to permit Pakistan to buy conventional arms and equipment as a deterrent against India's nuclear threat.

"We must have a sufficient conventional deterrent," he told one American interviewer. "If not, then we'll say we can't do anything but explode some sort of nuclear device. We are not racing for the bomb," he added. "If we get even a modest contribution, we shall not find it necessary to proceed."

In the other interview, Bhutto said much the same. "If we can get conventional weapons, we would prefer it," he said. But if not, "we take the big step forward and concentrate all our energies on acquiring nuclear capability."

Bhutto mentioned that the reprocessing plant was "in the pipeline," but hinted that "the pipeline can still be dried up" if the arms embargo were lifted. He also announced that Pakistan had acquired a "second line of defense"—some $450 million in loans for the current year from Iran and the Arab countries, which, he said, "was just the beginning."

The Americans apparently gave Bhutto the benefit of the doubt, and lifted the embargo in February 1975. They also put most of their antiproliferation energy into the London Club, where they pushed the French and other exporters to stiffen the general approach to safeguards, including those to be applied to the Chashma plant. The French proved receptive, and when the final safeguards agreement for Chashma came before the IAEA Board of Governors in February 1976, the American delegate had to vote to approve it.

But the Ford Administration still had "reservations," as it told the French the following month, and in June 1976, the U.S. Congress passed a rider to the Foreign Aid Appropriations Bill barring all economic and military aid to any nation involved in importing or exporting reprocessing or unsafeguarded enrichment plants. This was the Symington Amendment, named after its author, the senior Democratic Senator from Missouri, Stuart Symington, and it set the stage for much of what would follow.

In the meantime, the Pakistanis were quick to defend the Chashma plant, with its industrial capacity to reprocess some one hundred tons a year of spent nuclear fuel.

"Anybody can make a bomb," one Pakistani engineer told the authoritative *Nucleonics Week*. "You don't need sophisticated technology for that."

"We ourselves have enough technology for dirty reprocessing, for reprocessing which would produce plutonium for a bomb and nothing else," said another Pakistani.

Building a bomb would jeopardize further imports for Pakistan's peaceful nuclear industry, the sources insisted. "We're not going to barter away our future, and the nuclear power program is Pakistan's future," one of them added.

Washington remained unconvinced, and on August 8, Secretary of State Henry Kissinger flew to Pakistan for a showdown with his old friend Ali Bhutto. Dr. Kissinger had worked closely with Bhutto in building the bridge to China and in trying to contain the Bangladesh crisis, and found the Pakistani "of world stature." But this time Kissinger was coming to put his foot down.

In an off-the-record briefing on the plane, he told the reporters flying with him that the United States would use the Symington Amendment to cut off all aid to the Pakistanis if they persisted in going ahead with the reprocessing plant. With Bhutto himself, he brandished the same stick, and also held out the carrot of as many as 110 Corsair A-7 jet fighters, fully equipped with assorted missiles, rockets, and cannons. This was one of the most flexible American jets, and it had already caught the eye of the Pakistanis.

Bhutto himself told two different versions of the meeting. In one, he raised the nuclear issue rather elliptically.

"Dr. Henry Kissinger, the Secretary of State for the United States, has a brilliant mind," Bhutto later wrote in his final political testament. "He told me that I should not insult the intelligence of the United States by saying that Pakistan needed the reprocessing plant for her energy needs. In reply, I told him that I will not insult the intelligence of the United States by discussing the energy needs of Pakistan, but by the same token, he should not discuss the plant at all."

In this same passage, Bhutto openly acknowledged that his goal was a nuclear capability, and made his famous statement that all of the other great civilizations—the Christians, Jews, Hindus and Communists—had the capability, and now the Islamic civilization would have it too.

Bhutto gave a second, bloodier version of his meeting with Dr. Kissinger in a dramatic speech to Pakistan's National Assembly in April 1977. Here Bhutto claimed that Kissinger had personally threatened him. Drop Chashma, he quoted Kissinger as warning him, or else "we will make a horrible example of you."

Later, the threat would seem prophetic, especially after General Zia-ul-Haq overthrew Bhutto and then hanged him as a murderer. But in spite of any warnings, Bhutto held firm. Pakistan was not Korea. It was not even the old Pakistan, the West's "most allied ally," and Washington no longer pulled the strings. Not when it came to the Islamic bomb.

Kissinger left Pakistan empty-handed, and flew off to France, where he hoped to take a small holiday near Deauville. But he also found time to press Paris on the Pakistani contract, apparently not with any direct threats, but with a promise that if the French would cooperate, he would find some way to make it worth their while.

The French reacted sharply. The Quai d'Orsay called in the American

Chargé d'Affaires and expressed its surprise and displeasure at Kissinger's attempt to break the contract between France and Pakistan. The Gaullist Jacques Chirac was still Prime Minister, though not for much longer, and he too blasted the interference.

"This is a question of sovereignty," he declared. "It is not for a third country to intervene, especially the United States, which approved the contract in question on March 18 through its representative [at the IAEA]."

On Pakistan, the old imperial arm twisting was not yet out of season. Despite French protests, the attempt appears to have born fruit, if not in forcing Pakistan to cancel the contract, then at least in triggering a marked change in French policy.

The change came surprisingly quickly. Less than three weeks later, on September 1, the French President, Giscard d'Estaing, announced that he would personally head a high-level Council on Foreign Nuclear Policy, which was intended to open policy to considerations beyond the rather limited export orientation of the Ministry of Industry and the Atomic Energy Commission, the CEA. Dr. Kissinger then met personally with Giscard on September 7, and in October the new Council signaled that France would refrain from any more "cut-throat competition."

As one source summed it up for *Nucleonics Week*: "This means nobody should say 'Buy with us and we'll go easy on safeguards,' or 'Buy reactors from us and we'll throw in a reprocessing plant.'"

This came at the time President Ford called for a moratorium on any further exports of reprocessing technology, and in the following weeks French officials began the first in a series of leaks to well-placed journalists. France would not break the contract with Pakistan, the officials whispered. That would cause far too much of an uproar from the Gaullists, and especially from M. Chirac, who had just resigned as Prime Minister in a fight with Giscard. But if the Pakistanis, like the South Koreans, wanted to withdraw from the contract, France would not object.

These were only the whispers, not the official policy, and on December 16, the Council for Nuclear Foreign Policy issued a new statement. France would finally agree explicitly to stop selling reprocessing technology abroad, the Council declared. But, it insisted, the new ban would *not* affect old contracts, and especially not the contract with Pakistan for the reprocessing plant at Chashma.

On January 20, 1977, Jimmy Carter became President of the United States, and one of his biggest priorities was to stop the spread of dangerous nuclear technology, not least to America's former ally Pakistan.

From the start, Carter and his advisers understood that the United States could never do the job single-handedly.

"France in particular was well placed to lead a coalition that could defeat U.S. views," recalled Dr. Joseph Nye in a recent essay on his experiences in the fight to curb nuclear proliferation. "With its strong nuclear program and domestic political support, France was a leading country in the nuclear field.

French leadership would be essential in any refurbishing of the international [antiproliferation] regime. Our views on plutonium use had to be expressed in a manner that encouraged France to play a central part in supporting the [antiproliferation] regime."

France was especially central to the problem of Pakistan, where the French firm SGN had the contract to build the industrial reprocessing plant at Chashma. As the Americans saw it, the plant made no sense economically in Pakistan's still limited nuclear power program. And it posed a decided military threat.

"A large commercial-scale reprocessing plant can provide a large amount of weapons-usable materials very quickly if safeguards are broken," the well-informed Dr. Nye told us in April 1981. "It's the difference between having quite a large arsenal of weapons-usable material quite quickly, as opposed to having to eke it out in small quantities at a time. I imagine the materials that would be available from this plant if safeguards were broken would be somewhere between fifteen and twenty bombs straightaway, as opposed to much smaller amounts that would have to be done through clandestine means, or by other means."

As Nye recalled, the Carter Administration began discussing the threat with France in early February 1977, and the French seemed receptive to what the Americans had to say. But the French Government could not be seen to be giving in to American pressure, not with M. Chirac and the Gaullists now in opposition.

The new French Prime Minister, Raymond Barre, summed up the position in a statement on February 10. France would carry out the contract with Pakistan, he declared, "unless Pakistan does not wish to continue with it."

The French attitude reflected a keen reckoning of their own interests. Selling a reprocessing plant was not that big a deal financially. Its main importance was as a sweetener to win the sale of reactors. And if the United States and other main competitors would refrain from offering reprocessing, then France could go along without losing very much at all.

"The sale of a reprocessing plant in itself is a pretty small affair on the scale of nuclear contracts; a few hundred million francs . . . where a power plant is figured at several billions," explained the journal of the French Atomic Energy Commission, *Les Echos.* "Such a sale could only be thought of properly if it makes possible the simultaneous sale of power reactors, as was the case in the fabulous German-Brazilian contract."

No reactors, no great interest in selling reprocessing plants, especially if the Americans were so opposed. That is how the French were coming to see their contract with Pakistan in the first months of 1977. As far as they were concerned, it was up to the Pakistanis.

For the Carter Administration, this seemed a good start. Washington was already discussing the contract with Pakistan, arguing that building nuclear weapons could actually weaken the country's security, especially if India responded by building up its own nuclear arsenal. The Americans also maintained a steadily mounting pressure on the Bhutto government, while holding open the offer of the 110 A-7 Corsair attack planes if Pakistan dropped the reprocessing plant.

As Dr. Nye explained it, the American goal was twofold: first, to stop the plant if possible. If this were not feasible, the Americans at least wanted to delay it in the hope that the Pakistanis could be convinced in time to change their minds.

In pressing the Pakistanis, the Carter Administration got a big assist from the Canadians, who had been going through a long period of soul-searching ever since the Indians used the Candu reactor to get plutonium for their nuclear test. As a result, the Canadians were putting tough new restrictions on all their nuclear exports and, paradoxically, this came down hardest on India's chief rival, the Pakistanis.

Ottawa demanded that the Pakistanis promise not to follow India in making nuclear explosives, and that they agree to open all their nuclear facilities to safeguards. The Canadians also demanded that Pakistan agree to keep safeguards for the life of the Candu reactor in Karachi, even if Canada and Pakistan were to end their bilateral nuclear relations. Predictably, the Pakistanis refused, calling the demands "totally unreasonable," and in late December 1975 the Canadians cut off all spare parts for the Karachi reactor and all shipments of natural uranium fuel rods.

All this hurt badly, further limiting the operations of the Karachi reactor. But the biggest pressures on the Bhutto government were coming from inside the country, and they were not necessarily nuclear.

The Pakistanis held national elections on March 7, 1977, and in a bitterly fought campaign, Bhutto's People's Party won an overwhelming victory over the Pakistan National Alliance, a right-wing coalition dominated by the ultra-religious Jamaat-i-Islami. The opposition immediately charged that Bhutto had rigged the election, and their militants took to the streets, staging riots, burning buses, and attacking Bhutto personally as a drunk, an atheist, and a man not fit to rule an Islamic country.

Most observers believed the elections had been less than honest, though almost everyone agreed that Bhutto's party would have won a good majority even without the fraud. But his opponents were no longer fighting about the election. They were out to bring Bhutto down. Bhutto saw their opposition as having outside support, a replay of the destabilization of President Salvador Allende in Chile in 1973, neatly staged, in his view, by the American CIA. He saw the same hand operating in Pakistan.

In his mind, this was Dr. Kissinger's threat come true. The Americans were using the Islamic right wing "to make a horrible example" of Bhutto, and this was mainly because he had refused to give up the Chashma plant.

"The bloodhounds are after my blood," he warned the National Assembly in April. Foreign dollars were pouring in to pay for the agitation against him. A foreign hand was trying to force him out.

Mr. Bhutto even brought these charges to the attention of the new American Secretary of State, Cyrus Vance, and according to Pakistan's then Attorney General, Mr. Vance never refuted them.

Whatever the truth of Mr. Bhutto's allegations, neither he nor his followers ever provided any serious evidence of CIA involvement, and it seems unlikely on the face of it that the new Carter Administration would have resorted so quickly to covert action. But whoever was behind it, the destabilization worked, and in the early hours of July 5, the Army Chief of Staff, General Mohammed Zia-ul-Haq, staged a bloodless coup and brought the military back to power.

General Zia declared that the military would preside over new elections in October, and both Bhutto and his opponents would be free to run. Before the new campaigning could start, however, Zia had Bhutto arrested and charged with ordering the killing of a political opponent. Instead of elections, the Pakistani nation was treated to a highly publicized murder trial of its best-known leader.

As for General Zia himself, he turned out to be "a true soldier of Islam," closely allied to the right-wing Jamaat-i-Islami, and as the Chief Martial Law Administrator, he worked hard to make Pakistan a model Islamic republic, complete with puritanical laws and public floggings.

Bhutto was convinced that a chief purpose of the coup was to stop the Chashma Plant. This may be so, but the evidence indicates that the new Pakistani leaders made no change in their country's negotiating position about the plant, even as an international controversy began to grow on the issue.

As the political pressure against Bhutto mounted in June, the French had given the impression that they were dragging their feet on fulfilling the Chashma contract. According to one story, they stopped the shipment of essential blueprints, including plans for the chopping machine needed to break up the irradiated fuel rods before they could be chemically treated. Another story indicated that the French government agency that guarantees export credits was holding up credits and guarantees on any equipment for Chashma.

On the other hand, the SGN chief, François-Xavier Poincet, later told *Nucleonics Week* that his firm had already sent Pakistan "about 95 percent of all plans," including the plans for the chopping machine. The rest of the plans were "without significance," he insisted. The Pakistanis had what they needed to build the plant themselves.

Nucleonics Week added that construction had begun on the site at Chashma, and also carried reports from Karachi that Saudi Arabia would provide a loan to cover the purchase of the plant, in return for training by the Pakistanis in nuclear power techniques.

In a later interview with us, Poincet confirmed the 95 percent figure, and insisted that the Pakistanis already had what they needed, without any further help from SGN.

In the meantime, President Giscard announced once again that "the contract will be honored," while the Bhutto government, in one of its last acts, allocated $40 million for Chashma in its budget for the coming year. Only when all of the world's nuclear weapons were destroyed would Pakistan abandon the reprocessing plant, Mr. Bhutto declared.

That was before the July 5 coup. Afterward, the plot thickened. At the end of July, the American antiproliferation chief Joseph Nye made an unpublicized trip to Pakistan amid charges that the CIA had backed General Zia's coup. Word of Nye's visit leaked out, and the ousted Mr. Bhutto went on the attack. Dr. Nye's visit proved the international conspiracy, he claimed, and all because the Bhutto government had refused to abandon the Chashma plant.

The former Prime Minister was grasping at straws in order to buttress his weakened political position. Using Dr. Nye's visit for his own purposes, General Zia announced that he would continue with Chashma and brook no delays of any kind. According to the official statement following Nye's talks with the new government, the positions of Pakistan and the United States "remained as divergent as before."

If the Americans had backed the coup to stop Chashma, they had backed the wrong horse. The Pakistanis were committed. Whoever ruled in Islamabad—Bhutto or Zia or the Prophet himself—there would be no turning back on the Chashma plant. The nation's pride was at stake. No Pakistani leader could now give in to foreign pressure, and especially not to pressure from the United States.

For the Americans, the lesson was still to be learned. Washington continued to put pressure on Pakistan's new military government, and cut off economic and military aid in September 1977, the first use of the Symington Amendment. If there was to be any stopping Chashma now, the initiative would have to come from France.

In September, Pakistan's leading diplomat, Agha Shahi, flew to Paris. An aristocratic and highly polished performer, Shahi had proved himself a wily survivor through all of Pakistan's political wars, and now with the confidence of General Zia, he had come to press the French to stop their delays and get on with the Chashma contract.

One of Shahi's first calls was on SGN and its then President and General Director, François-Xavier Poincet, who described the meeting to us when we interviewed him at his home outside of Paris. A storyteller above all else, the jolly Poincet was at the top of his form.

"We met, and Agha Shahi explained for a full hour why we should keep on working for Pakistan," Poincet told us. "I told him I fully agreed with him, but that I was not the right address. I told him he should tell the same thing to the Foreign Minister."

After seeing Poincet, Shahi did get to the Quai d'Orsay, home of the French Foreign Ministry, which was the right address. He saw Foreign Minister Louis de Guiringaud, and the skillful Pakistani put the case for better French cooperation on Chashma. Unlike Poincet and SGN, M. de Guiringaud already had a different course in mind. He wanted Pakistan "to study a modification of the fuel reprocessing so that it would not produce pure plutonium."

The idea was to change the technology at Chashma. The new process would still treat the spent fuel. But instead of extracting pure plutonium, it would yield a mixture of plutonium and uranium, which could not be used in making nuclear weapons.

The Americans had been studying this "co-processing" for some time, and the U.S. Arms Control and Disarmament Agency saw it as a possible alternative to the standard reprocessing and recycling of plutonium. But the whole idea was "iffy." No one had tried co-processing in practice, and the Pakistanis would not be able to use the new mixture of plutonium and uranium as a nuclear fuel except in a fast breeder reactor, which they would not have until the 1990s, if then.

This is what the Quai d'Orsay wanted the Pakistanis to consider, and Shahi did not like it at all. From Bhutto's first meeting with his scientists under the tent in Multan in 1972, the goal of the Pakistani nuclear program was to get plutonium for the Islamic bomb, and Shahi, as the envoy of Pakistan's new military government, was not about to go back on the original commitment.

The two diplomats—Agha Shahi and de Guiringaud—put a good face on their disagreement over the new French proposal.

"I have confirmed to Mr. Shahi that the contract will be honored by France," declared de Guiringaud.

"Cooperation between our two countries is proceeding according to plan," replied Agha Shahi. He had been "strongly impressed by M. de Guiringaud's comprehension," and sure that there would be "a tightening and a deepening" of Pakistan's relations with France.

The ringing declarations completely fooled the press. In November 1976, almost a year before, *The New York Times* had reported that French officials wanted secretly to kill the Chashma contract. Now the same paper reported that France had just given "a seemingly irrevocable pledge" to go ahead with Chashma.

In fact, the opposite was true. Before, the French were leaving the decision to Pakistan. Now, for the first time, they were trying to kill the contract, or at least to cripple it by insisting on the new co-processing, which would deny to the Pakistanis the weapons-usable plutonium they wanted.

This was the real turning point in French policy toward the Chashma plant, and a rather subtle sign of the new direction came in November 1977, when the French Government took control of the firm doing the actual work, M. Poincet's SGN. The government did this by the simple expedient of buying 66 percent of SGN's shares from the Saint-Gobain holding company, shifting majority ownership to the French Atomic Energy Commission through its industrial subsidiary Cogema (Compagnie Général des Matières Nucléaires). M. Poincet remained top man until June 1979, and continued to push for fulfilling the original contract. But his power in the new SGN—now Société Générale pour le Technique Nouvelle—steadily diminished in the face of official French policy.

As diplomats in Washington saw it, the French were finally joining the good guys, and the new spirit of cooperation was especially clear when President Jimmy Carter flew to France in January 1978 for talks with President Giscard d'Estaing. According to official statements, the two men were drawing ever closer together in their talks about proliferation. Skeptics were quick to point out, though, that Mr. Carter had taken steps only days before the visit to secure landing rights at New York's Kennedy Airport for the controversial supersonic airliner, the Concorde, and the two Presidents had managed a neat trade-off involving the Chashma plant and the French-built airplane.

Within months it became clear that even as Paris was drawing closer to Washington, its growing strains with Pakistan were finally breaking into the open. Once again the voice was that of Agha Shahi, talking to the international press from Islamabad. "We are not satisfied with the rhythm of French deliveries for this plant," he declared on January 7, 1978. The French had not met their obligations for nine months, he claimed. And the Pakistanis were not happy.

On co-processing, the suave Shahi was even sharper. "Pakistan will not accept any change or modification in the agreement signed with France for the supply of a nuclear reprocessing plant," he announced. "Pakistan has adhered to all the safeguards suggested by France. We are ready to discuss additional measures. But we are counting on France to honor her signature."

The French were on the spot, and on February 20, Giscard sent a special envoy to Pakistan to meet with General Zia himself. The man chosen for this delicate mission was the Secretary of the Council for Foreign Nuclear Policy, the distinguished former civil servant and business executive, André Jacomet.

We visited M. Jacomet at his elegant Paris apartment on four different occasions, and on one he told us the story of his first trip to Pakistan.

"My message was that we didn't want to go ahead with the plant as it was," he told us. "That we wanted to find a solution to change the plans so that the plant did not produce plutonium."

Jacomet discussed the proposed change with General Zia, and also with Munir Ahmed Khan, who had managed to survive the military coup and stay on as chief of the Pakistan Atomic Energy Commission. Neither of them wanted the revision. According to Jacomet, the best Munir Khan could offer was to suggest a different modification, which in the end would still have given the Pakistanis access to plutonium.

For the French, the moment of decision was at hand. The Pakistanis were insisting on plutonium. The French knew better than anyone that the Chashma plant had no economic justification. And the Americans had compiled a secret intelligence dossier on Pakistan intentions, which French officials had seen by this time.

"We were convinced that Pakistan wanted the atomic bomb," M. Jacomet confided to us. "The only way was not to pursue the contract." His colleagues on the Council on Foreign Nuclear Policy agreed, and France set out to break the Chashma contract.

What happened next is not reflected in the secret diplomatic correspondence in our possession. But, according to SGN's Poincet, the government sent the firm a letter in February or March 1978 telling it to stop work on the project.

"We had no indication that the French Government would submit to the pressures of the American Government," Poincet told us. "After Kissinger raised problems in August 1976, the first French reaction was that it should honor its commitments and its contracts."

Poincet suggested to us that the Americans' interest in Chashma was motivated not by concern about nuclear proliferation, but by commercial jealousy. "It's devilish, you know," he mused. "The Americans are backward in reprocessing. They cannot bear to see the world market taken over by another country before they are ready. They believe they have a God-given right to tell others what to do, but their real God is American business. It's absolutely devilish."

Pressure or not, the French Government had ordered the now state-owned SGN to stop, and according to Poincet, "We had to notify Pakistan. The Pakistanis then started a diplomatic action with the French Government."

The diplomatic action included threats to block all commercial contracts with France. According to one published account, the Zia government postponed payment on the sale of some Renault-Saviem trucks, and also threatened to suspend negotiations for the purchase of several French Airbuses.

Paris replied with typical French elegance and public deceit. On June 14, at a packed press conference in the Élysée Palace, President Valéry Giscard d'Estaing led the entire world to believe that the contract was still on, though under continuing negotiations.

"The sale of nuclear technology to Pakistan has no military application," he told the reporters. "The Pakistani authorities have repeatedly pledged that the plant would be used only for peaceful purposes. That is why negotiations are under way to increase the safeguards concerning the peaceful use of the installation."

It was all an act. Giscard was sounding positive "just to mix the deck," Jacomet later admitted to us. The very next day, June 15, 1978, the Council on Foreign Nuclear Policy formally decided to break the Chashma contract once and for all.

According to the secret minutes of the meeting, which we managed to see, the decision sounded resolute: "To stop definitively the execution of the contract of 18 October 1974 between the Pakistan Atomic Energy Commission and Saint-Gobain Techniques Nouvelles for the design and construction of a plant for reprocessing irradiated fuel in Pakistan."

That left only one problem—to minimize the reaction from the Pakistanis. Once again, Giscard turned to Jacomet, who set off on his second trip to Pakistan in mid-July.

On route, Jacomet stopped first in Tehran, where he sought help from the Shah's government. The Iranians told him that they were not in favor of Pakistan having the bomb. "But the truth is that they were not ready to put any real pressure on Pakistan. They just weren't interested," he told us.

According to Jacomet, the French also urged Saudi Arabia to help. But the Saudis were not willing to press the Pakistanis either. In fact, they had earlier backed Bhutto's nuclear project, and only a few days before Jacomet headed East, General Zia appealed to the same Islamic sentiments in an interview with two Saudi newspapers, an Nadona and al Medina. The French Ambassador in Saudi Arabia had sent translations to his counterpart in Pakistan, and copies would have been available at the French Embassy in Islamabad when Jacomet arrived on July 17. The English translations from the French came from the American Embassy in Islamabad, though not with the Embassy's knowledge.

"The United States Government wants to pressure France not to deliver to Islamabad plants for peaceful use," General Zia declared in the interview. "But Pakistan . . . is a free country, proud of its history. I let the French Government know that they had to respect the agreements made."

"But France keeps quiet," he went on. "China, India, the U.S.S.R., and Israel in the Middle East possess the atomic arm. No Muslim country has any. If Pakistan had such a weapon, it would reinforce the power of the Muslim World."

Not vintage Bhutto, perhaps. But Zia was singing the same song, and only days before André Jacomet landed in Pakistan.

Jacomet told us the story with great feeling. This had been one of the most important missions of his long and distinguished career, and he liked to think he had represented France well. He recalled with a smile that he met first with Agha Shahi and then later with Zia at the General's home. Shahi and Munir Khan were both there, and Jacomet vividly remembered being offered coffee by a servant "dressed in a colorful costume, though I don't exactly remember why."

Jacomet was carrying with him a personal letter from Giscard to Zia. As the Pakistanis remember it, the French letter urged "a new effort" at nuclear cooperation and offered to give aid to Pakistan "to help her to meet her nuclear energy needs and to acquire mastery of the necessary know-how."

The words were wily, but the meaning clear. The French were still waiting to help Pakistan with what it needed, which was reactors for nuclear power. They were unwilling to help with what was not necessary, which was a reprocessing plant.

Jacomet added a little speech of his own, in which he insisted that the new

French policy was not to sell any reprocessing technology, and that Paris was not discriminating in any way against the Pakistanis.

Jacomet had expected a sharp, even violent reaction. But Zia was cool, firm. As Jacomet told us, "After I spoke, Zia said, 'You are breaking a contract. I never thought the French would do this.'

"He was full of self-control," Jacomet recalled. "Surely, he's not the most clever man in the world. But he was a good diplomat, a politician. During all the negotiations, he was more a diplomat than a simple military man."

In all, the meeting lasted forty minutes. Zia asked Jacomet to stay an extra day so that he could prepare a letter for Jacomet to take back to Giscard. This was Pakistan's official reply, and it has remained secret to this day. But Pakistani sources recall it with a smile.

"I must state in all frankness that we find it difficult to agree with the justification offered by your government for this far-reaching denial," General Zia wrote to Giscard. "Taking into account the possible impact on the future course of relations between our two countries, I hesitate to accept the decision as the last word on the subject."

In the months that followed, Zia's words would take on a hidden meaning. If the French were not ready to say something else, and carry out the terms of the contract, the Pakistanis were ready to take the initiative themselves.

12

The Kindly Dr. Khan

Dr. Abdul Qadeer Khan . . . the most successful nuclear spy since Klaus Fuchs and Alan Nunn May took their secrets to the Kremlin.

—*The Observer*,
London,
December, 1979

He was an amusing person. For instance, he was always offering cookies and sweeties to the secretaries because in his idea a girl should be a little fatty.

—Dr. Georges van der Perre,
Catholic University of Leuven

Plutonium is the easiest way to nuclear weapons. That is what the Americans used in the bomb they dropped on Nagasaki, and what the Pakistanis were hoping to get from their reprocessing plant at Chashma. But there is a second way—highly enriched uranium. That was the nuclear explosive in the bomb that devastated Hiroshima. And that was what the Pakistanis saw as their next best choice. For even as they argued with France over the fate of Chashma, they were secretly getting their hands on that latest, top-secret European technology and quietly buying the finest industrial components to build their own supersophisticated enrichment plant in the tiny village of Kahuta, near Islamabad.

This was something that none of the developed nations had expected. The enrichment process had been a costly, complex technology to master, even within the most advanced Western countries. Only a few of the major industrialized nations had ever built their own enrichment plants, and both the technology and the construction had proceeded under the strictest secrecy. How could poor, backward Pakistan ever hope to do it?

Yet they were doing it, largely by slipping in between the West's carefully structured set of nuclear regulations. The major components of a uranium enrichment plant were classified, and subject to export regulations in most of the countries concerned. But the individual parts were not classified, and the Pakistanis went about buying their enrichment plant by proceeding systematically from country to country, buying the essential items—part by part—from dozens of companies in at least five different Western European nations.

Pakistan was going both ways: plutonium *and* highly enriched uranium. Either would give the Pakistanis enough nuclear explosive material for several nuclear weapons. If both succeeded, the Pakistanis would soon become a serious nuclear rival to both the Indians and the Israelis. And they were pursuing the uranium enrichment route on a clandestine basis and with a skill and daring that left the ill-prepared Western intelligence agencies and the international agencies always a step behind—even when they noticed what the Pakistanis were doing, which was not until 1978.

The story of Kahuta and its uranium-enrichment plant begins in Amsterdam in the early 1970s, and it is largely the story of one man—an expatriate Pakistani who ran circles around the lackluster security schemes of three nations and walked away with the secrets of one of the most highly classified nuclear processes in all of Western Europe. His name is Dr. Abdul Qadeer Khan.

A myth in a dozen languages, Khan has emerged in newspapers and magazines throughout Europe as a man of immense mystery—an Islamic blend of James Bond and Dr. No, using the magic of the East to steal the secrets of the West. Khan is a superspook: "The spy of the century." "The spy who stole the bomb for Islam." "The most successful nuclear spy since Klaus Fuchs and Alan Nunn May took their secrets to the Kremlin."

We do not see him that way. In our view, the now legendary Dr. Khan appears more a scholar than a spook, a family man without much mystery to him. Like so many others still in similarly sensitive situations, he was just a bright young man from the Third World, one who had been educated in the West and who found himself in a position to do what he thought best for his homeland.

That is also the picture that comes from a close reading of the Dutch Parliamentary report on the subsequent security scandal issued in the spring of 1980, and from a series of interviews by the BBC *Panorama* team—on which one of us was a member—with people who knew Khan in Europe. *

Born in 1936 in Bhopal, in what was then British India, Khan came to Europe to complete his studies in the early 1960s. He went first to Germany, to the Technische Universität in West Berlin, where he became fluent in German. Then to Holland, where he took a degree in metallurgical engineering at the prestigious Technical University of Delft between 1963 and 1967. And finally to Belgium, where he finished his Ph.D. at the Catholic University of Leuven in 1972.

One of those who knew him best during these student days was his mentor at Leuven, Professor M. J. Brabers. Interviewed there in the spring of 1980, Dr. Brabers recalled Khan as "a competent scientist," though "not really a

---

* Several interviews quoted in this section were conducted by the BBC TV *Panorama* team's Phil Tibenham and Chris Olgiati, and are quoted with their consent.

genius." But what Brabers remembered best about the young Pakistani was his ability to make friends.

Khan was outgoing, charming, and highly likable. Unlike many Pakistanis, whom Brabers found quite class conscious, Khan could get along with anyone, from the people who cleaned the workshop to the most respected scientists.

"I don't know how, but he managed to make friends all over the world," recalled Brabers. If Khan admired a scientist, or if he needed some information, he would sit down and jot off a note. His enthusiasm and willingness to ask questions won him access that few other graduate students could get.

At one point, Dr. Brabers worked with Khan in editing a book on physical metallurgy, a *festschrift* for an older professor at the Technical University of Delft. What amazed Brabers was how the young Khan made contact with top scientists around the world, and how he succeeded in getting them to contribute articles to the book.

Brabers also recalled that Khan, as a Muslim, would not eat pork or drink alcohol. But he was by no means a fanatic.

"He was proud of his country," Brabers remember. "He also had the same attitude as everybody else in Pakistan, that they were not well treated by other countries, particularly the Western countries. But Khan was "not nationalistic, not in the old sense. He had an international mind. He could live in any country, I think, and that's what he tried to do for his first job."

This was in 1972, and the job was in Amsterdam, at a specialized engineering firm, The Physical Dynamics Research Laboratory, or FDO. The post had not been advertised. A former fellow student from Delft headed FDO's metallurgical section and was familiar with Khan's talents. He jumped at the chance to put Khan on his elite team.

A subsidiary of the major Dutch firm Verenigde Machine-Fabrieken, FDO worked closely with one of the key nuclear projects in Europe. This was Urenco, a joint venture of the governments of Great Britain, West Germany, and the Netherlands. No longer willing to depend on the United States for nuclear fuel, the three nations had created Urenco in 1970 to guarantee a steady supply of enriched uranium to fuel their nuclear power plants. They were building a jointly owned uranium-enrichment plant in Holland, at the town of Almelo.

The plant was to use a new and highly classified technology—the ultracentrifuge. Made of finely machined, high-strength steel alloys, thousands of these ultracentrifuges would spin a gas of uranium hexafluoride at incredible speeds, as fast as 100,000 revolutions a minute. This would physically separate the two different isotopes found in natural uranium—the heavier, garden variety uranium 238 from the marginally lighter, far rarer, and very fissionable uranium 235. The plant would then bring the separated streams of uranium gas back together, but with a higher proportion of the uranium 235.

The process called for the finest precision. The difference in weight between the isotopes is minuscule, and the natural uranium contains only a very small proportion of the prized uranium 235, about seven parts in a thousand, or 0.7 percent. For fuel, the standard light-water power reactors require that the mixture be "enriched" to some 3 percent of the uranium 235. Many research reactors—and also nuclear weapons—require highly enriched uranium, which is enriched to as much as 93 percent of the uranium 235.

FDO, and now Dr. Khan, served as subcontractors and consultants on the ultracentrifuge process. For Khan, this was a unique opportunity. He could strengthen his knowledge and experience in his field of specialization, the use of exotic metals to withstand the strains caused by the immense speed of centrifuges. And he would gain knowledge and experience in the new top-secret use of ultracentrifuges in the enrichment of uranium.

Because of the secrecy surrounding the ultracentrifuge process, the three nations in Urenco had agreed on tough security, and as a major subcontractor, FDO was required to get security clearances for its employees, including the expatriate Khan. FDO recommended Khan strongly to the Urenco management and praised his talent as a metallurgist. The firm also noted that Khan had been in the West for eleven years and planned to settle, preferably in Holland, and that he was married "to a Dutch wife."

The Dutch security service—the BVD—took the information and ran a cursory check on Dr. Khan. The check found nothing suspicious, and the BVD quickly approved a limited clearance, "secret inclusive." Much to its later chagrin, the BVD missed a number of details, such as the fact that Khan's wife was not Dutch at all, but a Dutch-speaking South African with a British passport.

The Dutch Ministry of Economic Affairs gave its approval. From what we have learned, they were under the impression that the Pakistani metallurgist would not work directly on the ultracentrifuge project, and that he would only come into contact with low-security data.

Once cleared and at work, however, the likable Dr. Khan fit right in.

"He was an amusing person," another of his old friends, Dr. Georges van der Perre, recalled. "For instance, he was always offering cookies and sweeties to the secretaries because in his idea a girl should be a little fatty."

Khan's command of Dutch was adequate, even good. But, as Dr. van der Perre remembers, Khan had his own Pakistani accent that "sounded funny a little bit."

With his Dutch-speaking wife, Henny, and their two young daughters, Khan moved into the tidy suburb of Zwanenburg, not far from Amsterdam's Schipol Airport. The family blended easily into the community. Everything about their home at 71 Amstelle Street was normal and instantly forgettable, down to the lace curtains and potted plants in the windows.

The Khans were good neighbors and good friends. They were also a typical young family, taking trips to the seaside, to the Ardennes, and sometimes to his old university at Leuven.

On occasion, there were neighborhood volleyball games, and Khan is still remembered for his "special style." "He was smashing from all parts of the court," one of the neighbors related. "His way of playing was rather unconventional, but effective because his smashes were dangerous."

At work and at play, this seemed to be the most menacing thing anyone remembers about the charming Pakistani. But volleyball was not the only game that Khan would come to play.

FDO, his new firm, had a friendly, free-wheeling atmosphere, and Khan soon had the run of the place. In this, he was no different from anyone else. No one at FDO seems to have taken security as a serious matter, and this quickly opened the door for Khan to enter the Urenco plant itself.

According to the official Dutch report on the "Khan Affair," his first visit to the factory at Almelo was on May 8 and 9, 1972, only about a week after he started work. FDO wanted him to familiarize himself with the general procedures at Urenco, become knowledgeable about the operation, and also to look into an important aspect of his specialty, the strengthening of the metals used in the centrifuges.

It was all harmless enough. But it was also a breach of security. Khan and his employers had violated—perhaps unwittingly—the supposedly rigid security regulations agreed on by the three Urenco nations, and all this even before Khan could settle down to his normal routine.

In the following months and years, Khan was officially engaged in only limited metallurgical research for the ultracentrifuge project. But with the laxity in enforcing the security rules, he apparently visited Almelo repeatedly, and also had access to Urenco information without having to go to the plant.

One of his jobs was to translate technical documents, which Khan repeatedly took home with him, all with the permission of FDO. He had every opportunity to see Almelo's complete design plans, which were available at another section of FDO's parent company. And, in many ways most important, he gained an inside knowledge of the firms supplying components for the ultracentrifuges.

In retrospect, it is obvious that the Pakistani was in a perfect position to pry away the secrets of the ultracentrifuge. But there is no evidence to suggest that Khan took the job to spy, or that the Pakistanis had purposely planted him in FDO to infiltrate Urenco.

Instead, it appears that Khan began working for the Pakistani Government only as late as 1974, possibly after the Indian nuclear test in May. Neighbors remember that cars with diplomatic plates from Belgium and France began showing up in the later part of the year, and that the visitors often stayed until the early hours of the morning.

The neighbors noticed the cars, but hardly gave them a second thought. They simply assumed that Khan, like any foreign professional, had close friends in his country's various embassies. At least that is how they saw it until some five years later, when all the pieces began to come together.

Whether Khan sought out the Pakistanis, or they recruited him, is still not known. But one might expect a first-rate expatriate scientist to bring matters of interest to his government's attention, if only to guarantee a good job should he ever decide to return home.

In any case, Khan was almost certainly working for Islamabad by the fall of 1974, when he made his most important visit to the Almelo plant. Urenco wanted him to translate part of a top-secret technical report from German to Dutch.

The report concerned a major breakthrough in centrifuge technology, and one with a fascinating history. This was the vertical centrifuge method, and it went back to research during World War II, when Nazi scientists were rushing to forge the ultimate weapon for Hitler. The Russians later perfected the method with the help of some of the same Nazi scientists, and now the secret had returned to Germany, where scientists had developed it experimentally. Urenco hoped to incorporate the new method, and the report was part of the effort.

Officially seconded to Urenco to help with the technical translation, Khan worked at Almelo for some sixteen days over a period of three or four weeks. He worked inside the complex itself, and was given a desk in one of the most sensitive sections, where the final planning and design work were executed. The section was aptly called the "brainbox."

A temporary building set apart from the centrifuge facility, the brainbox was supposed to keep the tightest security. Regulations required that all desks and offices remain locked. All work was to be strictly compartmentalized. And all information was to be restricted to those with "the need to know."

Those were the rules. The practice was something else. According to the official Dutch report, the brainbox had a decidedly "free atmosphere." Just as at FDO, no one put any special emphasis on security. Technicians and engineers spoke freely. Anyone in the brainbox was assumed to have passed the strictest security check. And Dr. Khan, the nice Pakistani chap from FDO, was just one of the boys.

The brainbox was a separate building, but the lax security spilled over to the main plant. That is where the centrifuges were. It is also where the toilets were, and the canteen, where the boys from the brainbox gathered for snacks and coffee.

Khan could hardly have done better. For sixteen days he had access to both the brainbox and the centrifuges. It was a rare opportunity, and it appears that Dr. Khan made the most of it, even with his limited security clearance.

On one occasion, a colleague noticed that Khan was making notes in a foreign script. The man assumed that Khan was writing in his native language, and asked what he was writing. The friendly Pakistani smiled and said that he had been writing a letter to his family back home.

Another staff member repeatedly saw Khan touring the centrifuge facility, notebook in hand. The staff member thought nothing of it, and only reported what he had seen after the scandal broke.

Inside the brainbox, Khan shared an office with a technician who was also working on the same German centrifuge project. The technician was not always at his desk, and it is likely that Khan saw the documents the man was working on.

Khan finished his sixteen-day secondment at Almelo without arousing suspicion, and returned to his normal routine at FDO, where he continued to have access to information on the ultracentrifuges. But during the following year, Khan grew careless, and several incidents brought him to the attention of the Dutch authorities. In one of the more blatant, he asked an FDO colleague to come home with him to photograph some ultracentrifuge drawings that he happened to have.

The authorities did not seem overly concerned. Then in October 1975, the Ministry of Economic Affairs asked FDO to shift Khan to a new post where he would no longer have anything to do with the ultracentrifuge project. FDO agreed, and Khan's usefulness in Amsterdam came to an end, at least for his Pakistani friends. It was time for Khan to come in from the cold.

The rest is detail. Two months later, on December 15, Khan and his wife, Henny, and their two daughters left on a trip. According to a neighbor, their departure was sudden. Henny then wrote to several friends and neighbors. The Khans were in Pakistan taking a vacation. Her husband had fallen ill with yellow fever, and they would be staying for another eight weeks. Shortly afterward, Khan wrote to FDO. He had decided not to return to Holland, and was submitting his resignation, to take effect from March 1, 1976.

FDO was sorry to lose such a good metallurgist. The Dutch authorities took little notice. And the neighbors were not especially surprised. Their only concern was that Henny might find it difficult to fit into Pakistani society.

"We also knew that his family, the family clan, let's say, was urging him and putting pressure on him to come home to Pakistan," one of Khan's Dutch friends explained. "It wasn't so strange. We said, 'Okay, the family has won the boy back.'"

Everything seemed so natural. Henny returned to Holland for a short time to wrap up the family's affairs, and continued to send Christmas cards to the neighbors. Khan also stayed in touch, and let his friends know that he had taken a new job in his own country. A little hush-hush, perhaps. But clearly a big job.

"I was happy that he got the job in Pakistan," one of his closest Dutch colleagues recalled. "I had insisted already for several years that he should return to Pakistan because I saw his future more in Pakistan than in Holland."

It was only later that Khan's friends would come to learn what the kindly Dr. Khan was really doing.

From Ali Bhutto's first meeting with his top scientists under the tent at Multan in 1972, the Pakistanis had seen plutonium as their easiest way to the Islamic bomb. They had a stock of plutonium in the spent fuel from their Candu reactor at Karachi, and the reprocessing technology needed to extract it was widely understood, easily available, and relatively cheap.

But Mr. Bhutto and his scientists had also shown an early interest in the far more difficult and tightly guarded processes of enrichment. "We considered it as a possibility," recalls Mr. K., the Pakistani official active in the Paris meetings with Libya in 1973. "We wanted to find out what it was about, what it would mean for us to understand this kind of program."

The Pakistanis pursued their interest quite openly, especially in France. According to one of the secret aides-mémoires now in our possession, Bhutto's scientists asked the French Atomic Energy Commission in 1974 if it would train some Pakistanis in enrichment know-how, including the new laser and ultracentrifuge technologies. This was at the time the Pakistanis were concluding their final negotiations with SGN for the Chashma reprocessing plant, and the French refused. Reprocessing, maybe. Enrichment, never.

At this point, the Bhutto government saw enrichment technology as only something to think about. By the summer of 1975, however, the Pakistanis were showing signs of a major new commitment—to go for ultracentrifuge enrichment as well as reprocessing. And since no one was going to build an ultracentrifuge plant for them, they set about building it themselves, buying the components they would need piece by piece.

The first clue came in August 1975, while Dr. Khan was still at FDO. The Pakistani Embassy in Brussels wrote to a firm in Holland inquiring about high-frequency transformers, or inverters. These are sophisticated electronic devices needed to control the spinning of the centrifuges, and Pakistan's continuing pursuit of them would leave a trail from Holland to at least four other countries over the course of the next five years.

Once Dr. Khan returned to Pakistan in the fall of 1975, Bhutto and his scientists set out on a crash program. They would start with a small ultracentrifuge pilot plant in the town of Sihala, a few miles south and east of Islamabad. Then, a bit farther down the road at the little village of Kahuta, they would build a massive industrial plant, with as many as 10,000 ultracentrifuge units.

Both Sihala and Kahuta are virtually in the backyard of Pinstech, with its reprocessing pilot plant, all of which gives the Islamabad area a formidable "nuclear park."

In retrospect, the new scheme was amazingly audacious. It was an alternative in case the French pulled out of Chashma, as they later tried to do, and a way to get nuclear explosive material unhampered by any international agreements. None of the IAEA safeguards would apply to the Sihala or Kahuta projects, since the Pakistanis have never declared the existence of the facilities to the IAEA, and thus none of the enrichment equipment could be subject to international controls.

The Pakistanis called their new initiative Project 706, and as with the reprocessing program, it was under the overall supervision of the Pakistan Atomic Energy Commission and its chief, Munir Ahmed Khan. Bhutto also brought in the military's Special Works Organization to oversee the construction at Kahuta and to help with the purchases. Fresh from the field, Dr. Abdul Qadeer Khan took charge of the new Engineering Research Laboratory, where he worked on the design of the new ultracentrifuges and also put together a shopping list of the components needed to build them.

For Dr. Khan, no relation to his new boss, Munir Khan, this was a dream come true. He had already shown that he was quick and resourceful. Now he would prove that he could handle one of the Third World's most ambitious engineering projects, building a little Almelo in Pakistan.

"He had a good setup, a good organization," explained his old mentor, Professor Brabers, who visited Khan in Pakistan. "He could choose the people he really wanted. He knew who the good people were. He gave them good salaries so they would not want to leave the job.

"Also in buying equipment, he knew all the companies; he knew so many people abroad in many countries," Brabers continued. "Why, he knew so many languages, and he is so charming [that] he managed to buy many things that other Pakistanis would not manage to buy."

Much of the buying itself fell to a network headed by a superb man in the field, Mr. S. A. Butt. One of the participants at the original meeting in Multan, Butt had caught Ali Bhutto's eye when he jumped up and shouted that the bomb could be built in three years. He was obviously wrong but his enthusiasm won favor, and in July 1975, he was posted to the Pakistani Embassy in Brussels, in charge of science and technology.

In Brussels, and later in Paris, Butt spent much of his time working on the reprocessing side with Belgonucléaire and SGN. At the same time he also became the chief purchasing agent in Europe for the items on Dr. Khan's shopping list, and was almost certainly the man responsible for the inquiry about inverters in Holland in August 1975.

Far from a super secret band of smugglers, Butt and his colleagues pursued their purchases in a surprisingly open way, at least at the start of their buying campaign. Butt and some of the others were accredited diplomats. They worked out of the Pakistani Embassies or offices linked to them. They told many of the suppliers what they were buying the components for. They made no secret of their requests. But in so doing they acted with a blatant disregard for the various national and international agencies that were supposed to be stopping the spread of dangerous nuclear technologies.

The buying campaign began in earnest in 1976, following the initial inquiries the year before, and the Pakistanis made one of their first stops in

Switzerland. Their reception could not have been warmer, as we learned during extensive investigations in 1980.

The buyers—three still unnamed Pakistanis—went first to the little town of Haag on the border with Liechtenstein, to a firm called Vakuum Apparat Technik, or VAT. A widely known manufacturer of highly specialized valves, VAT exports to nuclear and other industries all over the world.

The Pakistanis were astonishingly frank. Would VAT supply them with high-vacuum valves for a centrifuge enrichment plant?

VAT was happy to oblige. As a good Swiss firm, however, they checked first with the government in Berne to see if such a sale was permitted. Berne answered by the book. The bureaucrats sent VAT a list of the regulations, including the "trigger list" laid down by the nuclear exporting nations in the London Club. Complete centrifuge units were listed, and could only be exported to safeguarded facilities, which the Pakistan enrichment plant was not. High-vacuum valves were not listed, even if expressly intended for a centrifuge enrichment unit.

The valves might be necessary to the centrifuge. But, in the logic of the London Club list, they were not part of the centrifuge unit itself. They were not "nuclear sensitive," and did not directly separate the two different uranium isotopes, uranium 235 and uranium 238.

Rules are rules, especially to the Swiss, and VAT sold the Pakistanis the valves.

"The parts for Pakistan were not crucial components," a VAT official told us. "They were not parts for isotope-separation equipment."

Well pleased with the robust and businesslike attitude toward free trade in Switzerland, the Pakistanis went next to the picturesque Chur Valley, where they found a new firm called CORA Engineering. This time the Pakistanis were not talking about minor parts. They wanted a major component—a gassification and solidification unit to feed uranium hexafluoride gas into the centrifuges, and then to transform it back into a solid at the end of the centrifuge process.

The Pakistanis told CORA exactly what they wanted, and what they wanted it for, and CORA checked with Berne. Once again the London Club had not listed the item as nuclear sensitive, and once again Berne saw no problem in the sale.

"We made sure we were not violating any existing agreements and existing regulations," CORA's Rudolf Walti told us, in an interview later broadcast on the BBC. "We were told this [sale] would not touch any of these restrictions. In fact, that it wouldn't even need an export permit."

Mr. Walti knew, as did officials in Berne, that the Pakistanis needed the CORA unit for the centrifuges to enrich uranium. Without it, the centrifuges would not work. But Walti was not troubled.

"We are not producing revolvers or cannons, and we are not producing bombs," he argued. "We are not involved in nuclear weapons in any respect, because we wouldn't even know how to make a nuclear weapon."

M. Poincet, at SGN in France, had said almost the same thing in defending the sale of the reprocessing plant to Pakistan. Only Mr. Walti, at CORA, was even more emphatic. "There comes really a question of nuts and bolts," he insisted. "What can lead to a nuclear weapon? That is the question, of course. Nuts and bolts can lead to a nuclear weapon. So where do you draw the line?"

For Mr. Walti and his firm, the answer was easy, and in the summer of 1978, CORA Engineering completed the "nuts and bolts." Elaborately designed and carefully engineered, the gassification and solidification unit was one of the largest single components that the Pakistanis ordered in Europe, and it took three specially chartered Hercules C-130 transport planes to fly the completed plant to Pakistan.

The Pakistani buying campaign also showed up big and brazen in Holland, where Dr. Khan knew many of the suppliers personally. As in Switzerland, the purchases appear to have started seriously in 1976, following the initial inquiry on inverters the year before, and most of the known orders were for specialized tubes and steel.

The obvious starting point was Khan's old employers FDO, though their exact role remains a mystery. We know that a member of the FDO staff went to Pakistan on an unspecified mission in September 1976. The following June, two of Khan's Pakistani colleagues returned the visit. They brought with them a letter from Khan asking for spare parts and certain data on the ultracentrifuge process. On Khan's behalf, the two Pakistanis suggested that they could arrange a trip to Pakistan for one of the FDO staff, and possibly make it worth his while financially. The Pakistanis also suggested that another of Khan's ex-colleagues might come along. In the event, FDO apparently discouraged the idea, and the two Dutchmen declined the kind offer.

The Pakistanis got a much better response from a second company, Van Doorne Transmissie, and in 1976, they placed an initial order for tubes of specially hardened steel. Dr. Khan himself showed up at Van Doorne the following year, and raised the order to 6,500 of the special tubes. This was a staggering amount and workers at the company began to call it "the Pakistani Pipeline."

The Dutch Ministry of Economic Affairs got wind of the order, and one of its officials came to the plant. He was told that the tubes were for use in a Pakistani ultracentrifuge process, and unlike the Swiss, the Dutch authorities told Van Doorne to stop. But the government could not invoke any specific export regulation against the tubes, and Van Doorne went ahead with the bulk of the order, shipping out the last consignment in September 1979. The order was just too big to turn down, even at the risk of government hostility.

The Pakistanis also placed orders with other Dutch firms for aluminum tubes, and in the spring of 1977, at a meeting of the International Atomic Energy Agency in Vienna, a Dutch engineer reportedly showed some amazed Indian scientists a photocopy of an enormous Pakistani order for martensitic steel, an alloy so hard and strong and expensive that it is used almost exclusively for jet plane engines and gas centrifuges. It was an obvious tip-off to Pakistani plans, but no one—not even the Indians—thought it worth informing the authorities or asking for an official investigation to stop it. In any case, to whom would they have been able to turn? That was one of the problems. The international agencies such as the IAEA had no policing power. And selling the martensitic steel was not in and of itself illegal, neither internationally nor in any of the individual Western nations.

The buying campaign in West Germany was even more shadowy, though the Pakistanis thought it important enough to have a special buying office in the country. This was in a small village called Watchberg-Pech, some twenty miles from the Pakistani Embassy in Bonn, and it was headed by an accredited Pakistani diplomat called Ikram ul-Haq Khan, who set up shop in January 1977. This Mr. Khan was from the military's Special Works Organization, and worked closely with a Minister at the Pakistani Embassy in Bonn, Mr. Abdul Waheed.

One of the few known suppliers in Germany was a firm in Hanau, Leybold Heraeus. One of the world's foremost manufacturers of vacuum technology, the company sold the Pakistanis vacuum pumps and equipment for gas purification, at a cost of 6 million deutschmarks. No special export license was required, and the firm later told the German magazine *Der Spiegel* that the equipment "could be bought anywhere."

A second company—Aluminium Walzwerke of Singen—supplied a reported 40 million deutschmarks of material, including rolled rods and some 10,000 small aluminum parts specially welded according to detailed plans supplied by the Pakistanis. None of it was on any "banned" list of nuclear equipment.

"Misuse of these parts cannot be [prevented]," a company spokesman told *Der Spiegel*. "Export business is not equipped to do that." He pointed out that the parts could be used in a variety of nonnuclear items, and it was not the job of his company to investigate the final use of standard items sold without restriction throughout the world. Several other German firms are believed to have supplied the Pakistani centrifuge project, but at least one turned them down. This was a firm that also acted as an agent for enrichment services from the Soviet Union, Rohstoff-Einfuhr.

The firm's president, Alfred Hempel, said that the Pakistan Atomic Energy Commission initially contacted him by telex directly from Islamabad. Mr. Butt, in Paris, then followed up with three or four telephone calls, explaining that he was acting on the Atomic Energy Commission's behalf.

The Pakistanis wanted ten to fifteen tons of uranium yellow-cake, or an equivalent amount in the form of uranium hexafluoride, which would have been needed only for the enrichment plant.

Hempel knew where to find the yellow-cake. That was in South Africa, and he telexed his contacts there to see what was available. At the same time, he needed to get permission to sell the uranium and got in touch with

German governmental authorities in Bonn to see if the deal was all right.

It was "no" all the way around. Bonn forbade the delivery because Pakistan had never signed the Nonproliferation Treaty and Germany's international agreements required that uranium yellow-cake—unlike the individual parts of the centrifuge technology—must be subject to IAEA monitoring. South Africa telexed back and asked who the customer was, and when Hempel said Pakistan, the South African Government refused.

"Butt called," Hempel confided. "And he pressed us and asked for our decision." The decision had to be no. Mr. Butt would have to find some other way to meet his urgent need for uranium.

The Pakistanis also ran their buying campaign in France, where Mr. Butt moved from Belgium in February 1977. As far as is known, most of the purchases in France itself were for reprocessing, and only a few for the enrichment project.

One is especially interesting. The Pakistanis had approached a well-known firm in northern France and arranged to buy as many as 10,000 bellows for the ultracentrifuges. French Customs officials forbade the sale, and according to one diplomatic source, who cannot be named, the company managed to send part of the order through a firm in Belgium, along with the dies to enable the Pakistanis to make the rest themselves.

But the best-known purchases were in Britain, where the Pakistanis placed at least three orders, two of them for those telltale high-frequency inverters. These were the same inverters that the Pakistani Embassy in Brussels had been pursuing in Holland in 1975, and the orders ended up creating such a furor that the press and television from a number of countries came to cover the story.

The Pakistanis gave the job of buying the inverters to a British subject of Indian Muslim origin called Abdus Salam. This is not the Abdus Salam who won the Nobel Prize in physics, but a small businessman living comfortably in north London. A British official we checked with told us this Salam was also an old friend of Dr. Abdul Qadeer Khan.

Starting at the end of 1977, Salam set up a series of new companies, among them Weargate Ltd. The companies were never much more than names, and in at least four of them, Salam had the same British partner, an engineer from South Wales called Peter Griffin.

Salam and Griffin first showed up on the Pakistani circuit with an order for thirty inverters. This was in 1977, and the order went to a British subsidiary of the giant American firm Emerson Electric, which shipped the inverters to the Pakistan Army's Special Works Organization in Rawalpindi in August 1978. The invoice went to Weargate in Britain.

For reasons that are still not clear, the Pakistanis placed the order through a commission agent in Leonberg, West Germany—Team Industries. According to Team's Mr. Pfiffle, he had been contacted by the Pakistanis in Paris, almost certainly Mr. Butt, who had told him that Pakistan needed the inverters for the kind of centrifuges used in a textile plant.

The Pakistanis—through Team and Weargate—placed two additional orders with Emerson in Britain, including one for about sixty high-frequency inverters. The Pakistanis also approached an Emerson plant in the United States, the company's Industrial Controls Division in Santa Ana, California, as confirmed to us by a company spokesman during the summer of 1981. The American division refused to accept the order, possibly at the intervention of the American Government. But Britain's Emerson Electric did accept. Did they know what the inverters were for?

A former engineer at the British plant in Swindon told us that anyone who was anyone in the firm would assume that the inverters were for uranium enrichment. But they were not overly concerned because they were convinced that the Pakistanis would never know how to operate such sophisticated equipment, and that the inverters would all sit in their packing cases until they rusted away. This was the attitude until a few days after the first shipment reached Pakistan, when Emerson received a telex requesting a long list of extremely complex modifications. As the engineer described it, this meant another Anglo-Saxon prejudice about Pakistani "incompetence" went down the drain.

Still, the Emerson plant filled the first two orders, and would have filled the third except for an unexpected intervention. This came in July 1978, when a leading Labor Party Member of Parliament, Mr. Frann Allaun, raised an embarrassing question in the House of Commons.

"Was the British Government aware that the firm Emerson Electric had supplied Pakistan with a quantity of special inverters for driving ultra-centrifuges in a uranium-enrichment plant?" he asked.

What were the inverters to be used for? he wanted to know. And had the export been approved by British Customs?

Allaun later told the ZDF-*Magazin* program on German television one of the reasons he was so troubled by the sale.

"These converters are of the same kind, and have the same frequency, as those ordered by the British Atomic Energy Authority," he explained. "They are unsuitable as a control system in a textile factory."

Perhaps the most interesting, and least known, part of the story is how Allaun learned of the Emerson orders. Allaun will not say. But some reports mentioned that a worker from the Emerson plant approached him during a labor dispute, while the London *Observer* suggested that the information came from the Israelis, though no one has suggested how the Israelis would have learned about it.

In any case, Allaun has a long history of interest in nuclear disarmament, and he pressed the issue with the like-minded Minister of Energy at the time, Mr. Tony Benn, who instigated a full-scale investigation.

One of the first things the investigation found was especially disturbing. The export of the inverters was *completely legal*, and Emerson actually shipped the first of them to the Pakistanis *after* Allaun raised the question in the Commons. The three months the Government took to examine the problem enabled the shipment to be made. The British then added high-frequency inverters to the export control list, which effectively stopped Emerson from supplying Pakistan with any more of them.

"In the end we used the trading powers under the embargo procedure that we had in order to stop this apparently quite innocent sale of inverters which were clearly intended for the purpose of building the Pakistan bomb," Benn later explained to the Canadian Broadcasting Corporation's *Fifth Estate*. "We acted in a way that was right and proper," Benn concluded. "But I have a sort of feeling it wasn't effective, and that what President Bhutto began and President Zia continued is going to be, if it isn't already, a nuclear weapon in Pakistan."

Benn's pessimism is easily understood. The new regulation was only a one-shot remedy. The Pakistanis continued to shop in Britain for other, non-prohibited items for their centrifuge project, and the British were forced to expand their export regulations twice in the opening months of 1979—first to stop the export of inverter parts and sub-assemblies, and then to prohibit the sale of any parts or equipment specially designed for the centrifuge process. The clever Pakistanis were staying a step ahead of the game by buying the individual parts and assembling more and more of the equipment themselves in Pakistan itself.

For all the difficulties, Allaun's question in the Commons started the ball rolling. Tony Benn's investigation uncovered much of what the Pakistani network was trying to buy in Britain. The British talked to their partners in Urenco and the London Club, who began their own investigations. The media followed after. In time, the new interest would pose the first significant challenge to the Pakistani enrichment project.

The case of the Emerson inverters signaled the first public recognition that the Pakistanis were pursuing enrichment as well as reprocessing as a way to nuclear weapons. Yet the Pakistanis had been openly inquiring about centrifuge equipment since 1975, nearly three years before, and various government agencies in Western Europe had done little to stop them or to spread the word about what they were doing.

In short, security was appalling, and the international guidelines of the London Club woefully inadequate. Here was one of the most dangerous nuclear technologies, and the Pakistanis were buying it on the open market, barely bothering to mask what they were doing. Their trail was everywhere. But no one had shown any interest in following it.

The biggest scandal was in Holland, where the new publicity in early 1979 finally opened up the story of Dr. Khan. What secrets had the Pakistani taken? And how had he gotten away so easily?

There was plenty of blame to go around. Urenco blamed FDO for hiring Khan. FDO blamed the Ministry of Economic Affairs, which had approved Khan's security clearance. The Ministry blamed Urenco for not informing the internal security service about Khan's repeated visits to the Almelo plant. And the Dutch internal security service blamed the Dutch overseas intelligence service for not making a proper assessment of Pakistan's intentions from the beginning.

"The fact is that in the Hague every responsible authority is shoveling responsibility for this onto someone else," recalled one of the first Dutch journalists on the story, An Salomonson of *NRC Handelsblad*. "The buck-passing is particularly bad between the Ministry of Trade and the Ministry of Interior."

The buck passing continued, and the Dutch Parliament finally set up an official Commission of Inquiry, which issued its report in the spring of 1980. The language was careful to the point of tedium. But the conclusion was clear enough.

"Although no absolute proof is forthcoming, it is accepted . . . that Engineer Dr. Khan has been able to assist Pakistan in acquiring essential ultracentrifuge know-how," said the Commission. Rather predictably, the report recommended a tightening up of security, a tightening up of export regulations, and the possible prosecution of Dutch firms that have exported to Pakistan. So far there have been some changes in export regulations, but no prosecutions.

In the meantime, Holland's friends and allies were reacting sharply.

Britain and West Germany—the other partners in Urenco—wanted to know why Holland had not brought the Khan affair to their attention back in 1975, when suspicions first arose. Or in 1976 and 1977, when FDO and others told Dutch authorities about Khan's centrifuge project back in Pakistan.

Israel was even angrier. In January 1979, Prime Minister Menachem Begin sent his Dutch counterpart a strongly worded letter. Why had the Dutch permitted the nuclear sales to Pakistan? And what steps would they now take to stop them? The Dutch promised to investigate. Under pressure from Begin and the other nations' queries and protests, they issued their formal study in the spring of 1980, as noted earlier.

Begin also raised a specter that later proved real—that the Pakistanis had received funds for their nuclear project from Libya's Colonel Qaddafi, whose attitudes toward the Jewish state and the West need no elaboration.

Only the French seemed secretly delighted at Holland's plight. The perpetual odd man out in the Western nuclear world, they had not been invited to join Urenco, and were now happy to see the Dutch and their Urenco partners carry the can for giving Pakistan the bomb. The French themselves had just taken the heat for their role in the Chashma Reprocessing Plant. Their attitude now was, "Don't blame us. Blame them."

But the strongest response to both the Emerson case and the Khan Affair came from the United States, where the Carter Administration once again took the lead in trying to stop the nuclear spread.

As in Britain, the first problem Washington faced was to try to tighten up the export regulations, which was not as easy as it might seem. American exporters do not like restrictions or added paperwork any more than do their

European competitors, and the Department of Commerce and other business-minded bureaucrats dragged their feet before adding any new items to the control list, especially where the parts or equipment had both conventional and nuclear applications.

In theory, the solution was easy: Define the items requiring special export licenses in the tightest terms possible. In practice, that created new problems. By specifying a special variation of an otherwise standard industrial product, the Americans would be telling a would-be nuclear nation exactly what it might need to get the bomb.

A U.S. State Department official explained to us that the international consultations required to establish permissible and nonpermissible items in itself created delays, so that it is likely that some essential equipment did get through to Pakistan, including some of the high-frequency inverters.

Trying to put their own house in order, the Americans also tried to find out just what the Pakistanis had bought and where. This was in part a job for the Central Intelligence Agency, as well as for intelligence and security services throughout Western Europe. The picture that the spooks finally put together from all the bits and pieces floored even the most experienced analysts. While Washington had been pressuring Paris over French help for the reprocessing plant at Chashma, the Pakistanis had been buying an enormous variety of parts and equipment for the ultracentrifuge plant at Kahuta. According to one Washington insider, Mr. Butt and his network had managed to get at least one of almost everything they would need, while back in Pakistan the kindly Dr. Khan was rapidly developing the capability to reproduce what could no longer be bought.

Pakistan's purchases challenged everything Washington had been trying to do through the London Club, especially as some governments were using the London Club guidelines as an excuse to sell to the Pakistanis. If a particular piece of equipment was *not* listed, these governments would permit their companies to export it, even if the bureaucrats and businessmen both knew that it was going to Kahuta. Quite naturally, the Americans expected everyone else to follow the spirit of the guidelines, even if the Americans themselves obeyed only the letter of the law.

In American eyes, the worst offenders were the Swiss, and in early 1979, Washington sent a strong diplomatic note to Berne.

The Americans were most concerned about two shipments—the high-vacuum valves from VAT and the gassification and solidification unit from CORA Engineering. Both firms were keeping resident engineers in Pakistan, advising and providing post-sale servicing, and Washington feared that CORA would sell the Pakistanis a second gassification and solidification unit, which they still needed for Kahuta. The American note also mentioned other firms, including one, Sulzer Bros., that was supplying limited technology to the reprocessing side of the Pakistani program.

In line with the general approach in Washington, the note to Berne carried with it the implied threat that the Americans might cut off shipments of enriched uranium to Switzerland, or delay permission for the Swiss to send any spent reactor fuel of American origin for reprocessing.

The note created great resentment in Berne, as did the threat. The Swiss had played by the rules, and now the Americans were trying to pillory them.

We got the story straight from the man now in charge, Dr. Claude Zangger, the Deputy Director of the Federal Energy Office and the chairman of the international committee that had drawn up the first "trigger list" even before the London Club.

"In the spring of 1979 we made an inquiry," Dr. Zangger told us. "We found that what was being imported was not on the list. It was on the periphery. There was no legal basis for us to deny a license to export."

It was the old problem. The Swiss exports were not on the list, and not "specially designed" for the centrifuge enrichment process. "VAT is outside the gray area of the nuclear list," Zangger told us. "VAT produces valves. They have a catalogue, and the ready-made parts come off the shelf. CORA's unit was also "a conventional process. They are making this for many different uses. It's not part of the nuclear sensitive process."

Zangger disclosed that Berne sent this clarification to Washington promptly. He believed that Washington "accepted" it, because he did not hear back from Washington immediately on his reply. American diplomats expressed to us their surprise that Zangger would draw a conclusion that Washington was "satisfied" with the Swiss response, and the Americans say they continued to press the Swiss for clarifications.

The Americans also pressured the Pakistanis directly. At this juncture, Pakistan was gaining fresh importance in Washington's strategic thinking. The Russians appeared to be winning new influence in neighboring Afghanistan, where a coup in April 1978 had brought a Communist government to power, and with the weakening and fall of the Shah in Iran, the Pakistanis looked like the only available bastion in South Asia.

As a result, there was great pressure in Washington not to confront the Pakistanis too openly on their nuclear program, but rather to wean them away from it with offers of aid. In October 1978, Washington resumed the economic aid that it had cut off the year before because of Chashma. In November, the Americans offered fifty Northrop F-5 fighters, equipped with air-to-ground missiles. And there were also offers of civilian nuclear aid and diplomatic support for Islamabad in its dealings with India.

The theory was that the Pakistanis were going nuclear primarily because of the weakness of Western guarantees to help defend them against the overwhelming military power of the Indians. But by 1979 the Pakistanis felt that they had already put extensive groundwork into their nuclear program, and the Americans were offering far too little to make them give it up.

The Americans shortly changed their mind, deciding to pressure the Pakistanis by cutting off aid. In early March 1979, Deputy Secretary of State Warren Christopher visited Islamabad to warn the Pakistanis of the consequences of continuing their nuclear quest. The following month, on

April 6, Washington announced that it had cut off further economic subsidies to Pakistan. This amounted to a cut of nearly $40 million in the current year, and another $45 million in the next.

"U.S. laws require countries importing armaments components for atomic installations not subject to international security controls to be deprived of development funds," State Department spokesman Tom Reston announced in a formal statement. "Our information is that Pakistan is developing a centrifuge for the enrichment of uranium. In the long term this might give Pakistan a nuclear weapon capability. This would pose a difficult problem, and make for a grave situation. According to our laws, we have decided to cut back significantly on development aid to Pakistan."

The timing could hardly have been more dramatic. The Pakistani courts had predictably found former Prime Minister Bhutto guilty of conspiracy to murder, and in the face of appeals for clemency by nearly every world leader from Jimmy Carter to Colonel Qaddafi, General Zia ul-Haq had ordered Bhutto hanged on April 4, only two days before.

The father of the Islamic Bomb, Bhutto died convinced that his overthrow had been engineered by the American Central Intelligence Agency, and that the takeover by General Zia had brought about the stoppage of the Pakistani nuclear program. Pakistan, he thought, would henceforth be defenseless before the Indian nuclear threat. As he wrote in his last political testament from prison, "What difference does my life make now when I can imagine eighty million of my countrymen standing under the nuclear cloud of a defenseless sky?"

Bhutto's assessment of Zia was inaccurate. Zia was continuing the nuclear bomb program. Only two days after Bhutto died largely for what he believed was the nuclear cause, the United States cut off aid to his executioner for pursuing the same Islamic bomb that Bhutto believed had been stopped with his own overthrow.

A spokesman for the Pakistan Foreign Ministry claimed the Americans had singled out Pakistan because they believed—wrongly, he insisted—that the Pakistanis might develop nuclear devices for the Muslim World to use against the Israelis.

Over the following months, Washington continued the pressure, appointing a special task force to consider new options for stopping the Pakistani nuclear program, or at least slowing it down. The task force was headed by Ambassador Gerard C. Smith, and it suggested a series of carrot-and-stick options that became public in midsummer.

One option was to try again to wean the Pakistanis away from nuclear weapons by beefing up their conventional defenses, this time with the offer of the more advanced F-16 aircraft in place of the old F-5.

A second option was to use the stick of strict economic sanctions, restricting private American investment in Pakistan and blocking World Bank and other international loans.

A third option was the most surprising, and would have created great pressure on the Pakistanis—the use of covert operations, including a paramilitary attack to disable the Kahuta enrichment plant. When this possibility of covert action was published by *The New York Times* on August 12, 1979, the State Department immediately denied that it had ever been considered.

There is no evidence that Washington ever considered such an attack as anything more than an option, or that it was at all taken seriously. But the Pakistanis took the possibility very seriously indeed, and formally protested to the American Ambassador in Islamabad. At about this time they also installed French Crotale missiles at Kahuta to deter any surgical airstrikes by either the Americans, the Indians, or the Israelis.

Probably more to the point, the Pakistanis also surrounded Kahuta and other key locations with plainclothes security men, and with the growing tension throughout the country, this led to a series of very nasty incidents.

In late July, the French Ambassador and one of his First Secretaries were driving along the road to Kahuta—just to see a nearby historical site, they later insisted. As they drove past the high walls of the enrichment plant, a mob surrounded the car and severely beat both men. The Pakistani Government later apologized. But the message was clear: Foreigners should keep their distance from any of the country's nuclear facilities.

A few days later, in August, a young British journalist named Chris Sherwell tried to interview Abdul Qadeer Khan at his home in a garden suburb on the outskirts of Islamabad. A small group of men jumped Sherwell and beat him rather badly. The Pakistani Government then threatened to prosecute the journalist, and he was forced to leave the country.

In the words of an editor on Sherwell's newspaper, the *Financial Times*, "They did a very professional job on him."

Though unreported, we learned from the British Embassy in Islamabad that the son of a British diplomat was also attacked while passing in front of Khan's house on the way to a party, and there are stories of similar incidents that have never received any publicity.

In the meantime, Khan himself remained a man of mystery, unavailable to the Western press that had suddenly discovered one of the great espionage stories of the nuclear age. He was always guarded tightly by Pakistani security men.

Yet some of those who knew Khan best did manage to see him, and they reported that Dr. Khan remained the same genial person he had always been.

"He's now the normal house father," recalled his old mentor, Professor Brabers, who visited him in Islamabad. "He likes to do the cooking and to work in the garden. He has tomatoes and even peanuts. He likes to take care of his wife and his two nice children."

But there were signs that Khan was beginning to grow bitter at his treatment in the hands of the Western media, where major stories had already appeared in *Der Spiegel* and the London weekly, *8 Days*. A hero in

Pakistan, Dr. Khan had become an archvillain in Europe, and he did not like that at all.

"Western journalism takes pride in false and malicious reporting, especially when it covers the developing countries," he wrote in a fascinating and wholly unexpected letter to the German magazine *Der Spiegel*, as he tried to vindicate his actions to those who blackened his name—unjustly, he claimed. "The intensity is enhanced when it deals with Muslim countries.

"I want to question the bloody holier-than-thou attitudes of the Americans and the British," he continued. "These bastards are God-appointed guardians of the world to stockpile hundreds of thousands of nuclear warheads and have the God-given authority of carrying out explosions every month. But if we start a modest program, we are the Satans, the devils, and all the journalists consider it a crusade to publish fabricated and malicious stories."

Yet the facts are clear enough. The Pakistanis know that the goal of Western companies is to profit by the sale of their products. The marketplace does not ask them to analyze their customers' motives. Neither, in most cases, do their governments.

We soon discovered, in the course of our investigation, exactly what the Pakistanis had seen previously. The regulations and agreements that exist among Western countries to block the sale of "dangerous nuclear technologies" can be easily circumvented. The system of safeguards and controls is hopelessly vulnerable, easily evaded, and badly defined—many of the parts for uranium-enrichment plants could be bought individually on the open market and the regulations would not apply at all.

Most important, the Pakistanis knew that the mouthings of the diplomats against nuclear proliferation were hollow. The regulations were inadequate, the list of banned or monitored items incomplete, and there was no serious, comprehensive policing effort to prevent violations of the nuclear regulations that did exist.

Whether inspired by Satan or Allah Himself, the Pakistanis' "modest" nuclear program had advanced dramatically in the unexpected direction of uranium enrichment, and the West had done little to stop it. Partly, this was because of Dr. Khan's own skillful endeavors in getting the plans and the supplier lists for the needed parts. And partly, we concluded, it was because the community of nations simply did not have a system to prevent nuclear proliferation. It lacked the concerted will, the attention to detail, and the power of enforcement that would make one work.

13

More Bang for a Buck

Certain manufacturers are alleged to have, directly or indirectly, transferred or sold sensitive or nonsensitive material to Italian manufacturers. These have then sent the material on to Pakistan through a valueless kind of documentation.

—Georges Besse,
President, Cogema,
letter to F. X. Poincet,
May 29, 1979

We have no way of knowing if the Pakistanis have gone behind our backs and made whatever use of our documents in dealing with French or foreign firms.

—F. X. Poincet,
President, SGN,
May 31, 1979

We are supplying some vessels for Pakistan. But I don't know the uses of these vessels. . . . I am only a fabricator. I don't study the processes.

—Aldo Turci,
President, Alcom,
Milan, Italy,
May 1980

Somehow the Pakistanis always seemed to stay a step ahead. Back in June 1978, the French had decided officially to suspend the contract with Pakistan to help build the big one-hundred-ton-a-year reprocessing plant at Chashma. The decision appeared to mark a major turnabout in French nuclear export policy, and was widely praised, especially by the United States.

Yet even as the praise was still echoing, the American and possibly other Embassies in Paris began to pick up reports that work on the contract was actually going ahead. According to these rumors, as a French Government document later obtained by us termed them, French firms were still supplying equipment and technical advice for the Chashma plant. The chief suspect was the firm that held the original contract, the now state-owned SGN.

We had our own tip-off on the matter from an American official in Washington at the beginning of our investigation in January 1980. "Don't ignore plutonium reprocessing," he told us, even as the revelations about Dr.

Abdul Qadeer Khan's espionage in uranium-enrichment technology and the Pakistani purchases were making headlines in Europe. "The Pakistanis still want their reprocessing facility, and the same Pakistanis are doing the buying."

He would not be more specific, but the suggestion was intriguing in view of the highly publicized stoppage of the French contract for reprocessing. The building at Chashma was nearly completed. What the Pakistanis still needed was the nuclear-sensitive equipment that could make it run—items like mixer-settlers, dissolvers, evaporators and annular vessels. It was up to us to find out what the American official meant. In pursuing it, we had an extraordinary piece of luck.

Among the documents handed over to us outside Paris by a French scientist was a series of letters that constituted part of the correspondence of the French Government on the very subject. They make fascinating reading. They show a fine French regard for form, a subtle skill in the ancient art of bureaucratic self-protection, and a studied disdain for actually finding out what was going on.

The first letter was from French atomic energy chief Michel Pecqueur to Georges Besse, president of the CEA-owned industrial affiliate, Cogema. It was dated May 28, 1979.

"From various sides, French and foreign, there are rumors circulating implying that SGN could be encouraging the continuation of the transfer of know-how or of material to Pakistan, thus facilitating the completing of the reprocessing plant," Pecqueur wrote. "It is hardly necessary for me to stress the seriousness of such facts, should they be in any way confirmed, as transactions of this kind would call into question the national policy on nonproliferation that had been decided at the very highest level."

Besse wrote a strongly worded letter to SGN President F. X. Poincet asking for a detailed explanation. Poincet replied immediately. In his letter, dated May 31, he denied point-blank that SGN was sending any contraband materials to Pakistan. He admitted, however, that SGN had a limited continuing involvement in the "preparation of orders" for the Pakistanis, some of whom were still "resident" at SGN.

As late as the first four months of 1979, Poincet conceded, SGN still had four of its staff working on plans and designs; eight on requisitions, invitations to bid, and orders; and at least two on the site at Chashma. This was up to eight months after the supposed suspension of the contract. From the way Poincet wrote the letter, it seemed quite clear that M. Pecqueur and his nuclear authorities already knew that SGN had continued to honor the contract, at least in part.

But this was just for starters. In his letter, Poincet hinted rather broadly that SGN was doing a lot more.

As part of the original contract, SGN had worked as engineers and had also helped with procurement, he wrote. "We would prepare documents such as requisitions, conditions of sale, etc. . . . for the Pakistani Purchasing Mission, who would approve them before they were sent to the suppliers. . . ."

The Pakistanis had kept the lists of the French nuclear suppliers, and by 1979 had a detailed knowledge of who in the French nuclear industry could do what. It was already public knowledge, published in the nuclear industry's trade journal *Nucleonics Week* and confirmed by Poincet, that the Pakistanis had 95 percent of the design plans, and these could enable the Pakistanis to finish the reprocessing plant on their own.

Were they doing it? And was SGN helping them? While Poincet insisted in his May 31 letter that his company was no longer involved in the purchasing or subcontracting of the nuclear equipment for Pakistan (which would be "contraband materials"), he left one significant door open: "We have no way of knowing if the Pakistanis have gone behind our backs and made whatever use of our documents in dealing with French or foreign firms," insisted Poincet in his letter.

The hint could not be missed. Poincet was offering the perfect defense to the "rumors" and to a charge that no one had yet explicitly made—that SGN was helping the Pakistanis finish the Chashma plant on their own in defiance of the French governmental suspension of the contract. By denying that he or his company knew about Pakistani actions, Poincet was actually declaring himself and the company innocent of something that was common knowledge. For whether or not they had gone behind SGN's back, the Pakistanis were in fact using SGN drawings and specifications in a continuing effort to buy equipment for Chashma from French and foreign firms. And just about everybody in the French nuclear industry knew they were doing it.

The center for this shadowy buying campaign was a small, rather run-down office in the seedy Paris suburb of Courbevoie, about a three-minute walk from the old headquarters of SGN. Officially the Scientific and Technical Section of the Pakistani Embassy, this was actually the home of the Pakistani Purchasing Mission responsible for buying the nuclear technology to make the bomb. Its responsibilities included France and the rest of Europe. The Pakistanis had set the office up originally to coordinate with SGN on the Chashma contract, especially in sending out requisitions and invitations to bid to potential suppliers and subcontractors. Even after the supposed suspension of the contract in mid-1978, the Pakistanis kept the Purchasing Mission open. It was headed by a well-built, chunky, and highly energetic Pakistani diplomat named S. A. Butt.

This is the same S. A. Butt who had caught Ali Bhutto's eye at the secret 1972 meeting with the scientists at Multan, and who had later been sent to Brussels to head purchasing in Europe. Butt had moved his headquarters to Courbevoie in 1977, and was officially accredited by the French as a diplomat in the Pakistani Embassy with the senior rank of Minister. Using his front as a senior diplomat, Butt was actually the man in charge of buying components for both the enriched-uranium and reprocessing side of the Pakistani nuclear program.

After the suspension of the Chashma contract, the enthusiastic Butt continued to approach the nuclear suppliers for reprocessing equipment. From one of the businessmen involved, we obtained copies of several of the documents Butt used in his buying campaign. One is a "Requisition for Material," setting out the SGN specifications for some "spectrometry counting equipment" generally used in reprocessing facilities. According to the businessman, it was intended for Chashma rather than for the pilot plant next to Pinstech. The requisition explicitly called for the supplier to transmit a list of documents to SGN and to permit "quality control" on its premises by SGN inspectors. "After manufacture, SGN will check that the equipment conforms to the requirements set out in the present requisition as well as that supplied by the manufacturer in his tender," the document explained.

The requisition carries several dates, the last of them April 1978, which was before the French suspended the contract. But Mr. Butt was still sending the document out in 1979, the businessman told us, and also into 1980, setting out the same SGN specifications and conditions and stating that SGN would be responsible for quality control.

Butt asked for a competitive bid on this spectrometry equipment for the plant's control room from, among others, a company caled Aries based in Paris. The specifications for the equipment were SGN's, the president of Aries acknowledged to us in May 1980. He admitted he was bidding on the order, but said that his bid had not yet been accepted. He claimed he was not aware that the order was for the French reprocessing plant in Pakistan.

Another company approached by Butt was Robatel, in the Lyons area. Robatel had originally been slated to produce some of the nuclear-sensitive equipment for the Chashma plant. We visited Robatel, and the firm's head conceded that he had been approached by Butt, but denied that his company had accepted the order, which had been made after the Chashma contract suspension. "That would be against the law," he told us. "We wouldn't do that."

He added, however, that he found the Pakistani buyer, Butt, to be "personally charming, like many of the Pakistanis, and also a tough negotiator." He did not blame him for trying to get the rest of the parts to make the reprocessing plant function. That was the Pakistani's right. "But from our point of view, it's against the law."

As Butt continued in his buying campaign, with the sympathy of many French nuclear industrialists who wanted to continue to sell, the stories persisted that the French were continuing to supply the reprocessing plant. They appeared in selected publications like Nucleonics Week and even the major West German television public affairs program, ZDF-Magazin. The impression, shared by many, was that the French Government or SGN was playing a curious French game, and secretly helping the Pakistanis to do the job.

The situation was bizarre, judged only on the basis of obvious fact. Butt and the Pakistanis were trying to buy the needed equipment and they were doing it openly, even brazenly, both in France and possibly outside of it. But in so doing, they were attempting to induce French companies to violate an openly announced, and supposedly strict, governmental policy. They were telling French companies to break French policy and law.

This led to some interesting questions. In the first place, were the Pakistanis succeeding in getting the goods, and if so, what goods were they getting? Could the French Government itself be playing a two-faced Machiavellian game, pretending officially to suspend the contract while permitting SGN or some other firms to continue working on it? Could the French Atomic Energy Commission, with its penchant for exports, be openly defying the Quai d'Orsay and the stated policy of the French President Giscard d'Estaing? Or were the French simply muddling through by turning a blind eye on Butt and the Pakistanis, and letting the chips fall where they might?

The answers were as ambiguous as was French policy. The suspension was announced in August 1978. In the meanwhile—as we learned from the man who handled the contract suspension, French nuclear diplomat André Jacomet—the French were negotiating with the Pakistanis on other matters, including the sale of Mirage warplanes. The French wanted to keep in the Pakistanis' good graces, and perhaps more important, in the good graces of the Pakistanis' Arab friends, who were supplying much of French oil.

Almost from the moment they made the decision, French President Giscard d'Estaing and his officials began to make a series of compromises that watered down what they said they were trying to do.

"What we tried was not to break with Pakistan on the subject," Jacomet told us. "We felt Pakistan had a very strategic position in the world. We wanted to stay on good terms with them." Giscard reflected this concern in his July 1978 letter to the Pakistani dictator General Zia, telling him of the French decision to suspend the contract, but carefully holding open the door to further nuclear cooperation. In particular, Paris remained willing to press ahead with the alternative co-processing technology, which would have treated the irradiated reactor fuel in such a way as to extract a mixture of plutonium and uranium unsuited to making bombs. As the French played it, they were not breaking off the contract, or saying a final no. Rather, they were putting the ball back on the Pakistani side of the court. The decision of Chashma was not a cancellation. It was only a suspension, and there was a difference.

Aided by Jacomet's personal visit to Zia, the approach was French diplomacy at its elegant best. But to the surprise of the French, Zia went them one better, refusing to take Giscard's soft no as the last word on the subject. Zia's unexpected skill is best seen in his letter replying to Giscard, a copy of which we managed to see at one point during our investigation.

"The issue of the reprocessing plant has assumed political significance above and beyond its immediate economic implications," he wrote, admitting rather candidly his political vulnerability over the Chashma contract. "It is my fervent hope that Your Excellency will review the position presented to us by your special envoy and explore with us a mutually acceptable basis for the faithful implementation of the agreement."

The door was still open. The ball was back on the French side of the net. General Zia's political future was in French hands, or at least that is what his words implied. And in the ways of diplomacy, French officials were left in a rather strange limbo, unable to state publicly or to the Pakistanis that no was no and that the contract was dead.

This resulted in some strange decisions, which indicated that even the suspension was subject to question. The key one was that French engineers would continue to stay on in Pakistan to finish the "civil construction" of the plant, meaning the physical structure of the building itself. This decision was totally unpublicized, and French diplomats tell us it was made with American knowledge and consent. Because it was cloaked with such secrecy, and because French engineers were later found to be in Pakistan, it fed the rumor mill.

The suspension, it turned out, was only half a suspension. Completing the building would give the option of finishing the plant and starting up the plutonium factory at a later stage. Political fashions change, and the Chashma contract could always return to official favor. Poincet was admitting in his letter that SGN was still involved in requisitions for the plant. And SGN civil engineers stayed on in Pakistan at least until December 1979.

The governmental ambiguity left in a quandary the French firms holding contracts for the mechanical and nuclear-sensitive parts of the plant. Some of the mechanical equipment had already been delivered and was sitting in crates next to the factory. Some of it was under construction or in design in France. The companies with valid contracts got no help from the government in defining what they should do with these contracts—if they should fulfill them, if they should ship the goods, or whether and how they would be compensated if they did not. Finally, in February 1979, a full six months after the contract suspension, French Foreign Minister Jean François-Poncet tried to clarify the situation, and got the Minister of Industry, André Giraud, to issue formal instructions to the various firms involved not to supply anything further to the Chashma plant.

The French policy, welcomed with open arms by the Americans, was one of evasion, uncertainty, and compromise. The Quai d'Orsay wanted to offend neither the Pakistanis nor the antiproliferation-minded Americans. The Atomic Energy Commission did not want to overly restrict the French nuclear industry; it believed in reprocessing as a nuclear tool and was still unhappy about the stoppage of nuclear exports. And SGN, with an eye to the future, did not want to lose a good customer.

SGN's Poincet was particularly bitter about the way his government had implemented the suspension. "Various people in the government told us no, not to go ahead," Poincet told us. "I asked them to send me a letter telling me that. There was no policy on it. You know, there is a contract between two parties [SGN and the Pakistan Government], an international contract, and there is an International Court of Justice. These things cannot be decided arbitrarily. It's not just a question of the will of certain French officials."

Poincet fought the governmental decision and its ambiguity tooth and nail, and eventually lost his job because of it. On June 29—a month after writing the letter to Besse—he became the Honorary President of SGN and no longer its chief executive officer. Yet he continued to feel strongly that SGN had a valid contract with its Pakistani customers, not only to get the plant going, but in consultation, purchasing and subcontracting, quality control, and everything else that the contract called for. "The contract still exists. It is an international contract, it has not been cancelled. And by it our company still has the responsibility for the Chashma plant."

He was, however, as ambiguous as his government in his answer to our next question: "What exactly are you doing now?"

"We have Pakistani friends," Poincet replied. "And I keep in contact with my friends."

What did he mean? we pressed. Was he still in contact with S. A. Butt?

"I'm in contact with my friends," Poincet answered. "Mr. Butt is one of my friends." He conceded that he still offered advice and counsel to the Pakistani purchaser. But he was not willing to say what kind of advice and counsel.

This led to another question. Did Poincet know anything about his firm, or others, still supplying nuclear equipment to the Pakistanis?

This time his answer was firm. "I don't know anything about it," he stated categorically.

There was one intriguing hint in Besse's May 1979 letter to Poincet. This was the possibility of an "Italian connection," that French companies were using Italian subsidiaries or affiliates either to manufacture the equipment for the Pakistanis or as expediters to ship equipment, thus avoiding the customs authorities in France itself. "Certain manufacturers are alleged to have, directly or indirectly, transferred or sold sensitive or nonsensitive material to Italian manufacturers," Besse wrote in flawless bureaucratese. "These [Italian manufacturers] have then sent the material on to Pakistan through a valueless kind of documentation."

The Italian connection called for a follow-up, even though M. Poincet claimed to know nothing about it, both in his reply to Besse and in his interview with us.

From the initial rumors floating around Paris, we had our second extraordinary piece of luck. A friend of ours with close connections inside the French nuclear industry told us that it would be worth checking out a French company called Bignier Schmid-Laurent, or BSL, and its Italian subsidiary, a company called Alcom. BSL had produced some of the nuclear-sensitive equipment for France's own reprocessing plant at Cap la Hague. It had also been involved in the Pakistani deal, he told us, although this was only a rumor. He had no documents to back it up.

The story seemed well worth following. The Pakistanis needed the essential nuclear-sensitive equipment to extract the plutonium to make nuclear weapons. This could be the way they were getting that equipment. The information that BSL had an Italian subsidiary—which was quickly confirmed—fit with the rumors mentioned in Besse's letter to Poincet. The Pakistanis could now be hiding their hand behind a series of fronts and phony contracts. If the story could be told, complete with the proverbial "smoking gun," the Pakistanis would be hard-pressed to convince anyone that they were simply pursuing a civilian nuclear program.

We checked back with the American official who had first told us "not to ignore the reprocessing side" of the Pakistani program. He never liked to *offer* specific information, as this could be a violation of the oath he had taken as an officer within the United States Government. He would only *confirm* information, or at least tell us that he thought we were pointed in the right direction. Was it worth the effort going after BSL and Alcom? we asked. His answer was encouraging. "You may have hit pay dirt," he told us. "Don't stop."

We pressed him to be more precise. What kind of information did the American Government have? What kinds of leads could he give us? He would only say that the American Government had such information, and "thought it to be accurate," but still was not 100 percent certain.

Had the Americans brought the matter to the attention of the French? He would not answer, but the implication was that they still had not, that the Americans were in the process of doing their own checking. This was in March 1980.

We started our investigation both in France, where the results were at first meager, and in Italy, where we managed to establish some basic facts.

Sant'Angelo Lodigiano is located about thirty miles south of Milan, just off the Autostrada. It has a beautiful medieval castle, red-tiled roofs, a polluted stream, and a sleepy main street that would make a perfect setting for the final shoot-out in a spaghetti Western. It also has a small metalworking plant owned by the BSL subsidiary Alcom, which is headed by a short, tough, bald, and wonderfully excitable engineer named Aldo Turci.

Obviously flustered by our surprise visit, Engineer Turci explained in halting English that Alcom did a lot of export work for the Arabs, especially Libya, and also for the Pakistanis. "We are supplying some vessels for Pakistan," he admitted to us. "But I don't know the uses of the vessels. It's not important for me to know. I am only a fabricator. I don't study the processes."

"Who are the vessels for?" we asked.

"We have supplied a lot of material to Pakistan," he replied. "And we will supply a lot of material more to Pakistan, and it is all right."

But the present order for Pakistan—who is that for? we pressed.

Finally, after a great deal of pressing, he answered. The vessels were for a nitrating plant, he had been told. The order had come through his associates in France, BSL, and it involved twenty-six pieces of equipment.

And the client? we asked again and again. Who is the Pakistani client?

"Asiatic Chemical Industries," he told us. He insisted, and insisted again, the order did not have anything to do with nuclear weapons, that it was not his business to know what the equipment was for, and that if we had any further questions, we should talk to BSL.

Rarely had we seen a man act so guiltily, or hide it quite so badly. We hired a financial service in London to prepare a full report on the Pakistani company Turci had mentioned, Asiatic Chemical Industries Limited. The service reported to us that the Pakistani company had no nitrating plant and there was nothing to indicate that it was intending to build one. Our evidence was circumstantial, and it was possible that the Italian and French companies were being used by the Pakistanis without being conscious accomplices to the Pakistani scheme. But we were convinced that the information was true, and that we had found the "Italian connection" in the Pakistani quest for the nuclear bomb.

We turned our attention to BSL in Paris, making inside contacts in the firm. One of France's better-known fabricators in stainless steel and other exotic metals, BSL's company headquarters is in Ivry-sur-Seine, in the red belt of Communist-dominated working-class suburbs surrounding Paris. Its main plant is about an hour and a half's drive to the north, in the town of Soissons.

BSL also has subsidiaries abroad, including its 60 percent interest in the Italian firm Alcom. With slightly more than 2,000 employees in France and limited capital, BSL is by no stretch of the imagination a major multinational, or even a high-powered engineering firm like Poincet's SGN. It is rather an old-line family firm, widely experienced in metalworking and looking for new markets, particularly as a supplier and subcontractor for nuclear industry. From our contacts, we heard that Michel Gabeaud, the Vice President for Sales, had made a secret trip to Pakistan around Christmas 1978. (He later denied to us that this was true.)

At the plant in Soissons, we found signs, erected only after our visit to Italy, announcing that all photography was forbidden. We discovered that a contract for specialized nuclear equipment—originally slated to be produced in the company's Soissons plant—had recently been shifted to the Italian subsidiary, Alcom, by special order of the management.

This was early May 1980. Meanwhile, we learned that the American Government thought enough of the information they had about BSL to query the French. An American diplomat left Washington in late May for Paris. The replies he received were vague: The French Government claimed no knowledge about BSL involvement in shipping nuclear equipment to Pakistan. Another American diplomat—this one based in Paris—also raised the question with his French colleagues, and received similar replies. He was told that the French would "check into the matter." An American diplomat told us later that he believed the French officials really did not know. If true, this was symptomatic of the French Government's relationship to its own free-wheeling nuclear industry.

We finally decided to confront the company with the information. They would neither confirm nor deny the charge. On the telephone, a very nervous M. Gabeaud refused to say anything at all, while the aristocratic president of BSL, M. Robert Vitry, was outraged that anyone would even dare to call him at his home. At the BSL headquarters in Ivry-sur-Seine, a very frosty lady in her late thirties told us very politely and very precisely that the company would have no comment.

In short, BSL had nothing to add.

That was early June 1980. The story was broadcast on June 16 in its barest outlines by the BBC, for which one of us was working at the time. It was also published in some detail—as the facts were then known—in the leftist Paris daily *Libération*. Both stories were carefully worded: The Pakistanis, they stated, had cooked up a plot involving BSL and Alcom, and the companies had unsuspectingly accepted an order for a nitrating plant, not realizing that the materials were for the suspended Chashma reprocessing plant. There was no legal challenge—not even a comment—from either of the companies, and the world accepted the information as true. As it was.

The French took two quick actions in response to the story. One was extensive; the second quite limited.

The full-scale response was a massive police investigation to nail the source who had leaked the French governmental documents. A team of intelligence and security personnel spent days at places like Cogema, SGN, and even the French Atomic Energy Commission, interrogating at least seventy people—possibly more—often in a harsh manner, in an attempt to find the leaker. They did not find him. Nothing of this police inquiry ever reached the French newspapers.

The second action was small-scale and half-hearted in comparison. French officials met with the executives of BSL, the company involved in selling the nuclear-sensitive components that could give dozens of atomic bombs to Pakistan. They settled "the affair" quietly. They brought no criminal prosecution against a firm that had acted—wittingly or unwittingly—in direct contravention of French policy and law. BSL—according to both company and government officials with whom we talked—agreed to suspend its dealings with the Pakistanis.

The "smoking gun" and the full details behind the deal remained hidden until the end of the year, when a series of documents came in the mail to three different addresses—the French Ministry of Industry, headed by André Giraud; the President of the National Assembly; and the one journalist in France who had seriously covered the Pakistani nuclear story from the start, Fabrizio Calvi of the independent *Libération*. The documents included what purported to be the secret contracts behind the Italian connection, and they were accompanied by a strongly worded warning from a group calling itself the League for Protecting the Sub Continent (LPSC).

"We will not hesitate to use violent means to make those responsible for nuclear arms proliferation understand the seriousness of their actions," declared the self-proclaimed protectors. "We believe it better to eliminate a few individuals and destroy a few factories rather than risk the wholesale massacre of millions of human beings."

Unknown and otherwise unidentified, the document-wielding League had popped up from nowhere, and looked suspiciously like the creation of an interested intelligence agency, possibly the Indians, the Israelis, or the CIA.

The documents themselves—two signed contracts and an unsigned memo—appeared to us to be genuine, and we were eventually able to confirm their authenticity with officials in Paris and Washington. The details fit with what our own investigations had already learned firsthand, and also filled in the background on how the Pakistanis had tried to operate.

The secret contracts confirmed that the Pakistanis had formulated an elaborate subterfuge of international proportions, trying to interweave a series of companies in France, Italy, and Pakistan itself in order to get their reprocessing equipment. In the contract, BSL agreed to supply the Pakistanis with an extensive list of "nuclear-sensitive" equipment, including specially designed dissolvers, evaporators, annular vessels, and mixer-settlers. BSL was to produce them to the technical specifications originally prepared by SGN, and to see that they were properly installed in Pakistan. BSL was also to train four to six Pakistani engineers in the firm's own workshops, and to organize in Pakistan a special school of welders.

BSL's Vice President for Sales, M. Michel Gabeaud, signed the "protocol of agreement" with the Pakistani buying chief, S. A. Butt, in Paris on February 15, 1979, which led to a final contract on April 18.

The Pakistanis desperately wanted the last remaining items to get Chashma into operation, and they were willing to pay a high price for them. The contract was for a total of 39 million French francs, about $9 million. We found that the same equipment on the open market would cost an estimated 30 million francs, which means that BSL was getting an extra 9 million francs—more than $2 million—just for taking the risk.

BSL signed the agreement to supply the equipment two months after the French Ministry of Industry finally issued formal instructions to firms not to supply anything further for the Chashma plant. As a result, M. Gabeaud was personally very nervous about signing the contract. If everything worked out, he could possibly move up to become BSL's managing director. If it did not, he could conceivably end up in jail for violating a governmental ban and French law.

This fear was evident in the documents. The contract was itself marked secret, and it set out provisions for hiding BSL's role and the purpose of the equipment it was agreeing to supply. "BSL will never appear in official correspondence and purchase orders," stated the contract. The accompanying memo explained that it was essential to maintain secrecy "in order to avoid a possible identification of the final destination of the equipment."

To maintain the secrecy, Butt and Gabeaud created their elaborate fiction. The contract was headed "Equipment for a Nitrating Plant." The goods were to be shipped to a small firm in the Pakistani city of Faisalabad—Asiatic Chemical Industries Limited, which would act as a conduit for the Pakistan Atomic Energy Commission. And the shipments would appear to come from BSL's Italian subsidiary Alcom.

In addition, Alcom had a separate contract with another Pakistani firm, Arshad, Amjad and Abid Limited, which we had discovered from the financial service's report was controlled by the same Mohamed family that owns Asiatic Chemical Industries.

Gabeaud and Butt also arranged that Pakistan would pay for the equipment in French francs through the French-owned Bank of Suez in Milan. And everything was to be shipped either on a Pakistani freighter or on other ships going to Karachi "without touching Israel, South Africa and Indian ports."

The fiction also extended to the tricky area of quality control. In the original contracts for Chashma, SGN was to have the final say on whether equipment met the specifications, and SGN inspectors were to make the final checks and tests. That was no longer possible, however, and the contracts go to great lengths to spell out how the necessary tests could still be made "strictly in accordance with SGN's requirements" without letting anyone know that the equipment was intended for nuclear uses.

Smuggling high-technology equipment turns out to be a very complicated business.

These were the initial agreements, the way things were supposed to be done, all neatly laid out to meet what Mr. Butt called "the exceptional nature of this arrangement." But before any of the equipment could be delivered, Butt and his newfound friends at BSL and Alcom ran into the unexpected assault from the press.

The initial publication of BSL and Alcom involvement in the nuclear deal threw a monkey wrench into the Pakistani plan. The French outwardly continued to deny knowledge of the matter and refused to comment on it to inquiring journalists. The official spokesmen of both the French Foreign Office and the Atomic Energy Commission admitted to us that the French had taken their limited action—to settle the question quietly with BSL—only *after* they knew we had the actual contracts for the deal in hand.

Even then, they argued, France was not guilty in this "affair." "We stopped it quietly," said Alain Varneau, the official spokesman at CEA, who was always helpful in the course of our investigation. "We are sure BSL has stopped working on the order. But there is only so much we can do. We cannot control everything done in Italy."

Had the French consulted with the Italian Government on the question? Varneau's answer was vague, and he clearly did not have the authority to discuss this in detail.

In Italy, we got an opposite viewpoint. We spoke with a high official of the Italian Atomic Energy Commission, CNEN, Dr. Fabio Pistella, who is a chief aide to CNEN chief Dr. Umberto Colombo. "We heard about the contracts," he admitted, "but what can you do about an Italian company that is taking orders from a French parent company? How are they supposed to know what they are producing if the French give them the order and the plans? It was not their responsibility."

The French blamed the Italians. The Italians blamed the French. We learned most about the actual disposition of the contracts from the number-two man in the Italian company, Dr. Emanuele Poncini, the stepson of Alcom boss Aldo Turci.

"In July 1980, we decided to block the contract," he told us during an interview in our Milan hotel lobby in November 1980. "Before spending important money, we wanted certain assurances from the Pakistanis. If we have these guarantees, we could still continue. But we want to be sure this isn't nuclear-sensitive material."

Did he think he was selling the bomb to Pakistan?

"Absolutely not. We're just metal fabricators, a very small company. I don't know anything about making an atomic bomb, and I don't believe in people having them. We read the articles in *Libération* in June. We heard about Qaddafi backing this, and we don't want a person like Qaddafi to have the bomb. It's all a mistake. We make metal products, and I don't believe this equipment could go into a bomb. In any case, everything that we did was in consultation with our parent company, BSL, and we just got the orders."

What did you do? we asked. Did you ship any materials to Pakistan?

"No."

Have you gotten your assurances yet from the Pakistanis?

"No. Not yet. It is a delicate matter. There can always be pressure. If we go ahead, we would not want the order stopped. I read about the American protest recently to the Swiss. What if there is pressure on the Italian Government—from the Indians, or from the Americans, or from the Israelis? We don't want trouble. You know, you must remember what happened at Toulon—to what was going to the Iraqis. It was blown up. We don't want that kind of trouble."

As for the threat of violence, Dr. Poncini had a real fear, especially with the emergence [after our interview] of the League for Protecting the Sub

Continent. But the threat of intervention by his own Italian Government seemed unlikely. According to Poncini, no Italian official made any "intervention" with Alcom. He was probably right, and the reason was suggested to us by an Italian parliamentarian, Massimo Teodori of the Radical Party. He indicated that it would be extremely difficult for an Italian government to interfere in a work contract for a small town such as Sant'Angelo Lodigiano which depended for most of its employment on a company the size of Alcom.

A conversation with Poncini by telephone in July 1981 revealed more. He now said that the contract had been totally cancelled by Alcom in consultation with the officials at BSL, and that the final decision had been taken before the end of 1980. He also said that his company had lost "considerable sums" on the deal—somewhere around $1 million—because the Pakistanis had bank guarantees and letters of credit they had chosen to call. He still claimed that no equipment had been shipped, but he was vague about the actual disposition of the equipment we had found in production in the spring of 1980.

He was happy to say that Alcom was doing well nonetheless, and had found alternative work. But he said that the Pakistanis were furious with them, though he would not say with which Pakistanis his company had been in contact, or whether they had chosen to visit Alcom.

Michel Gabeaud, the BSL Vice President, who had not been immediately available for comment after the original exposé, finally spoke with us by telephone in July 1981. We asked for a meeting to question him about the documents, which he declined. He stated that his company had had a contract with the Pakistanis, but it had been stopped, "and the question is finished, *Monsieur.*" Contradicting Poncini of Alcom, he said he had no control over the Italian company and did not know for what they had contracted, or for how much, but his company was not involved in that arrangement.

Gabeaud also mentioned that he had had "a very serious heart problem in the meantime, and for months I have been unable to work." His tone called for us to take pity on him. We asked if his company had shipped any goods, or if it had lost any money on the deal, but he was reluctant to go farther. "That is all I can say, *Monsieur. C'est tout.*"

Shortly after the exposé, an American diplomat saw S. A. Butt at a reception for French President Giscard d'Estaing at the Palais des Congrès in Porte Maillot, Paris. Butt nuzzled up to the President to shake his hand, while an official photographer recorded the moment for history. The American thought that Butt could use the photograph as living proof of the continued good relations between the two countries. Butt had almost bamboozled the entire French Government and certainly the diplomats in Quai d'Orsay, but the aristocratic French President—the man on top—was still his friend. At least, Butt could say so when he showed the picture to his Pakistani bosses in Islamabad.

Other nations took a more serious view of the matter, as we learned from an Indian diplomat over lunch in Paris in July 1981. "The problem of Mr. Butt has been treated by the French with excessive leniency," he told us. "Our Ambassador has discussed the matter a numer of times with the French Foreign Office, and every time we raise the problem, they say it isn't really like that."

"Like what?" we asked.

"Like we think it is," the Indian diplomat explained.

Israel took a similar position. A Foreign Office official in Jerusalem pointed out that nothing surprised him anymore about the French nuclear industry, and the attitude toward Butt was "typically French." He would not define what being "typically French" meant.

Yves Doutriaux, the official spokesman for the French Foreign Ministry, seemed to reflect the French attitude toward the Pakistani diplomat best: "The actions of Mr. Butt were not illegal," he insisted. "It is the actions of French firms that were illegal."

Considering the evidence in its most favorable light, the French had shown an extraordinary—and highly atypical—lack of Gallic precision in implementing their decision to suspend the Chashma contract. Their policy was marked by carelessness and drift down the line.

The French already knew what the Pakistanis needed in terms of specific equipment to get the job done. They knew what companies could supply it, and they knew that the Pakistanis were approaching these companies. They did no intelligence work to stop it, and French officialdom and police demonstrated a remarkable ignorance about what was really happening in the French nuclear industry. They were also totally negligent in refusing to crack down on Pakistani diplomat S. A. Butt, who was and probably still is openly attempting to induce French firms to violate French law. And after the illegal deal was discovered—one that involved selling Pakistan the equipment to make an atomic bomb—they chose not to prosecute the French industrialists who made the deal. Rather, they preferred to settle the matter quietly, thus telling other businessmen that they could make similar deals and go similarly unpunished.

In the meantime, the Pakistanis still want to complete the reprocessing plant at Chashma, which has become a national political issue in Pakistan. They have continued their efforts to buy components for their entire nuclear program throughout Europe and, by now, the entire world. Chashma may not yet be dead. The BSL affair is just one case; there could well be others.

Down to Niger

Paris is a city of rumors. Some are true, like those about BSL and the Italian connection. Some are not. But even the tales that are not true often point the way to ones that are, as happened with a widely reported story about how

Libya's "mad Colonel Qaddafi" was hijacking uranium from the West African state of Niger to help the Pakistanis make their Islamic bomb.

The story first appeared in the confidential *Lettre d'Afrique*, a small newsletter published in Paris and known for its practice of printing tasty tidbits, true and otherwise, straight from the propaganda mills of several different intelligence agencies. That was late in 1979. The tale then traveled across the English Channel to a similar journal, *Foreign Report*, published in London by the widely respected *Economist*, and from there to the *Sunday Times*, where it ran under the catchy headline, "How General Zia Got the Makings of an H-Bomb off the Back of a Lorry."

The story went like this: A band of wandering nomads had found an abandoned truck in the blistering desert sands of northern Niger, about 150 kilometers from the Libyan border. The truck's cargo was missing—some 100 tons of uranium concentrate from the French-operated mines at Arlit in the Sahara. And, said variously unidentified sources, the culprit behind it all was Qaddafi, whose evil minions had hijacked the uranium and sent it to General Zia in Pakistan, there to make either an atomic or a hydrogen bomb, depending on how garbled the story became.

In fact, the story was a hoax. There was no evidence to back it up. But it had its effect, doing what it was most likely cooked up to do. Journalists in Europe at least, were sent scurrying to the ends of the earth in search of the long-rumored Libyan connection to Pakistan's Islamic bomb. To speed the search along, the reported hijacking forced a startling admission from French nuclear authorities, who effectively run the uranium mines in Niger and had known the real story from the start.

The head of the French Atomic Energy Commission, Michel Pecqueur, announced publicly that the Libyans had not hijacked a thing and for the best of reasons: They did not have to. With the full knowledge of the CEA's industrial affiliate Cogema, which owns a majority share in the mines, Niger had sold the Libyans 258 tons of uranium concentrate, or yellow-cake, and had sold 110 tons to the Pakistanis.

Later, an official from Niger offered slightly different figures—300 tons to Libya and 150 to Pakistan (and, according to *Le Monde*, in the first quarter of 1981, the Libyans purchased over 1,000 tons!). This was the uranium that would help the Pakistanis to make their Islamic bomb, and they were getting it with the help of the French, the Libyans, and the Islamic Republic of Niger.

Truth was emerging from fiction. The Pakistanis clearly needed the uranium. They had to provide fuel for their Candu reactor, both to generate electric power and to produce plutonium, which they would then extract from the used fuel either at the pilot reprocessing plant at the New Labs next to Pinstech or, when it was completed, at the Chashma Reprocessing Plant. This need had become particularly pressing ever since the Canadians cut off the supply of fuel rods.

But the Pakistanis had another need for uranium—for their enrichment plant at Kahuta, where it would be processed to produce bomb-grade highly enriched uranium. It was to meet this need that the Pakistan Atomic Energy Commission and S. A. Butt had earlier approached the West German firm Rohstoff-Einfuhr so persistently, seeking either natural uranium concentrate or uranium hexafluoride (UF_6), the compound in which the uranium would be pumped through the ultracentrifuges.

For their part, the Libyans had little use for uranium. They had only a single small research reactor, which got its fuel from the Soviet Union. Niger's position was more straightforward. It wanted to sell. Once among the most wretched of France's former colonies, this desert wasteland survived and even prospered from the sale of its single valuable natural resource, the uranium mined in the north of the country with the help of French engineers and technicians.

Eager to learn what had happened firsthand, and also to get some film of the picturesque uranium mines in the Sahara, Chris Olgiati of the BBC *Panorama* team flew to Niger in early 1980, and interviewed the country's rather austere military ruler, Colonel Seyni Kountche.

"Our policy on uranium is simple," Kountche insisted. "We sell our uranium to any country, regardless of its ideology or regime, on condition that it participates in our development."

The only other condition that Niger imposed was that the sale receive the blessings of the International Atomic Energy Agency in Vienna. "We expect our uranium to serve the interests of development, not the interests of war," Kountche went on. "And we require that the IAEA guarantee the sale. Therefore, we don't see why selling to one particular country should lead to complaints. We are selling, and will continue to sell, to Pakistan. If the International Atomic Energy Agency doesn't carry out proper supervision, then that's a matter for its own conscience and the conscience of the buyer country."

As one of the buyer countries, the Pakistanis agreed to accept IAEA safeguards on the uranium, meaning that the IAEA would record the transaction and monitor its use in any of the country's declared nuclear facilities. The Pakistanis also pledged that none of the uranium from Niger "shall be used for the manufacture of any nuclear weapon or to further any other military purpose or for the manufacture of any other explosive device."

This meant that the IAEA was supposed to keep track of the uranium that Niger was selling to the Pakistanis. Agency officials were convinced that none of it had gone astray, at least as of mid-1980.

"For the time being, the uranium ore is only stored in drums," the Agency's distinguished director, Dr. Sigvard Eklund, said at the time. "It has not been moved away."

In the case of the sales to Libya, the IAEA was not so confident. The Libyans had signed the Nonproliferation Treaty. But they had still not ratified it, or signed the separately negotiated safeguards agreement with the IAEA. And Colonel Qaddafi was still refusing to allow IAEA inspectors into Libya to check on the uranium he had bought from Niger.

"Libya is a Nonproliferation country," explained the ever diplomatic Dr. Eklund. "But they have not yet been able to conclude the safeguard agreement. This means that for the time being Libya has no obligation to inform us what it is doing with the uranium it has acquired."

Libya did sign the safeguards agreement in July 1980. But from 1978 to 1980, Niger was making the sales to Libya without any IAEA monitoring, and this was creating a most embarrassing problem on the Pakistani uranium as well. With the uranium that Pakistan was buying, Niger would send part by truck to the port of Cotonou in neighboring Benin, and from there it would go by ship to France and on to Pakistan. The rest of the uranium would go north from the mines at Arlit to a barren desert airstrip at Agadez, where the Libyans would fly it to Tripoli, and then to Karachi. This gave the Libyans the opportunity to add to the shipments some of the uranium that they themselves had bought, which would never be detected by an IAEA check.

According to sources in Niger, this is exactly what the Libyans were doing.

From his earliest offers to provide funding for the Pakistani nuclear project, Colonel Qaddafi had expressed fears that the Pakistanis would simply take the money and run, refusing to come through with what he thought they had promised, which was to share with Libya "full access to the technology." According to the former Pakistani official Mr. K., the Libyans had expressed these fears as far back as the meetings in Paris in 1973, and there have been reports of similar sentiments ever since.

The solution for Qaddafi was to find some continuing hold over the Pakistani program, and the best hold he could find was on their need for uranium. If the Libyans could control the supply of uranium, they could reinforce their claims for access to Pakistan's nuclear technology. In fact, this was perhaps the only hope Qaddafi had of getting a return on the hundreds of millions of dollars that he had already invested in the Islamic bomb.

The Libyans had two promising sources for the uranium. One was in neighboring Chad, where Qaddafi was backing a rebellion that has now given Libya control of vast uranium reserves. The other was in the Islamic Republic of Niger, where the Libyans had backed the 1974 coup that brought Colonel Kountche to power, and where they posed a standing threat to the uranium mining area in the northern part of the country.

Qaddafi chose Niger. We learned through one Niger official that Qaddafi even sent his trusted aide major Abdul Salam Jalloud to Niger to begin arrangements for the sales to Libya and Pakistan. The Libyans also took responsibility for transporting a good part of the uranium that the Pakistanis were buying, which gave Qaddafi the ongoing role he wanted in the Pakistani nuclear program, as well as a continuing opportunity to top up the shipments with the unsafeguarded yellow-cake that Libya had bought.

The Libyan relationship with Pakistan was put to the test in the turmoil following the coup against Bhutto, whom Qaddafi considered a personal friend. The Libyan leader was in the forefront of international Arab efforts to persuade General Zia-ul-Haq to spare Bhutto's life, and Qaddafi even sent Jalloud on a personal mission to plead for mercy. It was all in vain. No matter what Qaddafi or the other Arab leaders wanted, Zia could not run the risk of letting the charismatic Bhutto live, and the former Prime Minister was duly hanged in Rawalpindi Prison in early April 1979.

Qaddafi was clearly displeased. The Libyans held a national day of mourning for Bhutto, and in the following months there was a very obvious souring of relations with Pakistan. Several Libyan diplomats were expelled from Pakistan, and Qaddafi threatened to expel Pakistani workers from Libya. Zia's foreign policy adviser, Agha Shahi, rushed to Libya to cool the tension, and Qaddafi withdrew the threat. In part, the tension between the two countries was blamed on the hanging. In part, it reflected Qaddafi's larger dissatisfaction with the Pakistanis in the area of technical cooperation, especially in nuclear science and technology.

As far as we can tell, however, Libya never interfered in the uranium shipments from Niger to Pakistan. For all the ups and downs in relations between the two countries, this gave the Libyans a continuing role in the making of Pakistan's Islamic bomb.

Catching Up Too Late

Preparing for an underground nuclear test is a long and tricky process. It requires finding the right site, tunneling deep beneath the surface, ensuring that the radioactivity will be contained, and detonating conventional explosives to set the various measuring devices for the actual test. This is all hard to hide, especially from the prying eyes of America's spy-in-the-sky satellites, and as early as October 1978 the bomb watchers in Washington were picking up signs that Pakistan was preparing the ground for its first nuclear test.

Reports of similar sightings continue to appear with frightening regularity, both from Washington and from sources within Pakistan. As many as five different potential test sites have been mentioned, including one in the remote desert of Chulistan right across the border from where the Indians tested their "peaceful nuclear explosive." Another is the rugged mountains of Baluchistan some forty miles from Soviet-occupied Afghanistan. Pundits have also been quick to predict the earliest possible date for the big bang— and remarkably slow to eat their words after the appointed day has passed without any nuclear test.

In fact, many of the pundits and even the intelligence analysts have been crying wolf. No outsider really knows in advance when—or even if—the Pakistanis will test their first Islamic bomb, a decision that may not yet have

been made. Many scientists with whom we spoke told us it would be possible
for the Pakistanis to develop a nuclear device without any needs for testing.
The decision about whether or not to test or when to do it will depend less on
scientific necessities than on political factors such as Pakistan's relations with
India, with the Great Powers, and with its Islamic allies.

Even in the absence of a nuclear test, however, the threat of the Islamic
bomb can only grow. At Chashma, the Pakistanis have been pressing ahead
with their industrial reprocessing plant, still using the diagrams and
specifications from the French engineering firm SGN in an attempt to buy
the remaining equipment that they need. French and American officials
inform us that the Pakistanis are still trying to get many of the same pieces of
equipment that we caught them trying to buy secretly from BSL and its
Italian subsidiary Alcom.

Getting these last few items is the immediate problem. After that, the
Chashma plant will face another major hurdle, the start-up. The Pakistanis
will need outside help for the dry runs, tests, and other procedures that are
necessary to put the plant into actual operation. In the original contract,
SGN had the responsibility for this. Notwithstanding M. Poincet's conten-
tion that this contract is still valid, French officials assure us that SGN will
not help the Pakistanis to do it. Yet every major reprocessing plant in the
world has run into major problems during start-up, and the Pakistanis will
need the help of foreign experts; they do not have the experience or the
expertise to do the job themselves.

The enrichment plant at Kahuta is closer to completion. As early as
January 1980, an official in Washington told us that the Pakistanis already
had "at least one of everything they needed" for Kahuta, and that they were
putting together "copies" of many of the pieces of equipment. As a result,
Mr. Butt and his buying network have increasingly been looking for
specialized machine tools, as well as for individual components from which
Dr. Abdul Qadeer Khan and his team could put together the finished
equipment themselves.

The Pakistanis appear especially confident about their enrichment program, and Pakistani nuclear chief Munir Ahmed Khan told the former head
of the Iranian nuclear program, Dr. Akbar Etamad, that, as of the fall of
1980, Kahuta was on the verge of starting up. If Munir Khan was not simply
boasting and they begin operating Kahuta in the near future, the Pakistanis
could have enough highly enriched uranium for a Hiroshima-type nuclear
weapon by 1984.

The most likely source of the plutonium for Pakistan's first Islamic bomb,
however, is plutonium from the pilot reprocessing plant, the so-called New
Labs. This is the mysterious facility first designed by SGN in 1973 and
engineered by Belgonucléaire in the mid-seventies. Official analysts in
Washington have told us that the pilot plant could extract ten to fifteen
kilograms of plutonium a year, which is enough for two or even three

Nagasaki-type bombs. The plant was expected to go into operation sometime in 1981, which would give Pakistan the material for its first nuclear weapon by the beginning of 1982.

If the only goal of the antiproliferation efforts against Pakistan were to stop the building of even a single nuclear device, the battle would already be close to lost. There are still steps, though, that can be taken to delay the first bomb, if not to stop it, and also to limit decisively the total number of nuclear weapons that the Pakistanis can make in the future. Even at this late hour some of the chief nuclear exporting nations are beginning to impose the kind of export restrictions and to employ the kind of policing effort that are needed to stop the Pakistanis in their nuclear tracks.

These beginnings have meant a willingness to go far beyond the International Atomic Energy Agency and its safeguards, which have proved increasingly irrelevant to the Pakistani quest. Far more effective has been the use of arrests and arm-twisting to deny dangerous nuclear technology to the Pakistanis within the exporting nations themselves.

The skirmish between the Pakistani buyers and those who are trying to stop them has been clearest in the case of the Kahuta uranium-enrichment plant. As originally conceived by Dr. Khan, the plans for the facility called for as many as 10,000 individual centrifuge units with all the related valves, tubing, gassification and solidification plants, and electronic controls, such as the high-frequency inverters that the Pakistanis had attempted to get from Emerson Electric in Britain. To run the full 10,000 units, the Pakistanis needed a large and continuing supply of inverters. (It is impossible to say exactly how many or of what size or how often they would have to be replaced, since nuclear officials in all of the Western countries are extremely secretive about the exact power requirements of centrifuge technology, whether at Kahuta or at the Urenco plant in Almelo. The exact number of inverters needed to handle the electrical power at Kahuta would depend entirely on how clever the Pakistani technicians turn out to be.)

The ninety inverters that the Pakistanis originally tried to get from Emerson Electric was a start. They received only thirty of them before the British banned inverter sales in October 1978. The Pakistanis have been forced to look for more inverters in at least four different countries, where their trail has been dogged by an unprecedented posse of export-control officials, police, and international television journalists.

Soon after the ban in Britain, Pakistani would-be inverter buyers showed up halfway around the world in Japan. We learned of this effort in the fall of 1980, when colleagues from Japan's NHK Television asked us if we would work with them in getting the story.

The research showed that two Pakistani buyers had visited Tokyo in December 1978, right after the British forbade any further export of inverters. They said that they were from the Karachi Silk Mill Company, and one of them said jokingly that his name was Mohammed Ali. The Pakistanis wanted to buy high frequency inverters—"for a textile plant," they said—and a trading company specializing in South Asian trade put them in touch with the manufacturers, the Mitsubishi Electric Co.

This was the perfect choice. Mitsubishi Electric not only produced the kind of inverters used in textile plants, but also worked as a subcontractor producing the other kind of inverters for Japan's own ultracentrifuge enrichment plant.

The Pakistanis said they wanted 200 inverters, all within the course of a year. Mitsubishi was not sure if it could produce the inverters that quickly, and also had problems with some of the specifications. But before the exact terms could be agreed on, the whole deal fell through.

Officials of the trading company claimed to our NHK colleagues that they had stopped the contract after reading a newspaper story on the Pakistani nuclear program in the spring of 1979. They simply did not want to have anything to do with nuclear weapons, they insisted.

More likely, the Japanese Government stepped in, as we learned from a British official in London. The British had discussed the Emerson inverters and their new export restrictions with the Japanese as a normal part of the ongoing discussions between members of the London Club of nuclear exporting nations. The Japanese authorities then approached Mitsubishi Electric and warned them to steer clear of any inverter order from Pakistan.

The Pakistanis' next stop was Canada, where they found the authorities and the media even more sensitive about Islamabad's nuclear intentions. The story was taken up by Brian McKenna and Eric Malling of the Canadian Broadcasting Corporation's weekly television program *The Fifth Estate*. They reported that two officials of the Pakistan Atomic Energy Commission visited Montreal in July 1980. They came on diplomatic visas and, in their visa applications, gave their names as Anwar Ali and I. A. Bhatti. They would be working on "internal affairs" in the Pakistani Consulate, they claimed.

In Montreal, the Pakistani officials checked into the swank Queen Elizabeth Hotel. Instead of working at the Consulate, they made contact with three men, all Canadian citizens of South Asian or Arab background who were to act as the Pakistani buying network in Canada. The top priority was to buy the individual components from which the Pakistanis could put together their own inverters. This included various capacitors and resistors from the General Electric plant across the border in upstate New York, in the town of Hudson Falls.

In all, the trio made at least eleven shipments, worth some $170,000. The shipments were addressed to a firm called Tech Equipment in Pakistan, and at least some of them were sent through an agent in the Gulf state of Abu Dhabi, Khalid Jassam General Trading.

The Royal Canadian Mounted Police followed one of the trio, engineer Abdul Aziz Khan, to Montreal's Central Railway Station, where he took a suitcase full of documents out of a locker and tried to throw many of them into the trash. The documents all had something to do with nuclear technology, said CBC's *Fifth Estate* investigators, and "there were even actual plans and diagrams of how to make an atomic weapon." (*The Fifth Estate* offers no evidence to back up the juicy trash-can aspect of the story, and, while the rest of their report appears accurate, we find ourselves a bit skeptical about what was in the trash.)

Once charged, Khan made a mysterious flight to Pakistan, where he had a quick fifteen-minute meeting at the airport and immediately took the next flight back to Europe. He would have stayed longer, he later told Canadian authorities, but he had problems with the airline schedules.

This was the situation as of August 29, 1980, when the Mounties seized the last of the eleven shipments—some $56,000 worth of electronic components—at Montreal's Mirabel Airport. They also arrested the three men and charged them with violating Canadian export regulations. Many of the items had been imported from General Electric in the United States and thus required special export licenses, which the trio had failed to obtain. They were later charged under the Atomic Energy Materials and Equipment Act by which nuclear sales are regulated and through which the government exercised its authority to prohibit nuclear sales to Pakistan.

In retrospect, it seems that the RCMP had been on top of the case from July, and American officials in Washington tell us they provided the Mounties with information to help them in their search. The Mounties conducted surveillance on the two visitors from the Pakistan Atomic Energy Commission, but arrested the Canadian trio only after several of the shipments had gone through.

The three arrested men insisted that they knew nothing of any possible nuclear uses for the components they were buying for the Pakistanis.

"These parts are general parts that could be used for anything," the Egyptian-born Salam Elmenyawi told *The Fifth Estate*. "There is nothing special about them, so I cannot tell you anything about this. It is not for me to find out what these people [the Pakistani officials] are doing."

Officially the Pakistanis took the same position. In an interview with CBC Television, the Pakistani Ambassador to Canada, Altaf A. Shaikh, admitted that the two Pakistani visitors—Anwar Ali and I. A. Bhatti—had purchased parts for transformers and inverters. But what was wrong with that?

"It was not nuclear material," the Ambassador insisted. "What they bought was what anyone could pick up from a catalogue from the store, and that equipment was ordered. There is no ban on it."

The Ambassador also insisted that the two men had come to Canada openly, that they had declared their presence to the Canadian Government, and that the purchases were incidental to their "liaison work" with the Consulate in Montreal.

In the meantime, one aspect of the story still needs watching, and that involves the agent in the Gulf states to which the Canadian trio made their shipments—Khalid Jassam General Trading. Simon Henderson of the London *Financial Times* visited the firm in Dubai, and reported that it is little more than an office in the Arab Bank Building and the sole director is none other than Abdus Salam, the man behind the original attempt to buy the inverters from Emerson Electric in Britain. It is now clear that the British-based Islamic businessman had a hand in the Pakistani purchasing campaign in Canada as well.

For the most part, the outside world hears only of the well-publicized Pakistani failures, not of their secret successes. But as a British official told us, the Pakistanis are still approaching Western companies in an effort to buy inverters, which would suggest that they are still short of their goal and that recent efforts to stop them are paying off.

Far less successful have been efforts to stop the Pakistanis from getting an even more essential ingredient in their enrichment program—a continuous supply of uranium hexafluoride, the form in which the uranium is pumped through the rapidly spinning ultracentrifuges to separate out the isotopes of the highly explosive uranium 235. As early as 1976, the Pakistanis attempted to buy ten to fifteen tons of uranium in this form from the West German firm Rohstoff-Einfuhr, which had turned them down. The late Pakistani journalist Mohammed Beg, who had first told us of the Pakistani flights carrying hundreds of millions of dollars from Libya's Colonel Qaddafi to Mr. Bhutto, also reported that the Pakistanis had put the Kahuta plant through "a trial run" in the fall of 1979, using uranium hexafluoride flown in from the People's Republic of China. He had learned about this directly from one of the officials involved who told him the test had resulted in an accident.

The materials for that test run were only relatively small quantities of uranium hexafluoride, merely enough for the purpose of testing the centrifuge equipment. What the Pakistanis needed was their own highly complex "hex" plant, where they could produce the hundreds of thousands of tons a year that Dr. Khan and his team would need to keep their 10,000 ultracentrifuges spinning in order to produce an ongoing supply of bomb-grade highly enriched uranium.

From the start, this was always a major stumbling block for the Pakistanis, and a major question mark hanging over the success or failure of their entire enrichment program. Without a hex plant, Kahuta would never work, except perhaps as test facility, wholly dependent on outside supplies of uranium hexafluoride. Without a hex plant, Khan's dreams of an independent Islamic nuclear arsenal from enriched uranium would clearly be in vain.

Unlike the inverters, a hex plant was not something that the Pakistanis could buy off the shelf. The technology was as sophisticated and challenging as the centrifuge plant itself. The handful of companies around the world who could help them to build such a plant would know what it was for. Working with the highly volatile, dangerously toxic, and extremely corrosive fluorine gas would clearly push the Pakistanis to their limits.

This was the picture when we first began our investigation at the end of 1979. We quickly discovered that none of the Western government analysts with whom we spoke could answer the basic question: Where is the Pakistani hex plant?

The answer came in mid-1981. A German journalist, Karl Gunther Barth, received from one of his sources a set of documents showing that a chemical engineering firm in the West German city of Freiburg, CES Kalthof, GmbH, had helped the Pakistanis to build some fluorine facilities, which were completed and in production by April of 1980. Barth took this to be the long-sought-after hex plant, and in July 1981, he published a lengthy article in the magazine *Stern*, reporting that this was the key facility that allows the Pakistanis to make their bomb.

Barth was on the right track. We interviewed the head of the German company that set up the facility, Herr Albrecht Migule, as well as an American official who has followed the case. They both confirm that the Pakistanis now have a set of facilities capable of producing various fluorine compounds. This includes the all-important uranium hexafluoride, which could be used in the ultracentrifuges to produce highly enriched uranium for nuclear weapons.

The story turned out to be bigger than Barth first realized. The CES Kalthof–built facilities are only a small-scale pilot plant, which the Pakistanis are using as a stepping-stone to master the difficult chemical processes before moving up to a much larger industrial hex plant that could provide Kahuta with enough uranium hexafluoride to give the Pakistanis the material to build an entire arsenal of nuclear weapons.

The pilot plant is located about four hours' drive west of Multan, in the tiny village of Dera Ghazi Khan. From the figures that the plant's designer, Albrecht Migule of CES Kalthof, gave us in a telephone interview in August 1981, the plant could produce enough uranium hexafluoride in a year to make as many as three Hiroshima-size atom bombs.

As Migule put it to us, the plant can produce one kilogram of fluorine an hour, which would yield roughly three kilograms of uranium hexafluoride. If run twenty-four hours a day, 365 days a year—a rate that would tax both the equipment and Pakistani technicians to the breaking point—the plant would provide just over twenty-six tons of "hex," out of which the centrifuge plant could produce enough highly enriched uranium to make two or three bombs a year. Run at a more reasonable pace, the plant could produce enough uranium hexafluoride for a single bomb a year, according to Migule's figures.

Journalist Barth's documents suggest that Migule underestimated the capacity when he spoke with us. In a contract dated January 3, 1977, and signed by Migule, the plant's production capacity is given as 198 tons per year, or enough uranium hexafluoride to produce the highly enriched uranium for sixteen to twenty-four nuclear weapons.

Herr Migule would have every reason to downplay his plant's capacity in talking with us, especially if the Pakistanis are using it to produce material for nuclear weapons. On the other hand, the 1977 contract gives a projection of the maximum that the plant was supposed to produce, not an evaluation of what it was actually producing in practice.

Whatever the capacity of the present plant, it is only the beginning. Given the complexity of handling fluorine compounds, it is only sensible that the Pakistanis would start small, as they did with their pilot centrifuge plant at Sihala and their first laboratory-scale hot cells for reprocessing in the basement of Pinstech.

The Pakistanis are also getting the needed fluorine to make the hex from their own source of the mineral fluorspar, which Migule helped them discover in Pakistan in 1969. They have also been hard at work developing their own reserves of uranium, with help from the United Nations Development Program and the International Atomic Energy Agency. Two Agency experts were in Pakistan for a month in December 1980, one helping with uranium exploration, the other with the processing of uranium ore.

These mineral resources give Pakistan the perfect base for a large-scale industrial hex plant, and according to Herr Migule, the Pakistanis already have such a project in mind. Migule told us in a telephone interview that he was "very much hoping to get the contract."

"How much would the new plant produce?" we asked him.

"Some hundreds of thousands of tons of uranium hexafluoride," he replied.

And how much would your company earn if you got the contract? we pressed.

"About a hundred million deutschmarks," he answered. Or as much as $40 million at the present rate of exchange. According to Migule, his firm received only 5 million deutschmarks for its work on the present facilities.

Throughout our rather lengthy conversation, Herr Migule insisted clumsily that he knew absolutely nothing about the enrichment plant or about what the Pakistanis would want to use the uranium hexafluoride for. He also claimed to know nothing at all about one specific facility mentioned in the documents—a small plant to convert the enriched uranium hex-afluoride back into nearly pure uranium metal. This would take place after the hex had passed through the centrifuges, and would provide the bomb-grade uranium 235 in easy-to-use metal bars.

In fact, the Pakistanis have absolutely no conceivable need for Herr Migule's uranium hexafluoride except for the enrichment of uranium. Yet like so many other Western suppliers with whom we talked, Herr Migule defended himself by falling back on the old argument that the Pakistanis are not really capable of doing anything dangerous. "The equipment is already spoiled, I'm sure," he told us when we called him in August 1981. "Why, we even had to show them how to work a vacuum cleaner."

As a footnote to the story, we were particularly interested to hear from Migule about the intermediary that the Pakistanis used in the contract. This was the same front company that signed the phony cover contract for the reprocessing equipment from Alcom in Italy, Arshad, Amjad and Abid of Karachi and Faisalabad.

Migule subsequently admitted that the pilot plant was controlled by the government, and we have since learned that the facility is run by the Pakistani military, mostly likely the Special Works Organization, which also helps run the enrichment plant at Kahuta.

As opposed to their efforts to stop Pakistan from getting inverters for Kahuta, the nuclear supplying nations have been slow to pick up the trail of the hex plant. Officials in both London and Washington expressed surprise when we asked them about Pakistani interest in a full-scale industrial uranium hexafluoride plant. They said this was the first they had heard of it.

What we have seen of the beginning efforts to stop the sale of inverters suggests that similar or even stronger measures could be used to stop the Pakistanis from getting the full-scale hex plant and other equipment for their nuclear program. The Pakistanis are still dependent on outside sources of supply—for nuclear equipment, for components, and for the special machine tools to make "copies" of items they already have. For all their undoubted skill and doggedness, they are not yet self-sufficient, which means that they are still vulnerable to outside pressures and interruptions.

The Pakistani purchasing network is extremely easy to identify and pursue, as the Canadian Mounties proved when they followed the two employees of the Pakistan Atomic Energy Commission to their three buyers in Canada. From S. A. Butt in Paris to Abdus Salam and the firm of Arshad, Amjad and Abid, the big names are known, and targeting them and their contacts for surveillance should not be beyond the abilities of the Western intelligence services.

The Pakistani nuclear program still has important gaps to fill if it is to be successful. Most of these needs can be identified in advance, as can the handful of most likely suppliers, and the concerned governments have the power to take a whole series of steps—from enacting sweeping new restrictions with stiff fines and prison sentences to putting a quiet word in the right ears—to convince any would-be supplier that selling equipment to help Pakistan build a nuclear arsenal will henceforth be considered something akin to trading with the enemy in time of war.

This would be strong medicine, going far beyond the conventional reliance on either safeguards or the International Atomic Energy Agency. At least in the case of Pakistan, however, something more than safeguards is clearly needed.

The Pakistanis have never admitted that the Kahuta uranium-enrichment facility and the pilot hex plant exist. They are entirely outside of the safeguards system. There are no international rules against Pakistan or any other country enriching uranium if it wishes.

Safeguards on the Chashma reprocessing facility are officially in force, covered by the March 1976 tripartite agreement between Pakistan, France, and the IAEA. The French had insisted on the agreement as a condition for allowing the SGN contract to go ahead, and in a sense it was the IAEA's guarantee of the safeguards that enabled the Pakistanis to get their hands on the SGN sketches and specifications. Now that the French have suspended the SGN contract, the Pakistanis have an excellent case for claiming that the safeguards have been suspended as well. At present, no one is observing the terms of the safeguards agreement, and IAEA officials are trying their best to put a good face on a very embarrassing situation.

"The agreement is in force as far as we are concerned," the Agency's former Deputy Director, Mr. David Fischer, told us at the end of 1980 and again in August 1981. But he conceded that he is troubled about its implementation. He admitted to us that since the time that France officially suspended the contract in mid-1978, neither the French nor the Pakistanis have kept the IAEA "properly informed" about what has been happening in the continuing construction of the plant, as they promised to do. This is hardly surprising, as the French believe their role is terminated, and the Pakistanis have been conducting much of their recent buying campaign in secret.

Linked with the safeguards arrangements for Chashma is the New Labs pilot reprocessing plant. The tripartite agreement on Chashma specifically called for safeguards on any other facility based on the same reprocessing technology—the solvent extraction method which SGN initially provided for both Chashma and the pilot plant.

But the language of the agreement is so vague that it is not clear whether this provision really included the pilot plant, which was begun in 1973, three years before the Chashma agreement. One paragraph seems to say that it does, another that it does not. A third paragraph leaves it to the French and the Pakistanis to notify the IAEA that any second facility exists. Neither of them has done so, and IAEA officials have been forced to write to the Pakistanis at least twice—in October 1978 and March 1979—asking them if they are designing, constructing, or operating any facilities at all that should be covered by the safeguards agreement. The Pakistanis have denied that they are, and in their latest reply—June 18, 1979—they specifically stated that there was no reprocessing facility in Pakistan about which they were obliged to tell the IAEA anything at all.

In other words, the Pakistanis were refusing to accept that they had any remaining obligation to accept safeguards either on Chashma or on the pilot plant. What is more, the agreement is so badly worded that the IAEA is in no position openly to accuse the Pakistanis of breaking their safeguards commitments. The outspoken Mr. Fischer openly admitted to us that the Chashma agreement was not his or the IAEA's finest effort. . . . "The language of the agreement is a little obscure," he conceded with admirable candor and considerable understatement.

What this means is that the only check on the Islamic bomb that the IAEA can offer is the safeguards on the Candu reactor in Karachi and on the used reactor fuel, which is the only known source of plutonium that the Pakistanis have available to reprocess either at Chashma or at the New Labs. Fischer admitted to us in August 1981 that Agency officials were "deeply concerned" even about the effectiveness of these safeguards on the used fuel in Karachi.

"There were fuel rods everywhere," he told us, and he foresaw the possibility that the Pakistanis could divert a few of them from the storage pools and replace them with dummies without being noticed.

Those are the safeguards. We concluded that anyone hoping to slow down the Pakistani nuclear program would do well to look beyond the nuclear watchdogs at the International Atomic Energy Agency and face up to the harder option of stopping the exports before they ever get to Pakistan.

FIVE

IRAQ

14

The Secret War

We don't have any interest in killing French or Europeans, but if they persist in continuing to serve the godless and bloodthirsty regime, they alone will be responsible for the consequences.
—Committee to Safeguard the Islamic Revolution,
August 1980

The Zionist Mossad, and its Zionist collaborators in Europe, are hunting Arab scientists there and even liquidating them physically.
—President Saddam Hussein,
July 20, 1980

Some say Israel. Some say Iran. . . . It could even be two people sitting in a room with typewriters. We just don't know.
—Yves Girard,
Vice President, Technicatome,
February 1981

The explosions rang out in the early hours of Friday, April 6, 1979. The first blast came at 3 A.M. A few minutes later, two more blasts ripped through the dark.

The secret war against the Iraqi bomb had begun.

The setting for this sudden outburst of prenuclear violence was a town of some 50,000 people located on the French Mediterranean. It is called La Seyne-sur-Mer, and it is next door to the port city of Toulon, where the French Navy harbors much of its Mediterranean fleet.

As a place to visit, La Seyne is very much betwixt and between. To the east stretches the alluring Côte d'Azur, with its blue sea and bright sandy beaches. To the west lies Marseilles, with its gang-infested docklands and its sprawling power plants spewing filth into the air.

La Seyne-sur-Mer is caught in the middle, neither a great resort nor a major industrial center. It is a tepid mixture of both. The harbor is picturesque, crammed with small pleasure craft. But there are also warehouses and small factories. The busses to Toulon stop running at eight o'clock in the evening. The mayor is a Communist. The concerns are bourgeois—taxes and inflation, pollution in the sea, and hippies on the beach.

The explosions came from the area around the harbor, from a hangarlike building of La Seyne's biggest firm—Constructions Navales et Industrielles de la Méditerranée, or CNIM.

The name suggests little of anything nuclear. The bulk of CNIM's work is naval and industrial construction for a wide range of clients, from the French Navy to Algeria and Saudi Arabia and any of a dozen other countries, including Israel.

But CNIM also has a small, highly sophisticated nuclear department, and had just completed a difficult and extremely sensitive piece of work—the construction of the reactor cores for the two research reactors that the French had sold to Iraq, the Osirak, or Tammuz I, and the smaller, "critical assembly," Tammuz II. CNIM technicians had just put the finishing touches on the core elements, and they were sitting in Hangar No. 3, waiting to be shipped to Iraq sometime in the next forty-eight hours.

The first blast echoed through the hangar building. The two security guards, sitting in a corrugated aluminum hut only 200 meters away, were shaken. One of them called the local police, who arrived within minutes.

Inside the hangar, the police found the wreckage, a tangle of hard-to-identify metal shapes, blasted by carefully placed explosive charges. The twisted metal included the Iraqi reactor cores, as well as some machinery for handling nuclear fuel charges for a client in Belgium and a huge piece of equipment for a nuclear reactor in West Germany. Whoever they were, the saboteurs had damaged all three nuclear orders.

Three additional explosives had failed to go off, and sappers were called in to dismantle them. The explosives were heavy military charges, like the kind used to blow up tanks, armor, and other heavy metal structures.

A few hours later, the Communist mayor of La Seyne-sur-Mer, M. Maurice Blanc, issued a public statement. "This Friday, at three o'clock in the morning, a series of explosions went off in a workshop manufacturing nuclear materials at CNIM. Fortunately, no one was hurt," he declared. The mayor also asked the French Government for financial aid.

The French internal security service, the Direction de la Surveillance du Territoire, soon arrived and took over the investigation from the local police. The French President, Valéry Giscard d'Estaing, sent a special envoy from Paris to check on the progress of the investigation. The investigators themselves would not say publicly what they had found, possibly because they had found so little.

They had found few clues—a flashlight, some small batteries, a few detonators, a worn glove. Nothing to suggest who had set the explosives, or why.

The two security guards said that they had not seen anyone approaching by land, either on foot or in a vehicle, even though their hut had a commanding view of the only road that enters the area. Their view of the harbor was less good. But they said that they had seen and heard nothing from there either, and the police found no evidence to confirm the suspicion that the bombers might have come by sea. The guards also heard no sound of the huge hangar doors opening. So it was assumed that the attackers must have gotten in through one of the small side doors, all of which had been tightly locked.

The verdict—a very professional piece of sabotage, possibly with a bit of help or information from someone on the inside.

No one could even be certain of why the saboteurs had struck, though CNIM immediately assumed that the target had been the reactor cores for Iraq. This had been CNIM's most prized nuclear project, as the company's François Canellas had explained at length only the day before, on Thursday, April 5. In a rare coincidence, CNIM had given a special briefing to a reporter and a photographer from the area's leading newspaper, the *Var Matin République*. The old shipbuilding firm had wanted to show off its new nuclear projects, which had gone unpublicized and were largely unknown, even in the little town of La Seyne.

As Canellas told the journalists—the thirty-five-year-old Jose Lenzini and his photographer Michel Beault—the Iraqi contract had been worth some 70 million French francs, or about $17 million, and had provided some 300,000 hours of work. This was the first time CNIM had produced a complete nuclear component, and M. Canellas clearly had big ideas for the future.

"This is the first French experimental reactor for export," he boasted. "It shows that France, and French export industry, is capable of doing extraordinary work. It's proof that French manufacturing is absolutely first-rate."

Canellas gave Lenzini a sheet of technical details on the Iraqi reactors, which the now curious reporter carefully filed away. It could prove useful when he started to write.

Later the same day, Lenzini and Beault were invited to visit the nuclear department itself, in the specially designed Hangar No. 3. "The department has sixty workers," the journalists were told. "They work here in completely sanitized conditions. The temperature is maintained at a constant twenty-two degrees centigrade."

Lenzini and Beault looked around carefully. They were perhaps the first outsiders to enter the hangar—certainly the first journalists—and they were intrigued by what they saw. As they remembered the scene, there were three wooden crates sitting next to the entrance, all of them clearly marked 'IRAK.'"

"Each was about two meters long, and about a meter and a half high," Lenzini later told us. "We were told these were the core elements, and they were ready to be shipped in a day or two to Baghdad. The word 'IRAK' was stamped everywhere. It couldn't be missed."

Farther to the left, Lenzini saw another piece of equipment still under construction. That was also for Iraq, he was told. It was the core for the smaller reactor, Tammuz II.

The journalists also saw the fuel-handling machinery for Belgium and the reactor part for West Germany, an amazing piece some fifteen meters high, Lenzini recalled.

Pleased with the story, even if it was only a local piece of boosterism, Lenzini turned to Beault. It was time to take the photographs. But here the journalists had a problem. Beault had come fully equipped with his camera and lenses. But he had left the film back at the office.

No problem, replied their hosts. The journalists could come back and get their pictures the next day—at 10 A.M. Friday, April 6. "There will be plenty of time for picture-taking," one of the CNIM officials assured them. "The Iraqi things don't go out until after tomorrow."

Needless to say, the journalists never got the pictures they expected. In the following twenty-four hours the story changed dramatically, and the normally grumpy Lenzini found himself with an unexpected head start on a major international story of nuclear intrigue.

For the world's press, the big question was obvious: Who did it? Who were the saboteurs?

The first answer came in telephone calls to *Le Monde* and other French newspapers from a self-proclaimed "French Ecological Group." "We have succeeded in neutralizing machines that are dangerous for the existence of human life," the callers declared. "The Harrisburg catastrophe * proves once again the dangers of the atomic industry. We have gone into action and we will do whatever is necessary to safeguard the life of the French population and the human race from nuclear horrors."

French environmentalists, when asked by the police, said that they had never heard of such a group, and doubted that French ecologists would or could carry out such a professional job of sabotage. Most observers agreed. The ecology movement in France had staged some rather fierce antinuclear demonstrations over the years. But the sabotage at La Seyne was really not their style.

Who then? The papers had a field day.

France Soir reported that the police suspected "extreme leftists." *Le Matin* suggested a group of Palestinians working for Libya. *Le Point* pointed at the American Central Intelligence Agency. The *International Herald Tribune* said that it might be the French themselves—"by order of someone very high up in the French Government"—in an effort to slip gracefully out of a sale they no longer thought wise.

Others saw the machinations of the Iranians, the Syrians, Arab dissidents, even the Iraqis, who were supposedly trying to embarrass a wavering France in order to strengthen their own hand in new nuclear negotiations.

* This is a reference to the Three Mile Island nuclear accident in Harrisburg, Pennsylvania, in 1978.

"In this novel of espionage that we are living at La Seyne-sur-Mer, international interests are so enormous that all theses remain plausible," concluded the local reporter Lenzini, in one of his several articles in *Var Matin République*. The only thing certain was that the saboteurs "were not anonymous ecologists, but highly specialized commandos trained for this type of mission." A good conspiratorialist, Lenzini himself leaned toward the theory that the French spooks did it, in a desperate and ultimately unsuccessful effort to get out of the contract. But that was only a guess, he insisted.

Most of the speculation in the press, and in various foreign ministries, centered on the obvious choice—the world's most celebrated commandos, the heros of Entebbe, the villains of Lillehammer, the cloak-and-dagger men of the legendary Israeli Mossad.

"There is ample precedent for Israeli commando actions on French soil," recalled Ronald Koven in *The Washington Post*. "Ten years ago, Israeli seamen made off with five missile-launching patrol boats built for Israel in the English Channel at Cherbourg. Their delivery was being blocked by the French Government."

The case sounded plausible. The Israelis had the motivation: They clearly did not want the Iraqis to have their bomb or the reactor that could give it to them. They had the means: Their highly specialized commandos were far more able at sabotage than the best that French ecologists could conceivably muster. And they were rarely afraid to act, even on foreign soil, when they believed their vital interests were at stake.

The Israelis also had good friends in the French nuclear industry, many of them from the early days of Franco-Israeli nuclear cooperation. They (or any country with good intelligence) could have gotten whatever information they wanted on which firms were doing what and when on the Iraqi project. And after the explosions went off, Israeli spokesmen were quick to applaud. Said one Israeli diplomat in Paris to the press, "This will delay the Iraqis by a year and a half."

It seemed a persuasive case. The Israelis could have. They would have. They might have. But did they?

Only the proof was lacking. Not that proof was needed, or even wanted, when some of the more sensationalist journalists tried their hand at recounting the incredible adventures of the Israeli superspooks, and how they pulled off the sabotage at La Seyne-sur-Mer.

The best of this brand of zero-proof storytelling was an exciting "inside account" by the highly regarded Erich Follath, in the German weekly *Stern*. The story claimed to have come from an "inside source," presumably an Israeli official with some kind of link to the Mossad team who supposedly did the job. The details were wondrously precise. Many of them were also probably wrong.

According to the "inside source," three Israeli agents had flown to Toulon in early April the day before the attack. They checked into three different second-rate hotels. Then, at 11 P.M., they met in a dark street and a waiting Renault took them to an isolated house in the country. There they studied the detailed plans of the industrial dock at CNIM.

The raid itself ran like clockwork. Knowing that the guards at CNIM did not make their rounds between midnight and 3 A.M., Follath wrote, "the three men scaled a high wall, sprinted toward a storage shed, opened the gate with a duplicate key, and deactivated the alarm system."

Their intention initially was to steal the key components. They worked feverishly. But they could not take apart the complicated equipment before the guards were due to return. So they attached explosive charges, set the timers, and disappeared over the wall. "The amount of explosives was so precise that the other units in the shed remained undamaged," reported the knowing Follath.

A whopping good yarn, indeed. And one that was largely repeated in newspapers and magazines all over the world. The only problem is that whoever did the sabotage, and however they did it, they could not have done it that way, as a visit to CNIM quickly proved.

We spent several days in La Seyne-sur-Mer trying to discover the true story of what happened. We walked through the grounds of the plant, spoke with the guards and other company workers, and even retraced the possible routes of entrance into the plant. We came up with some specific conclusions that showed the Follath account to be wrong.

First, there was no high wall or even fence to scale anywhere near the nuclear hangar.

Second, there was no electronic alarm system to deactivate, CNIM's chief of security revealed.

Third, the amount of explosives might have been precise, and it can probably be assumed—though still only assumed—that the objective of the raid was the Iraqi reactor cores. But the saboteurs also placed explosive charges on the Belgian and German units, and damaged them quite severely.

"The damage was about equal for all the clients," CNIM's Russian-born boss Vsevold Dmitrieff told us later, when we interviewed him in his Paris office. "But it was an excellent job. *Très professionel.*"

The sabotage, that is. Not the journalism. To be fair, it is possible—we would even say probable—that the Israelis made the attack. It is also possible that Follath and *Stern* got the story from an Israeli or related source. Whether they had done the job or not, the Israelis may have wanted to be given credit for it, and even if they did it, they may have leaked a story with bogus details to throw investigators off the track.

The culprits were never found. The French authorities could never find enough evidence to make a charge. Even so, we learned that the Israelis really did not mind being blamed. As an Israeli press officer stationed in Bonn at the time of the attack told us at a coffee klatch in Jerusalem, "I didn't protest about the story to *Stern* because frankly, true or not, I thought it was a positive story for us. It showed us being able to reach our enemies wherever they are. And without killing anybody."

Whether the Israelis did it or not, the sabotage at La Seyne-sur-Mer sent shock waves the world over, and not knowing for sure who did it added to the impact. The mystery helped keep the story—and the threat of the Iraqi bomb—alive in the international press and on television, and also in the minds of those helping the Iraqis with their nuclear program.

The psychological fallout is obvious to anyone who has talked to the French scientists and engineers working on the project, but it operates in curious ways. Nowhere did we find the impact more telling than in the case of an engineer we met at CNIM, whose name we shall not reveal because his colleagues later told us that he could be fired for the sheer act of talking with us. For him, the sabotage wrecked the perfection that he and his colleagues had created, and the pride and faith with which they had created it.

"I'm not a nuclear scientist. I'm not a politician either," he told us.

Did he feel responsible in any way for the possibility that the Iraqis wanted to make plutonium, and the bomb, from this equipment? we asked.

The question struck him as somewhat bizarre. "That isn't the point," he said, echoing a familiar refrain. "I do my job. I'm a technician. I don't make atomic bombs. But the work we did for Iraq was a remarkable piece of craftsmanship, a proof that France can produce the highest-quality nuclear equipment in the world."

Now that wonderful piece of work was gone.

The Backroom Diplomacy

The explosion at La Seyne-sur-Mer blasted the Iraqi bomb onto the front pages of the world's press, which was almost certainly what the saboteurs wanted. But even before the back-alley bombers began their secret war, the diplomats of at least six nations had been carrying on their own closed-door battle against the French sale to Iraq. And here, at least, it was no secret that the Israelis were playing a leading role.

Officially, the Israelis claim that they began expressing their concern to the French from the time of Jacques Chirac's trip to Baghdad at the end of 1974. But their initial concern seemed a bit muted, at least according to Eli Maissi, the seventy-year-old Paris correspondent of Israel's leading newspaper, *Haaretz*.

"The Israelis were actually late in assessing the danger of the Iraqi purchases from France," the veteran Maissi told us. "Back in 1976, I saw a small item about the French-Iraqi contract published in a French newspaper. My reaction was quite casual. I went to the French Atomic Energy Commission to ask about it, and they said it was a purely commercial deal. But when I looked through the literature on the Osiris reactor that they gave me, I found out that it was fed with 93 percent enriched uranium, and enough, I found out, for an atomic bomb.

"With these facts, I sent my first dispatch to my newspaper. As far as I know, it was the first authentic story about the French-Iraqi contract. A few days later, *Tribune Juive* in Strasbourg published a story about the secret French-Iraqi deal. The French Foreign Office came out with a noisy denial, saying the deal was purely commercial and not secret since notification had been published in the *Journal Officiel*. After this exchange, the Israel Embassy was instructed to query the French Foreign Office, and they got the same answers I did. Then the Israeli Embassy Counselor, Zvi Maz'el, told me in private that my insistence on the danger of the reactor in the hands of Iraq was a 'mania' on my part."

Maissi became a crusader on the issue. He pushed his newspaper and the Israeli Government, especially over the proposed delivery of the bomb-grade highly enriched uranium fuel. But no one in Israel seemed to take the Iraqi nuclear program seriously, he believed.

This lack of concern apparently continued until late 1977, when the Israeli Embassy in Paris began to protest officially to the Quai d'Orsay. But the protests proved a waste of time. The French Government of Valéry Giscard d'Estaing simply turned a deaf ear.

"The Israelis had a tough time," Mlle. Simone Herpels, the Belgian Foreign Office official in charge of nuclear issues, told us during an interview in her Brussels office. "Iraq was an NPT state, and the Israelis had never signed the treaty. This was also just at the time that the revelations were coming out about Plumbat, and it was the Israelis themselves who looked like the nuclear outlaws."

Some friendly diplomats suggested that the Israelis should first sign the Nonproliferation Treaty, and then make the protest. But the Israelis refused outright. The treaty was worthless, they argued. Israel favored a different approach, at least diplomatically—the creation of a nuclear free zone in the Middle East or a regional agreement like the Treaty of Tlatelolco. The Israelis offered to sit down to discuss the idea with the Arab states, no strings attached. But as the Israelis knew all too well, many of the the Arabs—including Iraq—were still in a state of war with Israel and were not about to sit down at the same table. That would imply the beginning of some form of recognition, which most of the Arab states were not willing to grant.

The Arabs also suspected that the Israeli proposal for a nuclear free zone was a trick, designed to guarantee Israel's nuclear superiority, as there would be no way that the Arabs could know for sure that the Jewish state had destroyed all of its preexisting nuclear weapons or all of the material to make more of them.

In any case, the Israelis continued to express their concern about the Iraqi purchases. The French continued to ignore them. And this was the standoff in the somber halls of diplomacy when the saboteurs set off their first bombs at La Seyne-sur-Mer.

The Americans also moved to protest the French sale, and they moved far more quickly than the Israelis. The French signed the contract with Iraq in August 1976, and in November the Ford Administration raised the question with Paris rather vigorously, with backing from some of the Western European allies, including Great Britain.

The reaction from Paris was predictable. On December 3, the Gaullist former Foreign Minister, Michel Debré, spoke out sharply in Parliament. Those who criticized the sale of the reactors to Iraq were completely wrong, he countered. "We cannot let our American and European allies continue their offensive against our nuclear industry."

Nuclear sales were France's business, no one else's, and as Iraq had signed the Nonproliferation Treaty, the French believed it wrong to criticize the deal. Always ready to defend their own motives, some Frenchmen began to suggest darkly that America's real reasons for opposing the sale were themselves deserving of suspicion: America was losing out in the worldwide nuclear sales competition, and commercial jealousy prompted the strong U.S. antiproliferation stance.

In the following year, the new Carter Administration stepped up the pressure. Jimmy Carter and his antiproliferation man, Dr. Joseph Nye Jr., were already hitting out at French help to the Chashma Reprocessing Plant in Pakistan, and the French were beginning to back down. But on Iraq the French—even the "good" French—simply felt picked on.

"We did not perceive Iraq as wanting the bomb in the same way that the Pakistanis did," the former secretary of the Council on Foreign Nuclear Policy, M. André Jacomet, told us in one of our lengthy interviews with him in Paris. "On Pakistan, we had access to some documents indicating their intent. On Iraq, we only knew what we knew. And Iraq had signed the Nonproliferation Treaty."

So the French held fast. The Americans kept pushing. Tempers grew. Relations soured even more. Finally in January 1978 the split over Iraq took a new turn. The Americans were supplying the highly enriched uranium for France's own civilian research reactors, and the French had understood that fuel could be used for sale to the Iraqis. In fact, the French had already quoted a price and signed the contract with Iraq on the basis of their selling the cheaper American fuel.

Now the Americans issued an emphatic ruling forbidding any reshipment of the uranium to any third party without explicit American permission. If the French wanted the Iraqis to have highly enriched uranium, which was bomb grade, the Americans wanted it clearly understood that they would not be able to give them any of what the Americans supplied to France. The French would have to rely solely on their already overburdened enrichment plant at Pierrelatte, which produced primarily for the military *force de frappe*. And, added an unhappy spokesman for the French Atomic Energy Commission, the French plant produced the highly enriched uranium "at a price about three to four times more than the Americans charge us."

The Americans, with their considerable leverage, could not convince the French to discontinue the sale of heavily enriched uranium. Yet the campaign had some effect. In the end the French agreed to stage deliveries of the bomb-grade fuel so that only the actual amounts needed for the running of the reactor would be available to the Iraqis at any one time. This would make it very difficult, though not impossible, for the Iraqis ever to divert the fuel to military use.

It was hardly a surprise that by 1978 both the Americans and the Israelis could be found pounding on the door of the Quai d'Orsay. The Israelis totally distrusted the French by this time, and they had finally awakened to the consequences of the nuclear sale to Iraq. The Americans' antiproliferation approach under President Carter was already causing considerable friction among the European Allies, and they increasingly believed that Iraq wanted the Osirak reactor in order to make the bomb.

What is surprising is that they were not the only countries protesting. The French-Iraqi contract had aroused a sense of concern and anxiety among a curiously diverse group of countries. One of them was the country that Saddam Hussein had called "the number-one friend of Iraq," the Soviet Union. According to French diplomatic sources, the Soviets approached the French in early 1979 with a polite note asking for "details" on the Iraqi nuclear project. The note made no overt criticism. But as the Soviets had refused to give Iraq what France was now providing, their message was deliciously clear. The French responded, our sources told us, with some details about the deal, assuring the Soviets that international controls applied and that the reactor was intended strictly for peaceful uses.

Far more surprising, however, were the questions and protests from Iraq's closest neighbors in the Middle East, all of which were showing increased anxiety about the agreement. The French Government has kept these diplomatic flurries absolutely secret, and until now there has been little known about them. But they show the strong undercurrent of concern throughout the region, and not just on the part of the Israelis. As one French official explained to us, no Arab state, and certainly no Iranian government, wants any other state in the region to have the kind of technological advantage that would make it a regional superpower.

The Saudi Arabians were especially nervous on the subject, and first approached the Quai d'Orsay in 1978. According to the same French official, they asked for and received assurances from France that the Iraqi nuclear program would not lead to nuclear weapons.

The Saudis had many fears. The royal family run their desert kingdom as they please. They pray to a demanding God. And they reap the profits of the rawest kind of capitalism. Communism, atheism, radicalism, and the antiroyalist sentiment so strong in classic Arab nationalism all threaten Saudi rule and Saudi riches, and the Saudis saw shades of all these threats in the Iraqi Baath Socialists.

An Iraqi bomb, they feared, would only sharpen the threats. Not that the Iraqis would ever drop it on their Saudi cousins—that would be inconceivable—but simply having the bomb would make Iraq supreme in the entire Arabian Gulf. That, at least, was Saudi thinking in 1978.

Like the Saudis, the Iranians were also casting sideways glances at the rapid nuclear development in neighboring Iraq. Under the Shah, they also approached France to make known their fears. And in 1980, as war with Iraq began to threaten, the new Islamic government in Tehran renewed efforts with the French and other European governments to stop the Iraqi nuclear program.

"The French reactor for Iraq made us nervous," the former head of the Iranian atomic energy commission, Dr. Akbar Etamad, told us in a hastily arranged interview conducted in a discreet Paris café. Etamad, as a favored protegé of the deposed Shah, at the time of the interview literally feared for his life. He was one of the former Iranian officials whom the Islamic militants of Ayatollah Khomeini had vowed to track down mercilessly.

"In our time we didn't like the fact that the Iraqis were scheduled to receive highly enriched uranium," he told us. "It's relatively easy to divert this from the fuel cycle, and we expressed our concerns to the French. I don't believe that the present government feels any differently."

Indeed, in 1980 the Islamic militants had made uncharacteristically discreet approaches to both the French and the Italians to express their concern about Iraqi nuclear progress, and both governments had tried to reassure the Iranians.

Under Dr. Etamad's leadership, Iran itself had begun to build a multibillion-dollar nuclear program, ordering large power reactors from West Germany and France. The Iranians had also secured the promise of a reprocessing plant from the Germans, and the Americans were forced to offer the Shah the right to buy several billion dollars' worth of sophisticated conventional weapons to sidetrack Iran's interest in the nuclear option.

With the fall of the Shah, the country's nuclear potential was sharply reduced. The Islamic revolutionaries announced that they would stop the civilian nuclear program, and much of what Etamad and his nuclear scientists had built now stood unused, gathering rust in the hot desert sun.

Dr. Etamad told us that now, especially with the drawn-out war against Iraq, some of the people near the Ayatollah Khomeini—including at least one scientist, Dr. Ali Sekhavat, who had worked for Etamad—might push the Iranians into a nuclear weapons program. And, he added, they would be very tempted to do this if the Iraqi nuclear buildup continued unabated and it became clear that a nuclear bomb would be the result.

The Syrians also opposed the Iraqi nuclear threat, and approached France to complain as early as 1977. In view of the violence that would soon plague the Iraqi nuclear program, the Syrian opposition was highly significant. The two countries were already caught up in an extremely violent underground struggle, which would soon spill over onto the streets of London, Paris, Tripoli, Beirut, Kuwait, and Karachi.

Baghdad and Damascus had historically seen themselves as rivals in the Arab world, and the coming to power of competing Baathist cliques in the two capitals only made the rivalry more intense. The immediate conflict came to a head in late 1977 and 1978 over the Palestinians. Baghdad was backing two separate factions within the Palestine Liberation Organization, while Damascus had its own PLO unit, al-Saiqa, which effectively functioned as part of the Syrian Army. At least nominally, Damascus sided with the PLO Executive under Yasir Arafat, which Baghdad opposed.

As the bitterness between the factions grew, the Iraqis picked up the gun to back their favorites, and also to dispense revolutionary justice to Iraqi dissidents working for the wrong side. This became most dramatic in London in July 1978, when an Iraqi gunman shot and killed the former Iraqi Prime Minister Abdel Razak Naif, who was believed to be working with the Syrians and the PLO.

Following the murder, the British expelled five Iraqi diplomats. "Our increasing concern at the terrorist threats in this country," declared Foreign Secretary David Owen, "has led us to believe that the presence of known Iraqi intelligence officers here is not desirable."

Within days, the other side struck back, when a Palestinian gunman burst into the Iraqi Embassy in Paris and took nine people hostage. His demand— freedom for two comrades arrested in a London bombing. The French police quickly surrounded the Embassy and prepared to wait the gunman out. But the Iraqis could not wait. Against the firm wishes of the French police, the Iraqi secret service sent their own men smashing in with guns blazing. In the charge, the Iraqis accidentally killed a French policeman, Jacques Cappela.

This action put the French Government in a bind. Their own powerful police union was yelling that the assassins should be tried in a French court. But the government could not afford to offend the Iraqis, not with all the ongoing military and nuclear sales. So Paris decided to stay out of the squabble, and simply expelled three of the Iraqi secret service men, the cop killers, to be "arraigned by Iraqi justice."

"The way things are done in Iraq, I don't personally think there will even be a trial," complained the very angry head of the French police union.

The plotting and killing went on throughout 1978 and into mid-1979, when Saddam Hussein became the Iraqi President. Within weeks, Saddam charged that the Syrians were plotting a coup to unseat him, to be led by his longtime friend and comrade, the new Deputy Prime Minister, Adnan Hussein al-Hamdami. Saddam crushed the coup, arresting and later executing al-Hamdami, "killing his best friend with his own hands in order to become the sole ruler," as the Israeli Prime Minister, Menachem Begin, would later put it.

Saddam then turned the tables, opening links inside Syria with the extreme right-wing Muslim Brotherhood, who were already making problems for the Syrian President Hafez al-Assad. Saddam also offered Iraqi backing to dissident Syrian Baathists, including the former Syrian Prime Minister, Salah al-Din al-Bitar.

On July 21, 1980, in his Paris apartment, al-Bitar was killed by an unknown assailant, believed to be a member of a Syrian intelligence death squad.

The Syrians, the Iranians, the Saudis, the Soviets, the Americans, the Israelis—all had reason to fear Saddam Hussein's Iraq, and all had openly or secretly approached the French to protest their help in the making of a possible Iraqi atomic bomb. All of them would become suspect when violence once again touched the Iraqi nuclear program.

The el-Meshad Murder

The Meridien is a garish, air-conditioned hotel, the kind of ultramodern structure you might expect to see in Dallas or Los Angeles. But this one is in Paris, on a seedy side street right across from the Palais des Congrès at Place Maillot. The hotel is owned by Air France and frequented by wealthy executives and the occasional diplomat, many of them from the Middle East. Surprisingly, the Meridien is not a bad place to go in the evening to listen to traditional jazz, played at the far end of the open-plan lobby. It is also a good spot to pick up a woman. And with its long, anonymous hallways and soundproof rooms, it is the perfect place to get away with murder.

It was June 14, 1980. The "Do Not Disturb" sign had been hanging on the door of Room 9041 ever since the night before. Finally, the chambermaid let herself in. She looked into the room and immediately called for help. A few minutes later the police arrived.

The body of a man, still fully dressed in coat and tie, was lying across the bed. His head had been bashed in with a heavy, blunt object, and he had been left to die of his wounds. There was blood on the carpet and on the walls. Papers from his briefcase were scattered about. His money was still in his wallet, and only a personal diary seemed to be missing. There was also a bathroom towel, smeared with a woman's makeup.

"A romantic liaison," the police suggested.

The victim was an Arab, an Egyptian who had been recruited to work for the Iraqis. He was a nuclear scientist. His name was Dr. Yahya el-Meshad.

Trained as a Ph.D. in electrical engineering in the Soviet Union, el-Meshad had worked for the Egyptian Atomic Energy Commission from 1961 to 1968, when he became professor of nuclear engineering at the University of Alexandria. The Iraqis then recruited him following the big Atomic Energy Conference in Baghdad in 1975, and he split his time between

Baghdad University and the Iraqi Atomic Energy Commission, which had sent him to France on a very special mission.

The contracts between France and Iraq called for the Iraqis to make a final inspection of all goods before they were shipped, the procedure that the French call the *procès-verbal*. This included the much disputed highly enriched uranium fuel. El-Meshad came to France in June 1980 to make the scientific tests that would ascertain the quality of the very first shipment of bomb-grade fuel from France to Iraq. "His job was to receive and check the materials," confirmed an official spokesman of the French Atomic Energy Commission. "He was a frequent visitor here in Paris, and our scientists knew him well."

Because of the controversy surrounding the Iraqi contract, the details of el-Meshad's mission were shrouded in secrecy. The French did not make public any information about him or his itinerary, and they did not share the information with their American Allies. Nor, of course, with the Israelis, the Saudis, the Iranians, or the Syrians. We learned that he had gone first to the nuclear centers at Cadarache and Pierrelatte, and then to Saclay and Fontenay-aux-Roses.

In these centers of the French nuclear program, Dr. el-Meshad tested, examined, observed—and was well satisfied. It was a big moment for the Iraqi nuclear program, and el-Meshad signed that the 93 percent highly enriched uranium fuel met the specifications. The uranium could be shipped without further delay.

His work done, the quiet Egyptian scientist decided to stay over in Paris, where he was already staying at the Hotel Meridien. This was on June 12. What he did between then and the moment he met his death sometime the following night is still anybody's guess.

The police had only one real lead. From the makeup on the towel next to el-Meshad's battered body, they set out to check the prostitutes who worked the Meridien. After several days, they found what they had expected from the start. As Dr. el-Meshad came into the lobby of the Meridien at about 6:30 on the fateful evening, he had been approached by a woman, who had apparently followed him up to his room. Had she seen anything? Was she a witness to the murder, or even a participant in it?

The woman's name was Marie Claude Magal, a thirty-two-year-old hooker who frequented the hotel and several of the nearby clubs. The police interrogated her on July 1, more than two weeks after the killing. She admitted that she had gone up to the Egyptian in the hotel lobby, and had followed him up in the elevator and along the hallway. But, she smiled, she had not gone into the room with him. Despite her many charms, the man had turned her down. "The affair was never concluded," the prostitute told the police. "He went into his room alone."

Marie Claude waited in the hallway, hoping he would change his mind or that something else would turn up. She heard noises in the room. There was another person in there with him. But, she insisted, she had definitely not heard anything to suggest an argument or a violent struggle. Nothing at all.

The police were not so sure. They thought the prostitute had something more to tell, and after a few days they asked her to come back for a second interrogation. But the police would never get to hear what more, if anything, she had to say. On July 12, Marie Claude Magal was hit by a car and killed.

According to the police, she had gone to a bar on the Boulevard Saint-Germain, a Left Bank hangout called The Old Navy, where she became drunk, or perhaps drugged. She left the bar barely able to walk, weaved across the sidewalk, and pushed her way uninvited into a car by the curb. The driver, a gas station attendant, got angry and threw her onto the street, and at that very moment a Renault 5 sped by and smacked into Marie Claude Magal.

Was the death of the prostitute linked in any way to the killing of the nuclear scientist? Was it perhaps an attempt to get rid of the only witness to the murder of el-Meshad? The police thought not.

"All hypothesis of a criminal act is dismissed," declared police spokesman M. Pierret. "It was a banal accident, like so many."

Others thought differently. Marie Claude's mother insisted that the girl did not like to drink or take drugs, though that was possibly just a mother talking. And she recalled that in the days before Marie Claude's "accident" there had been several menacing telephone calls, all from the same unidentified stranger.

Not much to build a case on, or even to suggest a connection to the killing of the scientist. And nothing at all to answer the question: Who killed el-Meshad? And why?

Again, much of the speculation in the press centered on the Israelis. But this time observers had their doubts.

"It just wasn't their style," one French official told us. "They don't beat a man over the head and leave him to die."

The Israelis were also unusually vigorous in denying the killing. "It's getting so that whatever happens in the Middle East, we're blamed—for what we don't do as well as what we do," an official of the Israeli Foreign Office complained to us in Jerusalem. "But I assure you that we don't bludgeon people over the head with hammers and leave them to die."

Self-serving, perhaps, but probably true. Even in their publicized killings of the suspected Arab terrorist leaders following the massacre at the Munich Olympics, the Israeli hit teams tended to do their work in a professional, almost clinical way. Leaving a badly wounded man to die, or perhaps to live, is hardly the way a pro sets out to kill.

In fact, the killing did not look like the work of any first-rate secret service—unless the killing was unintended. From Marie Claude's testimony to the police and the scatter of papers in the room, it seems likely that the intruder had slipped into the room while el-Meshad was out in order to go through his documents, and possibly his personal diary. El-Meshad returned. He caught the intruder in the act. There was a brief struggle. The intruder hit el-Meshad in the head, put the "Do Not Disturb" sign on the door, and quietly went on his way.

All of which does not say who, but might say how and why.

Other speculation has centered on the Syrians, who were already spilling blood with the Iraqis. *Rose-al-Yousseff*, the well-connected Egyptian weekly, suggested that the killers might have been Syrian agents backed by a Communist-bloc intelligence service. Their object—to get inside information on the progress of the Iraqi nuclear program.

According to the weekly, the night before his death, el-Meshad was seen at an Arab restaurant near his hotel. He was dining with men who were "either Syrian, Lebanese, or Palestinian in features." There was a loud argument in Arabic. The story suggested that the men were trying to pry information out of el-Meshad about "the exact stage that Iraq had reached in its atomic project."

Rose-al-Yousseff offered the story only as speculation, and it is likely that much of it comes from Egypt's energetic and often imaginative intelligence service. Even so, our own research suggests that the Syrians would have been in an excellent position to get a great deal of inside information about the expatriate Egyptian Yahya el-Meshad. Their source—a second Egyptian nuclear scientist, who is now working in Syria, Dr. Esmet Zain el-Deen.

We traveled to humid, hot Alexandria in the Nile delta to speak with el-Meshad's friends and former colleagues, among them Dr. Mohammed Nagy, the thirty-eight-year-old current chairman of the University of Alexandria's Nuclear Engineering Department. He told us that both el-Meshad and el-Deen had been co-workers, but also longtime rivals, on the Alexandria faculty.

The two men differed radically in both temperament and politics. El-Meshad was "quiet," "a family man," and "rather apolitical." El-Deen was "outspoken," "a political showoff," and "a left-wing troublemaker." El-Meshad had first gotten a post at the university when el-Deen was forced to resign for political reasons in 1968 and had to go into exile in Syria. When el-Deen returned in 1972, el-Meshad stood in his way. And just after el-Meshad went to work for the Iraqi nuclear program, el-Deen took a similar job in Syria.

As with speculation about the Israelis, there is absolutely no hard evidence to link Dr. el-Deen in any way with the death of el-Meshad. But the Syrians had a life-and-death interest in the Iraqi nuclear program. They were already engaged in a great deal of violence and bloodshed against the Iraqis. And in Dr. el-Deen they would have had a firsthand source of information on the scientific skills and personal habits of the ill-fated el-Meshad.

Again, the whodunit went unsolved, while the impact on those working for the Iraqi nuclear program grew even larger.

When Yahya el-Meshad was found murdered in his room at the Meridien Hotel, the French scientists and technicians who had worked with him were shocked and alarmed. Who, they wondered, was stalking in their midst? But in a strange way, many of them were even more worried when they heard about the possibly unconnected death of the prostitute Marie Claude Magal.

"It seemed that whoever it was, they would reach anywhere, go to any lengths," one French scientist told us. "When they hit the whore, I had the feeling we weren't safe anymore. If they could find her, and even the police had a hard time, who knew what could happen next?"

The Islamic Committee

Rome. August 7, 1980. It is in the very early hours, sometime between 1:30 and 3:00 in the morning. A small bomb explodes outside the front door of a third-floor apartment at Via Della Lungaretta 55. The owner is out of town. He is Engineer Mario Fiorelli, director-general of SNIA-Techint, the firm supplying hot cells and other nuclear labs to Iraq.

At about the same time, two more bombs rip through the first floor of a building at Via A. Bargonia 34, the offices of Engineer Fiorelli's firm, SNIA-Techint.

The bomb at Fiorelli's apartment had been placed in front of the door in a small vase with a plastic plant. The damage was minimal. A hole in the door. Some plaster shaken loose from the surrounding wall.

The two bombs in the office—some 800 grams of mining powder each—did considerably more damage. They destroyed the furniture and the air-conditioning and electrical systems within an area of 450 square meters. They shattered the flimsy office partitions, and left gaping holes in the walls.

The bombers also went through SNIA's Iraqi files, and company officials concluded that they had photographed them.

Both the apartment and the offices were empty at the time of the explosions. No one was hurt, and no one saw anything. There were no watchmen. No alarm systems to deactivate. No antiburglar gadgets.

As in the bombing of the reactor cores at La Seyne-sur-Mer, the new bombings were claimed by a group that no one had ever heard of before—this time the wonderfully named "Committee to Safeguard the Islamic Revolution."

We spent days, and a researcher we employed in Rome spent several weeks, trying to dig out the facts behind what happened. We spoke with Italian nuclear officials in the government, with concerned company officials, the police, and some of the people who actually received the threats. We finally managed to obtain actual copies of the letters and even transcripts of the telephoned warnings.

A note on the landing of Engineer Fiorelli's apartment building told why the bombings had been done, and what might be expected in the future if Italian nuclear aid to Iraq continued. "We have been given the mission to protect the glorious Islamic Revolution and to fight against all its enemies, and all who help the enemies of the Revolution will be our enemies," the note began. "We know of your personal collaboration. . . . We implore you immediately to stop your activities, which we see as an act against us and our Revolution."

The note ended with a threat: "If you don't do this, we will strike out against you and your family without pity."

Later that morning, somewhere between 7 and 8 A.M., the bombers repeated the warning, this time on the telephone. Engineer Fiorelli was still out, and the message was left on his answering machine.

"We the Committee to Safeguard the Islamic Revolution warn you to give up your aid to the enemies of the Revolution at once," the voice demanded. "Do as we say before it is too late for you and for all those close to you. Long live the Islamic Revolution."

The voice was studied and overdramatic, the Italian stilted and foreign, according to a top SNIA official who heard the tape.

A few minutes later, there was a second call. It was the same voice, and roughly the same message. But this time he was no longer reading, his Italian was riddled with grammatical errors, and he used the Spanish word *vida*, life, for the Italian *vita*.

Some 300 miles away in Genoa on the same night, the bombers apparently tried to strike again. The target this time—SNIA-Techint's partner in supplying nuclear labs to the Iraqis, the giant Ansaldo Mecanico Nucleare.

According to the police report we obtained, the company's twenty-seven-year-old watchman, Vittorio Piccolo, saw a youth approaching Ansaldo's headquarters at Via Gabriella d'Annunzio. The young man was carrying a suspicious-looking brown sack. Piccolo yelled at him to halt. The youth began to run. Piccolo pulled out his pistol and fired into the air. The youth scampered around the corner and disappeared into the night.

The bombings and the incident in Genoa were quickly followed by a series of threatening letters, all signed by the same "Committee to Safeguard the Islamic Revolution." One of the letters came to Dr. Silvio Cao, the head of the fuel cycle department at the atomic energy agency, the Comitato Nazionale per l'Energia Nucleare.

A soft-spoken, gentle man, Dr. Cao was shaken, as were many of his colleagues. The Italian Government insisted on providing full protection, including an Alsetta car specially equipped with thick bullet-proof glass, a two-way radio, a siren, and a souped-up engine. For months after the threat, the car picked Dr. Cao up every morning at his elegant villa in the exclusive Olgiata suburb, a Roman equivalent of Beverly Hills, but one surrounded even in normal times by a high iron gate and specially hired guards. The car also drove Dr. Cao home at night. He was advised never to leave home without checking with the police. His eyes were always on the lookout. So were those of his wife and children.

Further threats were sent to Ansaldo and SNIA officials, as well as to the trade unions of both companies.

The threatening letters and the bombings at SNIA-Techint and the apartment of Engineer Fiorelli received scant attention in the press. As terrorist incidents go, they were small potatoes in the Italy of the neo-Fascists and the Red Brigades, and they were also poorly timed. Earlier that same week a right-wing group had placed a bomb in the railway station at Bologna. It had killed more than a hundred people.

The "Committee to Safeguard the Islamic Revolution" could hardly compete with that—except perhaps in the troubled minds of those working on the Iraqi nuclear project.

But Italy was only half the story. The "Committee" also struck in France, and they did it on the same August night that they bombed their targets in Italy.

The intended target in France was the home of M. Jean-Jacques Graf, a top official in the French Atomic Energy Commission, the CEA. Graf, who was forty-eight, had previously handled the design of the Osiris reactor at Saclay. Now he directed the Osirak project at the CEA subsidiary Technicatome, and had just been awarded the coveted Legion d'honneur. The bombers placed a small *plastique* just outside the apartment of Jean-Jacques Graf, and it went off in the early morning hours, causing little damage and injuring no one.

The bombers explained in a telephone call to Agence France Presse: "Jean-Jacques Graf received the Legion of Honor for his work in atomic armament, and we have given him what he merits for his work against our Revolution. We shall take care of all collaborators with the renegade regime in Iraq."

The coordination between the bombings in Italy and in France was impressive. But the bombers in France made one slight mistake. They got the home of the wrong Jean-Jacques Graf. Instead of the nuclear scientist, they somehow found another man of the same name, an older man who runs a *petite librairie* in the Paris suburb of Saint-Germain-en-Laye.

The old bookseller had absolutely nothing to do with "atomic armament" or with Iraq, and he really could not understand why anyone would want to bomb his home. But the mistake scarcely softened the psychological threat to the right Jean-Jacques Graf, who was heading the Osirak project at Technicatome and was in Iraq at the time.

As in Italy, the bombers also sent threatening letters to top officials and technicians at the major companies involved in the project. The letters proved that the bombers knew the names of many of the key people. Their list for Technicatome, which was the main contractor and designer on the Osirak, was particularly complete. Other letters were sent to technicians and engineers working in Iraq at Tuwaitah. One French official told us that these letters had been mailed within Iraq and carried Iraqi postmarks. Two of the SGN people in Iraq received such a threat. One was the top man, the project manager. The other was the stockkeeper, the lowest-ranking person on the project. The detailed knowledge of who was working on the Iraq project really made people scared.

As in Italy, there were also a series of letters to the syndicates, the trade unions. The letters, mostly printed by hand, were a strange mixture of Marx, Muhammad, and Charles Manson. We obtained copies of the letters through our own sources in French nuclear officialdom and the unions.

At Technicatome, the letter to the workers told them that management had received warning letters "not to carry out the shameful and danger-filled work of the bood-splattered dictator of Baghdad."

"We warn you now that if your company's employees leave for Baghdad in spite of our warnings, their blood will be spilled. And we won't be held back by the presence of foreign personnel, as we have been up till now," the letter said. "If you wish to avoid spilling the blood of your employees, you should vigorously oppose their leaving for Baghdad."

At Comsip, the elctronic controls firm, the union officials got an even juicier version. Their letter posed a question: "Is it that the workers of your company want to eat bread soaked in the blood of women and children? It seems that the directors of your company don't care about spilling innocent blood while they fill their pockets. But you, the workingmen, have a human conscience."

The letter called on the Comsip workers to give their cooperation. "We ask you to halt the fascist Iraqi conspiracy that has poured extravagant sums into the pockets of your bosses to obtain the materials illegally to fabricate atomic bombs. You cannot tolerate the genocidal extermination of the masses," the letter proclaimed. "We ask you, in the name of humanity and your own conscience, to help us in our campaign against the Iraqi bomb. It is necessary to rouse the workers, who should certainly be allied against the fascist and corrupt Iraqi plan."

For all its purple prose, the letter had its effect. The Comsip workers formally brought their fears to the attention of the management. They asked their bosses some tough questions in writing:

Did the company think that the threats would be followed by action? If the workers were attacked, would management assume responsibility? Could a worker leave the project voluntarily without losing his job? Could the company and the CEA assure the workers that Iraq was not going to build *la bombe islamique*, either with the enriched uranium or by irradiating other fuel in the reactor?

Comsip and the other French companies tried to play down the risks. But the campaign of bombings and threatening letters was beginning to take its toll. Many workers and technicians were wondering if the double and triple salaries they were paid for working in Iraq were really worth the risk. Some of the trade union officials were asking out loud if the companies really were helping the Iraqis to build the bomb. And if they were, a few were saying openly that they wanted no part of it.

Who, then, was responsible for all the threats and bombings? Who was carrying out this psychological war against the French and Italians working on the Iraqi contracts?

The "Committee to Safeguard the Islamic Revolution" had come out of nowhere, and the skill and the care and the subtlety of its campaign seemed out of step with the open militancy of the Islamic revolutionaries in Iran and Iraq. Unlike the bludgeoning of el-Meshad, this was a very professional piece of work indeed, the kind of psychological warfare that is waged only by somebody's first-rate secret service.

That, at least, was the thinking of many of the nuclear officials in both France and Italy, and some of them told us openly that the Israelis were to blame.

"The Israelis are responsible, not just for this, but for many of the problems in the Middle East," a top official at SNIA-Techint exclaimed. "They have mistreated the Palestinians and now they're trying to get at us for providing a standard, commercial piece of equipment."

"The knowledge of our nuclear industry is too good," confided an official of the French Atomic Energy Commission in Paris. "We've never heard of this Islamic Committee before, and maybe we'll never hear from them again. It has to be the Israelis."

He had no proof, of course. Later he tried to backtrack on his statement out of fear that we might quote him by name. He believed the Israelis were superintelligent, superefficient, and he pointed to the attack on the wrong Jean-Jacques Graf as an example. For him, this was a telling illustration of Jewish cunning, not Islamic incompetence.

"Very clever," he declared. "Far too intelligent to be Islamic."

Again, there was no evidence, which only increased the sense of fear. But as one observer pointed out, the campaign of threats did recall a known Israeli operation in the early 1960s. The target then was the Egyptian rocket program.

In July 1962, Egypt launched four rockets, two of them with a range of 350 miles. The Egyptian President, Gamal Abdel Nasser, announced that he could now hit "any target south of Beirut."

Nasser meant Israel, of course, and the Israelis were worried. They had launched their own Shavit rocket only the year before, and they had no intention of losing their advantage to an enemy which seemed as determined then as Iraq seems today to destroy the Jewish state.

But that was only part of the worry. The Egyptians had recruited former Nazi scientists to help build the rockets, and the Israelis heard rumors that the Egyptians and their ex-Nazi helpers were planning to use the rockets to attack Israel with warheads of the deadly cobalt 60 or even nuclear weapons.

The Israeli Mossad set out to scuttle the entire Egyptian program, and they did it by using terror against the German scientists. This included threatening letters, personal visits, and small bombs sent in packages through the mail.

The results made headlines all over the world. One of the bombs sent to Cairo exploded and blinded a secretary in one eye. Another bomb killed five people. And in Switzerland, police arrested an Israeli official and his German informer for allegedly threatening the daughter of one of the

German scientists. The campaign worked. It scared off many of the scientists. But it also gave the Israelis a bad name.

The present campaign of the "Committee to Safeguard the Islamic Revolution" looked very much like an updating of the old tactic. Only this time the secret warriors seemed to be taking much greater care to protect life and limb. And if anything went wrong . . . well, there were always the Islamic followers of Ayatollah Khomeini to blame.

But the Israelis were not the only ones who could have written the letters and sent the bombs, as several of the French and Italian scientists and technicians were quick to admit.

"It's a racist reflex to blame the Mossad for everything," warned a French scientist in a conversation held in a Paris restaurant. "Here in France, we just don't think the Arabs are capable of doing anything. We also forget that the Iranians are well trained and capable. Many of their people receive first-rate training. I wouldn't underestimate them."

"There's absolutely no proof of anything," added Yves Girard, the Technicatome Vice President. "Some say Israel. Some say Iran. We're looking hard to find a proof. But we do not have one. It could even be a small organization. A few people in Paris or Baghdad could do the job. It could even be two people sitting in a room with typewriters. We just don't know."

They just did not know, and that is what has made the secret war so scary. They did not know who was attacking them. They did not know if it was one group, or several. They knew only that they were the targets, the ones under attack in a Middle Eastern war that they claimed not to understand, in which they thought they did not play a part. They still did not realize that by helping to provide bomb-making technology to one of the countries involved, they were now at center stage.

15

A Bomb in Time

The torture was quite cruel. Dr. Sharastani has been seriously injured by it. And we are still not sure if he is dead or alive.
—Mme. Lison Vallet,
Amnesty International (French Section),
July 1981

I am persuaded that Iraq is preparing itself to have an atomic bomb.
—Dr. Francis Perrin,
Former head, French Atomic Energy Commission,
September 1980

What's been done about Iraq is unfair. They have accepted the Nonproliferation Treaty. They have accepted safeguards. They fulfill all the conditions. The criticism is not just and more than that, it tends to destroy the basis of NPT.
—Dr. Claude Zangger,
Swiss Federal Energy Office,
November 1980

For Saddam Hussein, it was all coming together and it was all coming apart. Long the driving force in the ruling Baath Socialist Party, the one-time terrorist from Takrit formally became President of Iraq in July 1979. He was now the supreme leader, the man up front in Baghdad's headlong rush to become the "radiant center" of the Arab world and the number-one power in the entire Middle East.

The stakes were enormous, and nowhere more so than in Iraq's ambitious nuclear buildup, which Saddam Hussein himself had described in his September 1975 interview in *al-Usbua al-Arabi* as "the first Arab attempt at nuclear arming."

The nuclear center at Tuwaitah was already the most advanced in any Arab country, the proud beginning of a research and training program that would make Iraq a full-fledged nuclear nation, fully able to pursue both the peaceful uses of atomic energy and the military applications as well.

But the nuclear program also had big problems. The sabotage attack at La Seyne-sur-Mer had wrecked the core elements for the new Tammuz research reactors, setting back their scheduled start-up dates. Diplomatic protests and stories in the Western press were warning that Saddam intended to build nuclear weapons. And the French were trying to pull back from their agreement to supply highly enriched uranium fuel, which could also be used to build nuclear weapons.

That was not all. As we learned in the course of this investigation, Iraq is riven by internal religious, ideological, and ethnic conflicts that sometimes threaten to split the country apart. These not only made the prospect of an atomic bomb in the hands of its leaders that much more frightening, but also had a dramatic effect on the nuclear program itself. The background is instructive, as it has influenced so much of Iraq's recent history under the Baath Socialists.

The political "ins" in Iraq, Saddam Hussein and his closest coterie, come largely from families, many of them interrelated, who have their roots and their loyalties in a single part of the country, the area around the provincial town of Takrit, to the north of Baghdad. The Takritis include many of the key military officers who back the Baath regime, a surprising portion of the Revolutionary Command Council and of top government ministers, and much of the leadership of the Baath Party itself.

Several long-standing social and historical reasons have led to this strange preponderance from a single town. But Saddam Hussein has personally favored old friends and relatives from Takrit for top posts, which has tended to shut out other towns and regions from their share in government, and this has fueled several political conspiracies, which Saddam has brutally suppressed.

To make matters even worse, the Takritis and those with whom they cooperate are overwhelmingly members of the same Islamic sect—the Sunni. This is far and away the majority sect within Islam as a whole. But the Sunni are a decided minority in Iraq, where over half of the population belongs to the more fundamentalist Shiite sect, which is all but excluded from political power.

The conflict has been growing for years. Shiite rebels claim that the Baath regime exiled 70,000 of their coreligionists between 1971 and 1972. In 1977, Shiite religious processions in the holy cities of Narjaf and Karbala turned into bloody demonstrations against the regime. One of Iraq's leading ayatollahs, Muhammad Bakr al-Sadr, led a series of demonstrations against the government in February 1979 and again in May and June. When he was arrested for brief periods, Shiite militants staged massive and at times bloody protests in several Iraqi towns. The Shiites also took a leading role in the clandestine Islamic Call Party, which gave the movement a decidedly revolutionary tone.

This Shiite upsurge was partly a response to the Baath Socialists and their repressive monopoly of political power. The Shiites also took inspiration from the Islamic Revolution next door in Iran, a revolution led by the ayatollahs, who are Shiite clergy.

The Shiite populations of the two countries have strong personal and religious ties. These were further strengthened by Ayatollah Khomeini during his fifteen years of exile in Iraq, from 1963 to 1978. So dangerous was his presence in Iraq that finally the Sunni-dominated regime ordered him to leave. And this was before the Islamic Revolution had toppled the Shah.

Once Khomeini had taken power in Iran, in early 1979, he hit back. He sharply attacked the Baathists in Baghdad for their atheism and socialism, and openly incited his fellow Shiites across the border to follow Iran's by overthrowing the Baath government and setting up an Islamic republic in Iraq.

"The people of Iraq," he urged, "should rise as one man to topple the regime of tyrants and establish the rule of divine justice."

"We will be sure the Iraqi regime will be overthrown," proclaimed Abolhassan Bani-Sadr, who was later elected and then deposed as President of Iran. "We shall say that the Islamic nation will overthrow you."

To the Baath regime in Baghdad, this incitement made every Shiite a possible subversive, a counterrevolutionary, a turncoat in the service of Iraq's historic enemies, the Zoroastrian Aryan Persians. In response, Saddam Hussein and his comrades called down a bloody wave of arrests and executions against the Shiite majority.

At the time of the Shiite demonstrations in May and June of 1979, they arrested thousands of Shiites and executed several Shiite teachers, engineers, and clerics. Amnesty International has the names of twenty-three of those executed. We spoke with Shiite sources in London who claim there were as many as eighty-six.

There were widespread reports of torture—both of Shiites and also of Communists and Kurds. Finally, Saddam staged mass expulsions of as many as 35,000 Iraqi Shiites, herding them across the border into Iran. Then, in April 1980, he took the enormous risk of ordering the execution of the Ayatollah Bakr al-Sadr.

This was the price of Saddam Hussein's minority rule, the cost of his repressive hold on power against all opposition, whether from the Shiite minority, from the Kurds, or simply from those out of favor with his personal clique of followers from Takrit. It was also the prelude to his most bellicose ambitions, as the religious rivalry of Sunni against Shiite merged into the racial conflict of Arab against Persian.

"The ruling clique in Iran persists in using the face of religion to foment sedition and division among the ranks of the Arab nation despite the difficult circumstances through which the Arab nation is passing," declared Saddam Hussein in Septembr 1980, on the eve of launching war against Iran. "The face of religion is only a mask to cover Persian racism and buried resentment for the Arabs."

Whatever the mask, this new face of age-old racial hatreds and Islamic schisms also came to haunt the most modern of Saddam Hussein's developmental ambitions, the making of the Iraqi bomb.

Some of Iraq's top scientists belonged to the Shiite majority, and Saddam saw some of them as a threat to his rule. In September 1979—only five months after the sabotage of the Tammuz core in southern France—he sent his secret police to the Iraqi Atomic Energy Commission to arrest one of the key men in the nuclear program, the widely respected Dr. Hussein Sharastani.

Generally regarded as one of Iraq's most brilliant nuclear scientists, Sharastani had originally studied chemical engineering at London's Imperial College from 1962 to 1965, and had completed his Ph.D. in Canada at the University of Toronto. He returned to Iraq in 1969, and was soon picked as a Scientific Advisor to the President and Director of Research at the Iraqi Atomic Energy Commission.

This was no everyday arrest, and when the secret police arrived, the head of the Atomic Energy Commission refused to allow them to take Sharastani without direct authorization from Saddam Hussein himself. The policemen returned later that afternoon with Saddam's explicit orders, and arrested Sharastani on his way home, along with his Canadian-born wife, two daughters, and three-month-old son.

As far as is known, Dr. Sharastani had not personally played any major role in the growing Shiite opposition. But one of his cousins was among those executed following the disturbances in May and June of 1980, and Sharastani himself was a close friend of the Shiite leader, Ayatollah Bakr al-Sadr.

Four months later, in January 1980, Sharastani was briefly seen in the al-Rashid military hospital. He had been severely tortured.

In a report on torture in Iraq, Amnesty International disclosed details of the kind of government Saddam Hussein was running, and of the kind of treatment the nuclear scientist was forced to endure. "Political prisoners are tortured during interrogation as a matter of routine, either to force them to confess to membership in an illegal party or to sign a declaration that they will never join a political party other than the Baath Party," Amnesty reported.

"Methods of torture known to be used are: beating all over the body with fists, feet or a rubber truncheon; beating sensitive parts of the body with an electric stick; beating the soles of the feet (*falaka*); rape or threats of rape; threats of execution and mock executions. There have been many reported cases of death under torture."

"The torture was quite cruel," added Madame Lison Vallet, of Amnesty's French Section, when we interviewed her in Paris in July 1981. "Dr. Sharastani has been seriously injured by it," she told us. "And we are still not sure if he is dead or alive."

In trying to find out something about Sharastani's condition, Madame Vallet and a small group from Amnesty managed to meet with the Iraqi Ambassador to France on June 17, 1981.

"The meeting was very strange," she recalled. "The Ambassador told us that he didn't know anything about Sharastani, that he didn't even know his name. He was obviously not telling the truth. He asked us why we were so interested in this man. And he kept repeating that the talk against his country came from a mixture of Zionists, Americans, and Iranians, and he lumped them all together."

Amnesty International's investigation had proven difficult, Mme. Vallet related. Iraqi dissidents were often afraid to speak to Amnesty directly, and she sometimes received anonymous telephone calls tipping her off on bits of information. Those who mustered the courage to come to Amnesty's Paris office often insisted on using their first names only, and asked that no notes be taken which would indicate who they were or what they looked like. In one case, Mme. Vallet told us, an Iraqi dissident in Paris had been found out, and then chain-whipped and severely crippled by men believed to have come from the Iraqi Embassy.

The Iraqi Government has so far refused to reveal the charges against Sharastani or to offer any evidence against him. Like many others in Saddam Hussein's Iraq—Communists, Kurds, and religious opponents of the regime—Dr. Sharastani simply vanished from public view. All that is known is that a secret "revolutionary court" found him guilty of treason and sentenced him to death. Numerous press accounts have since reported that the Iraqis carried out the execution. But in July 1981 a Canadian Government official announced publicly that Ottawa had received information that the nuclear scientist was still alive.

Sharastani was the first. In about February 1980, Saddam ordered the arrest of a second nuclear scientist, the man who had been in charge of nuclear coordination with the French, Dr. Jaffar Dhia Jaffar.

A friend and colleague of Sharastani, Dr. Jaffar was a nuclear physicist, well respected by scientists in Western Europe and one of the top men in the Iraqi nuclear program. Like Sharastani, he was a member of a well-known Shiite family, and was also the son of a former minister under the monarchy, which was overturned in 1958. According to his colleagues, Jaffar had spoken out against Sharastani's arrest, and had even gone personally to protest directly to Saddam himself. Amnesty International told us that Dr. Jaffar is still in prison.

Sharastani and Jaffar had both received the finest Western educations and were among the best nuclear scientists anywhere in the Middle East. Both had helped to develop the new Osirak reactor project, working closely with the French Atomic Energy Commission and its subsidiary Technicatome. The French scientists with whom we spoke saw Sharastani and Jaffar as first-rate scientists, and had come to know them personally when they visited many of France's nuclear facilities, including the plant at La Seyne-sur-Mer, where engineers from CNIM were building the reactor cores, and where unknown saboteurs struck in April 1979.

Why then did Saddam Hussein have the two scientists arrested? The decision could not have come lightly. Not with their key roles in the nuclear program, in which Saddam himself had invested so much. There are three possibilities.

According to one French scientist, Sharastani was believed to be at the very heart of the secret war against the Iraqi bomb and had been arrested and tortured for having conspired in the sabotage bombing at La Seyne-sur-Mer, probably by furnishing inside information to those who had carried out the attack. In the words of the scientist, "Sharastani had sold out to the Israelis."

If that is true, the Iraqis are the only ones to have found out enough about what had really happened at La Seyne-sur-Mer to arrest anyone at all for the attack. It would also mean that the Israelis had co-opted the Shiite opposition in Iraq, which is not totally out of the question. But the story seems unlikely. If the Iraqis had any evidence that the Israelis had carried out the sabotage, they would have shouted it far and wide. And if they charged the unfortunate Sharastani with being part of a "Zionist conspiracy" without any evidence, they were simply singing the old ritual song.

There is, however, one fragmentary piece of evidence that could support speculation that Sharastani's arrest was related to Shiite opposition against the nuclear program. Both in January and April 1980, United Press International reported from "intelligence sources" that armed men had attempted to penetrate and sabotage the nuclear installation at Tuwaitah. The attackers had been arrested, the report said, and their fate was unknown. They were presumably Shiite. When we checked the story with the Iraqi Embassy in Paris, they claimed to know nothing about it.

A second possibility we draw from our own investigation. Sharastani had been one of the top Iraqi scientists who did the main negotiating with the French. According to Technicatome's Yves Girard, the scientists sold the Osirak to Saddam Hussein and the Iraqi generals on the basis of their being able to deliver an atomic bomb from it. But the scientists did not really believe that the job could be done, not in the short run. Saddam may have called their bluff. When the scientists said they would not, or could not, deliver according to Hussein's timetable, the Iraqi leader may have seen it as a threat and tried to nip the opposition in the bud.

The third account of the arrests rings truest. According to opposition sources with whom we spoke in London—who were in contact with the Shiite opposition inside Iraq—the arrests had nothing to do with either Israel or France, or even directly with the Iraqi nuclear program. They were simply part of Saddam Hussein's far broader crackdown, especially on Iraq's Shiites, who had become increasingly rebellious in the months following the early 1979 victory of Ayatollah Khomeini's Islamic Revolution in neighboring Iran.

Other Iraqis paid the price as well. This was especially obvious in France, where many of the nuclear technicians came for specialized training. "They come to Saclay, and they are doing the work," a French scientist told us.

"But for every six or ten Iraqis, there's a political controller, a commissar.

"He watches them for disloyalty. They have very scrupulous checking into all aspects of their activity. With their families in Baghdad, they don't want to make a wrong step."

The French scientist observed that the surveillance over the Iraqi technicians became particularly noticeable after the bombing at La Seyne-sur-Mer. One of the "political commissars" would often sit around the cafeteria at Saclay, the French nuclear center near Paris, where he would studiously read Arabic newspapers, pretending not to speak French. However, right after the attack at CNIM the Iraqi was found reading with great interest the French leftist newspaper *Libération* with its detailed account of the action. From that moment, the French scientists assumed the Iraqi spoke French as well as they did.

The arrests, the stories of torture and possible executions, and the prying eyes of the commissars must have weighed heavily on the Iraqi scientists and technicians. Whatever the impact on them, the heavy hand of Baghdad also deeply depressed the French who were working at their side.

The French scientists and engineers had come to know Sharastani and Jaffar personally. They had respected them, trusted them, liked them. Now the two men were in jail, or possibly dead. Why? What kind of people were running Iraq? asked the French nuclear people. And should we in France really be helping them to gain nuclear expertise?

"The arrest of their top scientists had an affect on our morale," admitted Yves Girard, the Vice President of Technicatome. "Our people have worked in Iraq for five years. They were very proud of their work. And suddenly everything collapsed. Now they were feeling sad to see all that effort wasted.

"In 1976 and 1977, there was a much nicer feeling," he told us. "Now there are so many internal problems. It's better to think of Iraq—as we could in 1976—as a nice country."

An engineer from CNIM in La Seyne was similarly depressed. He had worked on the reactor core for Tammuz I, which he thought an excellent piece of craftsmanship. Then he visited Iraq twice in the summer of 1980.

"Iraq was really a war country," he told us. "Everywhere you went, even in Tuwaitah, you saw more soldiers than scientists. I was there when the first shipment of enriched uranium arrived for Tammuz II. It was like an armed camp, with soldiers everywhere."

"What did you think about that?" we asked. "Did it bother you?"

"It wasn't pleasant. It was like a state of war. I was happy to get back to France."

We asked him to be more specific. He was not ready to do so. He had done his job, after all, a limited one, and he was not a politician, only a technician. Beneath the surface, though, it was clear that his visit to Iraq had a deep impact on his view of Iraq and its nuclear program.

The Enriched-Uranium Controversy

Jacques Chirac, in his thirty months as Prime Minister of France, had made the nuclear contract with Iraq a showpiece of his independent and avowedly Gaullist foreign policy.

"We will make you the most advanced nation in the Middle East," he had publicly told his great and good friend, Iraqi president Saddam Hussein.

But Chirac had slipped from power. He had broken with President Valéry Giscard d'Estaing in the autumn of 1976, and ever since the split, France had begun to show greater support for the American effort to slow down the spread of the more dangerous nuclear technologies to the nations of the Third World.

This was clearest in the case of Pakistan, where Giscard and his Council on Foreign Nuclear Policy decided to suspend the contract for the reprocessing plant at Chashma in June 1978. But the new concern with nuclear proliferation also extended to Iraq, as the French Government moved to reconsider the terms of M. Chirac's earlier agreement with the Arab nation.

The immediate concern was the fuel for the Tammuz reactors. In the original contract of August 1976, the French had promised to provide nuclear fuel enriched to 93 percent of the extremely fissionable uranium 235. This is the standard fuel mix for many of the world's research reactors, particularly those that the United States had provided to nations all over the world under the Atoms for Peace program. But the same highly enriched uranium could also serve as the nuclear explosive for atomic weapons.

The French had promised to provide Iraq with nearly eighty kilograms of the highly enriched uranium fuel, or six loads of a little more than thirteen kilograms each. The understanding was that the French would deliver the entire eighty kilograms by 1981—enough to make somewhere between four and nine nuclear weapons, depending on the skill of the Iraqi bomb makers.

The risk was obvious, and it is still not clear how or why the French had ever agreed to such a rash course of action. But once the details of the Iraqi contract leaked out, the question of the highly enriched uranium became the single most important target of criticism. The Israelis repeatedly raised the issue in their protests to the French. So did the Iranians and the other Arab states. And the Americans, who supplied highly enriched uranium for research reactors in France, flatly refused to let the French pass any of it on to Iraq.

In time, even the French themselves came to have second thoughts—or at least some of them did. As early as March 1978, French newspapers were reporting un désaccord profond between the competing bureaucracies on the issue. On the one side, the French Atomic Energy Commission was fighting to push ahead with the Iraqi contract as it had been originally agreed. On the other, the French Ministry of Foreign Affairs was battling to hold back on the agreement, hoping to rewrite it to avoid some of the more embarrassing risks.

In a sense, the two sides were waging their old, ongoing war. The nuclear mandarins of the CEA were pushing nuclear exports, while the foreign-policy poo-bahs at the Quai d'Orsay worried over nuclear proliferation and relations with their friends in Washington. And once again, the Foreign Ministry side urged a technical solution, this time an alternative fuel that could not be used for nuclear weapons.

The French called the new fuel caramel, as in the dessert. It was a fuel originally developed for France's fleet of nuclear submarines. It was enriched to contain just enough of the highly fissionable and extremely explosive uranium 235 to run the Osirak, but not enough to make a bomb. In the original version, the new mixture contained something under 20 percent of the uranium 235, but French scientists later reduced the percentage to under 10 percent, as against a minimum of 40 to 50 percent that would be needed to make nuclear explosives.

The French tested the "caramel" in their own Osiris reactor at Saclay, and the initial results looked promising, so much so that Industry Minister André Giraud publicly praised it as the perfect "proliferation-proof" fuel for research reactors. But there was still a big hitch. Would the Iraqis buy it?

France was already trying to convince Pakistan to accept an alternative technological fix at Chashma, the so-called "co-processing," which would have denied the Pakistanis the weapons-usable plutonium they so desperately wanted. And now the beleaguered French diplomats were going to ask the Iraqis to take caramel instead of highly enriched uranium. It was not an enviable task.

The discussions with Baghdad began in late 1977 or early 1978, and as might be expected, the Iraqis said no. The new fuel would have required certain modifications in the core of Osirak, and the Iraqis were not willing to risk the possible delays.

It was this refusal that sparked the *"désaccord profond"* between the Atomic Energy Commission, which wanted to push ahead with the highly enriched uranium, and the Foreign Ministry, which favored pushing the Iraqis until they accepted the necessary modifications to use the caramel. In the end, President Giscard's office was forced to step in with something of a compromise. The French would give Iraq the highly enriched uranium, as originally agreed. But they would ship only as much fuel as was needed at any one time, and French technicians would see that it was immediately put into the reactor and irradiated.

That was in March 1978, long before most of the world had even heard of the Iraqi nuclear project, and it is probably fair to say that the new shipping arrangements removed some of the more obvious risk. But the French did not stop there. They continued to test the new caramel fuel, hoping the results would be satisfactory for powering Osirak, and continued quietly to urge the Iraqis to give it a try. This was the situation in April 1979, when the explosion at La Seyne-sur-Mer wrecked the Osirak reactor core, the very core that the French Foreign Ministry wanted to modify for the new caramel fuel.

In fact, the coincidence led some observers to suggest that the French had staged the sabotage attack, in an effort to delay delivery of the reactor core and gain time to convince the Iraqis to accept the modifications. It was an intriguing theory. But if the French did blow up the reactor core, which seems highly unlikely, and if they did it to push caramel, the plan backfired completely.

In the real world, as opposed to the theoretical, the Iraqis were outraged by the attack, which they blamed on Israel, and they insisted more strongly than ever that France stick to the original contract. The Iraqis had ordered a high-performance reactor with highly enriched uranium, and they would settle for nothing less.

This was the message the Iraqis gave to the French Prime Minister, Raymond Barre, when he visited Baghdad in July 1979, three months after the attack at the CNIM plant at La Seyne-sur-Mer. Saddam Hussein had just become President of Iraq, and he made it absolutely clear to M. Barre that Iraq would not tolerate any further backsliding. France would provide the reactor and the fuel as originally agreed. Or the Iraqis would take their business—and not just their nuclear business—to someone else who would.

At stake were literally billions of dollars. One pending contract for military equipment included orders for tanks, antitank weapons, radar systems, Crotale and Pluton guided missiles, and speedy missile-launching patrol boats similar to those the Israelis had spirited away from the French port of Cherbourg after the French had cut off all military supplies. This contract alone was worth $1.5 billion.

The oil-rich Iraqis were also looking for Mirage aircraft, turnkey industrial plants, and petrochemical installations, as well as four naval frigates, which in a nice twist of irony the firm in La Seyne-sur-Mer—CNIM—badly wanted to build. Needless to say, the Iraqis were less than enthusiastic about the security arrangements at CNIM.

Finally, the Iraqis were actively shopping for a large nuclear power plant, another billion dollar project that the French firm Framatome was eager to supply.

The billions added up, and shrewd trader that he was, Saddam Hussein left the distinct impression that the whole lot depended on France's willingness to carry out the initial nuclear contract. This was petrodollar diplomacy at its sharpest, and Mr. Barre seemed to have no choice. The price of oil was rising. The French balance of payments was suffering a chronic deficit. All the Iraqis were asking was that France keep its word.

What could the poor French do? The answer was well summed up by the editorial writers of The Washington Post: "It was what the world has come to expect from the French: a token bow to statesmanship and a serious pursuit of profit."

Barre's first task in this pursuit was to soothe any fears about the damaged reactor core, and to assure the Iraqis that the damage could be repaired without any undue delay. Baghdad was pushing hard to stick as closely as possible to the original schedule, and somehow the French technicians at CNIM and Technicatome managed to deliver the repaired core for the Osirak, or Tammuz I, reactor in the fall of 1979, in all a delay of only half a year.

It was a stunning performance, especially for the generally slow-moving nuclear industry. But there remained a nagging doubt. To meet the Iraqi pressure, the French sent Iraq a piece of equipment that they never would have used in France itself. According to sources in the French nuclear industry familiar with the sabotaged reactor core, French law would not have allowed the repaired core to enter into service. As one nuclear official told us in private, "We would have had to make it over from new."

But the Iraqis were in a hurry, and the French did not have time to start from scratch. The old core would have to do. After all, Iraq was not France, and standards do differ. Or at least that is how the French came to rationalize their speedy repair of the damaged reactor core. It would not do for France, but it was good enough for Iraq.

For their part, the Iraqis seemed willing enough to accept the repaired equipment if the French would guarantee it. This created a slight hitch, as the French technicians were unwilling to give the required assurances. M. Barre stepped in, and to the great astonishment of the top safety engineers and others at the Atomic Energy Commission, he officially guaranteed the repairs for seven years. What would happen after that was anyone's guess.

Barre handled the question of the fuel in much the same way. His foreign policy advisers still wanted to convince the Iraqis to accept the caramel fuel. But they saw that there was no way the Iraqis would agree, not in the months following the sabotage at La Seyne-sur-Mer. For one thing, the caramel was not really as good a fuel as highly enriched uranium, and the French knew it.

"It's not giving peak performance," explained Technicatome's Yves Girard. "Enriched uranium gives a very high performance, and we were selling a high-performance reactor. When we sold it in 1976, that was the intention."

Behind the scenes, the French told the Americans that they were still trying to persuade Baghdad to permit a scaling down of the enrichment level. But, they said, they had to move cautiously.

"The French are as anxious as anybody to supply low-enriched uranium fuel in future shipments," confirmed an American nuclear diplomat. "But highly enriched uranium is the kind of uranium this reactor takes."

So the French continued to test and to talk about caramel, even as they told Iraq that they would stick by their original promise and supply highly enriched uranium. And during the week of June 20, 1980, as we discovered in our conversations with French scientists, the first shipment arrived in

Iraq—thirteen kilograms of uranium fuel enriched to 93 percent, or enough for an experienced weapons designer to build one atom bomb.

The Plutonium Way to the Bomb

Saddam Hussein had brought the French to heel. But that was only a minor victory. The Iraqis were looking far beyond the few kilograms of highly enriched uranium, which was only enough for a single bomb at best.

To be sure, even the prospect of weapons-usable uranium in Iraq had served to heighten tensions throughout the Middle East, bringing wide-ranging protests to France, even from other Arab governments. But in reality, the big to-do about the highly enriched uranium fuel always sounded a bit symbolic, and generally overstated the actual danger. If the Iraqis ever diverted the uranium fuel to make a bomb, they would shut the door on further purchases of the know-how and equipment that they still needed to meet their more sweeping nuclear ambitions.

The seventy-megawatt Osirak research reactor, rather than the fuel for it, gave the Iraqis a different, and far more practical, way to make the bomb, as we learned from the outspoken former head of the French Atomic Energy Commission, Professor Francis Perrin.

"I am persuaded that Iraq is preparing itself to have the atomic bomb," he told us during an instructive interview at his Paris office. "The first thing to consider is that the new Iraqi reactor uses highly enriched uranium, the same as in an atomic weapon. I doubt that Iraq would use this uranium directly to produce a bomb.

"But if Iraq is so eager to have such an experimental reactor, I think it's in order to prepare for the fabrication of nuclear weapons—but not necessarily by this particular fuel," he said. "They could, for instance, irradiate fuel from this reactor to produce plutonium, which they might eventually use to produce two or three bombs."

"This is against the NPT," he conceded. "But you know, a country can declare that it wants to leave the NPT."

Dr. Perrin's suggestion seemed worth following up. Almost any reactor can produce plutonium. All that is needed is an adequate flux of neutrons from the ongoing nuclear chain reaction, and enough natural uranium either in the reactor fuel or in a "blanket" properly placed around the reactor core. The only real question is how much plutonium a reactor can make, and that depends on several different factors, such as the power of the reactor, the intensity of the neutron flux, and the configuration of the core. How good a plutonium producer would the Osirak be?

The answer was a lot more difficult than we had expected, and not because of any great difficulty in the mathematics or the science involved. The difficulty lay in the enormous secrecy in France surrounding the entire Iraqi nuclear project—the secrecy and the infuriating habit the French nuclear authorities have of telling lies for no apparent purpose.

It all began when we tried to get some basic data on the Osirak. As the name suggests, it is largely a replica of the French Osiris reactor at Saclay, and that is how French nuclear officials always described it.

"I always thought it *was* the Osiris," one American diplomat told us. "That's what they told me."

"*Une copie conformé*," confirmed Alain Varneau, the spokesman of the French Atomic Energy Commission. "An authentic copy."

But that wasn't exactly true. In ordering the Osirak, the Iraqis had insisted on at least one major modification, which appeared to affect the reactor's capacity to produce plutonium.

According to one very alarmed French nuclear scientist who told us about the modification in the fall of 1980, the Iraqis wanted a high-flux reactor that would give off a greater number of neutrons than normally produced, and this led French designers to add a specially engineered modification, a "heavy-water tank."

This was an aluminum tank containing heavy water similar to that used in the highly proliferating Candu reactor that the the the Pakistanis were using. The tank was built by the same company that built the sabotaged reactor cores, CNIM at La Seyne-sur-Mer, and the firm's officials had written about it in the publicity release that they gave to the local journalist Jose Lenzini in April 1979, on the day before the sabotage bombing in Hangar No. 3. The company had mistakenly issued the document without the permission of the French Atomic Energy Commission and had thus unknowingly violated the secrecy clauses in the French-Iraqi contract. The CEA apparently knew nothing of this document until we showed it to them in early 1981, when their representative asked us if he could photocopy it. We—graciously, we believe—consented.

The document provided hard evidence of the Iraqi modification. Yet at least until early 1981, when we showed them some of the proofs we had, officials of the French Atomic Energy Commission flatly denied that Osirak was anything but an exact copy of France's own Osiris reactor, or that any modifications had been made in it. The vehemence of their denials added to our suspicion that the French had specially modified the reactor to give the Iraqis a greater production of weapons-usable plutonium.

In short, from where we were sitting, France appeared knowingly engaged in a purposeful conspiracy to give Saddam Hussein the bomb.

This was an extremely serious charge to consider, a possible scandal and scoop far beyond anything so far reported about the French and their nuclear exports. And the repeated failure of French nuclear officials to admit the existence of the tank, or to explain its purpose, only made our suspicions grow.

Why were they lying about it? What did they have to hide? Why all the secrecy?

The answers would not be easy. The only way to know for sure was to examine Osirak's technical specifications, and those were very secret indeed, tightly guarded by France's draconian atomic secrecy laws.

Diplomatic correspondence and secret minutes were one thing. As journalists, we saw those often enough, and without any major risk to ourselves or to our sources. But nuclear diagrams and calculations—that was something else, especially for anyone within CNIM, Technicatome, or the CEA who might, for reasons of conscience, be willing to make them available.

The search for the secret data took three months. In the end, we managed to get many of the actual designs and specifications for the reactor, which surprised and delighted us. But pride was a small consolation. We discovered that on the CNIM work orders for the heavy-water tank was written the assignation "CR," an abbreviation for Command Rouge, or Red Command, which meant that the buying of material for the tank was to be done outside the company's normal purchase system. This intensified our suspicions. If the numbers to be deduced from the specifications showed what we expected, the bloody-minded Saddam Hussein had a plutonium-producing machine far more potent than anyone had yet suspected.

To analyze the figures and the designs, we sought the help of scientists in France, Britain, and the United States, and they all came up with the same, rather surprising conclusion. From the design of the reactor core and the placement of the heavy-water tank, the modifications appeared to be for highly sophisticated neutron-beam experiments, and not for the greater production of plutonium. In fact, the presence of the tank in the reactor pool might actually reduce the amount of plutonium the reactor could produce, since it would close off part of the area that the Iraqis might otherwise use to blanket the reactor core with natural uranium.

Whatever the Iraqi military wanted Osirak for, the Iraqi scientists were out to get the most sophisticated research tool that money could buy.

"The Iraqis heard about it and they wanted it," Technicatome's Yves Girard later explained to us. "They always wanted the best, and they saw that we had this heavy-water tank on our Orphee reactor, so they ordered it as a modification."

Why, then, did the French nuclear officials persist in evading and denying the truth?

Baghdad had insisted on complete secrecy, they claimed rather lamely, after we finally put the information from their own secret documents on the desk and forced them to admit that the heavy-water tank did, in fact, exist. Secrecy was a condition of the contract.

And what of the reactor itself? we pressed. With or without the heavy-water tank, couldn't the Iraqis still blanket the Osirak with natural uranium and use it to produce plutonium?

Yes, they could, conceded the Atomic Energy Commission's Alain

Varneau in early 1981. "In ideal conditions, really ideal conditions, they could get about ten kilos a year."

Varneau's admission was startling. The French were giving the Iraqis the capacity to make one Nagasaki-type bomb a year, and maybe two, and the spokesman for the French Atomic Energy Commission was admitting it.

And there it was. In the arduous search for a journalistic scoop, the pursuit of the heavy-water tank may have produced only a damp squib. But in the effort, the documents that we got finally forced the French to admit that Osirak could indeed make atomic bombs.

Later, after Osirak was attacked by the Israelis, the French nuclear authorities backtracked from the ten kilograms and offered a much lower estimate. The ten kilograms had come from only "a perfunctory study," M. Varneau said, which was apparently all that the French had considered worth doing at the time. But now they had commissioned a study "on a realistic basis," and the most the reactor could produce was two to three kilograms a year.

"I officially protest that the reactor can produce up to ten kilograms a year," Varneau insisted. "It cannot. More likely, it is 2.4 kilos per year."

In fact, Varneau was right both times. The "perfunctory" and the "realistic" estimates were both correct. According to almost all of the scientists with whom we spoke, the Osirak would have a range of between two and ten kilograms of plutonium a year. It all depended on how the Iraqis would run the reactor and under what conditions. In the end, the results would still be deadly. The only difference would be whether the Iraqis ended up with one Nagasaki-type bomb in four years or two bombs in one year.

Yet Varneau's original figure of ten kilograms was especially interesting as this was the number that Israeli scientists came up with, and it was this estimate of Iraqi plutonium production, rather than the possible diversion of highly enriched uranium, that most worried the Israelis.

"I know that we've stressed the danger of short-term diversion of the enriched uranium," admitted the noted Israeli nuclear physicist Yuval Ne'eman. "And I'm not regretful. It's insane to give a country like Iraq enriched uranium.

"But," he told us, "we were equally, even more worried by the possibility that they would blanket the reactor and get plutonium."

How much plutonium could the Iraqis have produced? we asked.

After studying the plans of the Osiris reactor, Ne'eman had concluded that the Iraqis could produce as much as ten kilograms a year, which was the number Varneau had given us at the French Atomic Energy Commission. But, warned Ne'eman, they could have doubled that with a few minor adjustments.

"What they would have to do to get more is not that difficult," he told us. "To be able to use a larger blanket of natural uranium, they would have had to make only two changes. They would have had to block off the beam tubes.

And they would have to install additional cooling systems. Otherwise, they'd have a severe heat problem, and could have had problems with melting.

"It's a feasible operation," Ne'eman emphasized, possibly calling on his own experience with the Israeli reactor at Dimona. "The French could have produced these changes in a relatively short time, if asked."

Professor Ne'eman had no evidence that the Iraqis were making these changes or that they had asked the French to help them to do it. But he thought that this was the direction in which the Iraqis were likely to go, and he had absolutely no faith that the French would stop them.

"If someone were keen on discovering an infringement, that's one matter," he argued. "But I have a total distrust of the French. Especially when they have been so careless about the whole matter.

"The Iraqis would be the ones who fix the amount of radiation," he explained. "The French couldn't guarantee whether the reactor will work for an hour a month, or twenty days a month. It would be easy for the Iraqis to arrange a leaking pipe or an electricity failure to stop the reactor and to halt the process of irradiation. That's not a problem—and it wouldn't necessarily be noticed.

"To put our real safety in the hands of the French, and in a vague promise that someone is there watching the reactor, is not something we can accept."

The French naturally took a different view.

"I know the Israelis distrust the French, and international organizations," conceded Yves Girard. "And they are right from their point of view. If the Arabs were to occupy Jerusalem and Tel Aviv, what would the United Nations do? They would make some statement deploring it, and that would be the end of it. So in this I understand the Israelis."

But French technicians would be on the spot, at least until 1989, under the 1979 agreement signed with Iraq. As long as the technicians were there, we were told by French authorities, they would certainly notice any attempt either to blanket the reactor with natural uranium or to make any major modifications in the reactor design.

Those were the good intentions, at least. But in the actual fine print of all the agreements and safeguards, the nuclear mandarins had left several glaring loopholes. The most startling was that the Iraqis had every legal right to make as much plutonium as they wanted.

"Iraq had no legal obligation not to use the reactor to irradiate natural uranium," said one of the diplomats at Quai d'Orsay picked by the new government of François Mitterrand to work out a tougher approach. "They had no agreement of this kind with us or with the IAEA. The only thing the IAEA does is to keep track of fuel use. This is one of the loopholes.

"They could have done it," he conceded. "Osirak would have been under safeguards. But there was no legal obligation not to irradiate natural uranium."

A second loophole was in the agreement for French technicians to stay on the Iraqi project until 1989. This was primarily to help the Iraqis, not to watch what they were doing, and the agreement did not in any way guarantee the access of French technicians to the reactor itself. "Our men were there to be technicians, not inspectors," the diplomat emphasized.

These were two of the loopholes that the ten-man task force attempted to close in their report, which was on the desk of Foreign Minister Claude Cheysson only two days before the Israelis bombed Osirak.

Yves Doutriaux, the official spokesman at the Quai d'Orsay, took a more confident position on the role of the French technicians. "If a French technician would see something wrong in the Iraqi behavior, he would report it," he assured us. "If we had seen Iraq developing the bomb, we would have cut our aid. We would have cut the fuel supply. How would the reactor work?"

The debate goes on. In the end, the judgment comes down to a very sticky question: How much do you trust the French? And which French do you choose to trust?

From Rome to Vienna

The attack came out of the blue, a stinging exposé by the distinguished diplomatic correspondent Richard Burt on the front pages of *The New York Times* and its sister publication, the *International Herald Tribune*. The article was dated March 18, 1980. The headline told the tale: "U.S. Says Italy Sells Iraq Atomic Bomb Technology."

"The Administration has learned that Italy has quietly become a major supplier of nuclear technology and know-how to Iraq, providing that nation with sensitive equipment that U.S. officials said could be used to manufacture bomb-grade plutonium," the article began.

"U.S. intelligence agencies recently confirmed reports from other countries that Italy is establishing close nuclear ties with Iraq, officials said. Some officials believe that Italy, which imports about a third of its oil from Iraq, has agreed to provide nuclear assistance in exchange for long-term access to Iraqi oil."

According to the newspaper account, Washington's chief concern was an Italian-built "hot cell," a lead-lined laboratory that would permit the Iraqis to reprocess plutonium from used reactor fuel. The Americans saw no problem in the sale of a small nuclear hot cell to Iraq, explained an unnamed State Department official quoted in the story. But, said the official, "the Italian facility was of sufficient magnitude to permit Baghdad to obtain enough plutonium to produce a nuclear weapon in about a year's time."

This was hard-hitting stuff, and the article created a minor explosion in Italy, where nuclear officials saw it as a public slap in the face directly inspired by American Government officials.

Richard Burt, the author, had just come to *The New York Times* after serving as assistant director of the prestigious International Institute for

Strategic Studies in London. He was known to have close ties to both the Pentagon and Department of State (where he is now a high-ranking official). And he had gotten the story directly from official sources in Washington, simply quoting what they had told him.

"We were frankly quite surprised by the article," recalls Dr. Achille Albonetti, the Director of International Relations for Italy's atomic agency, the Comitato Nazionale per l'Energia Nucleare, or CNEN. "It really wasn't a very nice thing to do."

To be fair, Dr. Albonetti and his colleagues had good reason to be surprised, and even angry, at the article's appearance. They had never made any secret of their nuclear sales to Iraq. They had proudly announced them in various publications. And most galling of all, they had sold the radiochemistry lab with the three hot cells to Iraq as far back as April 1976, and had completed it in 1978, though it still was not operating. Where had the Americans been during all that time? And why the sudden public attack, with all the melodramatics of intelligence agencies and secret reports?

The answers are not easy, even with the advantage of hindsight.

In part, the Americans had focused most of their concern on the Iraqi nuclear program on France and the supply of highly enriched uranium, and had placed less emphasis on the whole series of Italian laboratories, including the three interconnecting hot cells. But by early March the French Government had publicly announced that it would soon make the first shipment, and Washington could no longer cling to any lingering hope that the Iraqis would suddenly show their good intentions by accepting the low-enriched caramel fuel.

A second factor was the failure of the Italians to respond to polite diplomatic discussions. The Americans had first raised the issue of the labs as early as the beginning of 1978. They had formally expressed concern in the middle of 1979, and they had held "high-level contacts" with the Italians at the beginning of 1980. But the Americans felt unsatisfied by Italy's official replies, and at least some American officials decided that they would get a better response by going public.

Third was the Israelis. Burt's article mentions reports from "other countries," and by spring the Israelis were already expressing concern at Italian sales to Iraq.

Finally, the Administration was facing a tough decision that would affect both Italy and Iraq. In February, the Italians had effectively clinched a massive order from Iraq for eleven naval vessels—six corvettes, a Stromboli support ship, and the four frigates that the French shipbuilders at CNIM had been so eager to build. The order was worth countless jobs and next to $2.6 billion to the economically strapped Italians, and was widely seen as payment for their willingness to supply Iraq with sensitive nuclear technology.

But the contract contained a catch. The four frigates—missile-carrying warships of the Lupo class—were to be powered by gas turbine engines from the giant American firm General Electric, and the engines required special export licenses from the U.S. Department of State, which was in the process of deciding whether or not to grant them. Not surprisingly, this had forced a new look at Iraq's ambitious military buildup, including its fast-moving nuclear program.

In the end, Washington granted the export licenses, possibly because the Italians could have gotten engines from GE's British competitor Rolls-Royce. At the time, however, the Italians saw the public attack on their nuclear sales to Iraq as carrying with it a hidden threat. Either they cut their continuing nuclear ties to Baghdad, or Washington would deny the export licenses on the naval engines. Yet if Italian officials showed any hint of giving in to American pressure on the nuclear contracts, the Iraqis could cancel the lucrative naval order.

"We can't withdraw from these contracts," CNEN's generally pro-American director, Umberto Colombo, told us. "The point is, should we not respect the contracts, could we ever sell the frigates? We are not the only supplier of frigates, you know."

The article by Burt and the implicit threats from Washington brought a violent response. This time the target was the Americans themselves. Shortly after the article appeared, the man in charge of monitoring Italy's nuclear industry, including its relations with Iraq, the American Science Attaché in Rome, Dr. Dan Sirwer, received a threat on his life.

Until now, the story has been tightly cloaked by the American security services, and Sirwer himself refused to talk to us about it. But two of his diplomatic colleagues have confirmed to us that Sirwer was put on his guard and the American Embassy took special surveillance and security measures to protect him.

"He's been under orders not to talk to anyone about it," one of the American diplomats told us. "Presumably the Iraqis didn't like what Sirwer was doing, and they tried to do something about it. The threat was taken very seriously."

In response to the threat, Washington also put other American diplomats on the alert, including Dr. Abraham Friedman, the highly respected Science Attaché in Paris, who was monitoring the Iraqi nuclear efforts in France.

Much as the Italians had feared, the Burt article also brought a swarm of reporters looking into the whole range of Italy's nuclear sales to Iraq. The Italian nuclear bureaucrats responded to their questions with unfailing courtesy and something less than a strict regard for the truth.

"Our five laboratories don't have anything to do with nuclear technology," Dr. Colombo told the Italian weekly *L'Espresso*, in an obvious overstatement. "Contrary to what has been improperly stated, they are not able to produce or treat plutonium. Not even their components used separately would be in a position to function for military objectives," he added smartly.

"Let's be frank. How can Italy, which does not have or want to have the technology for the atomic bomb, supply it to a third party?"

Dr. Colombo repeated much of that same soliloquy to us, and no doubt to several other journalists as well. But with time and a continuing flood of questions, we finally got the company that built the labs—SNIA-Techint—to clear up part of the confusion.

Italy did supply a radiochemistry lab with hot cells, "which could reprocess spent reactor fuel and separate out plutonium," a top SNIA official told us, insisting that he not be identified by name. "But not in significant quantities."

The dispute, then, was no longer a question of yes or no. It was now how much. According to the SNIA-Techint official, the absolute maximum would be 300 to 500 grams of plutonium a year. According to Washington, as Burt had reported, the hot cells would let the Iraqis reprocess enough for about a bomb a year, or some five to ten kilograms, which is just about the amount of plutonium that the Osirak could be expected to produce.

Five hundred grams or ten kilograms—there was quite a gap between what the Italian and the Americans wanted the world to believe. Which of them was telling the truth?

The Italians had every reason to downplay the capacity, while the Americans have continued to stick to their claim without offering any evidence or reasoning to back it up. They simply ask us to accept what they say on the basis of authority or faith in the American intelligence services.

Any independent evaluation is equally "iffy." The size of the facility—three hot cells 2 × 1.5 × 1.4 meters each—appears to be right on the margin. Some nuclear scientists with whom we spoke think this is too small to let the Iraqis reprocess enough spent fuel to give them the five to ten kilograms of plutonium a year needed to make a bomb. Others tell us that under certain circumstances it could just do the job.

As of now, we do not know. It is worth remembering what we were told by the same top SNIA official after he had visited Iraq. He related that the Iraqis could adapt equipment from their own oil industry to enlarge significantly the capacity of the Italian reprocessing labs. He believed this was technically feasible and within Iraqi capability. That is an admission from the man who sold them the goods.

In any case, the problem goes far beyond the capacity of three hot cells. As analysts in Washington were coming to see it in the last year of the Carter Administration, the nuclear danger in Iraq was not just the highly enriched uranium, or the amount of plutonium the Osirak could produce in a year, or the amount of plutonium the Italian labs could extract. The danger was the overall direction the Iraqis were taking, the wide-ranging way they were setting out to master so many different aspects of nuclear know-how, much as the Americans themselves had done in their own World War II pursuit of the ultimate weapon of destruction.

In other words, the Iraqis were not looking to sneak away with a single bomb, or even a bomb a year. They were going all the way. Step by step, and from the bottom up, they were building nothing less than what U.S. Senator Alan Cranston called "a Manhattan Project for the radical Arab world."

This view of what the Iraqis were doing came very close to the kind of comprehensive commitment to science that Saddam Hussein had consistently preached—that the Arab world had to master all aspects of science and that it was not enough even to master the nuclear field alone. As Saddam put it in January 1980, "Any state which wants to use the atom for military purposes should reach a special scientific and technical level in all fields, not only in the nuclear field."

Altogether, the Iraqis were striking out in several directions at once, and with an energy and ambition that raised a certain fear.

"The Iraqis have a mixture of ideas, both atomic arms and the most modern research facilities possible," concluded the former French nuclear chief, Dr. Frances Perrin. "I don't think that they want the atom bomb exclusively. Atom bombs—it's a question of prestige. But they also want to be able to say that they have the most modern research facility."

In many ways, this was a much greater threat than a bomb in the basement, and far more dangerous in the long run than anything Menachem Begin described in justifying his bombing of the Osirak. It also called into question the entire international nuclear system.

The reason was obvious. Whatever the Iraqis had in mind for the future, they were still pursuing it within the rules of the international nuclear game. Unlike Pakistan, Iraq had signed the Nuclear Nonproliferation Treaty, promising that they would not develop nuclear weapons. Iraq had also accepted safeguards from the International Atomic Energy Agency. Under the rules of the game, the Iraqis had every right to buy the facilities and the know-how that they were getting.

"Iraq is a signatory of NPT, and it is keeping all NPT conditions, and is only beginning its nuclear program," CNEN's Dr. Albonetti told us. "The idea that in two or three years Iraq can make at atomic bomb is laughable. There's no precedent for an NPT member making a bomb."

As Dr. Albonetti saw it, the Americans—not the Iraqis—were the ones in the wrong. In the area of nuclear technology, the Carter Administration was retreating into "a policy of denial." And that could only weaken the basic bargain behind the Nonproliferation Treaty.

"If you go to the States, you can't even talk with an expert in reprocessing because of security considerations," he complained to us. "It is also difficult to get books on enrichment technology in uranium. Even assuming such a policy can be effective, you enter into a very debatable area. You weaken the entire Nonproliferation Treaty."

Switzerland's Claude Zangger reacted to the Carter Administration's stance on Iraq in much the same way. "What's been done about Iraq is unfair," he told us during a long session at his office in Berne.

"They have accepted the Nonproliferation Treaty. They have accepted safeguards. They fulfill all the conditions. The criticism is not just, and more than that, it tends to destroy the basis of the NPT. A basic principle is that each country should have the same rights and obligations."

In Brussels, we heard the same from the antiproliferation expert in the Belgian Foreign Office, Mlle. Simone Herpels: "For NPT to be successful, you have to be nondiscriminatory. If you want to have categories of states, you can't have NPT. The treaty must be applied without discrimination and the technology must be made available."

Meanwhile, right under Mlle. Herpels' nose in Brussels, the Iraqis were negotiating with the Belgian reprocessing experts at Belgonucléaire for modifications and enlargements of their small Soviet-built reactor. The firm's managing director, Jean van Dievot, denied to us that the enlargements would affect Iraqi reprocessing capability, but experts we spoke with outside of Belgium felt differently.

The Belgians, like the French, wanted a piece of the Iraqi nuclear action. Iraq had signed the NPT treaty. Who was to deny them their right to nuclear technology?

Getting the Uranium

In Osirak, the Iraqis had bought a fine reactor to produce plutonium. In the Italian labs, they bought adequate facilities to reprocess it. But these were only a start. They still needed the natural uranium to blanket the reactor core. Where would they get it? And how would they keep it secret?

Mario Chimanovitch thought he knew. The Tel Aviv correspondent for one of the leading newspapers in Rio de Janeiro, the *Jornal do Brasil*, Mario had chanced to meet some people who identified themselves as "members of Israel's intelligence community." This was in June 1981, about a week after the Israeli bombing of the Osirak, and his new friends wanted to give Mario a story. Their only condition, he told us later, was that he leave them out of it. If he needed to mention a source for what they were about to tell him, he could refer to "members of Israel's scientific community."

Their story was a good mixture of smuggling, espionage, and modern-day air piracy. As the friendly spooks told it, the Iraqis had secretly sent two cargo planes—an American-made Boeing 727 and a Soviet Ilyushin 76—to Brazil sometime in January 1981. The planes had landed at an airfield outside of Sao Paulo, where the Brazilians loaded them with arms and eight tons of natural uranium dioxide, or UO_2. The planes took off for the long flight to Iraq, flying over Africa. But—and this is where the story gets good— somewhere over an African country that Mario's sources would not name, unidentified fighter planes buzzed the Ilyushin, which was carrying the uranium, and forced it to land. The attackers then unloaded the clandestine cargo of uranium and let the empty plane continue on its way.

Mario was enthusiastic. Here was a story that had everything, and coming so soon after the Osirak bombing, it proved that the Iraqis were up to no good. They had to be using the uranium to blanket the reactor to produce plutonium for nuclear weapons, and though his new intelligence contacts never told him exactly who had stopped the Iraqis in their flight path, the headline wrote itself: "Israeli Air Pirates Force Down Iraqi Uranium Flight over Africa."

Mario rushed the story to his paper in Rio, but his editors were not so easy to please. They checked the facts, failed to find confirmation, or so they said, and refused to print the story as it was. Instead, they wrote their own exposé of how the wicked men from the Israeli Mossad had tried to misuse an honest journalist, the hapless Mario Chimanovitch. At the same time, the rival *O Estado do Sao Paulo* ran its own version of the original uranium story, which the Brazilian Government angrily denied.

"The fact that the secret service of a country spreads slander against Brazil is in itself extremely serious," declared the Brazilian Foreign Ministry spokesman, Bernardo Pericas. "The episode could have serious consequences concerning relations between the governments of Brazil and Israel."

The Brazilians then called their Ambassador Vasco Mariz home from Tel Aviv "for consultations," and instead of scoring a scoop, Chimanovitch found himself at the center of an international diplomatic row.

On the face of it, the air piracy over Africa seemed unlikely, though certainly not beyond the bounds of possibility. Whether or not the tale was true, Mario's friends in the Israeli intelligence community were telling it in order to justify the Israeli bombing of the Osirak by throwing the spotlight on a much larger story that was undeniably true. With or without air pirates, Saddam Hussein's Iraqis were racing around the world buying up what one American official called "worrying amounts" of natural uranium, for which they had little conceivable use other than to produce plutonium. And the Brazilians were helping them in their quest.

For the Iraqis, the Brazilian connection was an obvious choice. The Brazilians depended on Iraq for some 40 percent of their imported oil. They were also in the midst of acquiring a complete nuclear industry of their own—including the technology for uranium enrichment and plutonium reprocessing. This was all part of the multibillion dollar deal with West Germany, the so-called "nuclear deal of the century," which the Americans had tried so hard to kill.

As a result, the Iraqi Government approached the more-nuclear-advanced Brazilians and asked if they could provide a wide range of help and material. This included equipment and engineering for the construction of new reactors, fabricated fuel elements, help with uranium prospecting in Iraq, and the much-needed supply of both natural and slightly enriched uranium.

For their part, the Brazilians responded with caution, in part because their controversial deal with West Germany restricted the transfer of sensitive technology to any third country. But the Iraqis pressed on, and in May 1979, a high-ranking delegation visited Brazil and literally demanded that the Brazilians sign a sweeping agreement for nuclear cooperation within twenty-four hours.

The Brazilians naturally balked, loudly protesting against the heavy-handed Iraqi approach. But the negotiations continued, and in January 1980, the hard-pressed Brazilians finally signed, giving the Iraqis most of what they asked, including a promise to supply natural uranium.

At the time, the Brazilians insisted publicly that the agreement excluded any transfer of the know-how that they were getting from the Germans, especially in the fields of enrichment and reprocessing. But many observers expressed the fear that the Iraqis would use the implied threat of an oil price hike or cutoff in an attempt to get their hands on the sensitive technology, and that if they did, the oil-hungry Brazilians would find themselves hard-pressed to refuse whatever help the Iraqis wanted.

As one Western diplomat put it in an interview with Jonathan Kandell in the *International Herald Tribune,* "The key question in the Brazilian-Iraqi deal may be technical assistance, particularly the exchange of information on fuel enrichment and reprocessing. I think that the French would be extremely careful not to give the Iraqis technical guidance on nuclear engineering with military applications. But many of us are not as sure about the Brazilians."

Now, with the Israeli leak to Chimanovitch, attention shifted from the long-range danger of sensitive technology to the more immediate supply of natural uranium, which was an open and acknowledged part of Iraq's January 1980 agreement with Brazil.

But Brazil was only one of the uranium sources that Iraq was tapping. In March 1980, only two months after their agreement with Brazil, the Iraqis signed a contract with Portugal for 138 tons of natural uranium concentrate, or yellow-cake (U_3O_8). In early 1981, they got another 100 tons from the Islamic Republic of Niger, which was also supplying Pakistan.

The Iraqis also approached the Italians and Canadians for yellow-cake. But we have found no record of any sales.

Far more alarming, the Iraqis were also shopping for "depleted uranium," which is what is left over after the fissionable uranium 235 atoms have been removed in the enrichment process. This depleted uranium is almost completely uranium 238, and has only two major uses. Because of its density, it makes excellent ballast for ships and airplanes. It is also perfect for blanketing a reactor core to make plutonium.

Acording to the International Atomic Energy Agency, the West Germans have supplied Iraq in 1981 with a ten-ton shipment including both natural and depleted uranium. And we have learned from official American and Italian sources that the Iraqis tried to buy the same thing from Italy, apparently without success.

We learned from one source familiar with the Italian nuclear industry that the request to the Italians consisted of four tons of natural uranium, two tons of uranium enriched at 2.7 percent, and six tons of depleted uranium. The head of CNEN, the Italian Atomic Energy Agency, Dr. Umberto Colombo, confirmed to us that an order had been placed, but he said it went to a private Italian company and he did not know the details. He did not believe the sale had been made.

What did the Iraqis want with all this uranium?

"We were puzzled by the quantities," admitted a French diplomat in charge of "closing the loopholes" in the French nuclear contracts with Iraq. "But it's almost too much to be worrisome. Within this reactor they couldn't use all that fuel. It would be more worrisome if they bought only twenty tons and hid it away.

"Possibly they were hoarding uranium for the future," he added. "The price of uranium is low. Or maybe they are thinking one day of their nuclear power plant."

We let the French diplomat's comment pass, but after some reflection we realized that the Iraqis would not need uranium for even a small-sized power plant before 1990 at the earliest, probably not until 1995. This was early purchasing at its most extreme.

Yet, we discovered, it was true that the Iraqis were looking far beyond their immediate uranium needs. With several other Arab nations, they formed in the late seventies a joint venture called the Arab Mining Company, which is headed by Dr. Colombo's old chum from the University of Missouri and the man he trusted to tell him what the Iraqis were really doing, Dr. Abdul Rizam el-Hashimi, the vice chairman of the Iraqi Atomic Energy Commission.

With headquarters in Amman, Jordan, and operations in the African Islamic states of Mali, Somalia, Niger, and Nigeria, the company is still in its early days. But it could give the Iraqis—and other Arab nuclear hopefuls—an ample, secure, and reliable supply of natural uranium in the coming years. One Western diplomat told us he believed the organization represented the beginnings of a nuclear OPEC, in which the Iraqis would attempt to corner and coordinate the world's uranium market.

The Israelis were far more worried by the immediate Iraqi purchases, and especially by the depleted uranium. They could think of only one reason why Iraq would want so much. When the time came to divert, the Iraqis would have adequate amounts of uranium on hand to weather the international storm that would follow, as well as ample material to make not one but dozens of Arab nuclear bombs.

And the safeguards? Irrelevant.

Portugal and Niger and West Germany all reported their uranium sales to Iraq to the International Atomic Energy Agency in Vienna, which keeps records of such transactions. But that is where the system stops. Even though Iraq has signed the Nonproliferatioin Treaty and agreed to open all of its nuclear installations to safeguards, the IAEA does not require safeguards on either depleted uranium or yellow-cake, and the Iraqis were not required to tell the IAEA how much they had, or where it was, or what they were doing with it.

The IAEA has no obligations to keep track of the yellow-cake inside Iraq.

It does not check the Iraqi inventory records. It does not even ask questions until the yellow-cake is reduced to the more usable uranium dioxide or uranium metal, which are what the Iraqis would use to make pellets in their Italian fuel-fabrication lab. And strange as it must seem, the IAEA has no way of finding out if the Iraqis have converted the yellow-cake into oxide unless the Iraqis tell them.

"So long as it does not report that the U_3O_8 has been converted into a material that is in the safeguarded category, you have no right to inquire of its whereabouts," explained the former IAEA inspector Roger Richter in his dramatic testimony to the Foreign Relations Committee of the U.S. Senate following the Osirak bombing.

Similarly, said Richter, the Iraqis could keep their Italian-built fuel-fabrication and reprocessing facilities completely off limits: "You are not entitled even to look at the other facilities if Iraq has not adhered to its obligation under NPT to report to the IAEA that material subject to the safeguards is located in these facilities.

"These facilities are not under safeguards," Richter explained. "And so long as Iraq maintains that it is not processing plutonium or fabricating uranium fuel in these facilities, they will remain outside of safeguards."

In other words, the safeguards would apply to the Iraqi uranium only if the Iraqis told the IAEA what they were doing. They could tell the Agency if they wanted. They could also decide not to.

16

Operation Babylon?

The precision of the attack was stupefying.
—Jacques Rimbaud,
French technician,
June 1981

Anxiety is a function of money. . . . We knew our people were bothered. So we tried to relieve their anxiety.
—Technicatome official,
July 1981

Never again. Never again.
—Menachem Begin,
Prime Minister of Israel,
June 1981

When Dr. Yahya el-Meshad was found bludgeoned to death in his hotel room in Paris in June 1980, the shock waves rippled throughout the Iraqi nuclear program and among the French scientists and technicians working with it. But whoever killed the Arab scientist, and for whatever reason, there was one place where his death was scarcely mourned.

"It will be difficult for Iraq to continue its efforts to produce a nuclear weapon," announced Kol Israel, the official Israeli radio. "This death is going to delay the start-up of the country's atomic weapons project by at least two years."

The broadcast was probably more propaganda than any accurate assessment of el-Meshad's importance to Iraqi nuclear efforts, and the prediction echoed similar statements that Israeli spokesmen had made following the sabotage bombing at La Seyne-sur-Mer, and statements they would make after the Phantom attack on the Iraqi reactor site at Tuwaitah. Somehow the Israelis always predicted a two-year delay, whether as wishful thinking or a conscious effort to weaken enemy morale. Seeing themselves as the eventual target of Saddam Hussein's bomb, the Israelis were not above counting off all the delays and then turning around and prematurely crying wolf to waken the world to the Iraqi nuclear threat.

"All the Iraqis now have to do is sit back and decide which sort of bomb they prefer," warned Israel's own nuclear expert, the outspoken Prof. Yuval Ne'eman. "They have everything else at their fingertips."

They could use the uranium directly, he explained on July 17, 1980 in a lengthy interview in the *Jerusalem Post*. Or they could use it in the reactor to irradiate natural uranium and produce plutonium, which they could then extract in the chemical laboratories they were getting from Italy.

"They can have a bomb put together faster with enriched uranium," he warned. "But the plutonium will give them more bombs. The French reactor can produce three to four bombs a year [sic] and, with foreign scientists, they can have a bomb ready in a year. These scientists can have a uranium bomb ready for use in from six months to a year."

In the interview, which appeared nearly a year before the Israelis finally bombed the Osirak, Ne'eman was especially scathing about the idea that the Iraqis wanted the sophisticated and powerful reactor for research.

"There are no rudiments of nuclear research in Iraq," he scoffed. "There is only one nuclear physicist in Baghdad, who is in any case no researcher. The last I heard of him he was in prison awaiting the execution of a death sentence."

The Israelis had awakened relatively late to what Iraq was doing, as despairing Israeli journalists in Europe were the first to point out. But now that they were roused, Israeli leaders would waste little time in trying to derail the entire Iraqi nuclear project, either by creating so much pressure that the French and Italian Governments would be forced to cancel the contracts, or by more forceful means if needed.

The Israeli anxiety, and the readiness to take action, were obvious to those who followed the situation closely, among them a Washington-based defense analyst named Edward Luttwak, with whom we spoke in the spring of 1980. "I don't think it will get to the point where Iraq will be within an ace of having a nuclear weapon because the Israelis will stop it," Luttwak told us with amazing prescience over a year before the actual bombing of Osirak took place. "Whether this means going out to third countries and interfering with the shipment of nuclear equipment or going right inside Iraq and bombing the facilities, the Israelis will do it."

In part, the Israelis did what they do best, quietly planting stories through sympathetic journalists in the Western press. This became a high priority in the summer of 1980, when a senior Israeli official went to the United States and gave background briefings to certain selected journalists, all on the condition that the Israelis never be mentioned as a source in the resulting stories. We have the official's name, but cannot reveal it without putting one of our sources in a difficult position.

The Israelis similarly circulated an unsigned three-page summary on "Iraqi Nuclear Activity," which the editor of a well-known American periodical was kind enough to pass on. With or without independent verification, much of this information found its way into print, with never a mention of its Israeli sponsors.

What the Israelis were doing was routine propaganda work, the kind of thing that America's Central Intelligence Agency and Britain's now-defunct Information Research Department used to do on a far grander scale. The Israelis used the approach to give apparently independent confirmation to their official statements, and to give credibility to information that was generally true, but which many people would dismiss as false or biased if they saw the Israeli label attached.

To be fair, the Israelis never hid their official concern. Far from it. By July, the French had shipped the first load of highly enriched uranium fuel to Iraq, and Israeli leaders were increasingly speaking out in public. Their anger was obvious, as was their warning. The Iraqis were building the bomb. France and Italy were helping them to do it. And the Israelis would take whatever measures they thought necessary to stop the Iraqi bomb long before Saddam Hussein could ever think of using it.

The Israeli warnings were clear to anyone who listened, from at least a year before the attack on Osirak. The French shipment of enriched uranium was "a very grave development," charged Menachem Begin in July 1980 as he left Hadassah University Hospital following treatment for one of his recurrent heart attacks. "A savage policy," added the former Prime Minister Yitzhak Rabin. "At times like that of the Vichy regime," said the Transport Minister Hayim Landau.

In an official briefing to the Knesset's Foreign Affairs and Defense Committee, a senior military intelligence officer warned that the Iraqis could have several bombs by the mid 1980s, and the Knesset Committee urgently called for "a diplomatic and information offensive."

"When an irresponsible, extremist and aggressive regime such as Iraq's gets nuclear manufacturing potential in this way, Israel must regard the development as a threat to its existence and security," said the Committee members, as paraphrased by the *Jerusalem Post*.

The fear and anger mounted. On July 14, Israeli officials pointedly boycotted the Bastille Day celebrations at the French Embassy, and on July 28, the Israeli Foreign Minister Yitzhak Shamir called in the French Chargé d'Affaires and formally expressed Israel's "profound concern." The Iraqi nuclear program, and the French help to it, could "reignite the flames of conflict in the region," declared Shamir.

In diplomatic terms, this was strong stuff, and to give credit where it is due, *Time* magazine got the message exactly right. "It was," they wrote, "an implicit warning that if they ever became convinced that Iraq was at the threshold of acquiring a military atomic capability, the Israelis might launch a preemptive strike against Baghdad's nuclear installations."

The French replied with undiplomatic haste, giving their answer the next day, July 29. They saw no reason to deny Iraq "the right to peaceful uses of nuclear energy." And they would "proceed as before, without yielding to pressure or manueverings."

The less polished Iraqis had not waited for any official Israeli protests.

During the entire month of July they had felt themselves subjected to a
massive press attack, especially in France, and on July 25 the Iraqi Embassy
in Paris issued a communiqué "*a toutes les plumes libres et honnêtes*"—to all
honest and independent writers.

With some justice, and a characteristic lack of subtlety, the Iraqi missive
lambasted the "tendentious," even "pernicious" press campaign, "fed and
organized in broad daylight by the Zionist milieu." The Iraqi nuclear
program was for entirely peaceful ends, the statement insisted. And the
prime purpose of the "Zionist press campaign" was "to create a favorable
climate for an aggressive military action against Iraqi territory."

The Iraqi communiqué ended by quoting President Saddam Hussein, who
had just issued some rather startling charges of his own against his Israeli foes
and their nuclear program. According to Saddam, the "Zionist entity" was
continuing nuclear relations with the racist regime of South Africa, and had
also staged a nuclear explosion "in occupied territories" in the Negev
Desert. *

With stunning foresight, Baghdad also warned in a separate dispatch that
the Israelis were planning "to launch a military aggression against Iraq,
particularly since the enemy possessed U.S.-made aircraft capable of striking
at the Iraqi land."

"The Zionist entity," read the official statement, "was perhaps preparing to
launch an air attack on the Iraqi nuclear reactor in an attempt to obstruct
scientific and technological development in Iraq, and also to prevent the
Arab nation from forging ahead in this field." The Iraqis believed at least part
of their propaganda counterblast, and took steps to strengthen security at the
reactor site at Tuwaitah. French and Italian technicians who visited Iraq
during the summer of 1980 told us that they had seen a vastly increased
military presence, especially at the time of the delivery of the highly enriched
uranium fuel. And there were reports—unconfirmed by the Iraqis—that
Saddam officially put the nuclear program under the direct control of the
Iraqi military, who, as Technicatome's Yves Girard told us, had been given
to believe that the reactor would give them nuclear weapons.

This was the state of tension in early August 1980, when the self-
proclaimed and otherwise unidentified "Committee to Safeguard the Islamic
Revolution" launched its dramatic campaign of bombings and threatening
letters to French and Italian firms and individuals working on the Iraqi
nuclear project. What Italian nuclear officals had called a *terroristico* press
campaign had given way to the real thing, a campaign of terror, and the
timing strengthened the impression that the "Committee to Safeguard" was
more Israeli than Islamic. But before the secret war could make its mark, the
Iraqis embarked on a far more serious shooting war, and not with their Israeli
foes.

*The Negev Desert is part of pre-1967 Israel. The Iraqis do not differentiate between
territories captured by Israel during the 1967 war and those that constituted the borders of the
state between 1949 and 1967.

Ever since the Ayatollah Khomeini and his Shiite revolutionaries had toppled the Shah of Iran in early 1979, they had been trying to stir up the Iraqi Shiites to overthrow the Baath government in Baghdad. On September 22, 1980, Saddam Hussein hit back, launching an all-out war to crush Iran and make Iraq the undoubted master of the Persian, or rather Arabian Gulf.

In fact, Saddam and his advisers underestimated their Iranian enemy. Even after two years of revolutionary disruption and the execution of many of the former Shah's military officers, the Iranians put up an unexpectedly strong defense, and well into 1981, as the intensity of the fighting lessened, neither side was able to win a clear-cut victory.

However it would end—and a political resolution of the war seemed unlikely—the Gulf War left its mark on Saddam Hussein's nuclear ambitions. This was most visible at Tuwaitah, where on the ninth day of the war, September 30, 1980, the two Phantom jets attacked the Osirak reactor.

The attack made headlines the world over. But according to the best available accounts from French engineers, the physical damage was less serious than many press reports had suggested. Only one of the rockets actually exploded, damaging the reactor dome and the cooling system. This set back the start-up of the Osirak reactor, which had been expected by December 1980. The engineers seemed fairly certain, however, that they could repair the damage without too much further delay.

This was the visible damage, which would soon be repaired. Less visibly, the attack also left a deeper mark, and one that was not so easy to measure.

The scientists and engineers at Technicatome and SNIA-Techint and the other French and Italian firms working on the Iraqi nuclear project had already suffered a series of sharp psychological jolts. The sabotage of the reactor core at La Seyne-sur-Mer, the jailing of Sharastani and Jaffar, the killing of el-Meshad and Marie Claude Magal, the terror bombings and threatening letters from the "Committee to Safeguard the Islamic Revolution"—these had all raised questions, dashed hopes, stirred fears. But the attack at Tuwaitah affected many of the technicians as nothing had before. This was especially marked with those actually working in Iraq at the time, caught up as they were in someone else's war, and at the heart of one of the most sensitive military targets.

This was not part of their contract, not as they saw it. They were scientists, technicians, engineers, skilled workmen. They had not signed on to be part of someone else's war.

In normal times, as many as 400 French technicians were working in Iraq, along with a handful of Italians. Once the war began, all but seventy of the French rushed back to Europe, and after the attack on Tuwaitah, only about seven agreed to stay on.

Far more than the damage to the reactor's cooling system, this sudden exodus of foreign technicians drastically threatened the nuclear program, and the Iraqis put enormous pressure on the French Government and the various firms to get their people back on the job.

In time, as the war settled down, many of the technicians returned. They were getting double or more their normal salaries, with added tax advantages, and it was going to take more than a war—or even an Iraqi bomb—to keep them away. But at the main contracting company, the state-owned Technicatome, several of the staff simply backed off. They were not going back to Iraq, they said.

"They had fits of conscience," we were told by a French nuclear scientist close to the dissidents. "Some of them were scared, others ashamed."

To add to their feelings, a new rash of threatening letters turned up in February 1981. As before, they were signed by the "Committee to Safeguard the Islamic Revolution." But this time they carried a new twist. Some were addressed directly to the wives of the technicians and scientists, and were accompanied by photographs of massacred children. The technicians would be responsible for thousands of such deaths, the letters warned, and would have to bear the consequences.

In a separate letter to French officials and the newspaper *Libération*, the "Committee" also claimed credit for the Phantom attack on Tuwaitah. "The bombardment that our planes have executed is only an additional warning, and we repeat once more that the French experts better never again set foot in Iraq," the letter threatened.

"We have warned the French companies Serbag, CNIM, Technicatome of what could happen, and we have urgently asked them to give up the business and evacuate all their employees.

"We don't have any interest in killing French or Europeans," the "Committee" concluded. "But if they should persist in continuing to serve the godless and bloodthirsty regime, they alone will be responsible for the consequences."

It was all getting very spooky, and the management of Technicatome called a meeting of the concerned staff, most of whom did not want to return to Iraq. The company officials explained that all of the other firms had gone back to work. Only the technicians at Technicatome had not. The officials also warned that those who refused to go back to Iraq could find themselves subject to dismissal, while those who went could earn themselves some extra money.

The approach seemed to work, at least for the time being, a high Technicatome official—who asked not to be identified—told us. "I'm a little bit cynical," he confided. "Anxiety is a function of money. The two have a relationship. We knew our people were bothered. So we tried to relieve their anxiety."

"How much did it cost you?" we asked. "Twenty percent extra? More?"

"No, not that much," he laughed. "The anxiety had not grown to those amounts."

By April, most of the technicians were heading back. Technicatome had signed a secret agreement in 1979 with the Iraqis to provide maintenance and supervision on Osirak for ten years, or until 1989. This guaranteed a French presence in the project, though not necessarily free access to the reactor itself. But the technicians and workers still had their fears, and with continuing threats and possible violence from the "Committee to Safeguard the Islamic Revolution," the nuclear project continued to sit on the time bomb of psychological terror.

"I knew anything could happen in Iraq," explained Jean-Francois Masciola, the electrician employed by the controls firm Comsip and one of the technicians who had been at Tuwaitah during the Phantom attack and had returned for a second round. "It's that kind of country. I was there for the first bombardment, but I thought this time it would be okay."

Those were the technicians. In a similar way, the first attack at Tuwaitah also shook the confidence of a far larger public that had counted on the International Atomic Energy Agency and its safeguards to keep the Iraqis in check.

As a signatory of the Nonproliferation Treaty, Iraq had agreed to open all of its nuclear installations to inspections. In theory, this covered the Osirak and its highly enriched uranium fuel, and the year before, in September 1979, Iraq and France had exchanged letters agreeing to provide the IAEA with design information on the reactor and other new facilities and also to notify the Agency of any unexpected transfer of sensitive nuclear materials.

The letters were in the place of a customary trilateral agreement between the seller, the buyer, and the IAEA, which the Agency generally insists on in order to set out the exact safeguards obligations that countries such as France and Iraq are expected to meet. Iraq's refusal to sign such an agreement had sounded the danger signal. Yet most observers kept silent, as France had guaranteed that its technicians would have their eye on the fuel at every step.

That was before the rocket attack at Tuwaitah and the mass exodus of French technicians. After the attack, the fuel was still there. But the technicians, and their watchful eyes, were gone.

To be fair, before leaving, the French had pre-irradiated the uranium, which would have made it more difficult (though not impossible) for any errant hands to use it in making a weapon. They also stored the fuel safely away in the very bowels of the reactor installation, where it was fairly well protected from any return of the attacking Phantoms. But the international safeguards system did not seem very reassuring on the morning after most of the technicians left, and the alarms really started ringing when the Iraqis informed the IAEA in Vienna that the war had made it too dangerous for any international inspectors to visit the Osirak or to see that the highly enriched uranium was safe.

The IAEA "would be informed as soon as safeguards inspections can be resumed," the Iraqis promised.

This was a situation that the nuclear mandarins had somehow never anticipated. How do you have safeguards when people are fighting a war?

"French officials are indicating extreme embarrassment over the uncertainty surrounding the reactors," reported Ronald Koven in *The Washington*

Post. "They say that places the whole problem of nuclear proliferation in a new light and that the problem should be carefully examined by the international community."

For once, the mandarins themselves had no answer. They had never even thought of the question.

"We are in a completely new situation that was not foreseen in any international treaties," one French nuclear source told Koven. "The problem is raised for international reflection just as sharply as it was in 1974 when India made its explosion."

In the end, Iraq let the inspectors in, and they found the uranium exactly where it was supposed to be. But for a time, a lot of once-confident people were holding their breath.

"We were worried whether the IAEA would come or not," Technicatome's Yves Girard told us in January 1981. "We were very relieved when they let them in just recently. We had pressed. But for a while there, we couldn't get the IAEA in."

Not exactly the kind of safeguards to inspire confidence. And certainly not in the middle of a war.

From the mysterious bombing of the reactor core at La Seyne-sur-Mer in April 1979 to the Phantom rocket atttack at the reactor site in Tuwaitah in September 1980, sabotage, terror bombings, threats, and even murder had plagued the Iraqi nuclear program, and each time the violence had escalated, the finger of suspicion increasingly pointed in the same direction. But now, with the final destruction of Osirak, those who dropped the bombs wasted no time in claiming credit for what they had done.

The announcement came the afternoon after the attack, straight from the office of the Prime Minister of Israel, Mr. Menachem Begin. "On Sunday, 7 June 1981, the Israel Air Force launched a raid on the atomic reactor Osirak, near Baghdad," read the official communiqué. "Our pilots carried out their mission fully. The reactor was destroyed. All our aircraft returned safely to base."

For Mr. Begin, this simple message signaled the climax of a long campaign, and in a sense it was the failure of the earlier violence that led Jerusalem to plan the aerial attack. The Israelis had seen how the sabotage at La Seyne had delayed the Osirak by only a few months, and how the French were continuing to help the Iraqis with their nuclear program. The only serious question was whether the French would stick to their proposal to supply only low-enriched caramel in place of the bomb-grade 93 percent highly enriched uranium that they had originally promised. By the first months of 1980, the answer was obvious: The French had once again given in. The Iraqis would get the bomb-grade fuel.

This was the point—in January or February of 1980—when the Israelis began to work out a plan to bomb the reactor inside Iraq itself. According to a source familiar with the planning, Mr. Begin asked the military to develop various contingency plans, including the option of making the attack covertly so that the planes could not be identified as Israeli.

All of this took weeks and months to work out, and in the meantime the Israeli Government was becoming more and more worried about what the French and Iraqis were doing. These fears reached a climax in early summer, when the French sent the first shipment of highly enriched uranium to Iraq. In response, the Israelis stepped up their propaganda and diplomatic efforts, boycotting the French celebration of Bastille Day and formally protesting to the French Chargé d'Affaires in Jerusalem. There was also a possibly unconnected, but nonetheless marked increase in direct action against the Iraqi nuclear program, with the killing of the Egyptian-born Yahya el-Meshad in Paris in June and the emergence of the "Committee to Safeguard the Islamic Revolution" with its terror bombings in France and Italy in August.

By September, the stage was set for the Israelis to make their big move. On September 22, the Iraqis launched a full-scale war against Iran, and that same week from Tel Aviv, the Chief of Israel's Military Intelligence, General Yehoshua Saguy, issued a strange and provocative statement. "If I were an Iranian," he said, "I too would be worried, knowing that Iraq will unquestionably be a nuclear power at the end of the 1980s."

A few days later, on September 30, the two Phantom F-4 jet fighters swept past the Osirak site at Tuwaitah and sent their rockets crashing into the dome, causing extensive damage to the reactor cooling system. Once again General Saguy spoke out, declaring that the bombing would put Iraq's atomic option back two or three years.

Iraqi officials blamed the Israelis for the attack, and several of the world's most authoritative newspapers and magazines rushed into print with "inside stories" on how the clever Israelis had sent unmarked Phantoms flying low across the desert to attack the Iraqi reactor.

Within a day or two of the raid, however, Iranian officials claimed credit for the attack, and according to French technicians who saw the hit firsthand, the Phantoms had not even attempted a major strike, but treated the reactor as a target of opportunity on their way home after bombing an electric power plant on the outskirts of nearby Baghdad.

In fact, the Phantom attack appears to have preempted whatever the Israelis might have been planning. As a result of the hit, the French firms in Iraq called their technicians home, and according to a senior Israeli source, the Israeli Government came to feel that the immediate pressure was off. Without the French technicians, the Iraqis could never start up the Osirak reactor. So long as the technicians stayed in France, the Israelis felt that they could hold back on their secret plan to bomb the reactor.

The respite was short-lived. In spite of a continuing campaign of intimidation by the "Committee to Safeguard the Islamic Revolution," the French technicians began to return in numbers in the early part of 1981, and that is when "Operation Babylon" went into high gear.

IRAQ

The timing was later confirmed by the Israeli Air Force Commander, General David Ivri, when he revealed that he and his colleagues had come up with the actual plan for the attack some six months beforehand, which would have been about January. It was at this point that a hand-picked team of Israeli pilots began training in earnest for the big event, perfecting specially devised dive-bombing tactics in secret practice runs over the Sinai Desert.

The most memorable images of the Israeli bombing of Osirak—and the ones the whole world read—came from a young French technician called Jacques Rimbaud, just back from Iraq and eager to tell the world exactly how the Israeli planes had bombed and destroyed the Osirak reactor. It was the morning of Wednesday, June 10, three days after the attack. Rimbaud had just flown in on the Iraq Airways flight from Baghdad to Orly Airport in Paris, where an enterprising French wire service reporter took down what he had to say. Rimbaud's description of the bombing appeared in newspapers and magazines all over the world as the first eyewitness account of what had really happened.

"I heard a plane pass very low without doing anything," Rimbaud recalled. "Then, all of a sudden, another let go with big cylinders about a third of the length of the plane.

"I saw the reactor's dome fly up in the air and explode into pieces, a little like a slow-motion movie. After the explosion, fire caught quickly. In the dust, I saw the concrete dome of Osirak collapse, and only a few meters of it showed above ground.

"The precision of the attack was stupefying," he declared. "The central building is completely collapsed. The atomic reactor is hit and the radiation shielding has disappeared."

It was the classic eyewitness account, full of firsthand detail and the sights and sounds and feel of the event, and most of what Rimbaud said was later confirmed by the other French technicians with whom we and other journalists spoke. But no matter how hard we tried, we could never find M. Rimbaud himself. When in desperation we finally visited the company that the initial reports had mentioned as his employer, the construction firm Bouygues just outside of Paris, we found that Rimbaud's story raised an interesting question.

"But Monsieur, we had no one at the site during the bombardment," insisted the man who had been in charge of the Bouygues workers in Iraq, M. Bernard Minitrier. "Our job was effectively finished in the summer of 1979. Before that, at the height of the construction, we had close to 1,500 workers on the site. But we left only a few people there. The civil construction was finished."

"But what about Rimbaud?" we pressed.

"He had absolutely nothing to do with Bouygues, or with any work at the site of Tammuz," Minitrier repeated. "*Absolument rien*, Monsieur. He had worked for us in Tanzania. But I don't know what he was doing in Iraq. Perhaps he was just passing through on his return to France."

"But how would he have known what had happened?" we stammered.

"Oh, we were told that he had been sitting at the Italian Club in Baghdad. He must have heard it there," Minitrier explained. "But he is not ours. And he saw nothing. It is very amusing, *non*, Monsieur?"

Amusing it was. Also a bit perplexing. But it was not worth the time to push the investigation any farther, especially after we found other technicians who were on the site and who essentially repeated what Rimbaud had said. Yet under the pressure of deadlines and the fierce competition for a breaking story, the kind of mystery and myth-making and rushed reporting surrounding Rimbaud quickly became the journalistic hallmark for many of the breathless accounts of the Osirak bombing and how the daring Israelis had done it.

Of course, this has become standard practice when it comes to reporting the undercover exploits of the Israelis, whether proved or vaguely attributed to them. Only this time the fibs and fabrications were front-page news.

Even the name by which the bombing became known—Operation Babylon—was suspect. Of all the code names that the Israelis might have used, that is the one that they would never have chosen. As any schoolboy will remember, ancient Babylon was the capital of what is today's Iraq. Where secrecy is key, no one in his right mind would have used a code that gave the game away.

"I don't know anything about that name," one Israeli military spokesman told us, even after the code name had been printed in such major American publications as *Newsweek* and the sensationalist *New York Post*. "Where did you hear it?"

An official in Prime Minister Begin's office said that he had not heard it either. But he had nothing against using it if we wanted to. "It's catchy," he smiled. "Why not? I like it."

"A bit too romantic for my taste," added Colette Avital, a public information officer at the Israel Foreign Office in Jerusalem. "But if you want to use it, why should I object?"

Nuclear proliferation was now in the news, as the entire world debated the rights and wrongs of Israel's "nuclear Entebbe." But even as the Israelis celebrated and most of the rest of the world condemned, it was hard to avoid a disturbing suspicion. However much we might fear the spread of nuclear weapons, especially in the explosive Middle East, had Menachem Begin called it correctly, even from the Israeli point of view? Did Osirak really pose as great a danger to the survival of the Jewish state as he claimed? And was the threat really so clear and present that the Israelis had to bomb first and ask questions later?

From all the evidence, the Iraqis *were* moving toward nuclear explosives, using their Osirak reactor, their Italian labs, and their otherwise unexplained purchases of natural and depleted uranium to produce weapons-usable plutonium. But they were still several years away from having even their first nuclear weapon. The threat was not immediate. The Israelis had time to wait, time to give the new French President, François Mitterrand, at least a few months or even a year to close the loopholes in the Iraqi nuclear contracts.

In other words, while the nuclear threats were real enough, the survival of Israel was not yet at stake. In much of what he said, Begin was simply crying wolf.

The easiest evidence comes from the Prime Minister's own overstatements, misstatements, and misquotations. Some of the gaffes were classic, as a bellicose Mr. Begin played fast and loose with the truth to justify a course that he had already taken. This was most obvious in the celebrated case of the missing laboratory.

On the Thursday evening following the bombing, at a farewell party for the departing British Ambassador, John Robinson, Mr. Begin dropped what he obviously hoped would be another bombshell. As he told the tale, the French had secretly built the Iraqis a mysterious installation beneath the Osirak reactor some "forty meters below the surface," or thirteen stories down into the earth. This was where the Iraqis were planning to manufacture their atom bomb, Begin explained. And this was the real target of the Israeli attack.

Mr. Begin's startling new revelation quickly appeared in wire service reports from the international news agency Reuters, sending diplomats scurrying to their cables and journalists to their sources. Editors everywhere wanted to know all about the mysterious lab, and one of our more enterprising colleagues—a well-known Israeli journalist who was sending his dispatches far and wide—managed to scoop the entire international press corps with an account from "inside sources" telling exactly how the quick-witted Israelis had managed to send their bombs hurtling deeply enough into the earth to destroy the secret lab those "forty meters below the surface."

That was Thursday night. Friday morning the story changed rather abruptly, as an embarrassed Menachem Begin was forced to call the Reuters correspondent in Tel Aviv to make the first of several corrections. He had misread the figures, Begin confessed. The lab was only four meters down, not forty. It was all an honest mistake—at least on the part of Begin, if not on the part of our journalist friend and his "inside sources."

That was just the beginning. In the following days, Israeli spokesmen admitted a second error. The clandestine lab itself was a myth. It did not exist. There was only a small, far-from-secret chamber under the reactor, and that had no great importance except to certain sophisticated experiments.

"The 'secret room' was underneath the number-one channel," explained the ever-helpful Yves Girard, Vice President at Technicatome, the state-owned firm that designed the Osirak reactor. "It was for preparing the spectrometer," he told us. "It would have been useful in monitoring the neutron-beam experiments."

Even more embarrassing was Begin's missing quote. In his rush to defend the Israeli raid, the Prime Minister had eagerly pounced on a statement by the Iraqi leader Saddam Hussein, supposedly made following the first air attack on the Osirak reactor in September 1980. According to Begin, the statement had been quoted in the October 4 issue of the Baghdad newspaper *al-Thawra*, the official paper of Iraq's ruling Baath Socialist Party. Begin claimed the statement proved beyond a doubt that the Iraqis were secretly intending to use the Osirak reactor to make nuclear weapons for use against Israel.

"The Iranian people should not fear the Iraqi nuclear reactor, which is not intended to be used against Iran, but against the Zionist enemy," Saddam had declared, according to the Israeli account.

It was a fat and juicy quote, and Begin milked it for all it was worth. "Well, what does it mean 'to be used against'?" he asked his internationally televised press conference on the Tuesday after the raid. "Should that reactor be used for peaceful purposes, let us say for electricity, how can electricity be used against anybody, whether Iranian or Israelis?"

Somehow, no one seemed able to track down the exact source of the guilty quotation. Journalists tried, with no success. American officials in Baghdad, Tel Aviv, and Washington could not find it either. Secret cables went madly whirling around the world.

One American diplomat, with whom we had just eaten lunch, telephoned to see if we might have found it our investigations. We knew the quote, all right. An Israeli official had given it to us several months before. But we had not been able to track down the source, as we explained to the Israeli at the time.

"Take it on trust," he had told us. "Believe us."

From other things the Israeli had told us, it seemed unlikely that he was purposely trying to mislead. No doubt, he believed in what he was telling us, as did Begin when he dramatically brandished the quotation as the final indictment of Iraq's secret nuclear intentions.

In fact, the quote was bogus. Saddam Hussein had never said any such thing, at least in public, and the newspaper *al-Thawra* had never printed it. The closest thing to sentiments of this sort had appeared in an editorial in the official Baghdad daily *al-Gumhuriya*, and the meaning was really quite different. As Israeli officials later explained it, the translator in Tel Aviv appears to have gone off half-cocked, and Mr. Begin and his colleagues were so eager to defend what they had done that they rushed to use the supposed statement without anyone stopping to look at the original.

Perhaps the most galling example of Begin's blatant bending of the truth came in his positively brilliant description of why he had to strike before Osirak went "hot." He had to act now before Osirak started up, he explained, as he would never have given the order to bomb a *running* nuclear reactor. That would have spread a deadly radioactive cloud over Baghdad, killing and maiming thousands of innocent civilians.

"We have had reliable information from the most reliable sources that either in July this year, or at the latest in September, the nuclear reactor Osirak is going to be operational and 'hot,'" he confided to the eager journalists. "The Iraqis, even the last few days before our operation took place, pressed the French experts to do whatever they could to quicken the pace in order to make it possible for them to turn the reactor into an operational one in July, in other words less than two weeks from today. If that had happened, we couldn't do anything whatsoever in order to prevent the Iraqi tyrant from developing, at least in the near future, between three and five Hiroshima-type nuclear bombs of twenty kilotons.

"If the reactor had become operational—and as the specialists use the word, 'hot'—we couldn't do anything forever. Because if it were 'hot' and we would open it by bombs, from planes, then a horrifying wave of radioactivity would come out from the reactor and cover the sky over Baghdad, and then in Baghdad hundreds of thousands of innocent citizens—residents, men, women and children—would have been hurt.

"I, for one, would have never made a proposal to my colleagues under such circumstances to send our Air Force and bomb the reactor."

As Mr. Begin laid out the facts, the dilemma seemed harsh, his choice inevitable. Short of creating terrifying casualties among the citizens of Baghdad, he had to destroy Osirak before the French and Iraqis put it into operation. It was literally now or never.

"Therefore, we chose this moment," he concluded. "Now, not later; later may be too late, perhaps forever. And then we will stand by idly: two, three years, at the most four years, and Saddam Hussein would have produced his three, four, five bombs. What should, what could we have done in the face of such a present, direct, horrifying peril? Nothing. Then this country and this people would have been lost. After the Holocaust, another holocaust would have happened in the history of the Jewish people.

"Never again," he proclaimed. "Never again."

It was enough to make one cry, or to think how very lucky all those innocent Iraqis were that the kindly Mr. Begin had not waited a single day longer before he ordered the Osirak reactor bombed.

In fact, the real considerations were somewhat different. As Begin indicated, the Iraqis *were* putting pressure on the French to start up the reactor by the middle of July, when the Iraqis celebrate the anniversary of the 1968 Revolution that brought the present Baath regime to power. The French had initially agreed, and by the third week of May, it was known in Paris that they were planning to send a special team of technicians and a new load of highly enriched uranium fuel to Iraq to make Osirak operational in July.

This is the date we were later given by sources in the American

Government, who had received the information from the French. One American diplomat told us, "I assume Mr. Begin has the same kind of access to information sources that we have."

Alain Varneau, the official spokesman for the French Atomic Energy Commission, also told us later that the start-up had been set for July, though he said he was not certain, while Yves Girard, the Vice President of Technicatome, told us that the plan was to have the reactor "diverge" in July, though only at low power. The French technicians were still having trouble fixing the cooling system, which had been damaged by the September 1980 Phantom attack, so Osirak would not be able to go to full power until the fall.

Against all of this, the French Foreign Office insisted to us that July was off and that Osirak would not start up even at low power until September. Who was right? We wondered if the conflict between the Atomic Energy Commission and the Quai d'Orsay had become so bad that they could not even agree on a simple, if extremely relevant, point of fact.

We saw no choice but to go to the bottom. As we learned from one of our better inside sources in the French nuclear industry, the French Nuclear Research Center at Saclay has a little office that arranges the work schedules for the technicians who would have to do the actual work of turning the reactor on. The office was headed by a man called François Cherreau, and when we called, we spoke to his assistant, Jean-Pierre Jenthon, who had apparently never spoken to the press before and sounded rather stunned that we had managed to find his telephone number.

The team of technicians was originally scheduled to go to Iraq in July, Jenthon related. But the problems with the cooling system had forced a postponement until September at the earliest. The technicians would take their normal summer holidays in July and August, and only after that would they fly to Iraq to start up the reactor. The earliest start-up date possible was September, and it could be later.

Did the Israelis know of the delay? Did the Americans? Did all the French? From his speech at the Tuesday press conference, Begin indicated that September was a possibility. But there is no evidence that he or his intelligence people knew that July was off, and also no evidence that they ever tried to find out. By May, the Israelis were looking for a reason to act, not a reason to delay.

Actually, the start-up date was never the deciding factor in the Israeli decision to act. It was not now or never. The Israelis could still have struck, whether the reactor was hot or not. The Osirak was not a massive nuclear power reactor, but only a research reactor, which would be started up and stopped several times over the course of a year. Even if the Israelis should bomb it while it was operational, or "hot," there was only a minute possibility that the explosion would send a deadly radioactive cloud even over the reactor site, let alone over the city of Baghdad.

Warren Donnelly, a research associate at the Library of Congress in

Washington, undertook a study of the danger of radioactive fallout from a bombing like the ones the Israelis undertook at Tuwaitah, and came to this conclusion: "What you'd have to do for Baghdad to be in danger is take a plane, put the radioactive materials in it, fly it over Baghdad, and drop the stuff on it," he told us.

"It's hard to see how the radiation would cause even a single death," added Dr. William Higinbotham, of the prestigious Brookhaven National Laboratory on Long Island, New York. "Anyone who would be close enough to receive a lethal dose of direct radiation would be killed by the blast itself.

"In reality, even with the sizable, large high explosives which came down and blew up the top of the building and the top of the reactor, it's very unlikely that the explosion would drive out all the water and permit the release of significant amounts of radioactive material. Even if it did, what we're talking about would be far from a lethal dose to people in the immediate neighborhood, much less ten miles away, and would probably hardly be measurable thirty miles away."

How many people would die? we asked.

"Nobody," replied the distinguished scientist.

Even on the site?

"In any case, nobody would die from the radiation. A few people nearby might conceivably develop thyroid cancer sometime twenty or thirty years from now. But even that seems very unlikely."

Our amazement must have shown.

"Of course," he added with a smile, "this is a very, very different thing from a power reactor, which could have something like 3,000 megawatts rather than 50. In that case, there would be a substantial release of energy and a large inventory of radioactive material that could cause a number of deaths and contaminate a big area. But the Osirak wasn't a large power reactor."

The Israelis still insist that Begin was right, and they have even distributed an official study purporting to show that bombing the Osirak after it had started up might have caused a "large-scale nuclear disaster." But the scientific assumptions do not stand up to scrutiny, and Israeli officials have admitted to us that, as Dr. Higinbotham also suggested, they were seriously concerned with the public-relations aspect of any attack on an active nuclear reactor. We learned that a few months before the bombing, Begin's Government consulted the one-time head of Israel's own nuclear program and former Deputy Director of Military Intelligence, Professor Yuval Ne'eman.

"They asked me about that," he told us a few days after the raid. "And I recommended against bombing a hot reactor. You know, there's a taboo attached to radiation. To have bombed a hot reactor would have caused us great harm. We would have broken a taboo. And it would also have put us in direct confrontation with all the antinuclear people. Do you know what everybody would be calling us if we had done it? Whether scientifically justified or not, the accusations against us would have been terrible."

The wrong lab, the wrong quote, the wrong month, and a fear of bad public relations rather than deadly radiation—Begin was finding it hard to tell the truth. But the reasons were clear enough. As Begin put it, and as one of his closest aides confirmed to us, the Israeli leader had been "living a personal nightmare for nearly two years." He had become certain in his own mind that "that lunatic Saddam Hussein" was building nuclear weapons and that he intended to use them either to destroy Israel or "to bring her to her knees."

In much of this he was right. But the danger was not immediate, and he could have had the cool nerves to live with it a while longer. By acting unilaterally and rashly, he undercut the peace process with Egypt and embarrassed the one Arab leader who had had the courage to sign a peace agreement with Israel, President Anwar el-Sadat of Egypt. Begin had met with Sadat only three days before the raid: The coincidence of events gave an appearance of Egyptian complicity.

By acting when the danger was not imminent, Begin also undercut a psychological transformation that had begun to take place in the region, as confidence built between some Arabs, and many Egyptians, and the Israelis. Some Egyptians claimed that the Israeli "word" could not now be trusted, and that the Israelis would "use" the Egyptians for narrow political ends that could not be justified. They foresaw that Israel would rely exclusively on the force of arms to back up their political aims, and this would have repercussions on the Egyptian-Israeli peace agreement itself.

Begin also paid a price with France. The Mitterrand Government did intend to take serious action to close the glaring loopholes in the French contract with Iraq. In Mitterrand, the Israelis had a "friend" who was in the process of reversing the anti-Israeli policies of previous French governments, and at the least restore a certain neutrality in the French position toward the Middle East. The Israelis undercut Mitterrand before he had a chance to begin.

For all that, the Iraqi nuclear threat was real. Begin had lived with it during his term of office, and he had masterminded a campaign of diplomacy, propaganda, and direct action to stop it. This would build up to what he saw as his "supreme duty"—to save the people of Israel from a second, this time nuclear, holocaust. Now, when he finally decided to strike, the former terrorist leader was in the midst of a bitter election campaign, and it looked as if he would lose. Perhaps the bombing of Osirak might save the day. But Menachem Begin was not simply playing to the voters. He was playing to his own sense of destiny and purpose. If he waited, and lost the election, who then would save the Jews?

SIX

AFTER
BABYLON

17

The Threat of Nuclear Holocaust

> Israel should develop the capability and adopt an appropriate strategy and doctrine for overt nuclear deterrence.
> —Shai Feldman,
> Center for Strategic Studies, Tel Aviv University,
> *Foreign Affairs*,
> Spring 1981

> There is only one way in which India can keep its options open. That is to exercise the nuclear option.
> —K. K. Subrahmanyam,
> *The Times* of India,
> April 1981

> One has to make a distinction between the nuclear option and nuclear weapons.
> —James Buckley,
> U.S. Under Secretary of State,
> June 1981

> The road to military equality is first through nuclear proliferation in the Third World countries, and later through denuclearization for everybody.
> —Professor Ali Mazrui,
> BBC Reith lectures,
> 1979

For those like us who came of age in the shadow of Hiroshima and Nagasaki, the threat of nuclear war has become a presence, shaping the way we think and act. It is not something that most of us talk about. It is just there, warning that the future may never come, a quiet fear that everything we know and love could one day vanish under a mushroom cloud.

The possibility of nuclear holocaust is a fact of life. Yet a nuclear stand-off between the two Superpowers has developed, and the world has lived for thirty-six years with the bomb and somehow survived.

Now that world nuclear order is in crisis. The possibility of atomic war is looming—not only in the revived nuclear race among the Superpowers but especially as the weapons spread from a handful of stable and highly industrialized countries into areas of the world as unruly and turbulent as those of the Middle East and South Asia.

This is not to suggest that the leaders of those lands—whether General Zia, Saddam Hussein, Ayatollah Khomeini, Indira Gandhi, or Menachem Begin—are always less "responsible" than their Russian or American counterparts, or that they are always less cautious. Whatever one might say about mad mullahs, military dictators, or even mass murderers like Idi Amin or the Emperor Bokassa, no one should forget that a white European named Adolf Hitler unleashed horrors that his Third World counterparts could only dream about—or that it was the United States that dropped the atomic bomb on Japan.

Still, the new nuclear powers are more likely than the old to put their weapons to use. Zia's Pakistan is an unstable society. The chances of a coup or rebellion or all-out civil war are high, and the military themselves lack the sophisticated command and control systems to prevent a rash use of nuclear weapons. The same is true of Iraq, a dictatorship where Saddam Hussein is challenged from within by the Shiites and Kurds, and where his hold on power has been shaken both by the no-win offensive against Iran and the Israeli attack on Osirak.

Even the two democratic and internally stable countries with the nuclear option pose a danger by virtue of their having the weapon. The Indians still dream about a united Indian subcontinent under their aegis, and are highly nervous about the Pakistani nuclear effort—just as the Pakistanis dream and fear the opposite. The Israelis are a threatened state; with their Holocaust mentality, they have shown themselves time and again, especially with Menachem Begin at the helm, to be extremely quick off the mark in deciding that their very survival is at stake.

A campaign of threat and terror developed against the Iraqi program, possibly from different sources, but it had only a minor effect. It took the final bombing of Osirak by the Israelis to do the job. The program was a challenge to the international community and the entire system of safeguards against nuclear proliferation.

Now, in the absence of a workable nonproliferation system, individual nations or groups have decided to take direct action against the Pakistani nuclear program. A bombing and threat campaign—of so far limited scope—is under way against the European suppliers selling nuclear equipment to Pakistan. To date, there is no evidence to prove who is behind the attacks—the Israelis, the Indians, a group of Pakistani dissidents, or possibly in this case the American CIA. It is the type of campaign—as much as we would prefer an effective and aboveboard nonproliferation system—that in the present anarchic circumstances offers one option in slowing the nuclear spread.

On February 20, 1981, a bomb exploded at the home of Mr. Eduard German, the managing director of CORA Engineering, one of the Swiss firms that was building key components for the Pakistani enrichment plant at Kahuta. CORA had been specifically mentioned in the two American notes to the Swiss Government in January 1979 and August 1980, and had been featured prominently in the *Panorama* film on BBC Television the previous June. We learned that in spite of all the public exposure, the firm had signed a contract to supply a second gassification and solidification plant to the Pakistanis, a key unit in the centrifuge process and essential to the making of an enriched-uranium bomb.

The attackers at Herr German's house carefully placed the explosive to minimize any risk of hurting anyone, and after it went off they telephoned the CORA office, warning the firm not to continue the sale.

"They called themselves the 'Group for Non-Proliferation for South Asia,'" the federal police officer in charge of the case told us during a long-distance telephone call to his office in Berne. "Nobody knows this name, and all we can say is that it's been very difficult to try to find out who are the people behind it."

The police official told us that he had heard of the two similar groups—the "Committee to Safeguard the Islamic Revolution," which was conducting the terror campaign against the Iraqi nuclear project, and the "League for Protecting the Sub Continent," which had released the secret contracts for reprocessing equipment between the Pakistani Atomic Energy Commission and the French firm Bignier Schmid-Laurent. But the group that struck in Switzerland had a different name, and he knew of no connection. He also told us that the group had not sent any threatening letters, confining its threats to the telephone.

"For sure we can say that it's not an English-speaking person," the Swiss police told us. "Not an American, and not English. From the voice, it is a Pakistani man, who speaks English as a foreign language."

At CORA, we spoke with Mr. Rudolf Walti, the man we had interviewed previously. He told us that the same voice called back two months after the bombing and warned CORA not to attempt to send the new order through any back-door channels. The implication was that this is exactly what CORA had been intending to do, though Walti never said so in so many words. He did say that he was most impressed with the inside information that the terrorists had.

"It could be the CIA," he speculated. "When the Swiss Government called us to Berne about the note the Americans sent, the Americans had such good records of what we had been doing that if we ever lost our own files we could always go and ask them if we could use theirs."

As a result of the attack, CORA announced publicly that it had canceled the contract, and Mr. Walti assured us that he was finished doing nuclear business with the Pakistanis. The lesson was pointed: Where American diplomacy had failed to halt the Swiss sales to Pakistan, a small bomb and a few telephone calls had done the trick.

Another incident seemed related. Alcom, the Italian firm that had been working on the secret contract to build reprocessing vessels for the Pakistanis, told us that they had canceled their contract with the Pakistanis at the end of 1980, and lost substantial sums on the deal. While denying that the equipment they made could be used for the bomb, they said they did not want to be involved in "nuclear dealings with Pakistan that could lead to the Pakistanis having a weapon."

We pondered the meaning of this noble act, and on a hunch we telephoned back to the man who had given us the information and been helpful in explaining Alcom's delicate situation, the company's number-two official, Dr. Emanuele Poncini, who is also the stepson of Alcom's boss, Aldo Turci.

"Yes, it is true," he told us. "Mr. Turci received an unsigned letter warning us not to continue the project."

"Had this influenced you?" we asked Poncini.

"The letter did not play a part in our decision to cancel the contract," Poncini claimed. "We had suspicions, and we did not want to continue it. That's all there is to it."

We had a different suspicion about at least one of the reasons why Alcom cancelled the contract with the Pakistanis (and our investigation revealed no evidence that work was going on either in Alcom or their parent company, BSL in France). It had nothing to do with Dr. Poncini's, or Mr. Turci's concerns about whether their equipment would help Pakistan get a nuclear bomb. It did have something to do with the threat they had received.

Meanwhile, in the southern German town of Markdorf, an attack similar to the one at CORA took place on May 18, 1981. The target was the Hans Waelischmiller Company, a small family firm that sells highly specialized lead shielding for protection against radiation and special remote-controlled equipment to move and manipulate radioactive substances, all essential equipment for "hot cells" and reprocessing plants.

The bomb was placed against the outside wall of the factory, we learned, and exploded in the early morning hours. There was no security to speak of, and the bombers had easy access to their target. We phoned the company in July 1981 and spoke with one of the three family members who run things there, the thirty-seven-year-old son, Wolfgang Waelischmiller. "I think it was a psychological pressure on us," he told us. "It didn't affect any delivery to Pakistan. We have no ongoing orders."

Under questioning, Waelischmiller admitted that the firm had previously sold the Pakistanis some radiation shielding and hot-cell manipulators. The order had come through two other companies, one in France and one in Belgium, he explained.

We hazarded a guess. "SGN and Belgonucléaire?" we asked.

"That's right," he exclaimed, surprised. "How did you know?"

We told Herr Waelischmiller that we had old friends in both companies, men we had interviewed at length for our book—the venerable F. X. Poincet at SGN and the dynamic Jean van Dievoet at Belgonucléaire. Waelischmiller became more talkative after our disclosure that we had associates in common, and he related some of his company's history with the Pakistanis. It turned out that his firm was a missing link, at least in terms of our own investigation, in the chain of Pakistan's most important purchases.

The first Pakistani order came in 1976 via Belgonucléaire, Waelischmiller told us. It was for a pneumatic transport system vital in a reprocessing facility. This and other small materials ordered from the company were for the New Labs near Islamabad, which we knew from American intelligence sources to be the pilot reprocessing plant from which the Pakistanis hoped to get the plutonium for their first bomb.

The orders placed at the instigation of SGN were for the same type of equipment—manipulators and transporters of sensitive nuclear materials within a reprocessing facility. Waelischmiller stated they were for the Chashma Reprocessing Plant. In all cases, he related, the company's contracts were signed directly with the Pakistani Embassy in Paris. The man Waelischmiller most remembered was S. A. Butt, with whom his firm had done most of the negotiating.

As Herr Waelischmiller explained it, the explosion in the early morning hours of May 18 did minor damage to an order for one of their German medical customers, and afterward Wolfgang received a threatening telephone call, as did his father, Hans, and the local correspondent for the Reuters news agency. The calls were in German, and the voice identified the attackers as the same group that had attacked CORA Engineering. In translation the name came out "Organization Against the Proliferation of Nuclear Weapons in South Asia."

"I hope the police have some ideas who did it," he told us. "I don't believe it was a government—not the Israeli or Indian government. It's some private group.

"I'm not sure if someone wants to develop a political situation against Pakistan," Waelischmiller went on. "But it was not an explosion against us only. It was one for the press. At the moment we don't have any contract with Pakistan."

He went on to explain that "if a country like Pakistan, or anybody else, is getting nuclear technology, you can't say no to them just because they are possibly doing something wrong with it.

"Not to give nuclear technology to an underdeveloped country is to help proliferation, because they will look for means to find the technology in any case."

In other words, do not stop them because they will just want to get the nuclear equipment even more. We thought to ourselves that the firm would still sell to Pakistan. But were they making a sale now? Herr Waelischmiller denied any current business with Pakistan. But if not, why would this so-called Organization Against Proliferation bother to bomb them?

We learned why some two weeks later during a visit to an official in Washington. We explained the problem and the reply was a bit cryptic. In the words of the American official, "Why don't you ask Mr. Waelischmiller who from his company was recently in Pakistan, and what he was doing there?"

Impressed that the American Government knew the travel itinerary of the executives of a small company in a German province, we called back to Waelischmiller to see what he had to say. The truth emerged quickly enough.

"Yes, I was in Pakistan in April," Wolfgang Waelischmiller conceded. "But I never made any attempt to hide this. I went to New Labs in Islamabad."

"Were you negotiating for new business?" we asked.

"No, I was checking on some equipment that had been there already, and some other equipment that was on the way but was stuck in shipment in Karachi," Waelischmiller said, reversing his earlier position.

Herr Waelischmiller revealed that the equipment was remote-control machinery for low-active liquid waste, and that it was to be part of the hot-cell system within the New Labs project. He asked us how we had known he was in Islamabad, and when we told him that we had received the information from "official American sources," he was rather shaken.

"I never made it a secret. Maybe they know about it because I have an American Express card, and they check the bills," he suggested. He also said he had a visa in one of his passports for travel to the United States and possibly the Americans knew of his activity in that way. He said the surveillance "was not a pleasant feeling," and his company would not now consider new business with Pakistan, "not in this situation, it's just not possible."

The American official, we should add in fairness, did not in any way imply that the United States was responsible for the bombings and threats. He suggested that possibly the Israelis could be. But he did tell us that "frankly, these bombings are having an effect in slowing down the Pakistanis' buying program. That's what we've been trying to do all along. Now it seems to be working."

India could also be responsible. An Indian diplomat with whom we lunched in Paris, who had the role of reporting to his government on the Pakistani nuclear efforts in Europe, told us candidly that his country wanted to stop the Pakistanis from having the bomb. Otherwise, he said, the Indians would have to develop one themselves. "That's what our military men want to do in any case," he admitted.

"What about the bombings?" we asked. What did he know?

"What do you know?" he questioned back.

"What we know isn't the question," we countered. "What we'd like to know is what you know."

"I know nothing," he answered.

It could also be the Israelis. If the Israelis were in fact responsible for some or all of the violent incidents against the Iraqi nuclear program, it could be that they were updating the old tactics and applying them to Pakistan. The

Israelis were concerned about the Pakistani nuclear progress, as Professor Yuval Ne'eman summed up for us during our interview following the Osirak bombing. "I have no objections to the Pakistanis getting a nuclear option, because it's containable locally," he said. "My worries are about Pakistan becoming a supplier of nuclear technology to the Arabs." Israeli officials—like those of the other countries, India and the United States—deny any knowledge of or involvement in the campaign against Pakistan's Western suppliers.

Again, there is no proof. And there are additional possibilities. It could even be that a small group of Pakistani or Indian dissidents have banded together to form a small organization against "the Proliferation of Nuclear Weapons in South Asia."

Whoever is responsible, it is only symbolic of a larger international disorder with disastrous implications. In the absence of a workable and effective nonproliferation system, the buying and the selling seem likely to continue, and as they do, so will the violence and the threats. The potential for violence grows, until the secret sabotage and preemptive strikes can no longer hold the line. Then Pakistan—and others after them—will have their own nuclear weapons.

The Second Greatest Danger: Going Openly Nuclear

The first big nuclear threat to the peace of the Middle East and South Asia is that Pakistan and Iraq may get the bomb. The second biggest danger is that their rivals, India and Israel, may go public with what they have and openly declare a "nuclear defense strategy." It would make the first inevitable. The nonproliferation battle would be lost. Yet both countries have been thinking of doing just this.

September 22, 1979. It is about 3 o'clock in the morning. An American VELA satellite is hurtling through space over the southern Indian Ocean, somewhere in the region of Prince Edward Islands off the coast of South Africa. Suddenly, in a fraction of a second, the VELA's highly sensitive sensors record two almost simultaneous flashes—the standard signature left by a nuclear fireball.

On the same morning, at the United States observatory at Arecibo in Puerto Rico, a new radio-telescope detects a "ripple" speeding through the ionosphere that could have been produced by a nuclear blast in the southern Indian Ocean. The U.S. Naval Research Laboratory also registers two "pings" reverberating off the Antarctic ice shelf, possibly from a nuclear explosion near Prince Edward Islands.

Was there a nuclear explosion? The Naval Research Lab and the Defense Intelligence Agency were convinced that there was. A specially appointed White House panel studied the data and proclaimed the evidence to be "inconclusive." They could find no sign of the telltale radioactivity produced by nuclear explosions, and they thought that something else could have caused the apparent satellite sightings, perhaps a speck of microscopic dust hitting the VELA sensors.

The debate goes on. The questions remain. If it was not a nuclear explosion, what was it? If it was, who did it? The speculation pointed mostly at the predictable—the nearby South Africans, possibly in cooperation with everybody's favorite candidate whenever clandestine operations of any kind occur, the always likely Israelis.

Concerning the South Africans, there was some evidence. The U.S. Central Intelligence Agency discovered that South Africa had been conducting a secret naval exercise in the area at the time in question. The U.S. National Technical Information Service also reported that a South African naval attaché had earlier requested a computer search for information on nuclear explosions and their seismic detection.

If there was a nuclear blast, the South Africans had probably been involved. As for the Israelis, there was really nothing to link them to the event, although that did not stop rumors from continuing to circulate. Nothing, that was, until February 1980, some five months after the mysterious event, when CBS Radio in the United States carried a spectacular scoop from its junior correspondent in Tel Aviv, an Israeli-American named Dan Raviv. In order to avoid Israeli military censorship, Raviv flew to Rome to file his report.

"CBS News has learned that Israel exploded a nuclear bomb last September, in the Atlantic Ocean off the coast of South Africa," reported Raviv. "Informed sources [in Israel] confirm that this was an Israeli nuclear test—conducted with the help and cooperation of the South African Government."

Raviv's story echoed around the world, winning the young broadcaster instant renown. But as with so many stories on Israel's secret side, Raviv was leaning entirely on unidentified sources, without any hard evidence to back them up, and many of his colleagues among the foreign correspondents in Israel openly expressed skepticism about his sources and doubts that the story was true.

As Raviv told us when we later spoke with him in London, where he now works for the CBS Bureau, he had originally been doing a story on a book that the Israeli censor was threatening to suppress—a fictionalized but well-researched account of the nuclear program called *None Will Survive Us: The Story of the Israeli A-Bomb* by two Israeli journalists, Eli Teicher and Ami Dor-on. The book contained a review of nuclear relations between Israel and South Africa going back to the 1950s, when the Israelis agreed to trade technology for South African uranium, and this brought Raviv to chat with two sources—"spooks," he says—who told him that the September 22 test was "our event" and "a Zionist bomb." Their story was that Prime Minister

Begin had ordered the test to make 100 percent sure that Israel's nuclear arms actually worked.

"I looked and wasn't able to find anything to back up what they told me," Raviv confided to us. "But I trusted what my two sources told me."

The Israeli Government furiously denied Raviv's report, especially the suggestion that they were cooperating militarily with South Africa's *apartheid* regime. Israeli officials insisted that while there had been earlier links, they had stopped all contracts to supply military equipment to the white South Africans in November 1977 in response to a resolution of the United Nations, and that they had no other military links.

"It's like being accused of having a whore for a sister when you don't even have a sister," one Israeli official complained to us. "How can you deny her being a whore? First you have to prove you don't have a sister."

The Israeli Government Press Office hit back by taking away Raviv's press credentials, ostensibly for violating military censorship, which forced CBS to transfer him to London. The Censor's Office also went ahead and suppressed the fictionalized book by the two Israeli journalists which had started the whole affair. As might be expected, the Government's overreaction only added weight to Raviv's report about the possible Israeli nuclear test.

Test or no test, the real bombshell in Israel was still waiting to explode. And in the spring of 1981—before the bombing of Osirak—it seemed that it would.

From their earliest efforts to build the nuclear complex at Dimona with the help of the French, the Israelis had purposefully pursued a clear nuclear option. But in the wicked ways of the world, they had also helped to maintain an international norm that going nuclear was wrong, at least for the lesser powers.

They kept Dimona secret. They denied having nuclear weapons, even as they admitted to a certain "capability." They never made the bomb an open part of their military strategy against the Arabs, though they left little doubt that they would use it as a last-ditch defense if they ever felt their survival at stake. In all this calculated uncertainty, they helped to preserve the anti-bomb taboo.

This was a pretense, or as the Americans preferred to call it, a policy of "deliberate ambiguity." Everyone was convinced that the Israelis had the bomb, especially the Americans after the CIA sniffed it out in 1968. But as long as everyone kept the secret, no one had to face up to the fact, whether to compete against the Zionist bomb as in the case of the Arabs, or to impose sanctions against the Israelis as the United States and others did against India and Pakistan.

By early 1981, however, there were signs in Israel that the ambiguity might go, and that the bomb might come out of the basement.

"If unlimited quantities of ultrasophisticated arms continue to pour into confrontation states, Israel will be forced to adopt a new military posture," declared the *Jerusalem Post*'s savvy military correspondent Hirsh Goodman, in an article on April 3, 1981. "With increasing frequency one hears about the desirability of going nuclear—something that could not be talked about until a few months ago."

The new talk inevitably reached the pages of the influential American quarterly *Foreign Affairs*, in an article by Shai Feldman, a top analyst at Tel Aviv University's Center for Strategic Studies.

"By the end of the decade, Arab conventional challenges may be supported by nuclear weapons," argued Feldman. "Iraq may possess enough fissionable material for a nuclear weapon by 1985, and it is likely to enjoy a rudimentary deliverable force by 1990. Other Arab countries will follow suit, and—with possible imported short cuts—may even precede Iraq. This will dramatically extend the spectrum of threats facing Israel in the years to come.

"Therefore, Israel should develop the capability and adopt an appropriate strategy and doctrine for overt nuclear deterrence."

Feldman wasted few words in making clear what he meant, though his language echoed the bloodless jargon of the academic war games that nuclear strategists like to play.

"The suggested doctrine is counter-value—that is, threatening the destruction of cities and resources," he wrote. "It should consist of a simple but intentionally vague declaration that any attempt to cross Israel's borders by significant military force would be countered with extremely high levels of punishment. The strategy's purpose would be to deter the Arab states from pursuing most forms of violence against Israel by letting them know that she now possesses the means for devastating punishment."

In the past, the Israelis had shushed any open talk of the nation's nuclear weapons. Now, if the new doctrine were followed, they would openly wave them in the Arabs' faces.

"A balance of terror would develop," another of the new-line strategists, Professor Shlomo Aronson, told us in an interview at his Hebrew University office in Jerusalem. A close adviser of the former Defense and Foreign Minister Moshe Dayan, Aronson often reflects Dayan's strategic thinking.

"It's worked with the Superpowers," Aronson tried to convince us. "Why shouldn't it work with us. If the line is properly drawn, and understood, a major war is not a logical policy alternative in this area."

This assumed that Arab leaders would respond rationally, which was the very opposite of what Israeli propagandists were suggesting about "that lunatic" Saddam Hussein in Iraq. Yet here was Aronson the Israeli telling us face to face that the Arabs—and the Israelis—would always react in only the most rational way.

"Rather than looking at the bomb as a factor that is subject to irrational use, you have to look at it as a strategic reality," he told us. "And the Arabs, just like us, appreciate strategic reality—so long as they know what it is."

Another Israeli who has closely followed official thinking on nuclear policy, but who has asked that we not use his name, made the same point in a different and even more chilling way. "Why should any Arab leader make peace with Israel if Israel can be defeated?" he asked. "Sadat realized that he could not defeat Israel militarily, except at tremendous cost to his own country, and that's one reason the peace process began. There has to be no option except peace. And that is what the atomic bomb makes possible."

The former Israeli Defense Minister under Begin, Ezer Weizman, put the argument a bit more cagily in his book *The Battle for Peace*, published in 1981. "The Arab world—Egypt included—is very concerned over the possibility that Israel has a nuclear option," he wrote. "It may have been one of the considerations that induced Sadat to undertake his journey to Jerusalem. Certainly everyone dreaded the appalling prospect of the Middle East entering the 1980s in the shadow of the mushroom-shaped cloud. . . . Some of their leaders were beginning to realize that they must not force us into a corner where we might—albeit reluctantly—have no recourse but nuclear weapons."

Even with the peace treaty with Egypt, however, some of the new Israeli nuclear strategists believed that Israel should go open with its weapon. This was because of the cost—literally the economic cost—of not doing so. However much some Arabs, including the potentially most dangerous state, Egypt, were coming to accept Israel, they were using their vast income from oil to buy more and more highly sophisticated and extremely expensive conventional arms. The advocates of the new nuclear line feared that the Israelis simply could not keep pace. By early 1981 the Israeli economy was already showing severe signs of strain because of massive arms spending, and no one saw any end in sight.

"The Israeli military used to be prepared to accept a three-to-one edge against itself in equipment," the *Jerusalem Post*'s knowledgeable military correspondent, Hirsh Goodman, told us over coffee in a Jerusalem café. "In the October War of 1973, for example, the Arabs had three times as many planes. But the Israelis could turn their planes around and send them back into action three times as fast.

"But today's weapons are so sophisticated that they're idiot-proof from the standpoint of maintenance. With the new F-15, a team of monkeys can change the engines in five minutes. To maintain a balance now, you have to have numerical parity. And Israel just can't afford it."

As Shai Feldman and Professor Aronson were coming to see it, only a nuclear defense held out any hope of ever escaping the ever-rising costs of keeping up with Arab armament. In Washington in the 1950s, Mr. John Foster Dulles and his Cold War co-pilots had spoken of nuclear weapons as "more bang for the buck." Now, if these new nuclear warriors had their way, Israel would be saving its shekels with the same big bang.

But the arguments for the new line were not all echoes of the past. At least for Shai Feldman, a nuclear defense might also pay an unexpected and surprisingly liberal bonus. It could give the Israelis a way to withdraw from most of the West Bank territory that they had occupied ever since the Six Day War of 1967.

"It would enhance the government's ability to persuade both the elite and the masses that it is possible to withdraw to borders not very far from the pre-1967 lines without jeopardizing Israel's survival," he wrote in his article in *Foreign Affairs*. "In general, a disclosed deterrent would decrease domestic opposition to moderate policies. Appreciation of the security provided by nuclear deterrence would reduce the sense of paranoia which so seriously afflicts Middle East publics and politics."

The Israeli analysts made a strong case for an openly declared nuclear defense, and their ideas reflected wider thinking within Israel's tightly knit defense establishment. As Hirsh Goodman suggested in the *Jerusalem Post*, such things would not even have been talked about until into the 1980s, and the new line was clearly on the agenda for serious consideration by Israeli policy makers when Mr. Begin ordered his F-16's to bomb the Iraqi nuclear reactor in June 1981.

Immediately after the Osirak attack, however, the debate on going openly nuclear faded into the background and the Israelis continued with their policy of "purposeful ambiguity." The noted Israeli nuclear physicist and former Deputy Director of Military Intelligence, Professor Yuval Ne'eman, told us why when we interviewed him at his home in suburban Tel Aviv a couple of weeks after the raid into Iraq.

"I'm totally against the arguments of these people like Shlomo Aronson and Shai Feldman, that young man," the soft-spoken Professor Ne'eman told us. "I know his mother and father. Very nice people, and he's very nice, undoubtedly. But on this one, he's all wet.

"Some Arab regimes are closer to rationality, but some are not," the Israeli-born scientist argued. "Sadat, in his memoirs, wrote that he was ready to take a punishment of 100,000 people to cross the Canal. King Saud said that it was worth 6 million people dead to get rid of Israel. Do you really believe that a balance of fear would preserve peace in the Middle East?

"There's no symmetry in this conflict," he went on, not waiting for us to answer. "We don't think we can eradicate twenty-one Arab countries, and we don't want to. They think we're a cancer in the midst of the Arab World. The question, and problem, is whether and to what extent they would really care about retaliation."

An adviser to the Begin government on the bombing, Ne'eman is most often described as the man behind the creation of Israel's nuclear arsenal. But that was an honor he disclaimed.

"I'm *not* the father of the Israeli bomb because Israel is *not* a member of the nuclear club," he told us. "Israel had to take steps so that, if the situation required, we would be ready to step into the nuclear club. We took those steps in the early 1960s.

"But we stopped somewhere," he smiled, refusing to tell us just where.

"And we have every interest in not crossing that threshold, and in keeping a low profile. We have nothing to gain from 'going nuclear.' It would only trigger a free-for-all arms race all around us, and what would we have gained?"

As with the Israeli advocates of open nuclear deterrence—Shai Feldman and Shlomo Aronson—Professor Ne'eman argued his thesis persuasively, and until the dust from the Iraq raid settled, it seemed likely that his position would remain the official Israeli policy. If nothing else, a low profile made it easier for the Reagan Administration to ride out the protests from the Arab world without having to tackle the problem of Israeli nuclear weapons as well.

The advantage of ambiguity rested largely on a single point: that the rest of the world—and particularly the Arab world—saw a significant difference between an Israel with "nuclear capability" and an Israel with nuclear weapons. But however the Arab leaders (or the Reagan Administration) might try to defend that distinction in the case of Iraq or Pakistan, by the time of the Osirak bombing they had all come to take it as an article of faith that the Israelis had the bomb.

In short, Professor Ne'eman's fears that "going nuclear" might fuel a nuclear arms race seemed a little late. The arguments of Shai Feldman and his like-minded colleagues appeared increasingly likely to win support, for economic reasons if nothing else. Just as "more bang for a buck" proved persuasive in the Washington of the 1950s, the hard-pressed Israelis could as easily take to the promise that an open nuclear deterrent might help cut the costs of an ever-escalating arms race in conventional weapons.

"The process itself seems inevitable," Feldman confidently assured us. "And the end result will be a nuclear stand-off in which both sides have a deterrent power that neither side could use."

His Israeli opponents questioned his logic. "Shai Feldman is crazy if he thinks the Middle East can support a stable balance of fear," Professor Ne'eman countered. "It's a very dangerous thesis, and you can't experiment with it. We've stopped the Middle East from going nuclear for twenty years. We can do it for another twenty years."

Feldman hit back against his critics some eighty days after the Israelis bombed the Osirak. He called the raid a "time-buying measure" only, one that was "exceedingly ambitious and unrealistic" because preventing Israel's Arab enemies from acquiring nuclear weapons is simply "not feasible." Instead, he said, Israel should concentrate on developing a "second-strike capability" which would deter its enemies from using nuclear weapons first. "If properly exploited, the . . . operation provided Israel with time to make sure that once the region finally becomes nuclear, she could enjoy a more stable nuclear retaliatory capability." *

*From a study published by the Tel Aviv University Center for Strategic Studies, August 25, 1981.

Either way—whether the Israelis do openly go nuclear or quietly stand pat with a disappearing ambiguity—the debate itself was a sad reminder of just how far the dynamic of nuclear proliferation had taken hold in the Middle East. Only radical action could stop the budding nuclear arms race. The Israelis, by going openly nuclear, would inevitably accelerate a process they have most feared—the emergence of a weapon of mass destruction in the hands of enemies vowed to destroy them, the kind of weapon that in one blow could destroy the living fabric of the small Jewish state. For all Shai Feldman's faith in the eventual stand-off of mutual deterrence, it seemed as likely that any one of the newly nuclear nations would miscalculate and find a way to use its ultimate weapon of destruction.

Elsewhere, one could hear the same debate, especially in India. In the past, the Indians had refrained, at least publicly, from going beyond their May 1974 "peaceful nuclear explosion," content simply to "keep the nuclear option open." But as in Israel, the spring of 1981 brought a series of public calls for Prime Minister Indira Gandhi's Government to exercise the option and to declare that India would make use of nuclear weapons in its military defense.

"There is only one way in which India can keep its options open," wrote K. K. Subrahmanyam in *The Times* of India in April 1981. "That is to exercise the nuclear option."

A former high official in India's Ministry of Defense and now Director of the influential Institute for Defense Studies and Analyses in New Delhi, Mr. Subrahmanyam was responding mainly to the impending Pakistani bomb and the seeming impossibility of stopping it. But he and many of his like-minded colleagues also saw an overt nuclear defense as a needed response to the renewed American military aid to Pakistan (including F-16 jet fighters), the American interest in an alliance including Pakistan around the Persian Gulf, and the continued neglect of India.

"The U.S. is contemptuous of an India which they see as a country with no will to power," argued Subrahmanyam. "If Pakistan were to go nuclear and India does not, it would confirm in the U.S. mind the image they held in the late fifties and sixties that India is a country to be abandoned. But if India became a nuclear power, the United States would come to realize that it could not ignore a nation of 700 million—just as Nixon discovered about China in 1971."

Subrahmanyam's call for India to become an open nuclear power reflected a growing nuclear lobby in and near the top levels of the Indian Government, and especially in the Indian military, in the spring of 1981. Indian newspapers and magazines carried a series of signed articles by influential strategists, all urging nuclear weapons, and in a defense debate in the Indian Parliament on April 9, Prime Minister Gandhi seemed to agree when she told the cheering house that if the Pakistanis exploded a bomb, India would "respond in an appropriate way."

This was all in the spring, and it looked as if the pro-bomb lobby was winning. But on July 10, a month after the Israeli bombing of Osirak, Mrs. Gandhi put a damper on the discussion by declaring that India would not develop nuclear weapons even if Pakistan did.

"We do not believe in the theory of deterrence," she told a crowded press conference in New Delhi. India would still pursue peaceful nuclear research. But, she insisted, there would be no Indian nuclear deterrent.

However welcome Mrs. Gandhi's statement in July, four factors still caused worry.

First, the Indians were in no way giving up the nuclear option that Mrs. Gandhi's earlier government demonstrated so dramatically in May 1974. There was really no practical way that Indian scientists could ever unlearn what they already knew or undo the fears they had already created. Even if New Delhi held to its present line, the nuclear option would remain.

Second, the Indians were reported by U.S. intelligence sources to be digging new tunnels near the old Indian nuclear test site at Pokharan, in the Rajasthan Desert. Intelligence officials generally assumed that Indian scientists had produced more than a single nuclear device at the time of the May 1974 test. If they wanted, they could probably detonate a second device even before the Pakistanis could set off their first.

Third, the Indians were still refusing to sign the Nuclear Nonproliferation Treaty, as were the Pakistanis themselves, and several of India's nuclear installations still had no inspections or other international safeguards.

Fourth, the Indians were continuing to press ahead with operations at their new reprocessing plant at Tarapur, near Bombay. This is a bigger facility than the thirty-ton-a-year Trombay Reprocessing Plant, where the Indians extracted the plutonium for their "peaceful nuclear device." It would allow the Indians to reprocess the 300 to 400 tons of used fuel that they already have on hand from their four research and four power reactors, giving the Indians the material to make literally hundreds of atom bombs like the one that the Americans dropped on Nagasaki.

This reservoir of plutonium was particularly embarrassing to Washington, as the United States had supplied some 250 tons of the fuel as part of a thirty-year agreement signed in 1963 to provide a continuing supply of low-enriched uranium fuel for the two American-built nuclear power reactors at Tarapur. In the same agreement, Washington had also reserved the right to have the final say before any of the used American fuel could be reprocessed.

The formula was standard in American fuel-supply contracts. The nuclear problems between the two countries began in 1974, after the Indians detonated their "peaceful nuclear explosion." At the time, the Indians managed to convince Washington that none of the plutonium in the nuclear device had come from the Tarapur reactor fuel, which was under international safeguards, and as far as is known, their assurances were accurate. But the tension remained, and came to a head in 1978, when the U.S. Congress passed the Nuclear Nonproliferation Act, which restricted the supply of fuel to countries that had not signed the Nuclear Nonproliferation Treaty and had not accepted safeguards on all their nuclear installations. As a matter of standing policy, the Indians balked. Either the United States would supply the fuel under the terms of the existing agreement or the Indians might turn to the Soviet Union for fuel and refuse to give Washington any say at all over whether or not they reprocessed the used fuel.

This created a real damned-if-you-do, damned-if-you-don't dilemma for the Carter Administration and its antiproliferation policy. If, under the terms of the Nonproliferation Act, Mr. Carter asked Congress to allow him to waive the restrictions and to ship the fuel, the Indians might use it to make a second "peaceful nuclear explosion," and other would-be nuclear nations might come to believe that the United States would back down in their case as well. But if Carter let the restrictions stand and refused to ship the fuel, the Indians would move closer to the Soviet Union and feel free to reprocess the old American fuel to provide plutonium for a possible nuclear arsenal.

Which course created the greatest likelihood of proliferation—standing firm or giving in? In many ways the debate was irrelevant. India already had its nuclear option, and the power of decision—whether or not to make the bomb—lay in New Delhi, not Washington. Persuasion, not coercion, was the only real American option.

The Indians were sitting pretty. If they decided to go back on Mrs. Gandhi's July 10 statement and to develop a nuclear deterrent, they could easily outdistance the Pakistanis in building a large arsenal of atomic weapons, and their standing reservoir of used fuel with all its plutonium would give them the possibility of becoming a significant nuclear power. That was precisely what many of India's leaders, especially its generals and leading defense analysts, wanted.

"I am one of those who feels that going in for nuclear weapons is not a moral but a practical question," wrote K. C. Pant, Mrs. Gandhi's former Minister for Atomic Energy, in a widely quoted article in the Indian International Center's *I.I.C. Quarterly* in 1979. "Therefore, the considerations should be practical, and we should not tie ourselves to a position that will limit our options to carry out any other kind of explosion that leads to a capacity to build a nuclear bomb."

In particular, Pant called for his fellow Indians to compete with Pakistan's enrichment plant at Kahuta and "to go in straightaway, in a big way, for enrichment." This would provide enriched uranium fuel for India's reactors, he explained. And it would also have an important added benefit.

"We will need enriched uranium to act as a trigger for thermonuclear fusion," he explained. The ex-minister was writing about the new thermonuclear fusion reactors that he foresaw in use in the twenty-first century. But when we read the article during a trip to New Delhi, we were struck by a second posssibility, and we arranged to speak personally with Mr. Pant, who received us in Colonial splendor on the back lawn of his beautiful residence in one of New Delhi's garden suburbs.

Was Mr. Pant also thinking of a military use for the enriched uranium trigger? we asked.

"Why yes," the former nuclear minister replied. "It would enable India to have a thermonuclear, or hydrogen bomb."

Either India *or* Israel going openly nuclear at this stage would only add fuel to the region's nuclear arms race. It would not add to the region's stability, nor would it add to the security of either country. The Islamic and the Arab nuclear bombs would become that much more inevitable.

The French Dilemma

François Mitterrand stepped into the Élysée Palace as President of the French Republic on May 21, 1981, taking the place of the defeated Valéry Giscard d'Estaing. The canny and seasoned leader of the Socialist Party, Mitterrand had run on a program of reform. In the nuclear area, he had committed himself to cutting back France's rapidly growing nuclear power program, the pride and joy of the international nuclear industry. He had also criticized the French nuclear contract with Iraq, and had promised to do something about it.

This was all before June 7, when Menachem Begin ordered his F-16's into Iraq to bomb the French-built Osirak reactor. Rather than wait to give the new French President the chance to prove himself one way or the other, Begin relied on the force of Israeli arms. The slap in the face could not have been more clear.

"Mr. Begin could have put his trust in the President of the French Republic, whose sentiments in this respect are well known," Mitterrand told *The Washington Post*, with an obvious sense of hurt. "I have always placed and I still place at the top of my concerns the security of Israel and the peace of the Middle East. The first act of M. Begin has impaired this stock of trust. That is a shame."

Though unknown to Begin at the time, the new French President had already moved to make good on his campaign promises. In his very first days in office, Mitterrand had instructed a special ten-man task force at the Quai d'Orsay "to close the loopholes" in the Iraqi contract, and as we have seen, the subsequent one-page report recommended six steps that would have made it almost impossible for the Iraqis to use the Osirak reactor or its fuel to produce nuclear weapons, at least to the end of the 1980s.

Now, in the wake of the bombing, the French Administration faced a totally changed field of action, one that made their new strict line either easier or harder to push, depending upon whom we asked.

"The bombing of the Osirak certainly gets the French off the hook," said an American diplomat—who cannot be named—one of whose jobs was to monitor the French nuclear industry and the Iraqi contract. "It's the same kind of business that happened after Toulon. I've heard my friends at the CEA tell me, with a sort of black humor, 'Maybe it's our own people who did it, just trying to get us out of the contract.' I heard the same thing from another person at Technicatome. When you hear enough jokes like this, you begin to wonder."

He was not suggesting that French pilots had flown the Israeli F-16's, or even that French spooks had sabotaged the reactor-core elements at the plant near Toulon. He was simply pointing to a feeling that he had sensed among French officials, and that we soon saw for ourselves: a feeling of relief that the bombing had created the new basis for a new era of reform, going even beyond the six steps recommended in the Mitterrand Government's secret report on closing the loopholes in the Iraqi contract.

"We are now in the third phase of the world's approach toward nuclear affairs," the French Atomic Energy Commission spokesman, Alain Varneau, told us in grand fashion when we returned to see him a month after the Israelis had destroyed the Osirak. "The first phase was Atoms for Peace," he related. "The second phase was after the Indian explosion. The third phase is after the Israeli raid on Baghdad.

"We will arrive at a new set of rules," he went on. "And by we, I mean not just the United Nations or the world, but especially the exporting countries. I think that the new elements will be an open publication of all nuclear contracts. There will be stricter controls. There will be a new look at the controllers themselves. And perhaps there will be a reform of the Vienna Agency."

"Open publication of all nuclear contracts?" we asked, pinching ourselves to remember that this was the same man who had repeatedly evaded our questioning by insisting that the French had not supplied Osirak with various modifications, such as the heavy-water tank that we had spent so much of our energy chasing down.

"The catastrophic aspect of the Iraqi contract was the secrecy," he replied with a smile. "This has been one of the big problems. I tell you frankly, it has made my life very difficult.

"The main point is that secret clauses in a civilian contract will no longer be accepted," he promised. "It will be necessary to publish a contract—and all the clauses to it."

Later we heard much the same from another old friend, Yves Girard, Vice President of Technicatome, the state-owned firm that had engineered and designed the now-destroyed Osirak.

"We know that one of the problems was the secrecy," he told us over drinks at the Paris Hilton. "We hope to do away with this. It helped create the atmosphere of suspicion around the Osirak contract."

We could only wonder at this sudden conversion to candor. But the logic was clear, and no one summed it up for us better than the American diplomat. "The French Government can't have it both ways," he said. "They can't say the Osirak reactor is routine assistance, and then surround it with secrecy. Either it's something routine, or it's secret. The suspicions were aroused by the secrecy built up around the project."

The French were even secretive with their American friends. "To this day, I haven't seen a detailed contract of the French-Iraqi deal," admitted the American diplomat, whose job included keeping an eye on the Osirak project. "I may have to ask for it, but so far I've avoided doing it.

"I, and the State Department, take the French at their word," he explained to us. "I don't know about other agencies. But the French have never lied to me. They may have said that they couldn't tell me something. But I don't believe they ever lied."

How far this new shunning of secrecy will go is still unclear, and after knocking our heads on so many closed doors we remain cynical about the prospects for open government and published contracts even in the Socialist France of M. Mitterrand. But if Varneau and Girard were on the right track, the prospects were hopeful that the French would use the changed situation caused by the Israeli bombing to move in a very positive direction, holding the Iraqis to a strict set of rules and opening any new contract to public accountability.

The question—assuming they did not backtrack on their new position— was how much control the French could actually exercise. This was complicated by Saudi Arabia's promise to pay for Iraq's new nuclear reactor. The announcement came on July 16, straight from the Saudi Minister of Information, Mohammed Abdo Yamani, following talks between King Khalid and the Iraqi Oil Minister, Tayeh Abdel Kerim, at the Saudi resort of Taif. According to the official statement, the decision had been "based on our belief in helping our brothers," and Saudi officials told reporters that it had been communicated to President Mitterrand.

From a position of extreme wariness about the Baath Socialist regime in Baghdad, and official statements of concern to the Quai d'Orsay about the original Osirak contract, the Saudis would become the nuclear paymasters for Iraq. If Saddam Hussein agreed, this would also give the Saudis at least some control over the Iraqi nuclear program.

For Mitterrand and his commitment to nonproliferation, the problem was obvious. The Saudis were France's number-one supplier of petroleum, providing nearly 53 percent of the country's needs, and a growing market for French exports, especially in high technology. That was a formidable combination to confront. In his very first week in office, Mitterrand had sent his brother Jacques, a retired Air Force general and now head of the national aerospace company, SNIAS, to Saudi Arabia to reassure King Khalid that France wanted to maintain friendly relations with the Arab world. Khalid had returned the visit, coming to France in the week following the Osirak bombing, and Mitterrand was clearly on the spot to prove his good intentions not only to the oil-rich Iraqis, but to the even richer Saudis and their allies in the Gulf.

The pressure would be enormous. Even under Giscard, the French had suffered doubts about the nuclear contracts with Baghdad. But the cost of pushing the Iraqis too hard appeared to be too high. And that was at a time when the Saudis were knocking at the door to express concern about the Iraqi project, not offering to pay for it.

"France is recognizing that the Iraqi sale is worrying," André Jacomet, the distinguished former Secretary of Giscard's Council on Foreign Nuclear Policy, told us in an interview several months before the Israeli attack. "But we cannot say so publicly, and above all, we cannot cast doubts on the Iraqis' intentions."

"Atomic energy is very expensive and it's a way for us to get money," he went on. "We sell nuclear equipment to Iraq because Iraq is one of our biggest suppliers of oil. It's all linked."

Dr. Francis Perrin told us the same thing. "Why did France agree to help Iraq?" he chuckled. "Obviously it's because we receive so much oil from Iraq." Perrin suggested that one of the reasons the French Government had never published the Osirak contract was because it contained secret clauses tying the supply of nuclear technology from France to guaranteed supplies of petroleum from Iraq.

Now Mitterrand faced the Iraqis and the Saudis together, making it all the harder to require an end to secrecy or to cast doubt on Baghdad's intentions by insisting too strongly on the stiff new constraints his government's secret report had urged.

Even if the French did stick to their guns, the Saudis had a new weapon of their own. They had been supporting the Pakistani nuclear effort since the days of King Faisal. The Pakistanis, with their enrichment plant at Kahuta, would soon be in a position to replace the French as the supplier of highly enriched uranium fuel to Iraq. They could also give the two Arab countries access to weapons-usable plutonium.

With Saudi Arabia as the bridge, Pakistan and Iraq together would come close to being invulnerable to any outside sanctions, and there were already signs that the two countries were coming together in the wake of the Israeli attack.

According to a dispatch which was released by Agence France Presse on June 13, 1981, the Iraqis announced that President Zia ul-Haq had telephoned Saddam Hussein and offered him the "full support" of Pakistan, which "would do everything in its power, within the limits of its possibilities, to aid Iraq."

Without control of the fuel supply that Pakistani enriched uranium could give to Iraq, the new French constraints would have nothing to back them up. The only real barrier to proliferation would be the good word of Saddam Hussein and his new friend King Khalid. For all its good intentions, the new French Government would have only one way "to close the loopholes" and to prevent French technology from being used to build nuclear weapons, and that would be to stand up to both Iraq and Saudi Arabia and refuse to sell them the new reactor. This was hardly the kind of thing that any French

President would want to do, even the pro-Israeli François Mitterrand—but the political realities following the bombing of Osirak would make the sale of a new reactor likely.

Few people in 1981 were suggesting that the exporting nations should ban the sale of research or other reactors in and of themselves. This seemed too drastic a step. If the French did not sell, the Italians—or someone else—would. In this respect the nuclear genie was out of the bottle. By focusing on the safeguards that would be applied, and not on the sales themselves, the exporters were still avoiding a consideration of the only option that could halt the process of nuclear proliferation—a policy of denial, at least for the explosive Middle East.

The American Retreat

On July 16, 1981, six weeks after the Israelis bombed the Osirak reactor, the President of the United States, Ronald Reagan, told the world a truth that many of his critics had never expected to hear him utter. "The need to prevent the spread of nuclear explosives to additional countries" is one of the most critical challenges facing the nation, he declared in a statement released by White House officials. "Further proliferation would pose a severe threat to international peace, regional and global stability, and the security interests of the United States and other countries."

This was the prologue to the Reagan Administration's new policy of curbing the spread of nuclear weapons, a considerable change from Mr. Reagan's feeble rhetoric on the subject when he was still running for president.

At that time—on January 31, 1980—Reagan had declared that he did not think the United States should stand in the way of countries that wanted to develop nuclear weapons. "I just don't think it's any of our business," he said bluntly, and expressed skepticism about the ability of the United States to stop a country such as Pakistan determined to get the bomb.

Now, after his months in the White House, Reagan had changed his mind. Antiproliferation would remain "a fundamental national security and foreign policy objective."

The new Administration would continue to oppose the transfer of dangerous nuclear equipment and technology, and would urge full-scope safeguards as a condition for any new nuclear supply. The Administration would continue to back the Nonproliferation Treaty and the Latin American Treaty of Tlatelolco, as well as the International Atomic Energy Agency and the strengthening of safeguards. And in a new formulation, the Administration would "view a material violation of these treaties or an international safeguards agreement as having profound consequences for international order and United States bilateral relations and also view any nuclear explosion by a nonnuclear-weapon state with grave concern."

This was the bottom line of the new policy. It remained to be seen what the Administration would define as "a material violation," or how it would express its "grave concern."

There were significant differences from the policy of the Carter Administration. The new policy lacked any strong sanctions, especially as regards the American supply of nuclear fuel, the instrument which Carter had used to pressure other countries not to import or to export dangerous nuclear technologies. But the Carter Administration had often wielded the stick in a very clumsy fashion, and it had caused great resentment among America's Allies, especially when coupled with aggravating delays in giving needed approvals and export licenses by the Nuclear Regulatory Commission and Executive Branch agencies.

Now Reagan was throwing the stick away and promising that the United States would once again be "a predictable and reliable partner for nuclear cooperation."

The second shift away from the Carter policy was on reprocessing and the breeder reactor. Mr. Carter had opposed the development of breeder reactors and civilian reprocessing abroad and had dramatically suspended American development of the breeder reactor to prove the sincerity of his opposition to "the premature introduction of the plutonium economy." Mr. Reagan, who had already announced that he favored the development of an American breeder reactor, now promised that his Administration "will not inhibit or set back civil reprocessing under breeder-reactor development abroad," but this policy would only affect "nations with advanced nuclear power programs where it does not constitute a proliferation risk."

This implied rank, but welcome, discrimination. The Americans would not oppose reprocessing and breeders in Britain or France, or even Japan and Germany, but would oppose them in Pakistan, South Korea, Taiwan, and elsewhere.

A well-informed official at the State Department's Arms Control and Disarmament Agency summed up the policy with these words: "He'll get rid of about 80 percent of Mr. Carter's rhetoric, and keep about 80 percent of Mr. Carter's policy."

Yet the signs of serious slippage were already clear. For even as the new President promised "to give priority attention" to antiproliferation efforts, he was doing just the opposite, especially in the two major proliferation crises he faced at that very moment—Israel's bombing of the Iraqi reactor and Pakistan's fast-approaching success in getting its first Islamic bomb. In his approach to both, the new President beat a sharp and largely unheralded retreat from the most basic antiproliferation thinking of both the Ford and Carter Administrations.

More than any event in recent years, Prime Minister Begin's bombing of the Osirak demanded the "priority attention" to proliferation that Mr. Reagan was promising. But instead of seizing the opportunity, Reagan retreated. He condemned the attack, tried to distance the Americans from it, conceded that the Israelis "might have sincerely believed it was a defensive move," and delayed a shipment to Israel of four F-16 aircraft. In so doing, he and his officials were guilty of a dangerous obfuscation, which blurred one of the Ford and Carter administrations' most basic antiproliferation definitions. This could be seen in the testimony of Under Secretary of State Walter J. Stoessel Jr. before the House Foreign Affairs Committee.

"We had some concerns about the nature of the Iraqi program," Stoessel told the Congressmen. "But we had not made any definite conclusions that they were aiming for a nuclear weapons capability."

The Administration's tactical retreat on the meaning of the Iraqi nuclear buildup reflected a strategic withdrawal on how Washington would define the entire problem of nuclear proliferation. According to Under Secretary Stoessel, the Administration had drawn no definite conclusions that Iraq was aiming at "a nuclear weapons capability." Yet in response to questions from members of the Foreign Affairs Committee, the Under Secretary conceded that the Iraqis would eventually have acquired "a nuclear option," and that they would have gotten "the capability to build an atomic weapon."

In brief, the Administration was now suggesting that option and capability were one thing, weapons another. In terms of policy, this meant giving up the line that both the Ford and Carter Administrations had so carefully staked out.

Under the influence of Professor Albert Wohlstetter and other academic antiproliferators, both earlier Administrations had taken the view that it was necessary to draw the line before a country developed the nuclear option or, in other words, before it had a sufficient supply of weapons-usable plutonium, highly enriched uranium, or the capability to produce either. After that would be too late. Once a nation had the explosive material, it would only be a few weeks or months away from having the bomb.

As a result, the goal had been to stop any new countries from getting the capability, whether or not the present rulers expressed the intention to develop nuclear weapons. Rulers could change. Intentions could change. But the capability was the threat, and that is what Washington had tried to prevent.

Now, on Iraq, the new Administration was going back to a distinction that could not hold up in practice. It was trying to unlearn all that its predecessors had learned in the aftermath of the Indian nuclear test in May 1974—that countries like Iraq and Pakistan could all too easily build a military capability alongside a civilian nuclear program. In pursuing the distinction, the Administration would appear to be giving the Iraqis and the Pakistanis the same latitude that the Israelis now enjoy in their insistence that they have only the option and not the weapons themselves.

At the same time, the Reagan Administration made a similar retreat on Pakistan. Under American law, the Carter Administration had cut off military and economic aid to Pakistan in April 1979 because officials in Washington were convinced that the Pakistanis were secretly buying equipment for their enrichment plant at Kahuta to produce highly enriched uranium for nuclear weapons. The law—the so-called Symington Amendment to the Foreign Assistance Act—prohibited aid to any country getting (or giving) technology or equipment for an unsafeguarded enrichment plant or any reprocessing facility, or to any nonnuclear weapons nation that detonated a nuclear device.

The Symington Amendment is still law, and the Administration policy ignored the obvious fact that the Pakistanis are still moving ahead with their enrichment plant at Kahuta, the reprocessing factory at Chashma, and their pilot reprocessing facility, the New Labs.

On the face of it, this would appear to make Pakistan a prime target for the "priority attention" to proliferation that Mr. Reagan promised, and a most unpromising candidate for the resumption of American aid. Any aid to Islamabad would be seen as a major backtracking from American commitments to help stop the spread of nuclear weapons, and a signal to other would-be nuclear nations that they, too, could go for nuclear weapons without risking any lasting American sanctions.

Instead, Reagan was offering Pakistan a massive five-year aid package, totalling $3 billion, including $100 million a year in economic assistance and $400 million a year in loans to buy military equipment. As defined by Under Secretary of State James Buckley, who negotiated the final package in Islamabad in June 1981, Washington would also make available an unspecified number of the highly sophisticated F-16 aircraft, similar to those the Israelis used to bomb the Osirak reactor. One top White House official told us candidly that he believed the Pakistanis were pressing for the F-16's in order to get "nuclear delivery capability."

Why all the aid? And why the backtracking on antiproliferation? The answer was conventionally summed up in a single phrase: "The Russian Threat." Soviet troops had invaded neighboring Afghanistan, and Washington wanted to build up Pakistan as its chief anti-Soviet ally in the region.

Washington believed that by invading Afghanistan, the Soviets had taken a major offensive, and other nations in the area—from Saudi Arabia to the People's Republic of China—were waiting to see how the Americans would respond. For the Reagan Administration, as for Carter's, Pakistan was a good place to make a stand.

This was geopolitics at its most basic level. No one to whom we talked in Washington spoke that highly of General Zia ul-Haq and his regime, or of its stability, or of its popularity. Everyone admitted that by backing General Zia the United States was running the risk of turning the anti-Zia opposition against the United States. But for Washington, the ins and outs of Pakistani politics were clearly secondary. For reasons of history and geography and what the British used to call "the Great Game," and most of all because officials in Washington felt that "the United States has to do something," Pakistan was the place to do it—and to be seen doing it.

As we have tried to show in earlier chapters, Pakistan was increasingly central to the Arab world, and particularly to the oil-rich Gulf, which is where the most basic American interests are. Pakistani ports, whether at Karachi or Gwadar near the Iranian border, looked out over the Gulf, and could serve as possible staging posts for American Rapid Deployment Forces. Pakistani military officers and conscripts played an increasing role as advisers and mercenary troops within Saudi Arabia and the Gulf states. If Mr. Bhutto could see Pakistan at the center of an Islamic alliance with the Arab oil states in 1972, it wasn't really surprising that Mr. Reagan's advisers would see the same logic in 1981, and attempt to use it in building a strengthened American presence in the Gulf.

Even in its own terms, this new approach to Pakistan had three major weaknesses.

One was the danger, which State Department officials admitted, that General Zia's hold on power was weak and that American aid would turn the opposition even more against the United States. The strongest opposition within the country was led by Bhutto's wife and daughter, both of whom the General had put in detention in May 1981, while Bhutto's son Murtaza led the al-Zulfikar group, which hijacked a Pakistani airliner in April and also claimed credit for other attacks within Pakistan. In practice, any move to aid Zia would involve the United States in an ongoing commitment to help keep the Bhuttos and their opposition movements from ever coming to power, and that meant a continuing commitment to back a military dictatorship in Pakistan, whether led by General Zia or by another military figure.

The second weakness in Washington's aid to Pakistan was its impact on India. The rivalry between the two countries had long been a sore point for American policy; the Indians had generally felt that Washington "tilted" against them, while the Pakistanis tended to feel that the Americans, as allies, had not done enough to protect them against the Indians in the wars of 1965 and 1971. With the new aid proposals, the Indians complained that the Americans were purposely providing Pakistan with sophisticated weapons that were far better suited for use against India than for defending the border with Afghanistan. Mrs. Indira Gandhi's government in New Delhi specifically protested over the highly advanced, long-range F-16's as "a generation ahead of anything operating with other air forces of the area," and the Reagan Administration made matters worse by refusing to give any firm assurances that it would not permit the planes and other weapons to be used in a conflict between India and Pakistan.

In effect, it appeared as if the Reagan Administration had written off India as a Soviet satellite, which would only push the Indians closer to the Soviet Union, while increasing the chance that the United States would again be caught in the middle of a war between India and Pakistan.

The third danger was that of compromising the fight against nuclear proliferation by letting the world know that American sanctions against a proliferator were, at best, a temporary affair. The Reagan experts, though, did not see it that way. They had been arguing that one way to reduce nuclear proliferation was to give would-be nuclear nations a greater sense of security by offering them American protection and helping them to upgrade their conventional arms. In particular, this was an argument we had heard in an earlier interview in 1979 with Dr. Ray Cline, head of Georgetown University's well-connected Center for Strategic and International Studies and a former Deputy Director of the Central Intelligence Agency.

"What the Pakistanis have wanted all along is not a nuclear weapon, but a strong conventional defense," he told us. "They can't do anything with a nuclear bomb anyway, not really. But they are threatened by political and social fragmentation inside the country, and they need to be able to project a strong image."

Dr. Henry Kissinger had pursued the same logic in August 1976, when he offered to give Prime Minister Bhutto 110 A-7 jet fighters if Pakistan would give up the nuclear weapons project, an offer that Mr. Bhutto rejected out of hand. And the Carter Administration had similarly offered 50 F-5 fighters, which General Zia had rejected.

The Reagan Administration made the argument part of its official policy. As State Department spokesman David Passage announced in June, "This Administration believes that addressing the security concerns which have motivated Pakistan's nuclear program and reestablishing a relationship of confidence with it offer the best opportunity in the long run for effectively dealing with its nuclear program."

Off the record, at least one State Department veteran told us he did not think the idea would work. "There's really no buy-out option," he laughed. "We couldn't come up with an appreciably large enough amount of money to do that. It would be extremely difficult for Zia to abandon the nuclear program. There would be a great groundswell of opposition among the military elite."

Washington might still deter the Pakistanis from testing a weapon, he hoped. The Administration was already on record against any test, as was the Congress. But he knew of "no indication that they were slowing down" in developing the weapon, and he really did not expect that they would.

Under Secretary of State James Buckley then proved the point, however unintentionally, when he returned from talks in Pakistan with "absolute assurances" from the Pakistanis that they did not plan to make a nuclear bomb.

"I was assured by the ministers and by the President himself that it was not the intention of the the Pakistan Government to develop nuclear weapons," Mr. Buckley told a Senate Government Affairs Subcommittee on June 24, 1981. But, he added, the Pakistanis had not promised to forego a peaceful nuclear explosion, such as the one India staged in May 1974, nor had they promised not to develop the capability to build nuclear weapons. "One has to make a distinction between the nuclear option and nuclear weapons," Buckley told the Senators.

Once again, as with Iraq, the Administration was making the distinction between the option and the weapons. In the case of Pakistan this meant that the Reagan Administration had given in. According to American intelligence estimates, the Pakistanis were within a year or so of having that nuclear option, and Washington was saying that it was not going to make a fuss.

Perhaps Washington could still deter the Pakistanis from staging a test explosion. But short of the kind of military action the Israelis had taken against Iraq, it was too late to stop the making of the Islamic bomb.

In the end, it all came back to a question of priorities. Which was more important—to take a stand against nuclear proliferation or to take a stand against the Soviets in Afghanistan? On that, President Reagan's position was exactly the same as on that day in Jacksonville, Florida, when, as a candidate, he suggested that there was little the United States could or should do to stop Pakistani nuclear-weapon proliferation. "India next door has them," he had said. "And India's very hostile to Pakistan."

Even more to the point, candidate Reagan could not really understand why reporters kept harping on Pakistani proliferation when the Soviets were sitting in Afghanistan and threatening the Persian Gulf. "Right now there's an immediate crisis," he insisted. "And a crisis so great that very frankly I have to wonder why there's so much concern with this."

At the same time that he promised "to give priority attention to proliferation," Mr. Reagan gave far higher priority to the need to assert American power in the Persian Gulf against the Soviet presence in Afghanistan. The American bark on the nuclear proliferation issue showed itself far worse than its bite. Reagan had undercut his new Administration's policy on nuclear proliferation even before he had announced it.

The Spread Accelerates

With Ronald Reagan as President, the United States had clearly re-entered the world nuclear market, and just at a time when the race to buy—and to sell—supposedly civilian nuclear technology was picking up slowly but surely throughout the Middle East and the entire Third World.

The most interesting case was Egypt, where the bombing of the Iraqi reactor seriously embarrassed President Anwar el-Sadat, who had met with Israeli Prime Minister Menachem Begin only three days before in the Sinai and who was accused by some radical Arabs of complicity in the Israeli attack. As the most populous and still most militarily powerful Arab country, Egypt had long shown an interest in nuclear power, and was now negotiating to buy at least six large nuclear reactors from the United States, France, and West Germany. This was the first time that the Egyptians had the ability to pay for such costly purchases, and part of the money was coming from their new exports to Israel, stemming from the newly returned oil wells in the Gulf of Suez.

Like most of their Arab and Islamic neighbors, the Egyptians turned first to France, concluding a nuclear cooperation agreement in February 1981. The French power reactor company Framatome would prepare a feasibility study for the sale of at least two 900-megawatt pressurized-water reactors. A team from Framatome shortly visited Egypt for preliminary talks and the preparation of financial estimates.

The Egyptians then signed a similar agreement with the United States in June, in the wake of the Israeli bombing raid. The agreement called for two 1,000-megawatt power stations and set out the terms for the American supply of low-enriched uranium fuel. Secretary of State Alexander Haig called this a "model" nuclear agreement, as it forbade all reprocessing in Egypt and required safeguards on all Egyptian nuclear facilities. Egypt had just signed the Nuclear Nonproliferation Treaty in February. The Egyptians also looked for two more reactors in West Germany, where they conducted talks with the German reactor builders Kraftwerk Union. In all, current Egyptian plans called for ten power reactors, which would give Egypt the largest nuclear power capability in the entire Middle East. Significantly, in the very first of the new agreements, the French took the trouble to consult Israel before signing with Egypt.

"The Israelis blessed the agreement," the French nuclear spokesman Alain Varneau told us with a sigh of relief. "They gave it their approval. That's very good, and very important for us."

One of the unheralded results of the so-called peace process in the Middle East, the Israelis' approval marked a sharp turnabout from their earlier attitude. Back in 1974 and 1975, the Americans had promised nuclear reactors to both Israel and Egypt. But the Israelis had rejected the offer, which for reasons of American politics ended the offer for Egypt as well. In part, the Israelis were not willing to accept Washington's requirement that they open their entire nuclear program, and not just the reactor to be acquired, to inspection. They preferred to sacrifice their own hopes for civilian nuclear power in order to keep their freedom to exploit the "nuclear option." Above all, they did not want the Egyptians, potentially their deadliest Arab rival, to get even the possibility of producing weapons-usable plutonium.

In the meantime, the Israelis themselves were also considering their first nuclear power plant, a standard pressurized-water reactor to be located in the Negev. But the bombing of Osirak made any nuclear sale to the Israelis most unlikely. This was one price of the preemptive strike, and not one that the Israelis had seriously considered in their rush to destroy the enemy's growing capability. As an American diplomat involved in the negotiations told us, "Who would sell the Israelis a reactor now—when they haven't signed the Nonproliferation Treaty? It would be politically impossible."

(It was also revealed in September 1981 that the Americans had imposed an embargo on the supply of enriched uranium to Israel to power the small American-made research reactor at Nahal Sorek. The bombing made the lifting of this embargo most unlikely.)

Elsewhere in the region, the Pakistanis were finally pushing ahead with their long-discussed plans to build a 600-megawatt power reactor at Chashma, near their industrial reprocessing plant, and had hired a Spanish firm to serve as consulting engineers. The Libyans had a promise from the Soviet Union for a 300-megawatt power reactor. Syria and the United Arab Emirates both announced plans to build their own nuclear power stations during an Arab nuclear energy conference held nine days after the Israelis bombed the Iraqi reactor. The Saudis also declared that they intend to have a nuclear power reactor.

Beyond the Middle East, the same forces—regional rivalries, Third World nationalism, and the quest for secure sources of energy—were pushing in the same deadly direction. The list of likelies was all too familiar, and the same names that the U.S. Central Intelligence Agency fingered in its September 1974 report as potential weapons makers continued to pop up in the top ranks of civilian nuclear power development.

In South America, the Brazilians were pushing ahead with construction of three power reactors—one from the United States and two as part of their multibillion-dollar deal with West Germany. Brazil was also developing its own enrichment and reprocessing capabilities and had committed itself to helping Iraq with uranium and reactor construction, while their Argentine rivals were completing their second reactor and developing their own heavy-water plant with help from the Swiss firm Sulzer Brothers, who helped supply the ventilation system for the New Labs building in Pakistan.

In Asia, South Korea was actually constructing four new power reactors, with four more on order, while the Taiwanese were building three to add to the three they already had in operation. According to financial sources we consulted in London, the Saudis have offered financing to help Taiwan in further reactor purchases.

In Africa, the Nigerians have talked loosely of nuclear power, while the white South Africans have two power reactors under construction at Koeberg, with the major equipment presently coming from French companies, including Framatome and also BSL, the firm that had the secret contract to supply reprocessing vessels to Pakistan. South Africa also has had access to massive supplies of uranium, especially in Namibia (whose independence is still conjecture at this writing), and is building its own enrichment plant at Valindaba. American intelligence sources say the South Africans made preparations for a nuclear test as early as August 1977, but aborted them after Soviet and American satellites spotted the telltale construction work.

To the Western eye the drive for even "civilian" nuclear programs often seems a silly pursuit of prestige. "It's a little bit as with airlines," the Italian nuclear agency's Dr. Achille Albonetti told us during our first interview in September 1980. "Every country today needs its own airlines. Take Singapore, or Zaire, or any of the developing countries. It may not be profitable to have it. But it's essential. Even if you're starving, it's a necessity.

"For them, having a nuclear program is like having a jewel. It's a question of prestige. For the developing world, it's become an essential prestige item to have a research reactor and nuclear research facilities."

But, to those in the Third World themselves, however, nuclear facilities—and weapons—are far more than mere trinkets. They are the ultimate coin of political and economic equality, as Professor Ali Mazrui argued in his widely quoted Reith Lectures on the BBC in 1979. He openly called for Black Africa to have its own nuclear weapons.

"Africa should give up the idea of promoting itself as a nuclear-free zone except in terms of keeping outside powers and external bases at bay," urged the noted political scientist. "Those African countries who signed the Nonproliferation Treaty should review their positions and consider setting up a continental nuclear consortium allied to a strategy of developing a small nuclear capability, first in Nigeria and later on in Zaire and black-ruled South Africa.

"For these three countries, going nuclear would be a new initiation, an important rite of passage, a recovery of adulthood. No longer will the Great Powers be permitted to say that such and such a weapon is 'not for Africans and children under sixteen.'"

Just as Zulfikar Ali Bhutto had put it, all great civilizations had nuclear weapons. His Islamic civilization would have them, too. After the Islamic Bomb, was it not only natural for Black Africa to seek its own "black atomic bomb"?

The logic was that of further proliferation, and like those in the advanced countries who called for building new and ever more terrifying weapons as the only way to promote eventual disarmament, Professor Mazrui spoke of the African bomb as a shock that might help shove the Great Powers into accepting the need for a universal end to all nuclear weapons.

"The road to military equality is first through nuclear proliferation in the Third World countries, and later through denuclearization for everybody," argued Professor Mazrui. "African countries will not rise militarily fast enough to catch up with even the middle-range northern countries, but they could rise sufficiently fast to create conditions for substantial disarmament in the world as a whole." The leaders of the white world, said Mazrui, "need to be threatened with the danger of big black men wielding nuclear devices."

And so the dynamic of nuclear proliferation accelerates. What was once unthinkable now becomes "strategic reality," not just among the Superpowers and the Big Five, but in an increasing number of smaller countries, from Israel and India to Pakistan, Iraq, and beyond. The line against nuclear proliferation is fast disappearing as the deadly capability spreads.

Yet nuclear proliferation is not just another problem. It is a life-and-death challenge of the 1980s, for any unleashing of nuclear weapons in a region as strategically sensitive as the Middle East would instantly endanger Western interests and world peace. The choice is clear. If Washington finds the will, the Americans and their Allies among the nuclear exporting nations can still make their pressure felt, even at this late hour.

The nuclear genie has not yet wholly escaped its bottle. The Iraqis still have to buy their reactors from, and build up their reprocessing capability with the assistance of, one of a handful of countries, mostly in Western Europe. The Pakistanis are similarly dependent. For all their skill at putting together components and copying pieces and parts that they have already bought, they still have to buy their remaining components and their machine tools in the same handful of nuclear exporting countries. That is their weak point. If S. A. Butt and his Pakistani buyers have run circles around the present Western export regulations, it is not only because they are clever. It is also because the exporting nations have only just now set out to take the steps to stop them. Our investigation convinces us that a policy of denial can work—but only if there is the will to make it work.

"Pakistan is the watershed," an American diplomat told us at the beginning of this investigation. "It's not that I'm against Pakistan. But if they get it, it will affect the entire Middle East, and not only India. After them another eight to ten states will get it, and there'll be no holding back the spread of the weapon."

The line against nuclear proliferation must be firmly reestablished or the price will be incalculable. The nature of man has not improved, and the spread of nuclear weaponry puts the instruments of mass destruction into the hands of an increasing number of political leaders. The chances of miscalculation, and the use of the weapon, grow in each instance.

The nuclear arms race is one that cannot be won by anybody. Perhaps no one knew this better than one of those who helped to start it, and whose country has been the central instrument in selling the technology to make the bomb—France's greatest recent political leader, Charles de Gaulle. He once confessed to a man who had helped him build the *force de frappe*, the former French nuclear chief Dr. Francis Perrin: "You know, Perrin, there will be a worldwide atomic war. I won't live to see it. But you will."

Now in his eighties, Perrin smiled sadly as he told us of this earlier conversation. His sadness gave credence to some reports that reached us to the effect that he had worked on the *force de frappe* with reluctance.

Is it too late to stop it? Everywhere we went we found concern, but rarely the willingness to take the responsibility. Human beings had their reasons in each case—they wanted to buy, or sell, or improve their country's political position—but the concerted will to stop the spread of the most destructive weapon in the history of man seemed lacking. The nuts and bolts do add up to bombs, and still the particular nuts and bolts were being sold.

What could be done?

For a start, the Americans and other nuclear exporters must reject the unreal distinction between "nuclear options" and "nuclear weapons" once again being used by the Reagan Administration. The critical need is for the exporters to prevent any sales of technology and materials. The reality is that any country that has the nuclear option has the bomb.

The exporting nations could firmly draw the line against any new nation getting the capability to develop nuclear weapons, whatever the declared intentions about the use of nuclear technology by the present rulers.

The same nations could enforce a serious embargo on reprocessing and enrichment technology, on large research reactors, and to certain potentially dangerous countries, even on power reactors. This would be an embargo with teeth in it, rather than the present underfinanced, low-priority, and often half-hearted effort that we saw in too many places in our investigation.

The exporting nations could impose stiff fines and prison sentences on businessmen who sell the technology, and could withdraw diplomatic cover from foreign agents—like S. A. Butt and his Pakistani buying network—who are still going about their business.

They could press for regional bans and treaties that guarantee the security of all nations and simultaneously open any existing nuclear facilities to the fullest, and toughest, regional and international inspection.

The United States and the Soviet Union could set an example by stopping their own nuclear arms buildup, or what the experts call "vertical" nuclear proliferation, which is exactly what the two nations promised to do under the 1968 Nonproliferation Treaty. The spirit of that treaty has been violated most flagrantly by two of the countries that were its main sponsors.

And, if all else fails, the Americans, their allies, and even the Soviets could step in and say, in old imperial fashion, "Stop it, or else . . ."

They could do all of this if they would. But they have not done it in the past. If they will not do it in the future, the dangerous instability will grow, and nuclear weapons will be a live option in the conflicts that already afflict the Middle Eastern and South Asian regions.

The distinguished former American diplomat George Kennan probably summed up best how we ourselves feel: "For the love of God, of your children, and of the civilization to which you belong, cease this madness."

Or else. The evening is upon us. May the night never come.

Index